BETWEEN HEGEL AND KIERKEGAARD

Hans L. Martensen's
Philosophy of Religion

AMERICAN ACADEMY OF RELIGION
TEXTS AND TRANSLATIONS SERIES

Edited by

Terry Godlove
Hofstra University

Number 17

BETWEEN HEGEL AND KIERKEGAARD
Hans L. Martensen's
Philosophy of Religion

Translations by
Curtis L. Thompson
David J. Kangas

BETWEEN HEGEL AND KIERKEGAARD
Hans L. Martensen's
Philosophy of Religion

Translations by
Curtis L. Thompson
David J. Kangas

With an Introduction by Curtis L. Thompson

Scholars Press
Atlanta, Georgia

BETWEEN HEGEL AND KIERKEGAARD

Hans L. Martensen's
Philosophy of Religion

Translations by
Curtis L. Thompson
David J. Kangas

Library of Congress Cataloging in Publication Data
Martensen, H. (Hans), 1808–1884.
    [Selections. English. 1997]
    Between Hegel and Kierkegaard : Hans. L. Martensen's philosophy of
religion : translations / by Curtis L. Thompson.
        p. cm.— (Texts and translations series ; no. 17)
    Includes bibliographical references and index.
    Contents: The autonomy of human self-consciousness in modern
dogmatic theology—Meister Eckhart—Outline to a system of moral
philosophy.
    ISBN 0-7885-0348-0 (cloth : alk. paper). — ISBN 0-7885-0349-9
(paper : alk. paper)
    1. Religion—Philosophy.   2. Theology.   I. Thompson, Curtis L.,
1946–   .   II. Kangas, David J.   III. Title.   IV. Series: Texts and
translations series (American Academy of Religion) ; no. 17.
    BL51.M3516213   1997
    210—dc21   97-7157
                                                                                    CIP

Printed in the United States of America
on acid-free paper

Hans L. Martensen, Doctor of Theology. Photograph of a lithograph from a
painting by D. Monies, 1841. Reproduced courtesy of the Howard and
Edna Hong Kierkegaard Library, Northfield, Minnesota.

Contents

Preface

The present work consists of translations of three important treatises in the philosophy of religion by the nineteenth-century Danish religious thinker, Hans Lassen Martensen (1808–1884), together with an introduction to Martensen's life and thought. My original plan for this book included translating two of Martensen's works, *The Autonomy of Human Self-Consciousness* and *Outline to a System of Moral Philosophy*. My thought was to return to translating work that I had done as part of my dissertation research in Copenhagen during 1982. At that time I did close work on those two Martensen writings, so I was in possession of rough running translations which would be valuable as first-drafts with which to start my fresh work.

In the summer of 1995 I traveled to the Howard and Edna Hong Kierkegaard Library at St. Olaf College in Northfield, Minnesota to avail myself of their fine resources. While there I became acquainted with a number of other scholars doing research at the library, including David Kangas with whom I had much in common. We conversed at length about Kierkegaard, Hegel, and our projects. David was doing dissertation research into the influence of mysticism and romanticism on Kierkegaard, which brought him into an investigation of Martensen's very rich treatise on medieval mysticism. Originally, I had seriously considered including that text as a third treatise in this Martensen volume, but had finally decided against it out of a concern for the extra time it would take. As David worked on Martensen's book on mysticism he became increasingly enthusiastic over it, to the point of thinking it should be translated. He inquired about the possibility of his translation of that work being included in the book of translations on which I was working. I welcomed that possibility because I knew how much more representative of Martensen's early theological writings the *Between Hegel and Kierkegaard* volume would be with the addition of the Meister Eckhart piece. And it has been a joy working with David over the many months of preparing this manuscript.

Fortunately, during the same summer of 1995, I was able to make a brief trip to the Department of Søren Kierkegaard Research at Copenhagen University in Denmark in order to exploit their resources. My thanks are extended to the many people at the University of Copenhagen who were both hospitable and helpful. At the Hong Library at St. Olaf College, Cynthia Lund and Gordon Marino are to be given thanks for their assistance in this project, including overseeing the production of plates for the Martensen photograph and the three Danish manuscript title pages, and so too are Howard and Edna Hong for their support. At my own Thiel College, I am grateful for the backing provided by the Library, especially the Interlibrary Loan facilitator Dorothy Broenel. Faculty secretaries Jenny Williams and Jolene Campbell gave able assistance, as did my student assistant Marleen Griffith who tended to fine details of the manuscript. A number of people were willing to read over my translation work and some were of assistance on difficult passages. To be thanked are Terry Godlove, Editor of the Texts and Translations Series of the American Academy of Religion, who encouraged me to pursue this translating project, Warren Frisina, who also affirmed me in this task, Paul Sponheim, who first kindled my interest in Kierkegaard, Langdon Gilkey, with whom I studied Kierkegaard further and who served as advisor on my doctoral dissertation on Martensen, Ted Brelsford for his gracious and professional nurturing of the manuscript through to press, the anonymous reader for Scholars Press who made helpful comments, Sarah Thompson for her careful work on the Index, Ann Castro, Patrick Hecking, Peter Hodgson, Mark Dooley, Henrik Schon, Marsha Robinson, Udo Doedens, John Wise, and the members of the Fall 1996 Philosophy of Religion Seminar at Thiel College—Tim Claus, Hope Nelson, Briana Richardson, Gina Shongo, Dan Smail, and Jill Wiggins. Public thanks is expressed to the American Academy of Religion for awarding me an Individual Research Grant and to Thiel College for providing money supporting the summer 1995 trip to Copenhagen. I also wish to thank the American Scandinavian Foundation for granting me a George C. Marshall Fellowship which enabled me to do research originally during 1982 at the University of Copenhagen.

My biggest thank you goes to my dearest friend and colleague on the journey of life who also happens to be my wife, Kathy, who brought her critical eye to bear on the pages of the manuscript and who gave me the encouragement, reassurance, and hope to continue plodding until the project was completed.

CURTIS L. THOMPSON
January 6, 1997
The Epiphany of Our Lord

Introduction

What is the nature of freedom? Do we need to be liberated from the form of freedom advocated by the cultural values and social conventions of our contemporary capitalistic society? What is our assessment of the new, chastened form of autonomy struggling to burst forth on the other side of postmodern criticism of the Enlightenment conception of autonomy? How does one justify spending time in the philosophy of religion when seemingly bigger, more pressing, important issues of oppression, domination, and injustice call for participation in liberatory praxis rather than speculative theory? These are questions of relevance. Posed at the outset of this work on Hans L. Martensen's philosophy of religion, they are intended to indicate an awareness of the hermeneutical gap that exists between the writings and meanings of Martensen's time and those of our own.

Skat Arildsen has argued that a "new" era in theology began in 1835 with the publication of David Friedrich Strauss' *Life of Jesus*.[1] Over the unfolding decades of the nineteenth century, Arildsen maintains, Martensen followed the problems and issues of this new era of theology, but he consistently attempted to solve those problems from a theological point of view that belonged to the period before 1835. While I agree with Arildsen's assessment, I want to contend that Martensen's decidedly pre-1835 theological perspective worked out in relation to German idealism and romanticism is relevant to our contemporary situation. Martensen's theological standpoint sets forth a potent view of freedom. His theological point of view provides a basis for criticizing and liberating freedom as we find it in today's society. His theological perspective offers us a resource for developing a late modern conception of autonomy that recognizes

---

[1] Skat Arildsen, *H. L. Martensen. Hans Liv, Udvikling og Arbejde, Studier i det 19. Aarhundredes Danske Aandsliv* [*H. L. Martnesen: His Life, Development and Work, Studies in Danish Intellectual Life of the 19th Century*], vol. 1 (København: G.E.C. Gad, 1932), pp. 111–112.

1

both the limitations of reason and its dignity. Martensen's theological stance in an indirect way can contribute to our insistent concern that theology be in the service of liberating praxis. Martensen is relevant to the needs of our time.

Most scholars of religion who recognize the name of Hans Lassen Martensen (1808–1884) do so in connection with Søren Kierkegaard (1813–1855); they remember that Martensen was Kierkegaard's teacher and the target of his criticisms of Christendom. Few have examined Martensen's writings themselves. Even most Kierkegaard experts have been kept busy enough trying to work through his large corpus of writing, so that they have not taken the time to read any of the early works penned by Martensen. The fact that none of these early writings has been translated into English has not helped the situation.

Martensen stands strategically between Hegel and Kierkegaard. Along with J. L. Heiberg, he was one of the two most important intellectuals introducing Hegel into the Danish intellectual world of which Kierkegaard was a part. Scholarly interest in Kierkegaard has remained steady and strong over the past several decades, and the renaissance of Hegel scholarship over the past two decades has resulted in a fascinating corpus of Hegel interpretation. Many of the best Hegelian and Kierkegaardian scholars, however, recognize the value of interpreting either of these intellectuals in relation to "the other," that is, they recognize how Kierkegaard is best understood in relation to Hegel and how Hegel is profitably understood in relation to Kierkegaard. As this Hegel-Kierkegaard relation continues to gain increased attention, the value of looking at a figure like Martensen becomes more apparent. Kierkegaard's rather harsh polemic against Hegel leaves the impression that the two are merely opposites. In point of fact, there are many connections between them. When one enters into the world of Martensen's thought, one sees what an important link he is between Hegel and Kierkegaard. Martensen viewed his theology as mediating between supernaturalism and rationalism, but it is also the case that it can be seen as mediating between the German systematizer and the Danish Socrates. His early theological writings, the three most significant of which are translated here, are the focus of this mediating. A careful reading of these works should make possible a more nuanced understanding of the Hegel-Kierkegaard relation. One theologian of this century, Paul Tillich, who early on saw the worth of both Hegel and Kierkegaard, drew insight from Martensen and was referred to by Niels Thulstrup as "the twentieth-century Martensen."

This book has been generated out of the hope that Hans L. Martensen's thought might be considered by those interested in nineteenth-century theology in general, Kierkegaard research, or contemporary constructive theology. The three writings translated here provide a strong dose of Martensen's thinking from his early, formative period when he was concerned with issues in the area that can best be labeled "philosophy of religion." They are theological writings from around 1840, a time when the newly-emerging area of the philosophy of religion had recently been given definition by Hegel and Schleiermacher. However, these writings are the occasion for reflections on the philosophy of religion by a decidedly Christian theologian. The first writing is Martensen's work on the theme of autonomy as it is found in the modern thinkers Kant, Schleiermacher, and Hegel. Second is his work on medieval mysticism which provides a phenomenology of the mystical consciousness and shows the importance of the mystical tradition of the high Middle Ages for theological reflection. The third is his outline on moral philosophy published for use with lectures on that subject. Together these treatises disclose much about the shape Martensen's thought had taken as a young scholar in his late twenties.

Hegel scholars interested in Hegel's legacy, including followers who developed what has been called a right-wing theological interpretation of Hegel, should find these writings of interest. They constitute an interesting theological appropriation of Hegel's philosophical vision, which is itself a theological perspective as Martensen rightly maintains.[2] And Kierkegaard enthusiasts should definitely find these works fascinating reading. On the specific topic of Kierkegaard research, it is relevant to note how two camps of Kierkegaard scholars seem to have developed. On the one hand there are the purists who are into the writings and life of Søren Kierkegaard. This is the more scholastic type of scholar who is deeply committed to making sense of Kierkegaard's works within the context of his own authorship. They tend to show little interest in Kierkegaard's context, contending that it takes at least a lifetime to do a thorough study of Kierkegaard's authorship in and of itself. One hardly has the time to consider contextual questions very rigorously. This camp or perspective elevates Søren above his historical milieu, placing him on a pedestal and generally finds little to criticize in the brilliantly nuanced moves of this religious and philosophical genius. Kierkegaard, interestingly, did not go out of his way to put up road blocks to prevent this sort of idealizing of him; but such glorification has its consequences.

On the other hand there are the contextualizing Kierkegaard scholars who are anxious to take on the ambitious task of reading him in

---

[2] See the provocative work by Cyril O'Regan, *The Heterodox Hegel* (Albany, State University of New York, 1994), in which he makes the case for Hegel as a theologian, although a less than orthodox one. O'Regan argues that influenced by the mystics, Hegel, a sincere Christian and Lutheran, developed a theology marked by a narrative character and trinitarian essence which, while not excluding him from the ontotheological tradition altogether, did situate him within the heterodox margins of that tradition.

relation to his historical situation and to that of our own. This group of
interpreters recognizes the need for even the greatest minds of history to
be studied in terms of the questions, problems, ideas, and thought-world
of their socio-cultural setting, and therefore they are attentive to the
contours of "Kierkegaard's Denmark." They also realize the need to take
seriously the contemporary intellectual currents. Therefore, in this second camp many of those presently interested in Kierkegaard read him
through postmodern lenses tinted by the turn to language. As historical
research programs such as the one centered around Søren Kierkegaard
evolve, there is a natural transition that is made from an early, more
exclusive focus on the authorship of the one who is the object of scrutiny to a later, more broad-based historical sort of inquiry into complex
questions of influences and agenda-shaping. Thus, this second camp of
Kierkegaard enthusiasts is growing as additional scholars become interested in more comprehensive considerations and in the significance of
Kierkegaard as a resource for dealing with questions emerging in a late
modern time.

It is, of course, the second cluster of Kierkegaard researchers that will
most likely take an interest in the present work, although it would be
wonderful if these writings serve as an occasion for those in the first cluster to move toward the second. Precious little work has been done on the
early Martensen, especially in the English language.[3] His *Christian Dogmatics* of 1849 and his three-volume *Christian Ethics* of 1871–78 made quite
an impact in English translation in their time. However, the three treatises
translated here provide the reader with a thorough and complete presentation of Martensen's reflections on the philosophy of religion in the
formative period of his career. Hopefully this book will spark interest
among scholars to investigate at a more profound level the Martensen-
Kierkegaard connection.

Some readers might wish to turn directly to Martensen's writings.
Others could likely benefit from an introduction to him as a person and
thinker. The purpose of this "Introduction" is to present a narrative on
Martensen's life and career; to give a brief overview of the three treatises
that are translated here; to set forth affirmations of Martensen's philosophy of religion; to discuss Martensen's relation to Kierkegaard; and to
offer a remark on the translations and abbreviations.

---

[3] The only two manuscript-length works on Martensen in English are Robert Leslie
Horn's "Positivity and Dialectic: A Study of the Theological Method of Hans Lassen
Martensen" (Ph.D. dissertation, Union Theological Seminary, New York, 1969) and my own
"The Logic of Theonomy: Hans Lassen Martensen's Theological Method" (Ph.D. disserta-
tion, University of Chicago, Chicago, 1985). The latter is currently being revised and will
hopefully appear in the near future under the title *Recollecting Kierkegaard's Other: Hans L.
Martensen as Theologian of Theonomy*. The definitive work in Danish continues to be Arildsen's *H. L. Martensen*.

An Intellectual Biography of Martensen

Hans Lassen Martensen was born in Flensborg, Denmark in 1808, five years before Kierkegaard was born. He lived in that German-speaking community for nine-years until his family moved to Copenhagen where Hans attended primary and secondary school from 1817 until he entered the University of Copenhagen in 1827. During his pre-University years Martensen was exposed to the conservative Lutheran stance of J. C. Lindberg (1797–1857) and Andreas S. Rudelbach (1792–1862), both followers of N. F. S. Grundtvig (1773–1872). The late 1820s in Denmark was a time of intensifying rationalism, but it was also a period of Christian renewal through the impact of Grundtvig and Jacob Peter Mynster (1775–1854), both of whom influenced Martensen's religious life. Grundtvig presented a world-historical view shaped in part at this time by F. W. J. Schelling (1775–1854), and Mynster was effective in writing devotional material that edified religiously. Later, of course, Mynster would become Martensen's mentor and Grundtvig his able opponent on many issues. At the University it was especially Frederick Christian Sibbern (1785–1872), professor of philosophy, who contributed much to Martensen. Sibbern, really a philosophical theologian, knew Goethe, Schelling, and many of the time's romantic philosophers, and he exposed the young scholar to theology as marked by the romantic movement. At the center of Sibbern's thought was the notion of personality, which became for Martensen too the concept of central importance. Sibbern mediated to the impressionable student an appreciation for speculative theology.

Martensen earned a scholarship for educational travel during the academic years 1834–35 and 1835–36. This allowed him to spend time in Dresden, Heidelberg, Tübingen, Munich, and Paris and to study with such thinkers as Marheinecke, Steffens, Droysen, Tieck, Daub, Hegel's sons, Strauss, Baur, Baader, and Schelling. Most significant on this trip was the crisis that Martensen experienced while in Berlin. He became physically ill with which came a hypochondria, and the depression was marked with a spiritual skepticism.[4] He later describes that crisis as a fermentation of the contrast between theism and pantheism within his inner being. But as much as he was attracted to pantheism, he could not bring himself beyond the fact that the relation to the pantheistic God is finally a thoroughly impersonal relation. At the end of his life, Martensen concludes that the crisis was likely attributable to the onesidedly speculative tendency toward thought and knowledge that had engaged him all too exclusively: his faith had been repressed under the intensity of the

---

[4] H. Martensen, *Af mit Levnet: Meddelelser* [*From My Life: Communications*], 3 vols. (Kjøbenhavn: Gyldendal, 1882–83), 1:98–106. The next paragraph's references are to this work.

intellectual pursuit and he had lost sight of the truth that the deepest
knowledge is only a moment within experience rather than the result
of mere thinking, that the real riddle is not a riddle of knowledge but
a riddle of life which must be resolved not by thought but in life, existence. Here we see the centrality of personality in Martensen's new-
found theological stance; he left Berlin with a "natural faith in life, that
the creative and sustaining powers in existence are really stronger than
the disturbing ones."

It was Carl Daub (1765–1836) and Franz von Baader (1765–1841) who
nurtured Martensen along the road of speculative theology. Daub had
become an Hegelian in the early 1820s and for years thereafter poured
over Hegel's *Logic* and his *Phenomenology*. This Heidelberg professor
was most critical of the onesided emphasis on subjectivity that characterized modern thought. Using the *Phenomenology* as his model, he criticized
such theological forms as supernaturalism and rationalism as being
internally contradictory and looked for the presuppositionless thinking
of absolute doubting to produce the proper speculative insight into
the content of religion's revelation. Martensen, however, never discovered how Daub's thought moved beyond pantheism (1:117). In Munich
another speculative thinker made an impact on the sensitive, budding
theologian. Franz Baader, whose lectures were not impressive to the itin-
erant Dane, did shine in conversation. Martensen was struck by Baader's
insistence that philosophy should be religious philosophy. His criticisms
of the autonomous systems of modernity which ascribe self-legislation
to the human spirit were closely noted by Martensen who expressed that
viewpoint in his dissertation. Under Baader's influence, Martensen developed a view that he saw as in keeping with the church's *credo ut intelligam*, meaning "I believe, and under this presupposition I seek to know
(1:144)." The personal relation of faith contains a knowledge which can
be developed speculatively into a knowledge of the truth as truth (1:145).

The theological standpoint Martensen arrived at on his study-trip he
described as "theonomic." During his lifetime, this gifted theologian developed his theonomous theology in relation to the situation engaging
him. As he moves from theological professor to ecclesial spokesperson to
ecclesiastical bishop in society, his theological writing assumes different
forms in relation to the particular setting in life he is addressing. The three
respective publics of academy, church, and society which occupied him as
he progressed through his career led to three respective types of theology.[5]
Thus, we see his early writing during the years 1837 to 1841 addressed

---

[5] David Tracy has carefully worked out the relation of the publics of theology and types
of theology in his *The Analogical Imagination: Christian Theology and the Culture of Pluralism*
(New York: Seabury, 1981), especially chapters 1 and 2.

primarily to the academy as taking the shape of "philosophy of religion." The period from 1842 to 1850 finds Martensen preoccupied with dogmatic issues as he addresses questions being considered by the church; thus, his thought takes the shape of "dogmatic theology" during this time. Finally, during his years as bishop from the 1850s to his death in 1884 it is the social questions of the day that receive his attention, so his writing constitutes a practical or ethical theology during this era. Throughout these various periods, however, Martensen's theology is committed to the central root-metaphor of theonomy. Theonomy is the notion that human freedom rightly realizes itself when it uses its autonomous power of self-determination to acknowledge its dependence upon the divine power which is its source. We could say that when freedom, in relating itself to itself, relates itself to an Other, that is theonomy.

Martensen's consistent theonomic standpoint begins with his dissertation of 1837. But he wrote three theological works before that one. First, there was the prize-essay of 1833. The essay was in response to the question, "What is the basis of natural theology, its scope, and its relation to positive theology?"[6] Second, in 1834 Martensen published a review of E.G. Kolthoff's writing on the last book of the Bible, making the case for interpreting the Revelation as the result of the author's looking into the Idea and for the legitimacy of historical criticism on the basis of the Protestant principle.[7] Third, Martensen published the German version of his little book on Lenau's *Faust* in 1836.[8] Martensen had become friends with Niembsch von Strehlenau (1802–1850), the melancholy Austrian poet who later committed suicide, while in Vienna on his study-tour.

Arriving back home in Denmark, Martensen delivered lectures on the latest German thought and these were some of the most popular lectures in the history of the theological department of the University of Copenhagen. The first lectures, *Introductory Lectures to Speculative Dogmatics*, were given during the winter semester of 1837–38; another set, *Lectures on the History of Modern Philosophy from Kant to Hegel*, were delivered during the winter semester of 1938–39; and a third was *Lectures on Speculative Dogmatics* presented during the summer and winter semesters of 1938–39.[9] The first two sets of lectures dealt with the history of modern

---

[6] H. L. Martensen, "Forsøg til en Besvarelse af den theologisk Priisopgave [An Attempt at a Response to the Theological Prize Subject]," unpublished handwritten manuscript dated December 1833, in the Martensen archives of the Royal Library, *Ny Kg. Saml.*, 3435,4.

[7] H. Martensen, "E. G. Kolthoff, *Apocalypsis Joanni Apostolo vindicata*, "*Maanedsskrift for Litteratur* 12 (1834):1–31.

[8] Johannes M.......n, *Ueber Lenaus Faust* (Stuttgart: Cotta, 1836). Details of Martensen's relationship with Lenau are communicated in *From My Life*, 1:167–93.

[9] See *Forelæsninger over Indledning til speculativ Dogmatik, Søren Kierkegaards Papier,* eds. P. A. Heiberg and V. Kuhr, 2nd expanded edition, ed. Niels Thulstrup (København:

philosophy, concentrating on the primary figures in the German idealistic tradition, namely, Kant, Fichte, Jacobi, Schelling, and Hegel; the third set of lectures on speculative dogmatics treated the theological significance of German idealism. In his memoirs Martensen writes about these lectures: "I had to lead my listeners through Hegel, we could not remain with him but had to, as it is said, go beyond him. I had to, if possible, get them enthused about Hegel, and yet I had to oppose him and bring them to oppose him. Whether I always succeeded in this to the same degree, I must leave undecided. But I can assert with certainty that all the way through I have maintained my theonomic standpoint in contrast to Hegel's autonomic, that the intuitive view of faith and revelation was for me the *principal* thing in contrast to the autonomic in Hegel. I could not agree with a thinking which would produce its own content. I sought only a *second-order* reflection [*eftertænkning*] on that which is given in revelation. When it is often said that during this my initial period at the University I was a representative of Hegelianism, then this is a most uncritical assertion which totally ignores my explicit and justified declarations in my dissertation, and which has been refuted by each of my literary works."[10] Martensen never moved beyond his appreciation for the Hegelian dialectical method and for the contributions of the whole line of thinkers in the tradition of German idealism, but he did not adopt their insights without a critical assessment grounded in his own theological position.

During the period 1837–41, which I have characterized as the "philosophy of religion" phase of his theological development, Martensen published eight writings. These writings deal with different subjects, but their unity can be seen in that they all deal in some significant way with *the Idea*. This concept stands at the center of Martensen's philosophy of religion. We will want to offer a quick synopsis of Martensen's periods as dogmatic theologian and practical theologian. But first we must give a little more thorough treatment of his philosophy of religion. Since in the next parts of this Introduction we will be examining the three most important of his writings from this period, we here make mention of the other five.

Gyldendal, 1968–70), II C 12–24, *Referat af Martensens Forelæsninger over den nyere Philosophies Historie*, XII, II C 25, *Referat af Martensens Forelæsninger over "Speculativ Dogmatik,"* XIII, II C 26–28. The lectures entitled *Den nyere Philosophies Historie, i dens Forhold til Theologien* [*The History of Modern Philosophy, in its Relation to Theology*] as transcribed by F. E. Seidelin, are in the Royal Library of Copenhagen, *Ny Kgl. Saml.* 3439,4.

[10] H. Martensen, *From My Life*, 2:4–5. It goes without saying that the use of Martensen's autobiographical statements as evidence for his earlier positions needs to be accompanied with a healthy suspicion regarding the possibility of revisionist interpretations that are self-serving in character. After reading Martensen's dissertation it becomes apparent that this particular statement in the autobiography is certainly well-founded.

When Martensen began giving lectures in the fall of 1837 it was as a *Privatdocent* in theology. Since on the last stop of his trip he had been able to spend time in Paris with Johan Ludwig and Johanne Louise Heiberg, he read with interest Heiberg's published lecture introducing Hegelianism to students at the military high school. Martensen uses his review of that lecture not so much to deal with Heiberg's claims but rather to present his own view of why Hegel's philosophy is unavoidable for those who want to engage in modern scientific reflection.[11] Hegel strives to arrive at a point independent of experience and consciousness, that is, the infinite abstraction of thought from all determinateness; this is done by carrying dialectical doubt through to its logical conclusion. Martensen then iterates the moves Hegel makes in being able to speak of God's consciousness of Godself as the human's consciousness of God. Thus, the meaning of Hegel's speculative logic is that actuality is nothing other than the determinations of thought which have been revealed in the external world, so that knowing actuality is the same thing as knowing its categories. Martensen closes with critical comments on Hegel, maintaining that he sets the concept above other forms of truth and has no sense for the holy and the eternal.

Besides the Heiberg review article, Martensen also re-worked his essay on Lenau's poem in a Danish version for publication in Heiberg's new journal for the speculative Idea called *Perseus*.[12] The Danish re-working of *Ueber Lenaus Faust* involves a number of changes, the chief of which is the addition of a long introduction on apocalyptic poetry, under which genre Martensen sees Lenau's poem as falling. Our young reflector on esthetics sees poetry as striving to represent the speculative Idea. In Faust the Idea is deeper than in either Prometheus or Don Juan, for the Idea is revealed in an immediate way as that universal outside of which the

---

[11] H. Martensen, "J. L. Heiberg: Inledningsforedrag til det i November 1834 begyndte logiske Cursus paa den kongelige militaire Høiskole" [J. L. Heiberg: Introductory Lecture for the Course in Logic Begun in November 1834 at the Royal Military College] *Maanedsskrift for Litteratur* 16 (1836): 515–28. Already here at the outset of his career Martensen was speaking of the need to "go beyond" Hegel (p. 528): "The infinitely great in Hegel whereby he more than any other philosopher originating from a non-Christian principle draws near to Christianity, is, that he rose to the idea of the Logos as the creative ground and possibility of human reason. If, instead of seeking the eternal thought which the human has not itself conceived, he had sought the eternal Word which the human has not itself spoken, then he would have arrived at the Christian Logos, and instead of finding in existence only the concept and reason would have found the Word and revelation. The objective starting point of philosophy would have *gone beyond* [*komme ud over*] the abstract category. I hope on another occasion to be able to develop and justify this." [Emphasis mine.]

[12] "Betragtninger over Ideen af Faust. Med Hensyn paa Lenaus Faust," *Perseus* 1 (1837): 91–164, and printed in Julius Martensen, *Mindre Skrifter og Taler af Biskop Martensen. Udgivne med en Oversigt over hans Forfattervirksomhed* [*Minor Writings and Talks of Bishop Martensen: Published with an Overview of his Authorship*] (Kjøbenhavn: Gyldendal, 1885), pp. 29–88.

individual has no particular existence. The highest object of speculative poetry is not characters illuminated by the Idea but instead the religious-speculative Idea or the light itself by which the characters are illuminated. Poetry's conception of the revelation of the Idea becomes an absolute rather than a relative conception when it sees this light not merely within the confines of subjectivity but as spread over the entire spiritual universe. *Faust* represents the third and highest stage of poetry which concentrates on the principle of history, namely, the Idea, the Idea of Absolute Spirit which is freedom. In freedom the theoretical and the practical are united. The Faust-poem discloses the theological standpoint of theonomy in the artistic form of apocalyptic poetry, since in disclosing both the triumph of religion over mere secularity and the nothingness and vanity of the finite and worldly it anticipates the judgment of the End.

In the next year, 1838, Martensen provided further esthetic-theological commentary, this time on two of Heiberg's plays, "Alferne" and "Fata Morgana."[13] Henning Fenger points out that "Alferne" or "The Ferries," a one-act festival play written in 1835, is a dramatization of Tieck's fairy tale *Die Elfen*.[14] In his review Martensen focuses not on this play which was such a success, but rather on "Fata Morgana," the 1838 speculative comedy. In this five-act fairy tale-comedy, which was a box-office disaster, Fru Heiberg played the title role of the "Queen of Illusions," in whose pearl all people see their false ideals and secret dreams. Martensen praises Heiberg's effort to create a new dramatic genre of art, speculative poetry, which brings together the striving for the Infinite of the romantic poets and the concern for form of Goethe.[15] Poetry in this form leads reality to ideality, carrying forward the speculative Idea.

On December 22, 1838, Martensen was married to Mathilde Helene Hess. Communicating this in his autobiography, he says little more except that after nine years of marriage this daughter of a ship captain died, leaving him with two children, Julius and Marie.

A final writing on esthetics was Martensen's review of J. L Heiberg's four philosophical poems published under the title *New Poems*; the review was published on three consecutive days in January of 1841 in *The Fatherland*, the newspaper of academic liberalism.[16] The cultured commentator

---

[13] These two poetic plays are included in J. L. Heiberg's *Poetiske Skrifte* [Poetic Writings], ed. Fru Heiberg and A. F. Krieger, 11 vols. (Kjøbenhavn: C. A. Reitzel, 1862), 2:1–91 and 2:93–226. See the summary of "Fata Morgana" in George Pattison's *Kierkegaard: The Aesthetic and the Religious* (New York: St. Martin's, 1992), pp. 18–21.

[14] Henning Fenger, *The Heibergs*, trans. Frederick J. Marker (New York: Twayne, 1971), p. 111.

[15] H. L. Martensen, "Fata Morgana. Eventyr-Comedie af J. L. Heiberg" [Fata Morgana: A Fairy Tale-Comedy by J. L. Heiberg], *Maanedsskrift for Litteratur* 19 (1838): 361–397.

[16] J. L. Heiberg, *Poetiske Skrifter*, 10:163–324. Martensen's review, "Nye Digte af J. L. Heiberg" [New Poems by J. L. Heiberg], appeared in *Fædrelandet*, vol. 2, No. 398 (January 10,

notes that Heiberg's poems bear an unmistakable testimony to the actual presence of a poetic breakthrough of the spirit of modernity which sits in judgment on those who would deny it. The primary vehicle of emancipation is apocalyptic poetry, so the emphasis of the long review falls on Heiberg's "A Soul After Death: An Apocalyptic Comedy," which is generally acknowledged as a classic of Danish literature. In Heiberg's comedy it is the world of Copenhagen life in all its petty detail that has been resurrected for judgment. The result is a look at the kingdom of triviality and the metaphysics of triviality lying behind it. Concern for the insignificant is a manifestation of the bad as opposed to evil; the difference is that while evil is the spiritual contrary of the Idea which contains a reappearance of it, the bad is a more immediate or superficial contrary of the Idea expressing not so much a spiritual antithesis to it as perfect disinterestedness and indifference. The bad's kingdom is that of triviality, which is roughly equivalent to Hegel's bad infinite. If the spirit contains the unity of the Infinite and the finite, the spiritless or the trivial appears as the absolutely undialectical, the tautological, that which has lost the transition to its other. Therefore, Martensen notes that triviality is the consequence of a singularity of vision: "Genuine science and poetry, just like faith, sees all objects in a twofold way, sees them simultaneously under the *gestalt* of eternity and temporality. This double view appears on the whole in everything that is called witty. The bad, flat view of the world, on the other hand, sees everything in a single way." This contrast between the monistic and idealistic worldviews separates all artists and all intellectuals in the modern world. Martensen notes how this double-eyed view also leads to a viewpoint that is comical and even humoristic, where the humoristic is seen as a positive, speculative form of the comical; the humoristic is related to irony as profundity to acuteness.[17]

1841), Col. 3205–12; No. 399 (January 11, 1841), Col. 3213–20; and No. 400 (January 12, 1841), Col. 3221–24.

[17] In this writing Martensen also makes some fascinating comments on Heiberg's poems in relation to the theme of "Protestantism in Nature," and in the process acknowledges a philosophy of nature that anticipates the type of naturalistic theological understanding advocated by contemporary thinkers working on the relation between religion and science such as Philip Hefner in his *The Human Factor: Evolution, Culture, and Religion* (Minneapolis: Fortress, 1993), in which he develops a theology of freedom where freedom is understood as appearing naturalistically out of and through the evolutionary process. Cf. Martensen's comments in his review of Heiberg's new poem "Protestantism in Nature," and think of "the ideal" as referring finally to "freedom": "Since the essence of Protestantism in fact resides in the struggle of freedom toward the ideal, in continuously transcending immediate reality, then nature must be accorded the same Protestantism, which subjectively reveals itself in the spirit, insofar as it dimly and unconsciously strives to be transformed from its immediate nature to its ideal. Nature itself protests against every form of naturalism, be it esthetic or religious, be it in heathen or in Roman Catholic form." This quotation is included (p. 188) in J. H. Schjørring's "Martensen," *Bibliotheca Kierkegaardian*, vol. 10, *Kierkegaard's Teachers* (C. A. Reitzel's, 1982), pp. 177–207.

In 1839 a review of Martensen's dissertation by J. A. Bornemann appeared in a new journal.[18] The author made the case for the mediating character of Martensen's treatise on theological method and offered the statement: "In theology both rationalism and supernaturalism are absolute standpoints which belong to a by-gone age." Jacob Mynster, then Bishop Primate of the Lutheran Church in Denmark, responded to this article and in particular to the statement about the obsolete status of supernaturalism with an article entitled "Rationalism: Supernaturalism."[19] Mynster calls to mind the principle of the excluded middle and the principle of contradiction, arguing that "one can mediate between contrasts but not between contradictions." Martensen responded to Mynster's article with his essay, "Rationalism, Supernaturalism, and the Principle of the Excluded Middle."[20] Here the protégé and eventual successor of Mynster very respectfully disagrees with his critic in making the case for speculative theology as that new third type of theology demanded by the present situation. The article makes clear that Martensen's philosophy of religion is of the ontological rather than the cosmological type.[21] Mynster's insistence that no contradictions can be sublated leaves him with a God who is a remote Infinity beyond the world and human consciousness, claims Martensen. No, the understanding is left with contradictions, but speculative theology has the task of moving beyond the understanding and grasping a deeper identity of that which is contradictory for the understanding. The metaphysical necessity of the Christian doctrine of the Incarnation means that Christian metaphysics cannot rest in an either/or. The concept of the supernatural can become actual only by being mediated through the natural and consequently must contain the natural as its own moment. The important logical fact that every concept contains its other, its negative, which has been so fruitful for science, also demands its due in theology, insists Martensen. Theology must acknowledge both rationalism and naturalism as necessary intermediary standpoints through which the way to the standpoint of the Idea is

---

[18] J. A. Bornemann, *"De autonomia conscientiae sui humanae, in theologiam dogmaticam nostri temporis introducta," Tidsskrift for Litteratur og Kritik* 1 (1839): 1–40.

[19] Bishop Mynster, in *Tidsskrift for Litteratur og Kritik* 1 (1839): 249–67.

[20] Lector Martensen, "Rationalisme, Supranaturalisme og *principium exclusi medii*: (I Anledning af H. H. Biskop Mynsters Afhandling herom i dette Tidsskrifts forrige Heft) [Rationalism, Supernaturalism, and the Principle of the Excluded Middle: On the occasion of Bishop Mynster's treatise about this in this journal's previous volume], *Tidsskrift for Litteratur og Kritik* 1 (1839): 456–73. J. L. Heiberg also contributed an article in response to Mynster. See his "En logisk Bemærkning i Anledning af Biskop Dr. Mynsters Afhandling om Rationalisme og Supranaturalisme," *Tidsskrift for Litteratur og Kritik* 1 (1839): 441–56.

[21] For the development of this distinction see Paul Tillich, "The Two Types of Philosophy of Religion," *Theology of Culture*, ed. Robert C. Kimball (London: Oxford University, 1959), pp. 10–29.

prepared. Theology requires a dialectic or a logic with a living copula, where the thinking human spirit is reconciled with the mystery of life and the dualism of pantheism and theism is overcome; only the speculative spirit is capable of overcoming the either/or of life. This means that self- consciousness and revelation are finally one and the same: revelation is the very essence of self-consciousness. The Christian God, as an object of our knowledge, is in addition the one who manifests itself within the human. Martensen does not see this emphasis on the immanence of the divine in the human as ending in rationalism, for that immanence fully comprehended is transcendence.

In the next year, 1840, Martensen is promoted to the rank of *Professor Extraordinarius* or Associate Professor. That same year sees the publication of the work on the mysticism of the Middle Ages. Martensen had intended to submit that work to Copenhagen University for the degree of Doctor of Theology; however, before that could be done the University of Kiel bestowed on him an honorary Doctor of Theology degree on the basis of his dissertation on autonomy, and so he dedicated the Meister Eckhart piece to the theological faculty in Kiel.[22] In 1841 the *Outline to a System of Moral Philosophy* is published. It was the fruit of his lectures for the students who were preparing for the philosophical exam.[23] He would later use this writing in teaching theological students Christian Ethics.[24]

In 1841 Schelling was called from Munich to Berlin to combat the influence of the left-wing Hegelian school.[25] We find that in the early 1840s Martensen also came to see Danish life as having moved into a critical time due to the emergence of left-wing Hegelianism in Denmark. As a result, Martensen underwent a shift from being committed first and foremost to the public of the academy to that of the church. There were five factors that triggered this transition from theological professor to ecclesial spokesperson. Here we can do no more than mention these five. The first is three anonymous articles that appeared in *The Copenhagen Post* in January and February of 1840, attacking Martensen for introducing the theological students at the University to Hegel's philosophy.[26] The second

---

[22] H. Martensen, *From My Life*, 2:10–11.

[23] Ibid., 2:12.

[24] See, for instance, Martensen's 215–page handwritten copy [*Haandskrivet*] of *Forelæsninger over den christelige Moral efter Grundrids til Moralphilosophiens System* [*Lectures on Christian Ethics according to the Outline to a System of Moral Philosophy*], that were used during the winter semester of the 1845–46 academic year, item E650 in the Department of Søren Kierkegaard Research, the University of Copenhagen.

[25] F. Lichtenberger, *History of German Theology in the Nineteenth Century*, trans. and ed. W. Hastie (Edinburgh: T. & T. Clark, 1889), p.71.

[26] See "Nogle Træk til en Charakteristik af den philosophiske Aand, som for Tiden findes hos de Studerende ved Kjøbenhavns Universitet [Some Features of a Characterization of the

factor working to move Martensen toward the church is Copenhagen's version of Fichte's atheism controversy in Jena,[27] namely, the Hans Brøchner affair of December 1841 centering around the refusal to let this supporter of left-wing Hegelianism take the theological exam for ordination. Third, there is the factor of Martensen's article of April 1842 that appeared in *Intelligensblade*, published by J. L. Heiberg,[28] which must be understood against the background of the rise of left-wing Hegelianism among the cultured and the rise of sectarian born-againism among the less refined. Factor number four is two letters received by Martensen in the early 40s inviting him to take a leading role in representing Hegelianism in an ongoing debate, an invitation which he rejects because of the polarization in German philosophy of religion and complications that have arisen with the rise of left-wing Hegelianism in Denmark.[29] The final factor is the increasing influence of Jacob Mynster, a leading figure of Golden Age Denmark, on Martensen.

Interested, then, in the ecclesial question of the relation between faith and dogmatic knowledge, Martensen devoted most of his time over the next years to his major work, *Christian Dogmatics*. About this work, which was translated into German, Swedish, English, and French, it has been stated that it is the most representative single work of the main trend of Danish theology of the nineteenth century.[30] Because of the shift of concern from the academy to the church, Martensen's *Christian Dogmatics*[31] of 1849 is markedly different from his *Speculative Dogmatics* of a

---

Philosophical Spirit which is Found at Present Among the Students at the University of Copenhagen]," *Kjøbenhavnsposten* 14, No. 25 (January 26, 1840): 97–99. Martensen responds to this article with "Philosophisk Beskedenhed i *Kjøbenhavnsposten* [Philosophical Modesty in *The Copenhagen Post*]," *Fædrelandet*, vol. 1, No. 50 (January 29, 1840), Col. 259–61. The anonymous author responds with "Philosophisk Suffisance i 'Fædrelandet' [Philosophical Arrogance in *The Fatherland*]," *Kjøbenhavnsposten* 14, No. 31 (February 1, 1840):121–24. Martensen responds with a short article, "Erklæring [Declaration]," *Fædrelandet*, vol. 1, No. 56 (February 4, 1840), Col. 315–16. The final article then appears: "Sidst Indlæg: Sagen contra Lector Martensen som Mandatarius for Hegel & Comp. [A Final Plea: The Case Contra Lector Martensen as the Authorized Representative for Hegel & Comp.]," *Kjøbenhavnsposten* 14, No. 41 (February 11, 1840):161–63.

[27] Martensen says the incident in Denmark made him think of the Fichte affair, *Briefwechsel zwischen H. L. Martensen und I. A. Dorner, 1839–1881*, 2 vols. (Berlin: H. Reuter, 1888), 1:49.

[28] H. Martensen, "Nutidens religiøse Crisis [The Current Religious Crisis]," *Intelligensblade* 1 (1842): 52–73.

[29] The two letters are included in Jens Holger Schjørring's *Teologi og Filosofi. Nogle Analyser og Dokumenter vedrørende Hegelianismen i Dansk Teologi [Theology and Philosophy: Some Analyses and Documents Concerning Hegelianism in Danish Theology]* (København: G.E.C. Gad, 1974), pp. 34–35.

[30] Niels Thulstrup, *Kierkegaard and the Church in Denmark*, vol. 13 in *Bibliotheca Kierkegaardiana* (Copenhagen: C. A. Reitzels, 1984), p. 169.

[31] H. Martensen, *Den christelige Dogmatik* (Kjøbenhavn: C. A. Reitzel, 1849). *Christian Dogmatics*, trans. from the German by William Urwick (Edinburgh: T. & T. Clark, 1866).

decade earlier. In fact, after the transition to ecclesial spokesperson, as he grows more comfortable with his place in the establishment, Martensen's writings not surprisingly take on a more conventional flavor. In 1843 Martensen addresses the two issues of baptism and the church year with his book *Christian Baptism: Considered with Reference to the Baptist Question*[32] and his article "The Church Year."[33] In the book on baptism he makes the case that baptism is the action of the contemporaneous Christ. From 1845 Martensen serves as Court Preacher which means that he had the responsibility of proclaiming God's word to the King and Queen. In 1848, the year after Martensen's first wife died, he is married to Virginie Henriette Constance Bidoulac, the daughter of a French immigrant.[34] After his *Dogmatics* receives responses, Martensen publishes in 1850 his *Dogmatic Elucidations* in response to his critics.[35] In that year he is also given the rank of *Professor Ordinarius* or Full Professor.

Once Martensen is appointed Bishop of Sjælland in 1854 another shift takes place in the focus of Martensen's writings. If in the years up until the early 1840s Martensen as University professor directs his writings to the academy, and during the next period from 1842 to 1850 as ecclesial spokesperson he directs his writings to the church, then during the last three-and-a-half decades of his life as ecclesiastical representative he directs his writings to society. The transition to the public of society was occasioned by the February Revolution of 1848, an event that made 1848 a year of awakening in the whole arena of the social, as Martensen writes in his autobiography: "For this is the world-historical meaning of the February Revolution, that it was not as the July Revolution merely a political-liberal revolution, but was in addition a social revolution. *The fourth estate and its demands is the innermost feature of the February Revolution. The social problem is the question of rich and poor, of work and capital, of the destitution of society and of a more equitable and just distribution of the goods of the earthly life.* It was this problem which fermented and turbidly stirred at the bottom of the February Revolution."[36] Martensen states that at that time he came to realize the importance of the social, that if one did not consider and grasp the social side of a matter one would be unable to come to a full understanding of it. To some extent Martensen continued to be one of the shining stars in the established

---

[32] H. Martensen, *Den christelige Daab. Betragtet med hynsyn paa det baptistiske Spørgsmaal* (Kjøbenhavn: C. A. Reitzel, 1843).

[33] H. Martensen, "Kirke-Aaret," *Urania: Aarbog for 1844*, ed. J. L. Heiberg (Kjøbenhavn: H. I. Bing, 1848), pp. 161–88; reprinted in Julius Martensen, *Minor Writings and Talks of Bishop Martensen*, pp. 93–109.

[34] H. Martensen, *From My Life*, 3:218.

[35] H. Martensen, *Dogmatiske Oplysninger. Et Leilighedsskrift* [*Dogmatic Elucidations: An Occasional Writing*] (Kjøbenhavn: C. A. Reitzel, 1850).

[36] Martensen, *From My Life*, 2:127.

network of Golden Age Denmark, but it should be pointed out how he
did take a stand for Christian socialism. "[In 1848] I had to remember
what Fr. Baader had said several years back about the disrelation between
the haves and the have-nots. I had to be reminded of his word that our
present social culture resembles not a tree which spreads out its branches
to all sides, but a pyramid at whose top there is found some few favored
people, while its broad base forms an infinite swarm of possessionless
and destitute which is entrusted completely to itself and therefore relegated to every sort of self-help, because neither by heart nor stomach,
neither by duty nor honor is it tied to the state, to which it is related
with indifference if not hatred (2:130–31)." Years later, in 1874, Martensen published *Socialism and Christianity* in which he addressed the social
problem that had emerged in Denmark with the impact of the Indus-
trial Revolution.[37]

The last thirty-four years of Martensen's life, then, found him concerned with practical or ethical theology aimed at social issues, his most
important writing being the three-volume *Christian Ethics*.[38] The first volume is a general discussion of ethics and the next two comprise the special ethics, with the second volume on the individual ethic and the third
volume on the social ethic. However, Martensen did not leave behind
completely the interests of his youth during this period. In 1867 he published *Faith and Knowledge*, an engrossing work featuring an "Ethical
Concept of God" that shows the influence of Schelling and similarities to the thought of Dorner on the immutability of God.[39] Besides other
writings dealing with such matters as the Grundtvigians and the relation
between Roman Catholicism and Protestantism, Martensen also published during this period his work on Jacob Böhme of 1881 which includes
intriguing reflection on the Trinity.[40] Near the end of his life Martensen
wrote his memoirs, publishing the three-volume autobiography in 1882

---

[37] H. Martensen, *Socialisme og Christendom. Et Brudstykke af den specielle Ethik* [*Socialism and Christianity: A Fragment of the Special Ethic*] (Kjøbenhavn: Gyldendal, 1874).

[38] H. Martensen, *Den christelige Ethik. En almindelige Deel* (Kjøbenhavn: Gyldendal, 1871. *Den specielle Deel. Første Afdeling: Den individuelle Ethik; Anden Afdeling: Den sociale Ethik* (Kjøbenhavn: Gyldendal, 1878). *Christian Ethics*, vol. 1 trans. from the Danish by C. Spense, and vols. 2 and 3 trans. from the German respectively by William Affleck and Sophia Taylor (Edinburgh: T. & T. Clark, 1873, 1881, 1882).

[39] H. Martensen, *Om Tro og Viden. Et Leilighedsskrift* [*Faith and Knowledge: An Occasional Writing*] (Kjøbenhavn: C. A. Reitzel, 1867). See Isaak August Dorner, *Divine Immutability: A Critical Reconsideration*, trans. Robert R. Williams and Claude Welch with an Introduction by Robert R. Williams (Minneapolis: Fortress, 1994)

[40] H. Martensen, *Jacob Böhme. Theosophiske Studier* [Jacob Böhme: Theosophical Studies] (Kjøbenhavn: Gyldendal, 1881). *Jacob Boehme: His Life and Teaching*, trans. T. Rhys. Evans (London: Hodder & Stoughton, 1885).

and 1883. After his death on February 3, 1884, two volumes of correspondence between Martensen and Dorner were published as well as the equivalent of a volume of correspondence with Bishop Otto Laub.[41] Years later three further volumes of letters Martensen had sent to his close friend L. Gude were also published.[42] In his funeral sermon for Martensen, C. Rothe fittingly stated how Martensen had understood that "the human things must be known in order to be lived,—the divine things must be lived in order to be known."[43] We go now to a consideration of what Martensen's life had allowed him to know about the divine things in his early theological period.

Overview of the Three Treatises

The three translated treatises complement one another nicely. When read together they illuminate one another with the end result of enlightening our understanding of Martensen's philosophical and theological point of view. In the third section of this Introduction an effort will be made to communicate a sense for the comprehensive vision informing these particular works through the articulating of rudimentary and reflections affirmations of Martensen's philosophy of religion. Before attending to that comprehensive vision, a very brief overview of the three translated works is in order. It soon becomes evident just how central is the notion of personality in Martensen's philosophy of religion.

Personality or the idea of freedom anchors Martensen's theological view during the period in which he wrote the treatises included in this volume. It informs, first of all, *The Autonomy of Human Self-Consciousness in Modern Dogmatic Theology*. After returning home from his study-trip abroad Martensen set to work on his dissertation for the theological licentiate in the winter of 1836–37, defending the thesis "with flying colors" on July 12, 1837.[44] That work, which was submitted in Latin by Johannes

---

[41] *Briefwechsel zwischen H. L. Martensen und I. A. Dorner 1839–1881*, 2 vols. (Berlin: Reuther, 1888). "O. Laubs Brevvexling med H. L. Martensen" [O. Laub's Correspondence with H. L. Martensen], in *Biskop Otto Laubs Levnet. En Livsskildring i Breve* [*Bishop Otto Laub's Life: A Life Description in Letters*], 3 vols., ed. F. L. Mynster (Kjøbenhavn: Karl Schønberg, 1885–87), 1:299–2:407.

[42] *Biskop H. Martensens Breve* [*Bishop Martensen's Letters*], 3 vols., ed. Bjørn Kornerup (København: G.E.C. Gad, 1955–57.

[43] C. Rothe, "Dr. Th. Hans Lassen Martensen's Jordefærd—February 12, 1884," (Kjøbenhavn: Gyldendal, 1884), pp. 6–7.

[44] *Den Danske Kirkes Historie*, ed. Hal Koch and Bjørn Kornerup, 7 vols. (København: Gyldendal, 1954), 6:328, and Morten Borup, *Johan Ludvig Heiberg*, 3 vols. (København: Gyldendal, 1946), 2:175.

Martensen, set forth a criticism of autonomy as given expression in the stances of Kant, Schleiermacher, and Hegel. The charge is that these thinkers, especially the first two, have not taken seriously enough the notion of personality, the personality of God and that of the human. Kant's moral theology and Schleiermacher's theology of feeling are depicted as being onesidedly subjective. Martensen gives expression to a hermeneutics of suspicion that finds its basis in a theological epistemology which acknowledges the limits of consciousness in the conscience, "the most intense and primordial moment in the God-consciousness." The true relation between God and the human consists in human self-consciousness finding itself conceived by an "other" self-consciousness, namely, the divine, the source of all true revelation. God, as absolute Subject, can be known only "in God's *free* self-revelation." Such a divine Other makes room for human autonomy of a relative sort, but it does not authorize absolute autonomy such as has won the day in many of the most celebrated systems of modernity.

Martensen locates the substantial content of Christian dogma in the doctrines of Creation (communicating the ideal beginning of revelation in God's essence) and Incarnation (communicating the ideal end of revelation in God's kingdom). On the former, Martensen endorses the Hegelian move of placing the negative within the very self of God, i.e., with negativity becoming the eternal other by which God mediates the continuous divine passage from possibility to actuality. The dogma of Creation thus becomes the expression for God's alteration or othering, from which God returns to unity and restores Godself. As Creation points to God moving within the human, Incarnation points to God appearing before the human. Martensen claims that the human's need for an incarnation or for a visible God "is so deep-rooted and engrained in the nature of the human race that one can say about God's incarnation in Christ that if it had not actually occurred, humanity itself necessarily would have invented it." This claim reflects the Christological payoff of Martensen's view that pantheism is a necessary moment within theism. Martensen insists that nothing less than a full disclosure of freedom has taken place in the Christ event, a disclosure of that freedom which gives itself fully in love. His word for this is the absolute personality: the Christ embodies and makes known the absolute personality. The Idea is at the heart of Martensen's philosophy of religion, and this Idea is the absolute personality of the divine which is disclosed in the personality of the Christ.

This work on *The Autonomy of Human Self-Consciousness* was later translated into Danish (1841) and into German (1844). It is not difficult to grasp why Martensen regarded his dissertation as one of his better productions.[45] We can agree with Arildsen's assessment that it belongs with the most completely thought-through works of his authorship.[46]

The concern with personality is also central to the second treatise. Martensen's interest in mysticism is made public in 1840 with the publication of his *Meister Eckhart: A Study in Speculative Theology*. In this fascinating work, the subtitle of which is literally "A Contribution towards Illuminating Medieval Mysticism," Martensen attempts to enter into the phenomenon of mysticism by way of an investigation of the mystical spirit, which is allowed to give an account of itself and disclose its own mystery. Mysticism is presented as a form of Christian speculation to be accorded an important place in the history of religious reflection, and thus the legitimacy of the subtitle that we have chosen. Martensen concentrates on fourteenth- and fifteenth-century German mysticism, which he considers to be the richest and most fully-developed form of Christian mysticism in both a religious and a philosophical respect. The book is entitled *Meister Eckhart* because in the circle of German mystics Eckhart is the most eminent figure, the master of the whole school, the "patriarch of German speculation." The goal of the treatise is to offer a treatment of the mystical movement of the Middle Ages as a whole, considering its various moments. The disposition [*Gemyt*] of the mystic receives considerable attention, and thus the notion of personality occupies a central place in this second treatise as well. This work is very important among Martensen's early writings in that it deals more thoroughly with the ontology informing Martensen's thought than does any other of his minor writings.

The heart of this writing is its delineation of the three moments of the mystical consciousness, that is, mystery, revelation, and the highest Good. The deepest mystery is found in the Godhead [*Guddommen*], and mysticism is not content until it has passed beyond God to the Godhead or the God beyond God that is the mysterious ground and possibility of the divine personality. Through ecstasy the soul enters into a true unity with this mystery. To be the true mystery, the Godhead must disclose itself as revelation, the second moment of the mystical consciousness. The divine Essence separates itself from itself in order for self-disclosive personality to take shape out of the immediate mystery of Substance. The mediation of this difference in concept is revelation. Mysticism errs, according to Martensen, in placing the divine mystery higher than the divine revelation. The personal God is encountered in revelation, but the mystic holds the mysterious Godhead in greater esteem than the revealed God. In Christian mysticism, the creature's hunger and thirst for God leads to

---

[45] Martensen, *From My Life*, 2:2.
[46] Arildsen, *H. L. Martensen*, p. 140.

the imitation of Christ as an inward process of Christification. The resulting *Gemyt* or disposition is an intensified personality, and because of the emphasis on *Gemyt* the Western church has been profoundly interested in individuality. The third moment of the mystical consciousness, the highest Good, deals with mystical morality or the practical way in which the human is able to fulfill its destiny by revealing God, through becoming united with God's will by means of Christ as the Mediator. This progress cannot happen apart from a process of moral detachment from the relativities of life, a process involving a movement through the stages of nature, grace, and essentiality.

This second writing includes a discussion of the prophetic character of mysticism in considering the mystics as "forerunners of the Reformation." Martensen closes his presentation of mysticism with a brief treatment of the relation between mysticism and theosophy in which he concentrates on the post-Reformation thought of Jacob Böhme, a subject to which as we have noted above he returns at the end of his career. Martensen sees mysticism and theosophy as important because they teach us the necessary role of critical reflection in grasping the unity of religion and philosophy. The young Danish scholar's own theological understanding at many points shows the influence of the German mystics. A second edition of the work on mysticism, with minor revisions, was published in 1851.

The idea of personality is no less central to Martensen's understanding of the volitional character of religion than it is to his understanding of its cognitive character. This becomes apparent in the third treatise, the *Outline to a System of Moral Philosophy*. This brief writing is an extremely compact and yet rich abstract of the structure of Martensen's reflections on moral philosophy as they had developed up to 1841. P. Madsen calls Martensen's little ethics with its penetrating conciseness and systematic conclusiveness "a pearl among his writings."[47] About this work Arildsen writes: "In Danish literature the system of moral philosophy stands theologically-philosophically as a typical expression of the triumph of speculative philosophy, its faith in the infallibility of the system and its enthusiasm over harmony, identity: there is one ethic! In the realm of intellectual history it belongs in the same class with its contemporaries: H. N. Madvig's *Latin Grammar* ("Madvig's Greater) and J. L. Heiberg's *New Poems* as 'the canonical books of the humanities of the forties.'"[48] This schematically-presented Hegelian ethics of freedom is clearly a writing that was influential within Danish circles. The *Outline* gives systematic

---

[47] P. Madsen, "Biskop Martensen som theolog" [Bishop Martensen as Theologian], *Theologiske Tidsskrift* 1 (1884): 393–409, p. 404, and cited in Arildsen, *H. L. Martensen*, p. 203.

[48] Arildsen, *H. L. Martensen*, p. 203.

articulation to how it is that the human personality arrives at its proper destination.

In his long Preface to the *Outline*, Martensen makes a case for the value of Hegel's system as a contribution to ethics. In the *Grundrids* itself Martensen creates his own system of freedom. His introductory comments dwell on the concept of moral philosophy and the presupposition of moral philosophy or the teaching on human free will. Basic to Martensen's view of freedom is his distinction between essence and existence. Freedom "is and becomes only what it *makes* itself into." Possessing the ability to deny its essential self, the subjective will is capable of going against the essential will. The free will presupposes the creative will of the Godhead as its innermost ground determination. The Godhead is that pantheistic Substance that is the ground and essence of all things, including human freedom. God, as opposed to the Godhead, is the reality that emerges before the human as a result of contrasts within the life of the Godhead, contrasts that are necessary in the use of language and thought, and contrasts which Martensen believes are not simply ingredients of human cognizing but actually characterize the internal life of the Godhead. The Godhead is the unity of being or prius in which the distinction between free God and free human is set.

The threefold content of moral philosophy is determined by the end of the Good presenting itself to humans as the law, the ideal, and the kingdom of personality. The law is the Good as over against the subjective will of the human. The first part of the system, "The Good as Law," advances from (1) the law's inner relation to the will in the sense of duty conveyed by the conscience to (2) the will's self-determination as understood in relation to action and responsibility to (3) the will's conflict and reconciliation with the law. The second part of the system is on "The Good as Ideal." The ideal is the personal and living shape of the Good within the individual human. In this part of the system Martensen considers the ideal and the corresponding notion of virtue under a threefold point of view: God, the world, and the individual are treated under the form of the ideal. "The Good as Kingdom of Personality" constitutes the system's third part. The kingdom of personality is the Good as it is manifested objectively in the moral world of civil society. This part of the system of moral philosophy includes an examination of that kingdom in terms of its immediate actuality as experienced in the family, its reflected actuality as mediated by the state, art, and science, and its absolute actuality as realized in the spiritual communion or *Menigheden*.

This writing which sketches out a system of freedom, like the other two treatises, does not utilize an indirect mode of communicating. But its direct communication does manage to fill in gaps left in the reader's understanding of Martensen's construal of self, world, and God after having worked through the first two treatises. And the *Outline* continued to be read long after the first edition was published. A second edition, with no revisions except for the exclusion of the Preface, was published in 1864, and a third edition in 1879. It was translated into Swedish, German, Dutch, and Hungarian.

Having offered a brief overview of the three translated treatises, we take a step back to consider some of the affirmations of Martensen's position which carry us further into his perspective within the philosophy of religion.

Affirmations of the Philosophy of Religion

I have little at stake in designating the three translated works as falling into the area of the philosophy of religion. From another perspective it would make more sense to speak of these as "Martensen's Early Theological Writings." Martensen was a theologian. We will see that he refers to his position as "a metaphysics of revelation," which points to the overlap of philosophy and theology in his thinking. The decision to regard the three treatises as writings in the philosophy of religion is due to Martensen's own understanding and presentation of them. Early in his career he saw his work falling into that category of scholarly activity.

The three translated treatises complement one another nicely. When read together they throw light on one another with the end result of illuminating Martensen's philosophical and theological point of view. The summary that follows is given in the form of affirmations in the philosophy of religion drawn from Martensen's writings and lectures. The division is between the "rudimentary affirmations," which articulate the fundamental presuppositions of Martensen's philosophy of religion, and the "reflective affirmations," which express the structural declarations of his philosophy of religion. The former are from methodological statements he makes in his *Lectures on Speculative Dogmatics*; the latter are from statements that he makes in the three works translated below.

1. RUDIMENTARY AFFIRMATIONS OF THE PHILOSOPHY OF RELIGION

A critical resource for offering a complete overview of Martensen's philosophy of religion is his *Lectures on Speculative Dogmatics* from the summer semester of 1838, included in Kierkegaard's *Papirer* XIII, II C 26–27. In the early portion of those lectures (§§ 1–23) Martensen spells out his position on central issues in the philosophy of religion. Therefore, this overview will necessarily draw on those lectures, especially §§ 2–15, which are exceptionally rich in the way they state explicitly some of the fundamental philosophical and theological principles guiding Martensen's thinking on religion. Since those lecture transcriptions of Kierkegaard have not been translated into English, I have not hesitated to include a number of lengthy quotes in the synopsis which follows. The summary of that lecture material takes the form of ten "rudimentary affirmations" which will go far toward exhibiting the conceptual presuppositions on which Martensen's philosophy of religion as expressed in the three translated treatises is built.[49]

1. *The philosophy of religion affirms a distinction between itself and both dogmatic theology and metaphysics, since philosophy of religion considers the comprehensive realm of religion, dogmatic theology considers the more restricted terrain of ecclesial dogmas, and metaphysics considers the pure idea of God as the universal ontological foundation.* Of course, Martensen's philosophy of religion is Christian philosophy of religion, and so the question arises as to its difference from Christian dogmatics. At the end of his note to § 1 he states that to "understand something as idea is to understand it in its eternal possibility, to understand the rational in its eternal rationality (§ 1)." He then clarifies in § 2 of his speculative dogmatics lectures that while Christian dogmatics, as speculative science, is not different from Christian philosophy of religion, the two do differ insofar as the philosophy of religion "has as its task to understand Christianity as the absolute religion in the system of the various historical forms of the Christian religion in the developed system of its dogma. The domain of the philosophy of religion is thus the whole realm of religion, while dogmatics, which instead proceeds from the ecclesial-scientific interest, finds its peculiar domain inside the circle of ecclesial dogmas." Martensen writes that dogmatics proceeds from ecclesial concerns, but "philosophy of religion proceeds from the Idea of religion." "Every little concrete ecclesial determination must be able to be developed from the Idea; therefore, the philosophy of religion is necessary."

In Martensen's view the only true knowledge is a mediated type of knowledge, as opposed to an immediate type, for the mediated type is grounded in "a knowledge of something which is *other* than the known." Because of this dialectical character of true knowledge, Martensen contends that Christian dogmaticians must have a knowledge of the other religions. Furthermore, Martensen views the philosophy of religion as belonging to Protestantism, in that it was Schleiermacher who first defined it, Hegel who penetrated it more speculatively, and Baur who with his "Christian Gnosis" developed most clearly its distinctiveness over against dogmatics. The claim is that considerations in the philosophy of religion

---

[49] All quotations included under these "Rudimentary Affirmations of the Philosophy of Religion" are from §§ 1–15 of Martensen's *Lectures on Speculative Dogmatics*.

are a necessary part of the theological enterprise. In fact, the older dogmaticians such as Athanasius, Augustine, and Anselm could not arrive at
systematic completeness because they lacked a philosophy of religion.
Martensen also sees the philosophy of religion as differing from straight
metaphysics. He declares (§ 2, n.), "Every religion has its metaphysics."
It is this metaphysical foundation of each religion rather than the positive content of each which Martensen suggests should be introduced into
Christianity. For Martensen, then, philosophy of religion differs from
metaphysics, which "treats the pure Idea of God, the universal metaphysical foundation."

2. *The philosophy of religion affirms the fundamental existential relation of the
human to God as the essence of religion, so that religion has both a subjective and
an objective side to it.* A crisp statement about religion appears in § 3: "Religion is not merely consciousness of and knowledge of that fundamental
relation which exists between God and the human, but it is this fundamental spiritual relation itself as really existing. Thus, because the human
in religion stands not merely in an ideal but existential relation to God,
religion is considered as the essence of human nature or as that which
makes the human human." Elaborating further on this line of thinking in
the note, Martensen states: "Religion is a form of the human's consciousness of eternity, in which the human consequently is lifted from self-
consciousness and world-consciousness to the ideal religion." A final
statement in the same note makes it clear that religion is not merely a subjective experience but includes meanings that are shaped by objective,
metaphysical reality: "If it is said to the contrary that religion is God-
consciousness, not as theory but as sentiment and feeling, a proper, but
only psychological, determination is given of religion as a phenomenon
in the soul; but hereby the metaphysical significance of religion is not
seen. So we must again show the difference between religious and esthetic feelings."

In sum: "Thus, religion is the fundamental relation between God and
the human, the bond between the human's personal existence and the
Idea of God." Therefore, he notes, that the definition of religion is properly given in the term *"Forbindtlighed"* which includes the notions of con-
nectedness and obligatedness. Religion is that existential relation which
binds a person to God and obliges one to take this divine reality seriously
in the living out of one's existence.

3. *The philosophy of religion affirms the need to differentiate the religious
consciousness from other forms of consciousness, namely, the esthetic, the ethical, and the philosophical forms of consciousness.* Religion is distinct from art
and philosophy, even though these three are closely related, and philosophy of religion has the task of making clear just how it is to be distinguished (§ 3): "The essence of religion as a definite form of the human's

consciousness of eternity can only be conceptually grasped when it is understood in its qualitative difference from the other forms of consciousness in which the human enters into a relation to the absolute Idea. The absolute Idea is also the object of art, and in its highest determination as the Idea of God constitutes the essential content of philosophy. Art *can be* and philosophy *is* a consciousness of God, which is exactly also the general definition of religion. But its qualitative difference from art and philosophy consists precisely in the fact that these forms of consciousness contain the Absolute in its infinite objectivity, while religion is the infinitely subjective and real existence of the Idea of God in the human." Religion is the presence of the Idea of God within the human. But what is religion's relation to the Absolute? Martensen explains (§ 3, n.): "It is the absolute Idea (that is, that which comprises life in its infinitude, in which prosaic, actual life has its ground and returns), which appears in these forms (religion, philosophy, art)." We are told that the human is liberated from its self-consciousness by being taken up in that view of the world in which self-consciousness is both elevated and transfigured. He concludes that the absolute Idea, if it is carefully reasoned out, has to be on a par with the Idea of God. If then religion is to be defined by "God-consciousness," then it is on a par with philosophy and art. Martensen parenthetically establishes a boundary between art and philosophy: "However, art sees the Absolute not in its pure absoluteness, but through sensuality, the concreteness of beauty; but since the Godhead enters into sensuality, art raises itself to the representation of the Absolute. Philosophy has no other object than God and carries every form of consciousness back to this."

One way of looking at the differences among these three, the traditional interpretation of Hegel's understanding of the relation, is not affirmed by Martensen: "The difference then could be sought in that art has the idea of God in the form of beauty, as in Greek art; that religion allows the truth to appear as beauty; that philosophy finally allows the pure thought to step forward; so that it depends on the stage of development of consciousness, which appears. But then art and religion remain only intermediate links to philosophy." As opposed to this view, Martensen thinks: "In order to determine the qualitative difference we must not merely *describe* religion, but show its ground and possibility in the relation between the Idea of God and the human soul. Art and philosophy present the Idea of God in its objectivity, but religion is its real subjective existence in the human. In the former I relate myself objectively to the Idea of God, (that is, I contemplate the Idea itself, as it is in-and-for-itself apart from all relations); in the latter I relate myself subjectively (that is, I ask about its relation to me). Christianity, for example, can be considered both objectively in philosophy and subjectively in religion."

While religion is closely aligned with art and philosophy, so too is it intimately related to morality. "Since religion is the expression for the relation between God and humankind, it stands in close connection with morality. The moral idea is a moment in the religious idea; when it is separated from this, it only happens by an abstraction. The religious is the eternal, existential reality [*Existentielle*], which is realized in the concrete human as the moral." However, religion cannot be supplanted by morality, just as it cannot be supplanted by art: "Religion can not be replaced by esthetic or moral substrates (belonging to art and philosophy). Even if religion does not appear as conscious, it yet *is* in the human as the bond with God, consequently religion is human nature, makes possible the human's existence: 'The human is an independent rational being' is all too general a definition, not giving the human's essence. The idea of the human, as God has thought it, is to seek in religion, the human is a religious being."

4. *The philosophy of religion affirms that religion presupposes a self-revealing God, who objectivizes Godself for humankind, and this makes possible speculation's true thoughts about God.* For Martensen the metaphysical relatedness of the human to God is capable of bearing rich speculative fruit because the nature of divine Substance or Godhead is to reveal itself. We see this in Kierkegaard's notes on Martensen's *Lectures on Speculative Dogmatics* § 4: "The human's fundamental religious relation to the Godhead can be designated in general as a relation of infinite contrasts and dependence through which is mediated a relation of identity and freedom. But this depends on the fact that the human's real unity with God is only possible by this, that God, according to the eternal truth of God's essence, objectivizes Godself for the human in religion, that is, that God reveals Godself for the human. If God were not present in religion in God's infinite objectivity, if God could not be known by the human, then the human's subjective relation to God would be an untrue and unfree relation; for only *the true thought of God* liberates the human not merely from the human's dependence on itself, but also from *blind* unfree dependence on God. But the thought, in which in religion God is revealed for the human, is according to its origin different from speculation's true thought about God, because it is an integral and eternal moment in that human's fundamental existential relation to God, which constitutes religion's essence. Therefore, just as the human's life has its eternal presupposition and possibility in that original fundamental relation, so all human reflection and speculation has its eternal presupposition and possibility in revelation." There is thus a good and a bad form of being dependent upon God. The good, free form of dependence on God, which cannot transpire without the true thought of God, liberates the human from the bad, unfree form of dependence on God. The self-revealing God implies a Creator God and an epistemic distance between God and the creature. In

the note to § 4, Martensen is recorded as stating: "That the essential thing in religion is the human's subjective unity with God, is seen from the way every still pagan religion seeks to procure this or obtain salvation.—The relation is free, because it is not an outer relation, but united with the human essence. The unity presupposes real *difference*, if it shall be true, not merely abstract. Therefore the idea of reconciliation and redemption is the center point in every religion. Herein lies still not the Christian concept of sin, but only of a contrast, which shall be sublated. And all religions assume that the natural human is not in unity with God, but advances to this in a dependence on God. Therefore the idea of sacrifice is found in every religion. The truth of religion depends on the depth in the idea of reconciliation, the content of this."

For the difference to be transcended, God's self-revelation is required. "But in religion in addition an objective moment must be acknowledged, that is, the idea of revelation must be recognized. God must reveal Godself, in order that God can become known in God's contrast to the human, and in order that this thereafter can be sublated. Where revelation is not yet developed, no difference between God and the human and the infinite contrast between them can be recognized. Consequently, the concept of religion is inseparable from the concept of revelation." It is the case, though, that to "reveal Godself, that is, to objectivize Godself, to make Godself as an object," "God must also make Godself as an object for humankind (and in addition for Godself)" and this must be done "as God is according to God's eternal essence and not otherwise (or else it was indeed no revelation)."

And the Hegelian cast of Martensen's understanding of revelation is apparent in his insistence that this revelation must take place in thought. "The solitary medium through which God can objectivize Godself is *thought*; for to know an object in its objectivity is to know it independently of my subjectivity, to know it in-and-for-itself. Feeling is subjective, private; representation certainly has some objective reality in itself, but yet only grasps the object in a certain relation. If I only had a representation of God, I would only know God in a certain relation, not in-and-for-itself. Thought is the purely free, independent." He continues, "Only by knowing freely, through thought, am I liberated from dependence 1) on myself, my subjectivity, 2) on God (N.B. [note], the unfree dependence), while God is alien to me, a power over me." Therefore, the "objective is necessary in theology. Schleiermacher and his party have mistaken this, as if it only depends on *how* I believe, not at all *what* I believe. The truth of feeling depends on its content. In all religion therefore is a knowledge. Schleiermacher separates sharply between philosophy and religion; right, but he overlooks that there is given a knowledge *in* religion in addition to philosophy, that is, knowledge *of* religion." But what is the nature of the difference, then, "in the objective thought of God which is found in philosophy and that in religion? It lies in the origin; religion's thought about God is revealed, that is, an integral moment in the fundamental relation between God and humans. All founders of religion have also referred to a subjective relation to God; the enthusiasts with revelations as well. Philosophy mediates its knowledge through speculation and reflexion. Revelation is a presupposition for reflexion."

5. *The philosophy of religion affirms that a self-revealing God presupposes the personality of God, that is, the absolute Substance is to be understood as the infinitely free Subject.* In § 5 of his *Lectures on Speculative Dogmatics*, Martensen gives us a clear statement on the personality of God: "Religion and revelation are only possible under a presupposition of the ideal of God's absolute personality, in which idea God is not merely understood as the absolute *Substance*, but as the infinitely free *Subject*, who in God's absolute substantiality knows and wills Godself and stands in a free creative relation to the world as that which is itself really different from God. Only the self-revealing God is able to reveal Godself for the human, and only the God who infinitely affirms and wills its own eternal existence is able to will this its existence in the human, or enter into a religious relation to the human. If God were not personal, then the human's personality would be an unsolved and insoluble contradiction; for human knowledge only finds its true content in knowledge whereby it is itself known and the human will only finds its true end in the will by which it is itself willed. The system of religion and revelation allows itself therefore to be designated as the system of personality. The negation of the divine personality, which involves the negation of the human, abolishes the concept of religion and revelation in its deepest roots."

In the note to § 5, Martensen offers a number of clarifying comments. For instance, he writes, "Personality is the identity of subject and substance." Of course, it is Spinoza who has thought through the notion of substance: "God as the absolute standpoint is the standpoint of pantheism, in the way developed by Spinoza. This is a necessary moment in the understanding of God. The concept of Substance is the concept of the absolute Actuality, which contains all essence, all reality; if there were something outside God, different from God, God would indeed be limited. Therefore ἐν καὶ πᾶν [one and all]; *only God is.* Whatever in the world is reality, is only God. The other is a mere appearance existence. Pantheism is no atheism, but acosmism [Hegel]. The finite beings are only empirical, transient, modifications of substance.—'God and the world are one,' insofar as the world stands in a pure relation to God, as God is the actual reality therein; from the empirical standpoint the world is only mere appearance." This divine Substance is omnivorous, so there cannot be a genuinely free, centered, subject such as self-consciousness: "Here is no place for self-consciousness; for it presupposes a limitation. God is not conscious of Godself, does not see Godself, because God is the light; God does not think Godself, for God is the eternal spring of all thought. As if God should oppose something to Godself, which was not Godself."

Martensen, as we have seen, has an appreciation for pantheism: "It is right that pantheism thinks of God as Substance, wrong that it remains standing with this." But he sees the need for substance to become subject: "God as Subject. Subject is freedom, self-determination, intelligence, will. Substance is only product, effect. God must be carefully thought-through from Substance to Subject. Freedom is absolute independence and infinite self-determination. That which has itself in its power [*sui compos*]. Substance is thought of then as *causa sui* [self-causing]; for otherwise it would not be substance. Consequently, it is the free. But free is only that which has itself perfectly in its power, can make itself into an object, that is, is self-conscious. Substance must consequently become self-conscious. Spinoza thinks of substance essentially as power, but not as that which has itself in its power. It must will itself, posit itself as its own end. Freedom consequently first in the will finds its own fullness. Only as willing is God *sui compos* [fully self-possessing]. The concept of God's power must be thought-through as God's power over Godself, that is, Substance becomes self-conscious or Subject."

6. *The philosophy of religion affirms that the fulfilled personality of the human presupposes the personality of God, for the human I requires a divine Other who as Thou enables it to recover its proper personal depths.* Humans find the completion of their personality in the divine personality, according to Martensen (§ 5, n.): "Personality is the unity of substance and subject. The human, which shall be said to exist personally, must not blindly be an instrument for Substance (for example, the spirit of the times), must not have individuality alone, but at the same time must be peculiarly self-conscious in its peculiarity and in addition penetrated by the Infinite, by Substance. Luther, for example, was both subject, willing, and in addition one with Substance, that is, the idea of the age." In Martensen's view, individuality is equal to the abstract subjective reality, the finite; on the other hand, subject is equal to the substantial in the subject. He notes that other thinkers use the term "individual" for the human's personality. With the affirmation of God as Subject and the human as subject, the relation between God and the world becomes other than what one finds in pantheism, that is, one gets God as a free, creative reality who is the world's Creator: God posits the creation "with freedom, not with blind necessity. It is an action, not an occurrence." And this differs from the flowing forth of things affirmed by pantheism.

Kierkegaard's lecture notes make clear Martensen's claim that human fulfillment is thus dependent upon revelation. "Only now is the revelation-concept possible. That which reveals itself, must be itself self-revealing. If God were not personal, the human's personality would be a contradiction. For then the human subject would be without an object. The human is subject or *I*. No *I* could become self-conscious as *I* except in opposition to a not-*I*. Nature is the not-*I*'s first form. But this opposition must again be sublated and first by recovering itself in the not-*I* gains the *I* itself. Nature is found to be a wholly rational reality, in which the *I* always finds itself but only as an abstract thing." Nature is an other, but it is not personal in the same sense as are other people: "Next, I objectivize myself in the other human; with an object a self is here a subject, I objectivize myself in his or her knowledge. The end for my will, in which this shall recover itself, can not be nature, things, but only persons [Fichte conceived the object as a thing, not as itself a subject]." My fullness of personality is found over against a "Thou": "Finally, I objectivize myself in God, but I am personal, so the essence in which I find myself must be personal. In the revealed religion therefore is known no abstract determinations concerning God, but God's own knowledge and will; the human comes to participate in the divine Subject. (Not-*I* must be thought of as a 'Thou' as over against my '*I*.')" This I-Thou relation has been developed fully by other thinkers such as Martin Buber and Emil Brunner, but it is interesting to see it being incorporated by Martensen in 1838.

7. *The philosophy of religion affirms that human knowing as mediated in history is revelation, for just as the human's essence is not arrived at immediately but mediately in history, so too can God's revelation to humans proceed only as quickly as human consciousness is able to know it.* God's revelation is the unfolding meaning experienced by human self-consciousness. This becomes clear in § 6 of the *Lectures on Speculative Dogmatics* where Martensen claims that, just as it is necessary for knowledge that the human's essence must be posited in its personal unity with God, so too is it necessary for knowledge that this essence of the human be not "*immediately actual*" but achievable only through an infinite mediation. "This mediation is history, and not merely the human religious consciousness, but also the divine revelation follows the law of historical development. The basis of the necessary relation which takes place between the knowing one and the known, between subject and object, is namely God's revelation for humans conditioned by the level of human self-consciousness." God can only reveal, in other words, that which the human is ready to receive: "Therefore, as long as humankind finds itself at a relative standpoint of its development, God can only manifest a single abstract moment (phase), which corresponds with the human finite consciousness. But in the fullness of time when the essence of human self-consciousness becomes actual, and *the true human is revealed*, the true God reveals Godself according to the infinite content of God's essence." In the note Martensen explains:

"In the inner relation which takes place between God's revelation and human self-consciousness, the concepts of accommodation (συγκαταβα-σις) and anthropomorphisms have their ground. These concepts therefore have not merely subjective, but objective reality."

The identity of the knowing consciousness and revelation is made possible by the human's participation in the divine Substance or God-head which serves as a *prius* in which subject and object find their unity: "The essence of spirit consists in that it sublates its immediacy, that is, in mediation [*Vermittelung*]. History is the successive sublation of the spirit's immediacy, the spirit's liberation to its essentiality. According to the fundamental relation between subject and object, the spirit must reveal itself parallel with the human's self-consciousness. If the object is to be known by me in its essentiality, my self-consciousness must be equal with the object; there must be the identity of subject and object. In order to be able to be known the Godhead must be the principle in my knowledge, must be subjective, not only objective. The identity of subject and object, humankind and God, is still in its development. Therefore, only gradually can a single moment (phase) of God be known."

8. *The philosophy of religion affirms a progressive development of revelation that passes through paganism and Judaism, for the former manifests forms of spirituality corresponding to moments in the Godhead or divine Substance and the latter manifests God as Subject or as "God."* The unfolding revelation of the divine and the various developmental stages of the human spirit correspond to one another, suggests Martensen (§ 6, n.): "The history of religion therefore shows an inner coherence between individual stages; the divine revelation must have just as many stages as the human spirit has under its liberation to full self-consciousness and personality." The diverse manifestations of human spirituality in the pre-Christian religions "correspond to individual moments in the Godhead." Martensen points out that since a person's self-consciousness can never be transcended, one must always use anthropomorphisms; thus, anthropomorphisms are found in all religions. The traditional Western religions hold a special place in the philosophy of religion, as stated in the *Lectures on Speculative Dogmatics* "§ 7: "Paganism, Judaism, and Christianity are the fundamental forms in which the idea of religion and revelation has historically realized itself. In as much as we want to know the essence of these religions and their mutual relations, they must be considered according to the fundamental universal determinations of the religious idea." Martensen holds that the three major moments of the religious idea are: first, "the universal idea of God, the fundamental relation between God and the world, which constitutes a religious metaphysical basis"; second, "the idea of God's appearance, that is, finitude or the objective view of the idea of reconciliation"; and third, "the idea of the human's appropriation of reconciliation,

which is objectivized in the religious cultus." In as much as the philosophical consideration of religions knows each of these determinations in
its relation to the idea of personality, it conceives paganism and Judaism
as the elementary presuppositions and points of passage for Christianity,
because it shows that these systems contain only abstract moments of
God's and humankind's personality, over against which Christianity is
personality's actual system." According to Martensen (§ 7, n.), the idea
of God's appearance, that is, Incarnation, comes forth in all religions and
must come forth in them since religion is to contain the unity of God and
the world.

The distinctive mark of paganism (§ 8) is that it is "the spiritual standpoint of the natural human, namely, insofar as the human self-consciousness partly has not liberated itself from the objective power of nature,
partly still is imprisoned in its own subjective naturalness, in the barriers
of individuality and nationality. But so long as the human has not found
its own *I* and understood its own spirit's qualitative difference from
nature, neither will she be able to understand the divine Spirit's qualitative difference from the world. Therefore God can only reveal Godself for the pagan consciousness according to its substantiality manifested
in the world, but not according to its subjectivity and personality. In as
much as the divine Substance is reflected in the natural national-spirit's
consciousness, it is comprehended not in its pure universality in-and-
for-itself, but is viewed only in its immediate unity with the individual
national-spirit. Since then every people represents a stage of the development of human consciousness, the divine Substance is individualized
in this concrete form and every people must consequently view the Godhead under the form of the Idea, which constitutes its own spiritual
essence, and is reflected in the national individuality. The ethnic religions
or national religions thus present the divine Substance dispersed into a
multiplicity of moments. Their qualitative difference is determined by the
concrete form in which Substance presents itself, and the higher forms
separate themselves from the lower by the striving they express in developing that subjectivity which is hidden in Substance, a striving which
in paganism does not reach its goal." In § 9 we learn that paganism gives
rise to polytheism, which "can only present the Idea in the outer multiplicity of its moments." This yields "a circle of theophanies," but since the
qualitative difference between nature and spirit is unknown," the Godhead is manifested in an alternatingly natural and human form. "In none
of these theophanies does the Godhead appear as an actual person, but
the God figures are only finite, particular individualities or general symbols and superficial personifications." Only in the Greek view, where
the pagan nature symbols are elevated to mythology, does the consciousness arise of "the *human figure*" as "the essential form for the appearance
of God." The Greek gods are "actual living individualities."

Martensen continues his *Lectures on Speculative Dogmatics* by stating (§ 11) that in Judaism "the qualitative difference between nature and spirit" is "taken up for the human consciousness and God is revealed according to its subjectivity, that is, *as God*. The fundamental relation between God and the world is no longer the relation of substantiality but the relation of causality, which appears as the relation of contrast between the Creator and the creation. In this religion revelation *as such* first appears, because only the subject can actually be said to reveal itself. But this revelation is only relative and God's personality is only abstract and particular, not absolute; the divine subjectivity, namely, is not substantial, in the dogma of the Creator the ethical moment appears separated from the metaphysical and the Idea of God's unity is only comprehended negatively in contrast to polytheism. Finally, God is only this people's God, a determination which gives this people its great world historical significance but also unfolds the seeds of its ruin." In § 12, Martensen continues his depiction of Judaism, which he sees as the negation of paganism in that it lacks a subjective consciousness of God: "Since the Jewish idea of God contains the abstract negation of the natural and creaturely element, there is found in this religion no appearance of God. God is only present for the people in the law and in God's dealings with the people, which are accompanied by signs and wonders, but they are never allowed to look at God." A last comment on Judaism is in § 13: "Since creatureliness stands as an insurmountable barrier for the Jewish consciousness the character of the religious cult is the absolute dependence and fear of the Lord. The divine revelation has only objective and positive existence in the theocratic constitution but no subjective existence and development in the human individual. The human individuality is still not liberated to true personality, for the believing Israelite only mediates its consciousness of God through its national-consciousness and thus Judaism itself stands within the circle of national religions. Instead of the free individuality's personal relation to God, legality and external sacrificial cult prevail here. The deeper principle of subjectivity is developed only through the prophets, who by a deeper consideration of sinfulness and a more ideal conception of the promises considered universalism more closely."

9. *The philosophy of religion affirms Christianity as the religion which gives expression to the highest form of revelation, that is, the absolute interpenetration of Substance and Subject in the spiritual person of infinite personality.* Martensen is lecturing at a time when, under the influence of Schleiermacher and Hegel, Christianity was simply regarded as "the revealed religion." In a day when there is talk about "the parity of religions," this strikes us as a bit outdated, but this was also at a relatively early stage in the doing of the philosophy of religion. Martensen discusses the distinctive character of Christianity in § 14: "In the Christian idea of God, which finds its deeper explication in the dogma of the Trinity, thought of the subjectless

substance and the substanceless subject is denied. Namely, as the infinite personality is here thought of as perfecting itself through an eternal immanent genesis and process, it is thought of as the absolute penetration of the substantial and the subjective, that is, as the truly spiritual person. In the determination of God's relation to the world Christianity denies on the one hand acosmism, in as much as Christianity does not consider the world and finitude as a mere appearance, but ascribes to creatureliness a relative actuality and independence outside of God; on the other hand abstract dualism is denied, in as much as the creation is not merely from God, as its absolute *cause*, but in addition subsists by God, in as much as God in God's infinite personality has appointed itself as the substantial *ground* of the creation and in real presence essentially and actually is present in God's world, and not merely is the creation from God and by God, but also *to* God, in as much as God is mediated by Godself as its absolute *end*. Since God is thus the beginning, middle, and end and as Father, Son and Spirit not merely has revealed God's will, but God's essence, God stands through this God's essential revelation not merely in relation to the world, but also in an infinite relation to Godself." The internal life of God is not dependent on the world, as we see in the note: "God completes God's personality through an immanent process which is eternal, independent of time and creation." Even in Martensen's era there was a tendency to discredit the secular, so he notes that one "of our time's tasks is to ensure the world or not-God its right." In §15 of the *Lectures on Speculative Dogmatics* he writes: "The Christian idea of God's appearance is contained in the dogma of the Incarnation or the doctrine of God's real *historical* human-becoming in Christ. In this human-becoming the dualism between God and the creation is factually overcome, since the divine nature in this way has united itself with the human, that God not merely is revealed *by means of* or *in* but *as* this historical personality. The dogma of the Incarnation thus excludes the pagan consideration of revelation according to which this revelation is only to have been a mythical appearance or theophany. The doctrine of a mythical Christ, who as unhistorical would be in addition impersonal, namely, has its deeper ground in acosmism which is incompatible with Christianity. On the other hand the dogma of the Incarnation denies the Jewish consideration, which is able only to conceive the Christ through the categories of finitude and creatureliness."

10. *The philosophy of religion affirms the interrelatedness of reason and revelation in that each has its ground in the other, so that the immanence of God is seen insofar as the essence of divine revelation is what human self-consciousness arrives at and the transcendence of God is seen insofar as the depths of human self-consciousness is the divine self-consciousness.* This final affirmation summarizes Martensen's epistemological view of the relation between faith

and knowledge. In ancient times, Martensen explains (§ 2, n.), the two disciplines of philosophy of religion and dogmatics were strictly separated. The philosophy of religion was natural or rational theology in contrast to revealed religion, which was the subject of dogmatics. Interestingly enough, Martensen points out that "this difference presupposes a *now unacceptable* difference between reason and revelation; for both have their ground in each other." This affirmation of the interrelatedness of reason and revelation follows upon Martensen's understanding of human nature as essentially religious.[50]

2. Reflective Affirmations of the Philosophy of Religion

The three writings translated here together give a full view of Hans L. Martensen's philosophy of religion. They elucidate one another in a most helpful way. Time and time again when one of the works only mentions a notion and leaves it undeveloped, one of the other two writings will be found to develop the same notion more fully. The three treatises thus function as mirrors which reflect on the subject-matter in mutually complementary ways. Therefore, it is necessary to look at the statement the three of these corporately make about the philosophy of religion. In so doing, we will identify ten "reflective affirmations" of Martensen's philosophy of religion.

1. *The philosophy of religion affirms a method that proceeds dialectically as guided by the Idea or that final purpose of the teleological process in terms of which a given subject of inquiry is seen in relation to the totality or whole of reality.* The guiding notion for Martensen's inquiry into the philosophy of religion is the Idea, where the Idea is not understood in the Kantian sense of an unconditioned ideal of reason that is non-constitutive or unreal and therefore merely regulative. It is Hegel who mentors on method. If knowing something as idea is to know it in its eternal possibility, then following the dialectical method is following an approach in which through various piecemeal efforts one arrives at an all-embracing perspective on the subject-matter at hand. The dialectical method is the conceptual method in which every theorem is considered in its own right and as part of the totality. The total comprehensive knowing—in which varying, sometimes contradictory, representations are unified—is the concept.

---

[50] The remaining sections of this introductory material include statements on the Incarnation (§ 16), the Christian cult (§ 17), the relation of dogmatics to the various heresies (§18), the Protestant-Catholic distinction (§19), the relation of Scripture and tradition (§ 20), the nature of dogmatics as mediating theology (21), the notion of inspiration (§ 22), and the relation of dogmatics to church symbols or confessions of faith (§ 23).

2. *The philosophy of religion affirms a theonomous view of life which grounds a hermeneutics of suspicion in relation to the tradition of German idealism from Kant through Fichte and Schelling to Hegel and in particular in relation to that tradition's understanding of human autonomy.* Although the idealistic tradition presents itself as being presuppositionless, this is not the case. When it considers human self-consciousness to be self-sufficient, this is an incorrect claim because the self in actuality is dependent upon the divine self-consciousness. Idealism understands the human metaphysically as a being endowed with reason. Actually, it is the human's unity with God in religion that fundamentally defines the human, with reason or thinking included as an aspect of this specific character. This anthropological insight which is at the same time a theological insight points to the need for a positive consideration of the human spirit as opposed to the negative consideration of the line of thinkers from Descartes to Hegel whose metaphysical or logical approach has been onesided. The positive is what cannot be produced and construed by mere reason but must be received from outside itself. Acknowledging the centrality of the God-relation in the constitution of the human leads to a theonomous view of life. This theonomous view in turn yields a distinctive view of the human's knowing and willing which stands in judgment on idealism's view of autonomy.

3. *The philosophy of religion affirms a mediating or speculative approach which is differentiated from supernaturalism and rationalism in that the historicity of God means the history of the world is the setting in which the revelation of God unfolds and the world's history is integral to God's unfolding life.* God as a living reality entails difference or otherness within God, and that otherness reaches its full actuality in an actual world which becomes part of God's life. Revelation is the grasping of God's unfolding life. The basis for the human's appropriating of God's unfolding life is the indissoluble unity of the anthropological and theological moments of the human. Since the world is in God and its life is in God's life, the human's world-consciousness cannot be absolutely separated from its God-consciousness. Pantheism defines God as that which has existence only in the other, which makes it an external reality. It posits negativity within God, but sees this happening through a blind necessity. It also regards the history of the human race as the history of God. Theism, on the other hand, which defines God as that which has existence within itself as well as within the other, insists that God's freedom establishes difference or otherness within God. For theism the worldly principle is a moment within God, but it is by no means God's very self.

4. *The philosophy of religion affirms both that the Godhead includes contrast, difference, otherness in the form of the Son, who as inclusive of human nature and the principle of the world gives expression to negation over against the*

Father, and that the Godhead includes unity, identity, sameness in the form of Spirit, which gives expression to freedom by way of the divine will to love. The principle for the otherness within the divine life is the Son, who stands in contrast to the Father. Otherness therefore exists within the Godhead. God is the Subject in which this otherness is mediated, as the ongoing mediating activity makes real the unity of God. That which is one in the Godhead but differentiated in the two hypostases is again reunited in the mediating activity of love. This love of God is the expression of God's freedom. The free God who loves is therefore a God of othering, a God who others Godself in love. God as reuniting love is Spirit.

5. *The philosophy of religion affirms the first foci of theology's ellipse as the Creation of the world by God, which establishes both the difference between God and the world as the infinite qualitative difference between Creator and creature and the unity between God and the world as God establishes Godself as the Substance of the beings of the world.* The concept of creation is inseparable from the concept of personality: the creation has its ground in God's freedom. God as Creator is God as the free power who is the source of the world and of human beings. God creates out of nothing, that is, out of God's nothing or out of that in God which is not God. In establishing Godself as the Substance of the beings of the world, those beings have ready access to the presence of God. God's presence within the human takes the form of a primitive knowledge of God and is the basis for being able to acknowledge its dependence upon God. But this dependence must be determined qualitatively as well as quantitatively. The dependence of the world and the human on God is not simply that nothing falls outside of God's power. This simply claims the divine power in terms of size and dependence in terms of a natural and external reliance on the divine. Substance, the basis for quantitative dependence, exists only in the other, and is therefore an external reality. But God, as that free, spiritual reality which exists not only in the other but also in itself, is an internal reality. Qualitative or spiritual dependence is found only where there is an inner or free human being who in freedom is able to certify its dependence upon God by negating its own independence.

6. *The philosophy of religion affirms the second foci of theology's ellipse as the Incarnation of God in Christ, which is the actualization of the kingdom of God and the means by which the world is perfected.* If the Creation constitutes the beginning of God's revelation, the Incarnation constitutes the end. These two together comprise the center of that revelation. When one has properly thought through these two doctrines which disclose the most original features of religion, the remaining theological deliberations fall into place as a matter of course. Lying behind the Incarnation is the idea of God's appearance. Human consciousness can find nothing appearing externally in history except that for which it already finds the principle within itself.

The Christ as the constitutor of the human race and the true author of the new creation gives human consciousness an other. The Incarnation is the perfecting of the creation. The true idea of God is the idea of absolute personality and freedom, and the Christ reveals the ideal of personality as the absolute personality. Since absolute freedom constitutes his essence, the Christ is the principle of the human race.

7. *The philosophy of religion affirms that religion includes three forms, Religiousness 1 which is the metaphysical relatedness of the human and the divine, Religiousness 2 which is the existential, living religious relationship between the human and the divine, and Religiousness 3 which is the existential, living religious relationship between the human and the divine as mediated by the Christ.* At the heart of Martensen's philosophy of religion is the distinction between the *natural relatedness* of God to the human and the *religious relationship* of the human with God. This God-relatedness is conceived as being metaphysical or ontological in character. Theologically, it is the payoff of the human being as created in the image of God: God, the Essence and Substance of all reality, resides within the creature or the creature resides within God. However, metaphysical relatedness, or that which is ideally or essentially the case within the human, must be actualized in existence. Thus, ontological gift entails a religious task. Natural God-relatedness presents an ideal which awaits fulfillment in religious relationship. What is true essentially must become true existentially. Just as the more explicit manifestation of religion is centered in a subjective experience of the religious relationship between God and the human, so too the metaphysical God-relatedness enables one to speak of the human as possessing natural religious needs, thoughts, and imperatives. For Martensen, then, religion encompasses both of these aspects of the God-human relation, both natural relatedness and religious relationship. The stages of religion are three and not two in number, for the "religious relationship" aspect of religion may be of a natural or a Christian sort. Therefore, in looking at Martensen's reflections on religion, it is helpful to differentiate three types of religiousness: Religiousness 1 refers to that essential ontological God-relatedness which is intrinsic to human nature; Religiousness 2 refers to that existential religious (but non-Christian) relationship of the human with God; and Religiousness 3 refers to that existential religious (Christian) relationship of the human with God. Martensen's philosophy of religion, insofar as it focuses on the transition from Religiousness 1 to Religiousness 2 or to Religiousness 3 and on the divine empowering of that passage, can be seen as a theology of othering.

8. *The philosophy of religion affirms that the essential freedom of the human, as the metaphysical reality of its unity with the divine Substance or Essence of life, calls the human's subjective freedom to a life of love by way of the law (conscience as the co-knowing of the human and the divine), by way of the ideal (of*

the divine, of the world, and of individuality), and by way of the kingdom of per-
sonality in its immediate actuality (family), in its reflected actuality (state, art,
science), and in its absolute actuality (the spiritual communion or the kingdom of
God as such). The concept of freedom is of a piece with the concept of
spirit, self-consciousness, *I*. Human freedom is determined by the divine
to be self-determining. The essential will of freedom needs to be determined as actual. This happens through the human's subjective will or
freedom of choice. The reality of the human condition is that freedom
misuses itself or is estranged from itself, as the human falls away from its
essence and manifests the sinfulness of human nature. And yet the self is
called to be responsible. The freedom of the human must be considered
both subjectively and objectively in order to give a full account. From
the subjective side freedom can be considered in relation to the law and
in relation to the ideal. The law calls freedom to actualize its essence in
existence. The conscience plays an important role in this process of self-
actualization which ends in guilt and an unhappy consciousness. As freedom makes the Good its own it strives to actualize the ideal it sets for
itself, be that the ideal of God, world, and/or self. In its striving the self is
brought out into the world to contribute to the lives of others. From the
objective side freedom is shaped by the structures of society and culture.
Within the kingdom of personality, the primary moments of the communal cultivating ethos are the immediate actuality of the family, the reflective actuality of the state, art, and science, and the absolute actuality
of the church in the sense of the spiritual communion or the kingdom of
God as such.

9. *The philosophy of religion affirms that the human finds the fulfillment of an*
intensified personality (Gemyt) as it utilizes its striving freedom, which leads to
virtue, to humbly acknowledge its dependence upon God as the power undergird-
ing its existence. The intensification of personality takes place according
to that over against which one lives one's life. The "other" of the self
determines the level of its striving and the intensity of its selfhood. The
intensified personality is that spiritual center of freedom which is capable
of grasping truth; it is the way in which the objective, metaphysical truth
and the subjective, empirical *I* are able to be united. The intensified personality is the depths of the unified self or soul which holds together the
many contrasts of the self. The truth of the way things are calls for the self
to humbly acknowledge that divine reality which is its source. Humility is
the designation for such acknowledgement. The highest potentiation of
the personality happens as the self uses its self-determination or independence to humbly make itself dependent upon the divine power which
sustains and empowers its life.

10. *The philosophy of religion affirms mysticism's eschatological vision of the*
preservation of the essentialized self within the life of God, as the self's self-will is

destroyed while the goodness created by the self's decision-making is preserved in God's eternity. The freedom of the human being is important because in and through the decisions made by the self it constitutes itself. The self constituted by freedom is thus historical, but besides being temporal the self that is created in becoming is also eternal. The eternality of the self is owed to the preservation of the essential goodness created by freedom within the life of God. The God of love discerningly destroys the selfishness given expression by the self's freedom while graciously saving the goodness expressed by that center of freedom. The extent to which the self actualizes its freedom is the extent to which it essentializes itself. Such essentialization, which is itself dependent upon grace, provides the content for the self's eternal life within the life of God.

Martensen's Relation to Kierkegaard

Robert Leslie Horn concludes his 1969 study of Martensen's theological method with the claim that "until Kierkegaard's relation to Martensen is understood in detail we will have little chance to understand Kierkegaard at all."[51] Since that claim was made, scholars have given limited attention to Kierkegaard's relation to Martensen. But a relationship is a two-way street, and most of the attention to the relation has been given from the Kierkegaard side. Kierkegaard never mentions Martensen by name in his pseudonymous authorship, and when in those writings he does criticize the Hegelians he is careful always to refer to a Docent, of which there were none in theology at Copenhagen University when he was publishing his works.[52] But he does of course include many comments on Martensen in his *Papirer*, and these have been the primary means of access into this relation. A biased view is the inevitable result, with Kierkegaard the gifted analyst of culture marshalling all the armaments of his ideological critique and bringing them to bear on this one Martensen who is made out to be a babbling bourgeois buffoon. While the collage of Martensen that develops from the *Journals* is humorous and not without some veracity, it surely does not present a complete picture of either Martensen or the Martensen-Kierkegaard relation. The task set before us in this section of the Introduction is to examine this relationship from the other side, i.e., to consider it as much as possible from Martensen's perspective. This

---

[51] Horn, "Positivity and Dialectic," p. 268.

[52] Niels Thulstrup, *Kierkegaard and the Church in Denmark*, p. 196: "In the original manuscript of the *Concluding Unscientific Postscript* (*Afsluttende uvidenskabelig Efterskrift*) Martensen was mentioned by name in a number of passages, but before publication these were altered to read 'a lecturer' or 'a Hegelian.'"

will also likely be a biased view, coming as it does from the opposite direction, but hopefully the net contribution will be a more balanced view of Martensen and his relation with Kierkegaard.

There are four distinguishable moments in the relation that are especially worthy of consideration. They are Martensen's teaching of Kierkegaard, Martensen's ignoring of Kierkegaard, Martensen's infuriating of Kierkegaard, and Martensen's influencing of Kierkegaard.

1. MARTENSEN'S TEACHING OF KIERKEGAARD

During Martensen's years as a student, he later recalled, "there were two names that glittered in the scientific world and denoted the zenith of the era's knowledge," namely, Schleiermacher and Hegel.[53] In his own personal study, he felt a need to lose himself in their works. Martensen saw "the clue to understanding the worldview which Hegel carried through in such a splendid way into all spheres of existence" as residing "in his speculative logic, the system of existence's general determinations of thought, which were not our subjective thoughts, but divine thoughts, which penetrated and unfolded themselves in the universe." The challenge would be to find whether the Christian vision of life could be given expression within the Hegelian system. In his reading of Schleiermacher, on the other hand, Martensen encountered an alluring power of personality and a thinker whose theology grew out of a deep speculation on the whole of life.

In September of 1833 Friedrich Schleiermacher visited Copenhagen. Among the young academicians who had looked forward to Schleiermacher's arrival with great anticipation was the twenty-five year-old promising theological candidate, Hans L. Martensen, who engaged the great thinker in conversation a number of times during his eight-day stay.[54] In fact, Martensen says that this person "electrified" him: "For me shone forth from his essence a gentle earnestness."[55] Sibbern had informed Schleiermacher that Martensen had studied his dogmatics, so Schleiermacher invited the aspiring theologian to ask him anything he liked. The resulting conversations included the topics of the relation of theology and philosophy and whether the contrasts by which we think have a place

---

[53] H. Martensen, *From My Life*, 1:65–68.

[54] Skat Arildsen, "To Tyske Teologers Københavns-Besøog: I Anledning af Hundredaarsdagen for Fr. Schleiermachers Død. En Studie [Two German Theologians' Copenhagen-Visit: On the Occasion of the Centennial of Fr. Schleiermacher's Death: A Study] (København: Pamphlet, 1934). See also N. M. Plum's *Schleiermacher i Danmark [Schleiermacher in Denmark]* (København: Bianco Luno, 1934).

[55] H. Martensen, *From My Life*, 1:68. Martensen's account of this Copenhagen-visit is in 1:68–76.

within the inner life of God. We need not recount more details here but note that Schleiermacher made quite an impression on the young candidate. At a social gathering Martensen shared a German poem that he had written for the occasion, which the guest appreciated very much. Schleiermacher returned to Germany and died a few months later in February, 1834. This personal association with Schleiermacher provides background for the first close encounter between Martensen and Kierkegaard that we know about. It appears there was a certain "star" quality about Martensen that would have made nascent theological students desirous of establishing a relationship with him.

While attending graduate school, Martensen stayed in Copenhagen with his mother.[56] To help out with family expenses, during his last year he tutored in theology, by which he also hoped to refine his own form of theological discourse. Of those he tutored, Martensen discusses two individuals, one of them being Søren Kierkegaard. He describes his tutoring sessions with the young Kierkegaard as follows: "He had his own method of letting himself be tutored. Refusing any prescribed reading, he asked only that I should lecture to him and engage in conversation with him. I chose to lecture on the chief points in Schleiermacher's *Dogmatik* and to converse with him about it. I immediately perceived that here was no ordinary talent, but also one with an irresistible hankering after sophistry, a playing with overly subtle distinctions which exhibited itself on every occasion and frequently became tiresome. I am particularly mindful of how it displayed itself when we discussed the doctrine of predestination where there is, so to speak, an open door to sophists." It has been pointed out that as a young teacher, Martensen's personality surely had its impact on Kierkegaard: "Martensen's erudition and evident familiarity with even the most complicated concepts of German philosophy made an impression on his five-year-younger student. He virtually exemplified the optimistic and goal-oriented theologian who managed to keep abreast of theological developments both at home and abroad, and who additionally was able to pass on his knowledge by virtue of his considerable talents as a teacher."[57]

---

[56] H. Martensen, *From My Life*, 1:77–79. Just before this book on Martensen went to press, I gained access to the truly rich book, *Encounters with Kierkegaard: A Life as Seen by His Contemporaries*, collected, edited, and annotated by Bruce H. Kirmmse and translated by Bruce H. Kirmmse and Virginia R. Lausen (Princeton: Princeton University, 1996). Many of the quotations from Martensen's autobiography included in this section of the Introduction are found in Kirmmse's chapter, "Five Portraits by Contemporaries," pp. 196–205. I have been able to compare my translations with those of Kirmmse and Laursen and have made adjustments in a few instances where I preferred their renderings.

[57] Schjørring, *Bibliotheca Kierkegaardiana*, vol. 10, *Kierkegaard's Teachers*, p. 196.

These sessions took place in the spring of 1834, the year Kierkegaard began to make journal entries. That some of his earliest entries are on pre-destination leads one to think that they were made during the period of these tutoring sessions and that it might well have been Martensen's idea that Kierkegaard keep a journal. We can surmise that these tutorial sessions were instrumental in helping Kierkegaard to establish his intellectual agenda. In the *Levnet* Martensen proceeds to comment on his own mother and on Kierkegaard's mother: "In other respects he [Kierkegaard] was at that time greatly attached to me. My mother has told me that when I was abroad, he often came to her in order to ask about pieces of news from me. In addition, she mentioned, what I will not pass over here, that at times he remained sitting with her, and that she took great pleasure in his conversation. One time he was in deep distress and reported that his mother had died. My mother has repeatedly maintained that she, who really was not limited in experience, never in her life has seen a human being so deeply saddened as S. Kierkegaard was by his mother's death, whereby she presumed to be able to conclude that he had to have an uncommonly deep disposition [*Gemyt*]. In this she has not made a mistake. Nobody will be able to deny him that. Indeed the more he came to develop, the more his life and activity unfolded as a unity of sophistry and a deep, even if sick, disposition. But that the sickness in this deep disposition over the course of the years more and more took the upper hand, on this he has even given the most incontestable proof in the journals left by him, which some have had the tactlessness and unsightliness to exhibit before the public." Martensen here acknowledges the passion and depth of Kierkegaard, this one who early on was intrigued by Martensen's adventures of studying abroad, even while pointing to what he took to be a sickness.

Kierkegaard followed most intently the lectures that Martensen gave at the University after arriving back home from his study-trip. He attended the courses he could and obtained lecture notes from another student for both lectures he attended and those he had not. In 1836, a couple of months after returning home from his study-trip, Martensen's *Ueber Lenau's Faust*, which had been written the previous year while in Vienna, was published in Munich. The Danish version was published the next year, setting forth in the long introduction "the Idea of Faust in its full significance for the present age as the doubt unto despair," picking up on the "doubting sickness" which Martensen had experienced in the early part of his trip.[58] This latter publication was a major event in the Martensen-

---

[58] See Lee M. Capel's comments in Søren Kierkegaard, *The Concept of Irony*, trans. Lee M. Capel (Bloomington: Indiana, 1965), pp. 26 and 408, n. 6.

Kierkegaard relationship. For Kierkegaard had planned a writing project centering around Lenau's Faust. We thus find this undated entry from 1837 in Kierkegaard's *Papirer*: "How unhappy I am—Martensen has written an essay on Lenau's *Faust*."[59]

Carl Roos notes that Kierkegaard's despair is due to the fact that Martensen had stolen his thunder: the "new conception" of Faust that he had come up with was undercut on November 19, 1837, when in the course on speculative dogmatics Martensen's discussion of the principle of doubt, which had expressed itself in various forms, was depicted as finally revolving around the difference between Faustian haughtiness and the free thinking of the children of God, so that Faust is pictured as Luther's caricature, who misunderstands the Protestant human's right to think freely.[60] Thus, in Martensen Kierkegaard read and heard himself. This event seems to trigger Kierkegaard's "ironic barbs against the Danish Hegelians," and against Martensen in particular. So, for instance, we get Kierkegaard's play, "The Conflict between the Old and the New Soap-Cellar," written sometime after November of 1837, in which Phrase (Martensen) appears saying such lines as: "This is a totally onesided standpoint (clears his throat). Gentlemen, I have gone beyond Hegel; where to, I cannot yet say very precisely, but I have gone beyond him."[61] Worth noting is Capel's interesting speculative thought concerning this similar view of Faust that the two men shared: "Technically, it was possible for Faust as 'the personified doubt' to have entered into their free discussions in the spring of 1834, especially in connection with the problems of predestination and grace (the earliest theme in Kierkegaard's Journal and one he underscores in the folk book when Faust discusses it with the devil). Faust was, after all, paradigmatic for an individuality on the 'way to perdition' for both these theological students. The possibility remains technically open that Kierkegaard might have got the idea from Martensen as well."[62] The question of which person had the Faust idea first is not as important as recognizing the extent to which these two thinkers were giving shape to their reflection on life in very similar ways at this early point.

Three and a half years later, in June of 1841, Kierkegaard submitted his dissertation on *The Concept of Irony* for the Master of Arts degree (equivalent to a Ph.D. in the faculty of philosophy). While working on this

---

[59] *Søren Kierkegaard's Journals and Papers*, trans. Howard V. Hong and Edna H. Hong, 7 vols. (Bloomington: Indiana University, 1967–78), V 5225 (*Papirer* II A 597).

[60] Carl Roos, *Kierkegaard og Goethe* [*Kierkegaard and Goethe*] (København: G.E.C. Gad, 1955), p. 123.

[61] *Papirer* II B 1–21. See *Early Polemical Writings*, ed. and trans. by Julia Watkin with Introduction and Notes (Princeton: Princeton University), pp. 103–124.

[62] Capel's comment in Kierkegaard's *The Concept of Irony*, p. 359, n. 20. See also the discussion of this in Roos, *Kierkegaard and Goethe*, pp. 124–125.

dissertation Kierkegaard visited his teacher: "He once came to me in my home and wanted to read me something from his dissertation on the concept of irony, so far as I remember, a polemic against Friedrich Schlegel's onesided esthetic view of life. I had him read, but offered only a fairly cool recognition."[63] Recognition of the other, so crucial to bringing a relationship to a level of depth and substance, was not forthcoming at this time from Martensen in relation to his gifted student, nor, as we will see, will it ever be. Recognition from the other, especially one's gifted teacher, a recognition deeply needed for one reason or another, is not received by Kierkegaard. It is likely that this general "spurning" of Kierkegaard is a key factor in explaining why his treatise on irony contains many oblique and not so oblique references to Martensen. In the account of his tutoring of the young Kierkegaard, Martensen had referred to him as a Sophist. Now in this work on irony Kierkegaard had written that although the Sophists "did not give instruction in the particular sciences, the universal culture they practiced, the drilling with which they trained people, nevertheless seems to be most comparable to the capsule information that a tutor tries to convey to those being tutored."[64] Capel contends that from Martensen's point of view this passage "can scarcely be construed as anything but a personal attack to read here that the Sophists resembled nothing so much as tutors."[65] There are plenty of such references, and those who read the manuscript were not unaware of the target. Therefore, it was an awkward thought that Martensen should have to be considered as a reader for the dissertation. Besides F. C. Sibbern and P. O. Brønsted, a third reader had to be chosen, and the choice was between the newly-appointed Rasmus Nielsen and Martensen. Since Kierkegaard had been critical of the Nielsen appointment because he thought Nielsen was underprepared, the task fell to Martensen.

Roger Poole—who recognizes that Kierkegaard's "whole authorship is, in a sense, a constant war of attrition against the fashionable Hegelianism of J. L. Heiberg and of H. L. Martensen," that the "Danish Hegelians, rather than Hegel himself, were the target"—has given close consideration to these events surrounding the dissertation.[66] Martensen approved

---

[63] Martensen, *From My Life*, 2:142.

[64] Søren Kierkegaard, *The Concept of Irony: With Constant Reference to Socrates*, ed. and trans. Howard V. Hong and Edna H. Hong (Princeton: Princeton, 1989), p. 204. The Sophists appear in Kierkegaard's journals and papers as the eloquent philosophers who were "eaten up" by Socrates, and their position is compared to that of the thinkers of mediation in Kierkegaard's time.

[65] Kierkegaard, *The Concept of Irony*, p. 397, n. 24.

[66] Roger Poole, *Kierkegaard: The Indirect Communication* (Charlottesville: University Press of Virginia, 1993), pp. 2, 30–60.

the dissertation, but was not present at the defense. Poole offers a strikingly balanced comment on this situation: "Although Martensen has had
a bad press, due largely to our knowing him mainly through Kierkegaard's own eyes, he was a man of high principle. He could very easily,
things being as they were, have sunk the young Søren without trace. His
dissertation could have been turned down out of hand. Kierkegaard had
no allies on the faculty, except perhaps Sibbern. Martensen could have deprived Kierkegaard of his Magister Artium degree, hence of a career and
a living, and have made impossible that support from the rear during his
writing career that the high academic qualification afforded him."[67] Poole
continues, "He could also have taken revenge on Kierkegaard for what
must have been seven grueling years of being put to the test by his tal-
ented pupil. Many academics, alas, would have taken this opportunity of
revenge. To Martensen's credit, however, he allowed the dissertation, of
which he no doubt disapproved both the contents and the style, to pass
to acceptance without comment. Neither was he present at the defense
on 29 September. It was a high and grand gesture, and one that up to now
has gone unappreciated."[68] Well said. Martensen somewhere states regarding preaching that he found it generally the case that the more the
humanity the better the preacher. The same holds for teachers. Here we
see some humanity shining through Martensen the teacher.

2. Martensen's Ignoring of Kierkegaard

When Martensen's *Christian Dogmatics* was published in 1849 it had been
anticipated for some time. I can imagine that Kierkegaard was expecting
that his works would be cited by Martensen. He was disappointed that
the only apparent reference to his pseudonymous writings came in the
Preface where Martensen alluded to thinking "by axioms and aphorisms,

---

[67] Ibid., pp. 40–41.

[68] Ibid., pp. 41. Capel has likewise offered a positive statement about Martensen in his
translation of *The Concept of Irony*, pp. 397–98, n. 24: "One of the discernible features in
Martensen's autobiography is the wholly understandable yet undeniable strain of apology
running through it, whereby Bishop Martensen is concerned to present his side of the narrative covering an unusually long and brilliant public career, and one which, by the very nature of the offices he occupied, must inevitably have involved numerous conflicts, debates,
and controversial decisions on important cultural issues of the day. The impartial reader will
always be able to sympathize with Martensen in his confrontation with such a splenetic,
polemical, and satiric genius as Kierkegaard. It was, after all, the fact that the young Kierkegaard regarded him as a peer and rival which attracted him to Martensen in the first
place. Martensen's behavior surely requires no defence: literary, philosophical, theological,
and scientific controversies and rivalries are part of the intellectual scene and as old as the
muses themselves."

by flashes and impulse."[69] To be functioning as an intellectual in the intimate setting of Copenhagen and to publish a major work in the field of the Christian religion without mentioning the corpus of writing that Kierkegaard had been working on for nearly a decade was hard for Søren to fathom, as the *Journals* indicate. This blatant ignoring of Kierkegaard is surely another major factor in understanding the relationship. Martensen concludes the same in his autobiographical reflections. He pens an important line (2:142): "It is certainly possible that his hostility could have been mitigated if I had extended him a greater recognition." These two were not without their occasional opportunities for conversation, as Martensen notes (2:145–48):

> It was a Sunday afternoon that I walked to Christianshavn. Here I met S. Kierkegaard and could not avoid his conversation. We walked then together up Christianshavn's embankment, where we talked for a long time about Danish literature, the "Corsair," and our literature's miserable state, to which he often came back and which only interested me a little. We went back through the city and came to a standstill at Østergade, where I went up to the Athenaeum. But he went up with me and we sat down. And here—it came so to say by itself—there began a conversation on my conflict with Rasmus Nielsen. I declared without reservation my indignation over the reprehensibleness in R. Nielsen's conduct, namely, over the totally distorted, abortive, unwarrantable way in which he had employed Kierkegaard's Johannes Climacus, and from this work completely immediately and crudely had extracted sentences, which as a matter of course he had given dogmatic meaning and application. Kierkegaard contradicted nothing, indeed not a word of this and on the whole attempted not in the slightest way to defend R. Nielsen. On the contrary he criticized a few phrases in the Preface to my Dogmatics, which he thought I ought to have completely omitted. And then he said in the course of the conversation: "Our difference (Kierkegaard's and mine) is a difference inside the Christian." In this existed something revealing, which resembled an overture [*rapprochement*]. For a difference *within* the Christian must be able to be settled, and if the difference were inside the Christian, his opposition towards me indeed was not absolute. I sought to receive a further development, and he explained then, that according to his view one should not seek to work with the Pauline contrast between sin and grace, for whose appropriation the majority are still not mature enough, but that to the contrary one should seek to work with a radical use of the letter of James, since one thereby would be best able to plough up what should be ploughed up in the soul, in order that they could become susceptible for higher influences. There was indeed something to this, even if one might say that the same thing could be reached by properly

---

[69] H. Martensen, *Den christelige Dogmatik* [*Christian Dogmatics*] (Kjøbenhavn: C. A. Reitzel, 1849), p. iii.

employing Paul's teaching on the law, concerning which I will not disagree here; for if there were to be disagreeing on this, there would certainly be other and larger things to disagree on than this. By this contrast one did not arrive very far into the difference, which lay far deeper. This encounter perhaps might have been able to carry further, if it would have been advantageous for me, that is to say: if it actually had been in my heart to draw closer to him. But his experimenting and enclosed essence, which appeared to me necessarily to bring along with it the risk of an inner untruth in character, was distasteful enough to me that I could not feel a need for a closer relationship. The ghost of a *rapprochement*, if it can be called that, that I have just mentioned, was so feeble, that from this nothing further could be concluded, and his explanation of our difference was likewise very feeble. I could not gain confidence in him and was obliged to maintain the view that every one of us must sail his own sea.

Just why Martensen ignored Kierkegaard is a complex matter. On the surface of it, Martensen says that it was because he had his own projects that he was tending to (2:140–142):

S. Kierkegaard had in his nature a predisposition to blame, demolish, and put down—something Mephistophelian, something akin to an ambushing-nature. I was then picked out to be the object of his attack, and in all ways he sought to put me down, my abilities and my works, in order to destroy and extinguish every effect which went forth from me. He did not ever attack me directly. Certainly in his writings there were multifarious polemical and satirical tirades against speculation, of which I could take to myself my part. But he never attacked me in straightforward and open warfare. I also presume that he had been unqualified to take up a scientific fight in theology, since he was only qualified to fight in half-poetic, humoristic contexts, where he could serve himself by a sparkling and sniper-like discourse. The didactic, dogmatic discourse was not for him, for which reason he also continuously polemicized against "the docents" who are detested by him. His refinement forbade him to supply a companion piece to Rasmus Nielsen's crude attack. But his attack happened in the many conversations he held with an infinite number of people on the street, where he went around as a Mephistopheles and scattered his hateful seed. However he never presented himself personally to me as my enemy, was always friendly toward me and always sought my conversations on the street. Here I was yet quite stiff and reserved, since I was not fond of having anything to do with one about whom I knew that he everywhere went to work experimenting, while he himself was enclosed and undisclosive regarding his innermost views. Into his conversations he not infrequently brought up his own works, on which I could not enter into conversation, because of the fact among other reasons that I, as I expressed it in my dogmatic elucidations, had only a fragmentary acquaintance with this extensive literature. I was certainly aware of the principal concerns and familiar with what the whole was aimed at. But I was immersed in my own work, pursuing my own end, to which I felt myself called, and could not disperse my time on the alien work; while he all but demanded that one should drop one's own works, leave everything of one's own to rest, in order to immerse oneself exclusively in his new wisdom.

Ignoring Kierkegaard, for whatever the reasons, was not without its consequences. Martensen wrote his *Dogmatic Elucidations* primarily in response to Rasmus Nielsen's work, *Mag. S. Kierkegaard's "Johannes Climacus" and Dr. H. Martensen's "Christian Dogmatics": An Investigative Review*. This writing from Nielsen came as a surprise to Martensen, he tells us (2:137). Nielsen, a professor of philosophy at the University of Copenhagen who had been very much a Hegelian until his intellectual conversion through the writings of Kierkegaard, had been friendly and sympathetic toward Martensen. In fact, Martensen says he was pleased to have such a brilliant co-worker who was working for the same cause. He had even shared several parts of the work in dogmatics with Nielsen prior to its publication and had received his complete approval; but now suddenly Nielsen declared the whole dogmatics as a totally unsuccessful product because the problem of faith and knowledge had been completely misunderstood. In his autobiography Martensen summarizes Nielsen's polemic which on the face of it appears to be very similar to Kierkegaard's: "Against me he sought to argue that Christianity in no way is to be an object of objective knowledge, that the highest truth is the paradox, that the absurd is the only thing which can be believed, and that we can only believe in a power of the absurd; that faith is an infinite passion of intensity, and other assertions of this sort which are all well-known from the Kierkegaardian literature but about which I have to say that I have no use for them (2:138)." Martensen's rejoinder seeks to elucidate Nielsen's misunderstandings about faith and knowledge being "absolutely heterogeneous principles" and to clarify his own standpoint.

Because Martensen's *Dogmatics* ignored Kierkegaard, Rasmus Nielsen felt the need to criticize that major theological work. The Kierkegaard-Nielsen relationship is also one of complexity. In an undated entry of 1850 Kierkegaard wrote (JP VI 6630; *Papirer* X³ A 146): "I certainly am no Socrates and Nielsen no Plato, but the relation may still be analogous." Kierkegaard speaks of the two of them respectively as Socrates and Plato, and he is critical of Nielsen for inappropriately presenting Kierkegaard's corrective of the system in the form of a system. So we can surely not say that these two saw eye-to-eye on everything. But since Nielsen was such a devoted follower of Kierkegaard, we can see his critique of Martensen as being quite similar to that of Kierkegaard and surely as growing out of a Kierkegaardian perspective. Martensen himself definitely saw them as both occupying the same camp, namely, the camp that was opposing him, and so he likely understood the response he gives to Nielsen in his *Dogmatic Elucidations* as applying to Kierkegaard as well. His memoirs read (2:140): "In that first period of the attack stood S. Kierkegaard behind the whole thing as the inspiriting spirit. His relation to me at the beginning had been friendly, but more and more took on a hostile character. What moved him to this was in part the difference in our nature, in part the recognition I enjoyed with the students and with the public, in which he saw an undue overrating, regarding which he made no effort to conceal." Therefore, for our purposes, it seems appropriate to regard Martensen's response to Nielsen as being a response to Kierkegaard as well and as serving to enlighten us further on Martensen's relation to Kierkegaard. This 1850 writing, *Dogmatic Elucidations*, is about a decade after the period when Martensen was doing philosophy of religion, but his response is largely in keeping with his early theological viewpoint.

"Blessed are they who do not want to force their wisdom on others." With these words from Carl Daub, Martensen begins his response to Nielsen (and Kierkegaard).[70] He points out that in his dogmatics he has developed the thesis that "nobody can know the truth if she has not placed herself in a personal relation to the truth (p. 14)." So, naturally Christianity cannot be appropriated along the speculative way, if by speculation one means a disinterested, impersonal thinking, or a thinking that is altogether in the realm of the natural human: nobody can become a Christian by speculating (p. 15). But Martensen stands by his distinction between *fides, quæ creditur* and *fides, qua creditur*, or the objectivity and subjectivity of faith; the truth of Christianity possesses a certain reality apart from the faith of the individual (p. 16). Nielsen (and Kierkegaard) has claimed that the divine things are incomprehensible; Martensen questions whether they are *absolutely* incomprehensible, or whether in their incomprehensibility they are not *relatively* incomprehensible, so that Christianity, although it is a communication of and about existence, is also the communication of a doctrine, in the presentation of which is entailed a certain comprehensibility (pp. 20–21). The Christian thinker must surely strive to unfold what he or she experiences in life (p. 24). But when one takes a single element of life, as Nielsen does, namely, the experience of the paradox, and seeks to make it the fundamental basis for theology, then the approach is mistaken, for it only designates the divine truth from one side of the matter, only expresses the relation of contrast and the repulsive relation to human consciousness but not the relation of attraction and the relation of union (p. 26).

Nielsen's investigation of whether there could not be a different sort of objective knowledge gives occasion for Martensen to offer some reflec-

---

[70] Martensen, *Dogmatic Elucidations*, p. 9.

tions on the nature of objective knowledge. By objective knowledge Martensen means "a knowledge in which there is truth, a knowledge in which there is an agreement between thought and its object, so that the thinking is a true image of the matter (p. 27)." One can certainly imagine an objective knowledge that is impersonal and indifferent, although one can hardly imagine an absolutely disinterested knowledge; on the other hand, one can also imagine an objective knowledge which is conditioned by the most intense, most personal relation to the object, and so, Martensen asks, why should not a true knowledge of God be conditioned by faith? Faith is ultimately concerned. In genuine faith the subjective and objective concern is indissolubly united, although these certainly do not appear without an alteration of attitudes (p. 35). But theology is not faith. Therefore to the charge that in his dogmatics he has not repeated the Christian representations in their practical, applicatory meaning, he appropriately responds that "it is not the task of dogmatics to *preach reconciliation* but to present it as knowledge, to search the *content of revelation* contained in the reconciliation, to scientifically develop the contemplative moment of faith, which by no means excludes but includes the practical, namely, insofar as this becomes an object of the universal consideration of faith (pp. 39–40)." It is for this reason that Martensen maintains that the concept of revelation is the all-embracing concept in the dogmatics (p. 40).

Surely the experience of the religious life is requisite for an immediate and living intuition of the Idea (p. 8). But one cannot stop at the subjective side of faith, and that is why in his theological works he has "striven to show that faith is not merely a practical God-relation but also a contemplative relation which includes a comprehensive view of the world and human life in its relation to God (p. 40)." That is why he has not been able to be satisfied with a dogmatics which only wanted to give a doctrine of the religious subject, of piety, instead of a doctrine of God and God's revelation, only wanted to describe the human's experiences of the *effects* of Christianity, but not provide a doctrine of Christianity itself, as in its eternal truth it is addressed to the human and wants to be taken up by the human (p. 41). The dogmatic task is to develop scientifically the contemplative moment of faith. This surely entails "the *existential* thinking" Nielsen (and Kierkegaard) wants to emphasize, that thought which is one with the very life of religiosity that is had in the immediate religious experience, in the conscience, in devotion, in prayer, in worship, and religious action (pp. 41–42). Martensen believes this is the same as what he, with Daub and Mynster, has called knowledge *in* religion as distinguished from knowledge *about* religion, which when it is completely developed becomes theology (p. 42). Our Danish apologist refers to this latter sort of knowledge as a knowledge of reflection or an ideal knowledge, as opposed to the original, existential type of knowledge (p. 43).

Nielsen (and Kierkegaard) has suggested that Martensen's whole project has the effect of stripping faith of its "risk." Martensen responds that in by-passing critical reflection on the content of faith, one runs the real risk of believing that which is not true. For religion is not an isolated moment in the self, set off in a place of its own apart from the influences of other thoughts and representations; no believer is secure against delusions with respect to her faith. Therefore the church has regarded it as important to have the doctrines of the faith presented in their coherence, the most convincing of which have been those having their deepest roots in an existential grasping of the truth, which are yet conditioned by a reflective thinking. Thus speculative reflection as a reflective or ideal second type of thinking serves to condition that existential, immediately religious thinking that provides the final principle for theological formulation.

Professor Nielsen (and Kierkegaard), Martensen notes, presents the relation between faith and knowledge in such a way that one of these must always be on the descendent when the other is on the rise, so that one of these makes the other superfluous (pp. 47–48). In response to this Martensen gives one of his clearer statements of the relation between faith and knowledge:

> But if knowledge should make faith superfluous, then faith itself must be only a knowledge, a lower, vague and confused knowledge which deservedly becomes replaced by the higher. Now faith is of course also a knowledge, but mind you an *existential* knowledge, that is, a knowledge which is one with the religious life itself, a knowledge of religious experience, while theology is an ideal knowledge and must incessantly draw its nourishment from the former. A theology which understands itself will therefore never posit itself in the place of faith, since this would be the same as thinking that the river could make the source superfluous, by which it has its living origin, or that the top of the tree could make the roots superfluous. A theology which wants to posit itself in the place of faith would not merely misunderstand the meaning of faith's existential knowledge, but would also overlook the fact that faith is far more than a knowledge, namely, it is a life in God which not merely moves in thoughts but also in feelings and affections, in a holy relation of the will to God, so it assuredly cannot realize how any theology which knows faith from experience would be able to render itself guilty of such a misunderstanding. For true theology faith is absolutely irreplaceable, and to posit theological knowledge in the place of faith would be, as Sibbern has so strikingly expressed it, the same as thinking that one could warm oneself by an astronomical theory about the sun instead of warming oneself by the sunlight itself (p. 48).

The Middle Ages differentiated between a twofold certainty. On the one hand there is that certainty of religious experience which is given with faith, and on the other hand there is the certainty of ideal knowledge which is to be striven for in theology: *certitudo experientiæ* and *certitudo speculativa* (p. 49). The one of these by no means makes the other super-fluous, because they are each of a different nature. The theologian or any Christian, declares Martensen, can have the experience where states in our internal life are such that we do not believe what we know, that is to say, where we do not really believe it to be the case that there is real power in what is known: the work of knowledge, therefore, in no way makes the struggle of faith superfluous for theology. "The more perfectly the truth is presented as knowledge, the more earnestly does knowledge again put to us the question whether we now also possess the corre-sponding repose in faith, whether we now also perceive the correspond-ing certainty of experience—*certitudo*, not merely *per intellectum* but also *per affectum* (p. 51)." Theological knowledge thus leads one back to that other kind of work than the work of knowledge, namely, the work of faith which is the one thing needful both for the wise and the simple.

Martensen is convinced that part of Nielsen's (Kierkegaard's) difficulty with his use of the speculative method is that the reviewer is operating with a completely different concept of speculation than Martensen ac-knowledges in his dogmatics. The notion of speculation is understood by Martensen as having its roots in the intuition of faith and as striving in faith after a *relative* rather than *absolute* comprehension of the di-vine things, acknowledging that faith is far richer than knowledge and in-tuition far richer than the concept (pp. 51–52). One does not have to say either with Kant that God is absolutely incomprehensible nor with Hegel that God is absolutely comprehensible in order to be a systematic thinker (p. 52). Martensen writes: "The knowledge I have described and had in view is not the purely philosophical, but that theological or dogmatic speculation which proceeds from the presuppositions of the revelation of faith and seeks to clarify its intuition of revelation through the con-cept, although it certainly acknowledges that the conceptualization is the piecemeal in our knowledge, while the totality lies in the fullness of in-tuition which is not exhausted by a conceptual development (p. 66)." It is this type of speculation, Martensen claims, that is found in the most pro-found teachers of the church such as Origen, Irenaeus, Athanasius, the Gregories, Augustine, Anselm, and Thomas. Martensen maintains that even in Luther one finds essential features of an all-embracing speculative view and insights into a great coherent Idea which sheds light on the whole of existence, even as his writings invite the one who wants to seriously penetrate into them to a continuous pursuit of thought and dialectic (pp. 66–67). The concern is not simply to defend "speculation" as a mere name. Martensen is agreeable to describing the sort of knowl-edge in question as "a union of *contemplatio* and *meditatio*," as with Bona-venture and the Victors, where *contemplatio* is taken to mean that free intuitive overview of the whole and *meditatio* is taken to mean that discursive dialectical thinking which seeks to clarify the overview through the concept; nor does he mind if someone wants with the fathers of the early church to designate this sort of knowledge as Christian *gnosis* (p. 67). At the same time, Martensen does not understand why one should not dare denominate it as speculative, since speculation designates an absorption in the ideas, a beholding in the mirror of the Idea. Nielsen (and Kierkegaard) has merely adopted the concept of speculation from the systems of modern philosophy instead of from church history; dogmatic inquiry, as over against philosophical speculation, "has its own principle which is independent of philosophy, and therefore ought to be judged according to its own standard (p. 68)."

Martensen ignored Kierkegaard, both earlier in offering "only a fairly cool recognition" of the value of his dissertation and now again in not referring to him in the dogmatics. But he concludes in his memoirs:

> he seems not to have forgotten that I did not show a greater enthusiasm for his *opus*. And yet it is really very possible that I err when I presume that a greater recognition from my side would have been able to lessen his hostility. For his pretensions were unlimited and his demands exceedingly difficult to satisfy, if one would not make oneself into a blind admirer and parrot as some of our *literati* have undeniably done. For he laid claim not merely to the incredible, to being one of the world's greatest thinkers, perhaps the greatest, but also—and this even though he lacked all immediacy and was merely and sheerly reflection—one of the greatest poets. For me he was neither the one nor the other. For me he was only a humorist, who has elements both of the poet and the thinker, through which he develops his humor, which in Kierkegaard has a pessimistic character—the perfect contrast to Jean Paul, in whom everything is optimism and love. But the humorist can also certainly have his greatness, and far be it from me to deny the sublime, the many both profound and penetrating *aperçus* [insights] which are found in his writings. Neither should it be overlooked that behind all of it lies with him the religious, and that according to his most profound significance he is a religious author, concerning which his edifying discourses furnish testimony. The fundamental thought, for which he struggled, is that well-known individualism or the individual [*Enkelte*] and the individual's relation to God. He has made an attempt in the area of religion which deserves the utmost attention, but unfortunately this attempt has been lost in onesidedness and morbidity, in half-truths and false paradoxes. Soon it became apparent that the individual was completely severed from the community, that the Christian demand concerning self-denial and dying from the world was presented in such a way that the religious ideal, which was impressed upon us, became only a caricature of the holy. That would carry us too far, to go into this here, and I must point to the detailed expositions I have given of his standpoint in my *Ethics*. When in the past there was complaining over the fact that I have not sufficiently taken notice of him and gotten mixed up in what he had given, I believe that now there

will be able to be no more complaining over this. But it has surprised me much that among his supporters—in case such still be found—there has not been anybody who has done me or his/her champion the honor of contradicting me or to subject my assertions to an examination (2:142–44).

3. Martensen's Infuriating of Kierkegaard

Of all the key happenings in the Martensen-Kierkegaard relationship, that of Martensen's ascendancy to the office of bishop on April 15, 1854 has maybe been retold the most. Here we will simply attempt to allow Martensen's side of the story to receive expression. He points out how upon the death of Jacob Mynster the already tense relation with Kierkegaard turned to worse. "At Bishop Mynster's death it appeared also which spirits in him had gained a free hand. His personal relation to Mynster is not so well-known to me that I can talk about it. But it cannot be doubted that there must have come a point in time when Mynster, who for a long time had been in favor of him, must have shown coldness and displeasure with his production, and that his love had been transformed into hate (2:148)." At this time we find Kierkegaard getting infuriated over Martensen. But let us listen to Martensen (3:12–13) give us his account of what took place.

> In a sermon I preached in the Slotskirke shortly after Mynster's death, I included Mynster among the Christian "witnesses to the truth [*Sandhedsvidner*]," whom my talk had given me occasion to mention. This became the object of a violent attack from Kierkegaard's side, an attack which very soon was to put the whole country in a ferment. It was a long-premeditated blow, to be inflicted on me, and meant to be deadly. It was to destroy me utterly, and make me useless in the high position newly entrusted to me. If we are to view this event historically—and in a certain sense both this attack and its consequences can be regarded as a piece of church history in our small community—I suppose it may be explained as being due partly to a fanatical notion which Kierkegaard had formed of himself, about a high mission to which he had been called, and partly by simple personal enmity, not to say hate. However much, by literary and other contentions, one is accustomed to speak of objectivity, or of the "thing itself" and righteousness—personal feelings, often in the smallest forms, play an important role, and unless we take account of these, we cannot arrive at any satisfactory conclusion. To what degree personal feelings played their part in this affair, is shown by the fact that Kierkegaard was not ashamed to say publicly that I had preached this sermon in order to commend myself for the bishopric. One would hardly have expected a man of Kierkegaard's spirituality and intellectual gifts to have thus degraded himself to the level of penmen of the common and lowest kind. Yet both here and in other places he did descend to this kind of thing. Sibbern made a

most pertinent remark when he said that Kierkegaard had shown himself a Philistine.[71]

Martensen continues, saying that he will attempt to speak as briefly as he can about "the miserable affair."

> With regard to the phrase "witnesses to the truth," and my applying it to Mynster, I begin by saying that I have no intention whatever of making any apology for the expression, as though it were less than correct, or something which ought to be taken back. I would still use the same expression today. My expression was quite correct if it be taken in the right way, i.e., in its context. But Søren Kierkegaard was dishonest and audacious enough to tear it from its context, to push it to extremes, and to give the phrase the meaning of blood-witness or martyr. I need hardly say that neither I nor anybody else had ever thought of such a thing. I had in my sermon reckoned Mynster among the Christian witnesses to the truth when I was asserting his significance for our Fatherland. I was speaking of the barren period when he appeared, his fight against unbelief and rationalism, and how he had brought back the gospel to many hearts. Anybody who will think carefully about the concept "witness to the truth" must come to the conclusion that to be designated thus (and this is the point) a man must have witnessed to *the truth*. But suffering and persecution are no sure marks of such witnesses, since impostors and false teachers have often undergone great sufferings and have been martyrs. Besides, outward suffering and martyrdom belong to particular ages. They presuppose particular types of society, and special circumstances. They could not appear in every age. But we can find witnesses to the truth in every age and under all types of society.[72]

We can see that misunderstanding is present in the relationship at this point. As stern as Kierkegaard was on the notion of witness to the truth, it is not the case that he was restricting it to the meaning of blood-martyr as is here suggested. Martensen has clearly missed the point of Kierkegaard's critique. And if Martensen is seemingly incapable of seeing the religious and political shortcomings, no, the systemic injustices and oppressiveness of Golden Age Denmark, in which it was simply impossible for the figurehead of that cultural synthesis in any truly meaningful sense to be counted as a martyr or witness, then so too was Kierkegaard apparently guilty of playing the martyr, manipulating the world-historical, in order that his cause might be served. Robert Horn has drawn attention to Kierkegaard's "revealing remark that he could not have wished anyone other than Martensen to become bishop. Now the weakest side of the Es-

---

[71] T. H. Croxall, *Kierkegaard Commentary* (London: James Nisbet & Co., 1956), p. 241, although I have made minor changes in Croxall's translation.

[72] Martensen, *From My Life*, 3:13–15. Again this quote reflects minor changes in Croxall's translation in *Kierkegaard Commentary*, pp. 241–42.

tablishment is exposed. Like a fisherman waiting for a bite or a detective waiting for a conclusive clue before he moves in on the criminal, Kierkegaard says, he has waited for the elevation of Martensen to the bishop's chair. Had Martensen not become bishop, the 'attack' could not have been made. Now that it has, everything is fulfilled as Kierkegaard wished it."[73] Neither understood the other, and neither fully understood the cultural situation. Martensen needed some of Kierkegaard's critical acumen and Kierkegaard needed some of Martensen's affirmation of the natural.

After Martensen's sermon eulogizing Mynster, Kierkegaard wrote his "scathing denunciation of Martensen," but did not publish his letter for many months so as not to interfere either with Martensen's appointment as Mynster's successor or with the money-raising effort for building a monument to Mynster.[74] By December, Martensen had been appointed bishop of the primatial see of the Danish Lutheran Church and the monument-money had been raised, and so on December 18, 1854 Kierkegaard's letter was published in the *Fatherland*. On December 28, 1854, Martensen's single response to the attack Kierkegaard had launched against him was published.[75] That response included the following:

> Whoever accepts this article of faith also knows that in the church there is a testimony of truth transmitted from generation to generation and that at every instant and in every generation, in the community and among teachers, there arise people to hear this witness and to confirm the great event of Christianity in a living and personal way. Otherwise, the unity of the church through time would be destroyed. But it is useless to offer such consideration to Dr. Kierkegaard, whose Christianity is without church and without history.[76]

In his autobiography Martensen looked back on Kierkegaard's attack of nearly three decades earlier, and agreed with the many who had felt that his own answer to that attack was "more severe than it need have been." In fact, Martensen's final autobiographical comments on Kierkegaard include a strikingly positive assessment of his authorship and put a charitable construction on the reason behind his attack on Christendom:

> But it would be lamentable if the great richness of intellect and genius which we find in Kierkegaard's writings should be without fruits for the future. As yet we have only seen a run and a bad start. No author of impor-

---

[73] Horn, "Positivity and Dialectic," p. 267. The reference is to the *Papirer*, XI³ B 89, and Horn refers us also to XI³ B 159.

[74] Walter Lowrie, *Kierkegaard* (New York: Harper & Brothers, 1962), 2:565–566.

[75] Bishop Martensen, I Anledning af Dr. S. Kierkegaards Artikel i "Fædrelandet," Nr. 295 [On the Occasion of Dr. S. Kierkegaard's Article in *The Fatherland*, No. 295], *Berlingske Tidende* [*Berling's Times*], No. 302 (December 28, 1854).

[76] Louis Dupre, *Kierkegaard as Theologian* (New York: Sheed & Ward, 1963), p. 193.

tance has yet appeared who shows that s/he is really impregnated by the many brilliant distinguishing features in Kierkegaard's writings; for even though these are onesided, they are formed to incite, and to allay ferments. One may venture to hope such a writer may yet come, though certainly great patience and great affection is necessary in anyone who would work through all this mass of writings.

But before I take leave of him (for I shall hardly mention him again) I want, to his memory, to repeat a word which one of my friends uttered when expressing his appreciation for this remarkable and unique literary and religious phenomenon; words which seem to me apt: "He was a noble instrument who had a crack in his sound-board." This crack, alas, became greater and greater. To this I attribute his broken health, which increasingly exercised a disturbing influence on his psychological life.[77]

4. MARTENSEN'S INFLUENCING OF KIERKEGAARD

To speak here of "influencing" is obviously not to suggest that the "teaching," "ignoring," and "infuriating" dealt with above have somehow taken place apart from influencing. But it is to suggest that the general influence of Martensen on Kierkegaard's thought merits separate treatment.

The place to begin on this topic is with Martensen's view itself which can be discerned if one reads between the lines in the treatment he offers of Kierkegaard in his *Christian Ethics*.[78] In the late 1870s Martensen sees Kierkegaard's thought as centered in the contrast between individualism and universalism. Universalism, which holds the universal as the highest, was presented in the idealistic philosophy of Hegel in which every form of reality is regarded as a form or phase of thought. Interestingly, Martensen sees Hegel himself as not having carried out this idealism consistently in that his idealistic representations include a significant strand of actuality which leads to a certain ambiguity. But he admits that back in the late 1830s and early 40s, a time filled with speculative and esthetic intoxication with ideas, the one idea that had entirely disappeared was the religious-ethical idea which demands *existence*. Martensen writes: "Against this universalism must therefore come forth a reaction both from the side of philosophy and that of theology, a protest in behalf of ethics and religion, of personality and individuality, of the individual human and the individual thing." But the question is whether universalism should be rejected in every sense, or whether a higher union of universalism and individualism should be attempted. Martensen sees this whole problem as a modern form of the medieval debate over realism

---

[77] Martensen, *From My Life*, 3:22–23. Croxall, *Kierkegaard Commentary*, pp. 244–45.
[78] H. Martensen, *Den christelige Ethik*, 1:275–300; *Christian Ethics*, 1:217–236.

and nominalism: "what the Middle Ages called realism we call idealism, and what was then designated nominalism we style empiricism." In this debate Kierkegaard took up a peculiar position: "He finds that it is the misfortune of the age that it has received too much to know, and with all this knowledge has forgotten what it is to exist, and what inwardness means; that with the esthetic, the speculative, the world historical it has forgotten that the primary task is to become an individual human; that by becoming objective the age has forgotten that it is the task of every human to become subjective. He has therefore made it the aim of his life to carry forth and carry through the category: 'the individual' (1:278; 1:219)."

The distinctiveness of Kierkegaard's position is granted, but Martensen hints that he was not alone in making his protest: "At the time when S. Kierkegaard appeared, individualism was already in full activity by the side of universalism." He notes that the category of "the individual" is common to all those who in a much broader sense than Kierkegaard "desire to uphold the *principle of personality*, to maintain the personality of God and of the human in opposition to pantheism. 'The individual' is the category of nominalism—and when nominalism does not exclude but includes realism, then nominalism is the higher. The individual is higher than the abstract, the personal than the impersonal. Only the individual *exists*, has actual being (*existentia est singularum* [existence is singular] as the scholastics expressed it), while the universal has only ideal existence, and only in its union with the individual attains to actual being. 'The individual' is the category of Christianity and of theism." In Martensen's view God also is not the indeterminate universal but the individual, "not the abstract, but the perfect threefold one, which, though comprehending and embracing all the possible and actual, yet in the most decided manner is distinct from the universe." On this point, Martensen sides with Schelling rather than Hegel. "While Hegel says that it is the universal which individualizes itself, Schelling says that, on the contrary, it is the individual which universalizes itself."

But Martensen goes on to point out that that for which philosophy seeks, theology possesses, namely, in revelation. "It is undoubtedly the metaphysics of revelation that not the impersonal ideal but personal existence, not thought but will, not wisdom but love is the foremost in God; just as, on the other hand, it tells us that almighty love only exists and reveals itself in the form of wisdom." Further, this metaphysics of revelation is not empty and barren, for it has a bearing on ethics. "All metaphysical problems gravitate toward the ethical." The metaphysics of revelation poses precisely the key puzzle for the individual, namely, how does one express the unity of existence and the ideal, of individual life and social life. Our Danish Lutheran bishop agrees with Kierkegaard's assertion "that with the category of 'the individual' the cause of Christianity must stand and fall; that, without this category, pantheism had conquered unconditionally." Then Martensen states that given this situation, it seems that "Kierkegaard should have made common cause with those philosophical and theological writers who especially desired to promote the principle of personality as opposed to pantheism." Martensen is surely including himself among "those philosophical and theological writers" with whom Kierkegaard should have joined forces. The implication is that on the basic issue of the relation of essence and existence, Martensen sees his position as being on the same side as that of Kierkegaard.

However, Kierkegaard did not do this. "For those views which upheld the category of existence and personality, in opposition to this abstract idealism, did not do this in the sense of an either-or, but in that of a both-and." While in his authorship Kierkegaard attacked only Hegel *directly*, "for directly he has never entered on the subject" with Martensen and others, he did turn *indirectly* "to combat those philosophical and theological speculations which seek precisely to work out his own category, though in a far more universal sense than he has done. All these views he classifies together under the names of 'speculation' and 'mediation' without in any way permitting himself to institute a closer examination into their internal diversities, especially the diversity in the position they assume toward revelation." Here Martensen is again bemoaning the fact that in his "reckless polemic against speculation which in so many respects is entirely uncritical" Kierkegaard is overlooking the differences that exist among those who hold a speculative and mediating stance. From Martensen's perspective, Kierkegaard unfortunately "declares war against all speculation, and also against such persons as seek to speculate on faith and strive after an insight into the truths of revelation: for all speculation is a waste of time, leads away from the subjective into the objective, from the actual to the ideal, is a dangerous abstraction; and all mediation betrays existence, leads treacherously away from the decisive in actual life, is a falsifying of faith by the help of idea."

Martensen had affirmed in his early work the dialectical method. In Kant's first critique, the transcendental analytic was devoted to breaking down the knowing process into its various parts, but the long transcendental dialectic was intended to put the parts back together through the regulative ideas of reason. Hegel's philosophical position can be viewed as a further developing of Kant's dialectic. To Martensen's mind, Kierkegaard too knew the importance of dialectic. In fact, he suggests, everything for Kierkegaard is dialectic. "But his dialectic is a separating dialectic of existence, which develops the relation of the individual to the various spheres of existence, develops especially the inner contradictions in the problem of faith, and why it must be believed 'in virtue of the absurd.'" Predominating this form of dialectic, and serving as "the guiding viewpoint for the voluminous authorship of Kierkegaard," is "the individual in its personal relation to God." It is this concern that leads him to take up the task of "introducing Christianity into Christendom." But Martensen points out that in Kierkegaard's writings "a vast amount of *reflection* has been employed to attain his goal of the individual."

There is appreciation for Kierkegaard in Martensen's appraisal of him in his *Christian Ethics*. As he explains: "In every case we cannot but admire the rich psychological observation, the keen insight, the dexterity in psychological experiment, whereby he has become acquainted with the mysteries of existence, both actual and possible, which only few know, and fewer still are in a position to express; which he not merely has discovered in others, but also detected in his own inner life by a self-observation, which in this way can only be accomplished in a hermit life, with whose sufferings and temptations he has been very familiar." While admitting the profundity of Kierkegaard's probings into the nuances of existence, Martensen finally has to maintain a critical stance in relation to him. As he says, his teaching concerning the individual has been in many respects "a corrective to a onesided universalism, yet the corrective itself in all important points needs to be corrected." The primary difficulty is Kierkegaard's position on sociality. Martensen believes that if this existential thinker could have gotten "sight of the idea of 'the kingdom,'" then his horizon would also have widened, and he would have perceived a higher and nobler universalism than that which he at first combatted. What is needed is: "The individual and the kingdom of God; or rather: the kingdom of God and the individual."

One of the few places in contemporary scholarship where Martensen's influence on Kierkegaard has been dealt with is Arild Christensen's 1962 article, "Efterskriftens Opgør med Martensen" [The Postscript's Showdown with Martensen].[79] This essay is quite circumspect in its scope, concentrating on the influence of Martensen's dissertation dealing with the autonomy of modern thinkers on the pseudonym Johannes Climacus, but a few general comments about the influence on Kierkegaard are made as well. Christiansen notes that he is using the Danish translation of Martensen's dissertation which was largely worked up or prepared by Martensen himself, and there are several places where more detailed formulations are given in the translation than in the Latin original (p. 46). It is pointed out how in the *Concluding Unscientific Postscript* a polemical position is taken over against Martensen's theory of knowledge and experience of conscience (p. 53). But Christiansen sees similarities in the

---

[79] Arild Christensen, "Efterskriftens Opgør med Martensen" [The Postscript's Showdown with Martensen], *Kierkegaardiana* (København: Munksgaard, 1962) 4:45–62.

presuppositions of the two great Danish thinkers: The presuppositions of Kierkegaard and Martensen should not be taken to be so different that a fruitful comparison cannot be made between the demand for subjectivity of the one with the other's demand for objectivity (p. 54). And in comparing the concept of God one finds in the *Postscript* with Martensen's, two attributes are held in common, namely, God as subject and the unity of power and knowledge or being and thought (p. 59). Christiansen claims, on the other hand, that Martensen does not designate God as passion, although he admits that this characteristic might still be given with the creative will of God. Christiansen concludes that Johannes Climacus's standpoint, just as Martensen's, is theocentric: Human passion, human subjectivity is an approximation to the eternal, divine (p. 60). God's subjectivity is the perfect, and the human's subjectivity is accordingly derivative from this. Also, at the end of his comparison Christiansen notes that if other works of Kierkegaard had been considered, "one would have found in developed form in Kierkegaard Martensen's conception of God as 'the eternal eye.'"

Two other students of Kierkegaard have considered the Martensen-Kierkegaard connection. Paul Sponheim is one scholar who long ago offered a brief treatment of Martensen's thought.[80] Sponheim considers (p. 82) "the claim that Kierkegaard's debt to idealism is far deeper than he would have us believe," showing (p. 84) "that Kierkegaard does at times employ metaphysical notions which link him with idealism." Sponheim's intention is to make the case for "the systematic tendencies in Kierkegaard's authorship," tendencies which feature the divine-human polarity, the reflective rhythms of synthesis and diastasis, and the Christological center. Thus, this interpreter sets Kierkegaard "in relation to the work of another Dane [Martensen] who was troubled by some of the same points in the System which disturbed Kierkegaard (p. 58)." He concludes "that Martensen was by no means the simple disciple of Hegel he is often made out to be. The violence of the clash between Martensen and Kierkegaard should not obscure for us the significant measure of common critical concern present in their relationship to Hegel (p. 65)."

We can note that many might quite readily grant that Martensen's theological formulations are a resource for the synthetic reflective rhythm of Kierkegaard's thinking. However, less likely would be agreement on Martensen as a resource for the diastatic rhythm. However, when one becomes aware of the many "neoorthodox" themes running through the early theological writings of Martensen, such as his criticism of the German idealistic tradition, his emphasis on revelation, his stressing of the

---

[80] Paul Sponheim, *Kierkegaard on Christ and Christian Coherence* (New York: Harper & Row, 1968), pp. 58–65.

infinite qualitative difference between God and the human creature, his distinguishing among Religiousness 1, 2, and 3, his stress on Incarnation, etc., one then realizes that Martensen's theology likely served as a resource for the diastatic reflective rhythm in Kierkegaard's ponderings as well.

Gregor Malantschuk is another scholar who has made an interesting claim about Kierkegaard's possible dependence on Martensen.[81] In discussing Kierkegaard's working out of the stages from a phenomenological view, Malantschuk suggests that it might "be illuminating to mention H. L. Martensen's attempt to mediate between a dogmatic and a phenomenological view of the stages in his licentiate thesis." Malantschuk makes the point that in his dissertation on autonomy Martensen summarizes Schleiermacher's dogmatic view of Christianity's relationship to humankind under "three stages": "This view, which he [Martensen] calls subjective and regards as influenced by Kant, is compared with Hegel's formulation of three stages, which in contrast to Schleiermacher's subjective stages are called objective." Malantschuk continues: "In this way Martensen brings out an opposition between Schleiermacher and Hegel which is almost analogous to the one we find in Kierkegaard between Augustine and Pelagius. For Martensen the conflict he presents has no further significance; whereas Kierkegaard develops it and fills out Augustine's abstract sketch with concrete material."[82] Malantschuk is referring to a passage at the end of Martensen's treatment of Schleiermacher, where he writes: "This development [the necessary development of the human spirit] runs through three stages [*Stadier*]. The first is that where human self-consciousness has still not awakened to a knowledge of sin, where the difference between that which it immediately is and that which it ought to be, between its empirical state and its idea, has still not arisen for consciousness. The second stage is the state of sin, where this consciousness together with the need for reconciliation is awakened in the human. The third is the state of grace or communion with Christ, the Perfecter of the human race, the unity of the finite and the Infinite. These are the necessary forms through which the substantial feeling is developed. The entire history of religions—paganism, Judaism, and Christianity— presents to us the history of this feeling and forms the necessary moments in its development." Therefore, the three stages in Schleiermacher are those of: "the natural and immediate standpoint, the standpoint of reflection which involves the sin of finite spirit, and finally the spiritual stand-

---

[81] Gregor Malantschuk, *Kierkegaard's Thought*, ed. and trans. by Howard and Edna Hong (Princeton: Princeton University, 1971), pp. 146–147.

[82] While indeed we find the discussion of Augustine and Pelagius in Kierkegaard, we also find it in Martensen's *Lectures on Speculative Dogmatics* in *Papirer* XIII, II C 28, pp. 74–78.

point." In Hegel, Martensen suggests, the difference is that this history of religions is viewed not so much as "the history of the human as that of God, the self-mediation of the Absolute Spirit, more God's way than the human's way."

We can only agree with Malantschuk that we do indeed get the language of three stages being used by Martensen in this setting. However, we find the use of "stages" language elsewhere as well. In his 1840 work on mysticism, Martensen distinguishes three stages [*Stadier*] by which the human being moves deeper into virtue and the infinitude of freedom is won. There is, he writes, "the stage of nature, the stage of grace, and the stage of essentiality." This last stage has been designated by some as the stage of righteousness. Within these three major stages, Martensen claims, there are a number of sub-levels. And in the Preface to his *Grundrids* or *Outline* of 1841 he mentions the "classical development of the relative stages [*Stadier*] of morality" that is contained in Hegel's philosophy of right.

On my view Martensen's influencing of Kierkegaard in this area is to be seen less in terms of language use and more in terms of conceptual differentiation. Martensen clearly sees the need to differentiate many types of consciousness. A fascinating study would be to flesh out Martensen's understanding of the esthetic consciousness, the speculative consciousness of philosophy, the moral consciousness, the religious consciousness, and the Christian consciousness. He carefully distinguishes all of these in his writings. Furthermore, he discusses the nature of the relation between these forms of consciousness, usually concentrating on two of these at a time. But one could pull these comments together into a theory of "stages on life's way." In addition, he operates with very determinate understandings of irony, the comical, and the humorous. The particular content is there in Martensen's early writings. But one thing is not there, and that is an explicit rendering of the parts into a whole view. Martensen is surely not without a worldview; and it is one in which the notion of personality stands at the center. Martensen, no doubt, has a comprehensive vision of life, and he is remarkably astute in seeing the nuances of a coherent systematic vision and in recognizing the implications of particular claims for the comprehensive conceptual framework. And yet, while he operates out of what might be labeled a comprehensive vision of personality in which the differentiation of forms of consciousness constitutes a theory of stages of sorts, he does not thematize that worldview explicitly in terms of the stages of life.

Another set of Kierkegaard scholars has underscored themes in Kierkegaard pointing to Martensen's influence, even though they have not drawn out that line of dependence. First is Merold Westphal, who in discussing "Kierkegaard's Politics" claims "how deeply Hegelian Kierkegaard is on two points."[83] It is the first point that pertains here, namely, Kierkegaard's individualism, which Westphal interprets as being dialectical in character rather than compositional. The difference is that dialectical individualism acknowledges the essential relationality of the *I*, that is, how personal self-consciousness is always at the same time also a we and the we is always also an interaction of distinct *I*'s, while compositional individualism is based on "the view that complex wholes are made up of preexisting, self-sufficient parts." The thought is that in his *Phenomenology of Spirit* Hegel "renounces compositional individualism" in defining spirit as the "'I' that is 'We' and 'We' that is 'I.'" Thus, Hegel is indicated as the figure who has influenced Kierkegaard. And yet, there is no need to go all the way back to Hegel, when there stands another figure between Hegel and Kierkegaard who has also developed a radically social understanding of the self. Martensen writes in his *Outline to a System of Moral Philosophy*: "But if in this way, on the basis of the individual's infinite significance, society can be said to exist for the sake of the individual, then on the other hand the individual may just as well be seen to exist for the sake of society." That is not quite "I is We and We is I," but it is close; and many other statements could be cited to demonstrate that Martensen's theology gave expression to a dialectical rather than a compositional individualism. Kierkegaard learned much from Hegel, but Martensen's early writings in the philosophy of religion provided the most immediate causative force in Denmark by means of which Hegelian theology had an influence on Kierkegaard.

The second scholar is George Connell, who argues for the "theonomous" character of the ethics of Judge William in *Either/Or* II.[84] In a note (n. 5) Connell states that "[w]hile the term 'theonomy' was popularized by Tillich, Kierkegaard was well aware of the concept." Then he refers his readers to Kierkegaard's notes on Martensen's lectures on speculative theology in the *Papirer*. Connell does not explicitly draw out the line of influence from Martensen to Kierkegaard on the theme of theonomous ethics. However, it is clear that Martensen understands his *Outline to a System of Moral Philosophy* as being precisely that, a theonomous ethics in which human freedom arrives at its fulfillment only as it in humility acknowledges its dependence on its divine ground and goal. Martensen

---

[83] Merold Westphal, *Kierkegaard's Critique of Reason and Society* (Mercer, GA: Mercer University, 1987), pp.30–32.

[84] George B. Connell, "Judge William's Theonomous Ethics," *Foundations of Kierkegaard's Vision of Community: Religion, Ethics, and Politics in Kierkegaard*, ed. George B. Connell and C. Stephen Evans (Atlantic Highlands, NJ: Humanities, 1992), pp.56–70.

understands his authorship from the dissertation on as advocating a theo-nomic standpoint. His ethics stand in that arena no less than his other theological writings.

One last secondary figure needing to be considered has made an im-portant contribution to the topic at hand. Again this is one who has dealt directly with the Martensen-Kierkegaard relation, namely, J. H. Schjørring in his article, "Martensen," in the *Kierkegaard's Teachers* volume of *Biblio-theca Kierkegaardiana*.[85] Schjørring is convinced (p. 178) that presenting these two figures as antithetical is to overlook nuances in the relationship, which was not merely that they shared a historical milieu: "Both men took the same problem as point of departure for further research, yet they certainly arrived at completely different conclusions." Schjørring grants that "each conceived misgivings about Hegel's philosophy early on," and that their "reservations ran parallel": "Martensen's refashioned hegelian-ism became in the course of time an important factor in the spiritual cli-mate within which Kierkegaard came to maturity, since it was only after a lengthy and intensive preoccupation with these ideas that he was able to escape their allure and lay the foundations of his own philosophy." Schjørring adds (p. 197) that it is also "important to emphasize that both scholars reacted critically to Hegel on the same central issue," that is, in regard to Hegel's "claim to have established a synthesizing community of interest between theology and philosophy in place of the earlier bifurca-tion of or outright conflict between these disciplines." Martensen thought the Hegelian synthesis erased Christian revelation in opting for auton-omy rather than theonomy; Kierkegaard thought any alliance between Christianity and philosophy was inappropriate. However, Kierkegaard differs from Martensen in that he does not propose any kind of inter-mediate position. Martensen searches for a middle ground, a mediating theology; Kierkegaard insists on paradox, and no mediating. And yet, Schjørring maintains (pp. 202–3) that even into the early 40s a "structural parallelism" between Kierkegaard's theology with that of Martensen can be seen: "This applies first of all to the concept of God as *auctor* [author] in the relationship of faith, the rootedness of Christology in historical once-and-for-all events, and the significance of the individual in relation to the universal." Nevertheless, "this common ground did not lead Kier-kegaard to modify his criticism of Martensen," but rather he intensified his harsh polemics against Martensen's mediating or speculative the-ology. Schjørring concludes (p. 207) that one cannot include Martensen in a general overview of German and Danish Hegelianism, that special at-

---

[85] J. H. Schjørring, "Martensen," *Bibliotheca Kierkegaardiana*, vol. 10, *Kierkegaard's Teachers*, pp. 177–207.

tention has to be paid to the relationship between Martensen and Kierkegaard, and that the relationship "may not be simply subsumed under the rubric of Kierkegaard's general attack on "the system."

Schjørring's assessment of the relationship is sound. He sees Martensen influencing Kierkegaard, although he proceeds carefully and does not overstate the case. And yet, in reading the three treatises included in this text many readers will see more connections of influence running from Martensen to Kierkegaard than Schjørring points out.

It is interesting that the writings containing the most biting sarcasm over against Martensen are those penned under Kierkegaard's principal pseudonym of Johannes Climacus, i.e., *Johannes Climacus, or De omnibus dubitandum est, Philosophical Fragments*, and *Concluding Unscientific Postscript*. It makes one wonder whether there might not be a link between the pen name Johannes Climacus and Hans Martensen. Of course, it is the case that Johannes Climacus was a monk (c. 570–649) who wrote the work *Ladder of Paradise*. That is the most immediate reference for the name. But this name very likely carried another meaning for Kierkegaard. We recall that Martensen did publish both his licentiate thesis and the German version of his piece on Lenau's Faust under the name of Johannes M........n. The Latin equivalent for the Danish Hans is Johannes. One of Kierkegaard's major criticisms of Martensen was his claim to have gone beyond Hegel. It seems that one meaning of climacus is to go beyond; one can reach a climax which goes beyond another. Could it be that these writings contra Martensen were understood by Kierkegaard as "going beyond" Martensen, and the name Johannes Climacus refers to climaxing in relation to or "going beyond" Johannes Martensen?

It is also the case that Kierkegaard was thrilled over coming up with the pseudonym Anti-Climacus. One might argue that *The Sickness Unto Death* and *Practice in Christianity*, published under that pseudonym, came at a time when Kierkegaard is beginning to realize the need to go to a more direct form of communication. In that sense, those later works are *Anti*-Climacus. But they are also anti-Climacus in the sense of going against Martensen, whose mediating stance he now sees as dangerous to the faith, as completely at odds with his own position, and as calling for a more openly oppositional approach.

And yet, even in Anti-Climacus' *The Sickness Unto Death*, one can see the influence of Martensen. If one passage in Kierkegaard's writings has been central for summing up his position, it is the first few paragraphs of *The Sickness Unto Death* of Anti-Climacus.[86] This passage begins: "A

---

[86] Søren Kierkegaard, *Samlede Værker*, XI, pp. 127–128 (*The Sickness Unto Death: A Christian Psychological Exposition for Upbuilding and Awakening*, ed. and trans. Howard V. Hong and Edna H. Hong [Princeton: Princeton University, 1980], pp. 13–14.).

human being is spirit. But what is spirit? Spirit is the self. But what is the self? The self is a relation that relates itself to itself or is the relations's relating itself to itself in the relation; the self is not the relation but is the relation's relating itself to itself." Then a little later we get the sentence: "The human self is such a derived, established relation, a relation that relates itself to itself and in relating itself to itself relates itself to another." This long passage on the self comes to a close by offering a "formula that describes the state of the self when despair is completely rooted out": "in relating itself to itself and in willing to be itself, the self rests transparently in the power that established it." The claim is that the human self relates itself to itself, and in relating itself to itself relates itself to another power. In the Danish that would read" "*Menneskets Selv forholder sig til sig selv, og i at forholde sig til sig selv forholder sig til et andet Magt.*" Martensen—in discussing "Freedom and Dependence" under "The Ideal of Individuality" in considering "The Good as Ideal" in his *Outline to a System of Moral Philosophy*—uses strikingly similar language when defining virtue or striving freedom, which is the very heart of the human personality and thus the equivalent of his formula for the self. He writes: "It is virtue, striving freedom, which relates itself to itself as to that which does not exist in its own power." In the Danish it reads: "*Det er Dyden, den stræbende Frihed, der forholder sig til sig selv som til et, der ikke staaer i dens egen Magt.*" In other words, the human self relates itself to itself, and in relating itself to itself relates itself to another power. Kierkegaard's self which relates itself to itself is the actual self relating itself to the ideal self; Martensen is treating the human individual who relates itself to itself, that is, brings the ideal of individuality into relation to itself as the center of decision-making. Martensen's writing on moral philosophy is in actuality a beautiful statement on freedom. It articulates how the human personality needs to relate itself to an Other, to a Power, to God who as the Substance of the world's beings is the source of the human's freedom, but who is also the truly free personality who is able to make the human truly free as the human humbly acknowledges its need for God. Martensen has influenced Kierkegaard on the theological anthropology situated at the center of Kierkegaard's thought. If this is indeed the case, then it seems very likely that lines of influence might be found in other areas as well.

Martensen has influenced Kierkegaard not by passing on a paragraph here or a sentence there that gets incorporated directly into Kierkegaard's writings but by providing a general theological framework out of which to reflect on matters of ultimate concern and by lifting up certain themes and images which are then spun out in a more nuanced way. On the more comprehensive vision, one thinks of the anthropological viewpoint Martensen articulates. The understanding of freedom situated at the center of that viewpoint definitely influences Kierkegaard. The whole vision of historical existence as creating the actual self through decision-making of actuality in relation to possibility affirms a polarity of destiny and freedom, and this view of Martensen's clearly is influential upon Kierkegaard. The divine side of the God-human relation is also an area of influence. Kierkegaard says little explicitly about the nature of God, and yet it is as though he is presupposing a large share of Martensen's understanding of God. In grasping Martensen's theological perspective one is able to clarify many passages in Kierkegaard's works which otherwise remain opaque. There are also the more particular themes and images of Martensen by which Kierkegaard has been influenced. One thinks of such areas as Martensen's rich reflections on the relation of subjectivity and objectivity, the notion of qualitative as opposed to quantitative dependence, the theme of the self-limitation of God, the emphasis on the human's need for God, the concept of self-consciousness as including not being secretive and thus the ethical hearkening for the self to disclose itself, the theme of the imitation of Christ, the concept of the conscience and the power of life which undergirds the self, the notion of the intensified personality whose depth and potentiation is dependent upon that over against which it lives its life, the topic of preaching or Christian discourses as engaging the individual, the radical interiority of the self and its ultimate incommensurability with externality, the understanding of mysticism and its critique, the understanding of idealism and its critique, the notion of reduplication or repetition, the theme of humility as a critical theological virtue, and the idea of theonomy as central theological claim.

So is Martensen finally a "clairvoyant meditator" who speculates wildly in a fashion that leaves him unremoved from the actual world of existence, or is he instead a "clandestine mentor" of that one who stands at the origin of existentialism? Martensen is a meditator who mediates by way of speculation, but he does not advocate just any old form of speculation, as has been shown above. He advocates a type of speculating that has its roots in the intuition of faith, that strives after a *relative* rather than *absolute* comprehension of the divine things, and that acknowledges faith as far richer than knowledge and intuition as far richer than the concept, and that includes both *contemplatio* and *meditatio*. Therefore, we must say "No" to Martensen as a clairvoyant meditator, just as at the same time we must say "Yes" to Martensen as a clandestine mentor. For he was influential in helping Kierkegaard to establish his intellectual agenda. He was a mentor to Kierkegaard in the area of grasping an anthropological understanding, including the myriad possibilities presenting themselves to the human's freedom as well as the insidious forces at work in our lives to make us less open to the future. He was also instrumental in helping Kierkegaard arrive at a comprehensive theological vision, which Kierkegaard admittedly developed in a different direction from that of Martensen, namely, into a non-mediating position that would not stomach the both-and, mediating standpoint of his teacher but which nevertheless functioned as the overarching intellectual horizon or framework of meaning in which his view could be intelligibly brought critically to bear over against that of his mentor. Martensen influenced Kierkegaard, and until that influence is fully acknowledged and studied, the relation "between Hegel and Kierkegaard" will not have been fully understood.

A Word on the Translations and Abbreviations

Thompson has translated *The Autonomy of Human Self-Consciousness in Modern Dogmatic Theology* and *Outline to a System of Moral Philosophy.* Kangas has translated *Meister Eckhart: A Study in Speculative Theology.* We each worked independently in arriving at our translations. Then the completed translations were compared and negotiations were made where needed. Having attempted to make our translations consistent, we are confident that at least the major incongruities have been identified and dealt with by making the appropriate changes.

We have utilized inclusive language in the translations. This has led to a few places where the style and flow of the text have been sacrificed. We obviously are convinced that this minor loss is more than justified by the resulting reduction in sexist language and witness to the need for doing what can be done to overcome forces of oppression at work in and through patriarchal social structures.

The texts of the translations have been kept unencumbered with explanatory notes as much as possible. We hope the Introduction has provided adequate background information and comment to contextualize these three treatises. Most notes included in Martensen's writings are his own and most of those appear in the translations as they appear in his Danish texts.

The pagination of the original manuscripts has been preserved. Page numbers from the original Danish texts appear in brackets within the text. Italic font has been used to indicate emphasis in the original texts and for Danish, German, Latin, French, and Italian words, phrases, and passages.

Finally, it is necessary to remark on the "creative" manner by which Martensen on occasion quotes and cites other sources, usually German texts. We have worked hard to identify the sources that Martensen himself was using, and generally we have been successful in that effort. However, it is apparent that while Martensen sometimes quotes a source very faithfully, at other times he will make minor changes without using brackets or otherwise indicating his editorial work. We are convinced that these minor changes of his were made in good faith. We have attempted to use English translations of these quoted writings, where they were available. In a few instances this has led to minor discrepancies between the German and the English, which we think are sufferable in the interest of keeping the English in harmony with the texts familiar to the reader.

The following abbreviations have been used in the *Meister Eckhart* treatise:

Eckhart:

EPT   *Meister Eckhart, Preacher and Teacher*; Bernard McGinn, ed., Paulist (1986).

ME   *Meister Eckhart: The essential sermons, commentaries, treatises and defense*; Edmund Colledge O.S.A. and Bernard McGinn, trans., Paulist (1981).

Werke   *Meister Eckhart: Werke I, II*; Bibliothek des Mittelalters, vols. 20, 21; Nicholas Largier, ed. and trans., Deutsche Klassiker Verlarg (1993)

Other:

BPS   *Book of the poor in spirit*, by a Friend of God; translation of *Nachfolge des armen Lebens Christi* by C. F. Kelly, Harpers (1954).

HS   *Henry Suso: Selections*; Frank Tobin, trans., Paulist (1989).

ThG   *Theologia Germanica*; Bengt Hoffman, trans., Paulist (1980).

Den menneskelige Selvbevidstheds

Autonomie

i

vor Tids dogmatiske Theologie.

Af

Dr. H. Martensen,

Professor i Theologien ved Kjøbenhavns Universitet.

Paa Dansk udgivet

af

L. V. Petersen,

Stud. theol.

Kjøbenhavn.

Forlagt af Universitetsboghandler C. A. Reitzel.

Trykt i Bianco Luno's Bogtrykkeri.

1841.

The Autonomy
of Human
Self-Consciousness
in Modern Dogmatic Theology

By
Dr. H. Martensen

Professor in Theology at the University of Copenhagen

Translated into Danish
by
L. B. Petersen

Copenhagen
C.A. Reitzel
1841

Preface

The present writing was published originally in Latin as a dissertation for the theological licentiate at the University of Copenhagen. It is reviewed at some length in *Tidsskrift for Litteratur og Kritik* (Vol. 1, No. 1), more concisely in *Theologisk Tidsskrift* (Vol. 2, No. 1). It has also received considerable attention outside of Denmark; thus, in Germany it has been reviewed in *Theologische Studien und Kritiken* (1838, No. 4), and especially Dr. C. F. Göschel in his book *Beiträge zur Speculativen Philosophie von Gott und dem Menschen und von dem Gott-Menschen* has capably referred his readers to it (e.g., pp. 48, 78, 117–118, 257–259). It was the first writing that came out in Denmark in the modern speculative direction and heralded the era in theology from which people have now already begun to mark time.

The further reasons for my undertaking to translate this work I dare consider superfluous; as concerns the modern form itself, I hereby recommend it for the closer consideration of favorable readers.

July 18, 1841

L. B. Petersen.

Contents

On the Inner Connection Between Theology and Philosophy

§ 1.

"One must philosophize," says Clement of Alexandria, "even if one will allow absolutely no philosophy. That is to say, one can neither disapprove nor reject anything unless one first has come to know it. Therefore one must philosophize even if merely in order to realize that one ought not philosophize."

This reasoning, which was already advanced in the period of the early church, has always been manifested in theology, and one will not easily find any thoughtful theologian who asserts that theology can do without philosophy. Restricting oneself to the view that philosophy shall only be related to theology as a *negative* condition for the positive science, one will be accepted by many theologians of our time who surely permit the use of philosophy as a complimentary discipline, but are far from granting it any *intrinsic* significance in theology. At the same time, if one admits that in some sense there is a speculative understanding of God and the divine things—which shall not be argued here—, one cannot be other than united with the philosophizing Fathers of the church, as well as [2] with the scholastics of the Middle Ages who taught that theology was philosophy, that true philosophy was theology, and thus claimed a unity of both. The truth of this claim simply follows from the peculiar nature of the subject-matter. That is to say, what makes philosophy indispensable for the human race is the desire for *knowledge* of the truth; but what other than this has called forth theology? The absolute truth or God is the object of philosophy; but theology has no other object, and religion has no other content than God's revelation to humankind: thus theology and philosophy have the same object, and have emerged from the same inner necessity. If then there is still any difference between them, it can only lie in *the method*, or in the way in which their eternal object is appropriated by human knowledge [*Viden*].

This difference in method can be determined in several ways; but all modifications of this really seem to be able to be classified under the principal difference that theology has faith [*Troen*] for its principle of knowledge, while philosophy on the contrary has knowledge [*Viden*] for its principle of knowledge. We would gladly consider this distinction valid, if we could merely become convinced that method is an arbitrary and by no means a necessary matter. Method is, if we are not mistaken, that law which the truth itself has imposed on human thought in order to arrive at its knowledge, the eternal way along which the infinite truth will be found by the finite spirit; it is the necessary bond between the object of knowledge and the knowing subject. To doubt that there actually exists such an objective method would be the same thing as admitting that no transition or point of contact is found between God and finite knowledge, that, in other words, there is no knowledge of God and the [3] divine things. Now, if one does not admit this, then neither can one acknowledge the view that there should be two truths *about the same object*. This smacks grossly of a bad Scholasticism which feigns two truths, one theological and one philosophical, which not infrequently contradict each other. Therefore, the proper acknowledgement to be made is that the truth existing for the human can only be one because truth is only one. Now if faith is to be neglected when it comes to knowing the truth—a thesis we here merely put forward as an hypothesis, but which for that matter is endorsed by many philosophers; if the speculative concept or the knowledge of the truth in its truth can only be obtained along the so-called way of pure thought; if the complete revelation of the truth takes place not by means of faith but only by means of doubt: then theological inquiry, which has the absolute truth as its object, must be a thinking not *in* but *outside* of and *beyond* faith, in order to be able to agree with the object's nature. Thus theology becomes philosophy. It is precisely this complete harmony and agreement between form and content which constitutes the concept of every science, for which reason it does not allow any other limitation than that which follows from the object's own nature. It is therefore an arbitrary procedure to permit philosophy an absolute knowledge of the truth but allow theology to remain at a lower stage and be discredited by a relative knowledge.

On the other hand, if the human can know the truth only by means of faith, if this condition is not a whim of the theologians but a demand of the [4] truth itself, a necessary law which the truth in its self-communication follows, then one must also conclude that in no way can philosophy forego faith, but it must be an inquiry *inside* of faith. And thus philosophy becomes theology. In whichever way, then, the matter is resolved, whether the investigation of God's essence ought to have faith or also pure rational necessity as its principle, it always lies in the objective character of method that the theological method cannot be different from the philosophical.

The same thing will appear when one considers this difference in method under another form which frequently occurs; we mean that well-known distinction between *a priori* and *a posteriori* knowledge. Consequently, when one says that in theology knowledge arises from the bottom upwards, from phenomenon to idea, and in philosophy on the contrary from above downwards, from idea to phenomenon, then one must add a note that these two movements, in spite of their contrary directions, are still only moments in one and the same thing, namely, in that development whereby the divine Idea and human thought pass over into one another; they are therefore also so closely connected in every knowing which has a real content that they are not able to be divided. Such a distinction remains only naked and abstract, and can in no way be the basis for a two-fold science. On the whole it must be maintained that the different sciences find their various grounds of division only in the objective moments into which the truth itself has been divided. But all sciences are moments in the one general science, philosophy, whose culmination point is speculative theology. [5]

§ 2.

As the general and fundamental science, philosophy has not only objects of knowledge but *knowledge itself* as its object; it is the science of the sciences (the doctrine of science—the theory of knowledge). Questions such as these: how a science is put into order, how human consciousness is related to the object of knowledge, which meaning and reality result from the categories of thought—all of these accordingly fall under philosophy, not in its unity with theology, but in its independence as *fundamental* science. Such a science is a presupposition for the study of every positive science; a theory of knowledge can be extracted from every scientific practice, even if there has not been any theory in plain site. The theologians particularly have been obliged to recognize its necessity, and there is always tied to theology at least certain theorems borrowed from that fundamental science which is rightly called architectonic, even if it has not yet been brought into any system. Already among the theologians of the Middle Ages we find the first instances of a theory of knowledge, which would form a basis for theology. Here one is reminded of the celebrated *credam ut intelligam* [I shall believe in order that I may understand] of *Anselm* and *Augustine*, a maxim which had such great influence on the whole of medieval theology; on this one also hears much in the writings of *Thomas Aquinas*, for example, his learned treatise on the identity of the subject and object of knowledge.[1] Again indicative of this is the well-

---

[1] Cf. *Summa of the Catholic Faith Against the Gentiles*, tract. "*quomodo deus per essentiam videatur* [In what way is God seen according to essence?]."

known conflict between nominalists and realists, which contains such [6] sweeping consequences for theology. Finally, if we consult religion itself, we will find there many things that seem to show the necessity of this science, e.g., those Christian dogmas of Revelation and Inspiration, indeed even many statements in Holy Scripture (e.g., 1 Cor. 13:12 and 2:14) which register it explicitly. Even at the beginning of Genesis, by far the oldest tradition of the human race, we already hear talk about that mystical tree of *knowledge*. In all these we have a summons to shape our theory of *knowledge*.

Not dogma itself, but the knowledge entailed in dogma is consequently the subject-matter of fundamental philosophy. In this science one does not arrive at any dogmatic and theological knowledge in a strict sense but at the knowledge of this dogmatic knowing, at the consciousness of the theological consciousness. It is easy to see that the entire reality, value, and meaning of Christian dogma depend on this consideration. In order to remove all doubt in this respect one simply needs to reflect on which consequences for Christian dogmatics flow from the conflict between nominalism and realism, from the philosophical question of whether ideas have subjective or objective validity; one simply places in plain view the old question of the reciprocal relation between reason and revelation, of faith or reason as the principle for thinking. Neither can it cause astonishment that dogmatic theology in every age is changed by the theory of knowledge of that age. Thus particularly *Kant* in modern times with his *Critique of Pure Reason* which found its further development in *Fichte's* system, *The Science of Knowledge*, and later *Hegel* with his profound work, *The Phenomenology of Spirit*, as well as with his speculative logic provoked the [7] greatest change in theology's situation. With these theories the entire way of reflecting on Christian dogma has undergone a great metamorphosis, of which we shall see examples in the following.

Of course there is already found in the theological works of the Middle Ages, as indicated above, not a few *disjecta membra* [scattered limbs or members] of fundamental philosophy; but the development of this science into an independent system was reserved for modern times, which is a period from the Reformation to our day when philosophy's domination has attained a wider extension. For after the Reformation philosophy was liberated from theology and in pursuance of the Reformation's own principle claimed its own independent authority. That is to say, the Reformation was not merely a liberation from a yoke of slavery which unlawfully bound the free human spirit, but a positive development of freedom itself. In that great struggle, where spirit fought for its most sacred rights, where free access to God was again opened for the human, where faith and knowledge supported themselves exclusively on God's authority which in truth is liberating—there developed among humankind a fervent conviction about the dignity of the spirit, about its divine right to search and comprehend everything divine and human. Indeed, one claimed not merely what in the proper sense can be called *jus circa sacra* [right in respect to sacred things], not merely right over everything which the human finds in the outer world; but there was inculcated in human consciousness the highest meaning of that old motto: "*Know yourself.*" Consequently, knowing itself became the object of knowledge, and the theory of self-consciousness became the altogether essential task of modern philosophy. [8]

On the Religious Principle of Philosophy

§ 3.

Before the human spirit puts forward *its own* theory of *knowledge*, it must address itself to the important question of whether consciousness shall observe a limit it cannot transgress, whether it must—for we also in our way shall make use of this expression—conduct itself transcendentally, or not. That is to say, it must be settled whether thought itself is to be removed from the light of religion when it appoints its entire knowledge of divinity and humanity as subject-matter of reflection; whether it can complete its theory by its own power and ability, or whether in this undertaking it also needs divine assistance. At first sight this appears easy to decide; for already with a provisional contemplation it must be brought to consciousness that a doctrine of the highest principles of knowledge cannot dispense with *God*, since God is the constitutive principle for all things. The consciousness of God also plays the leading role here as the light which enlightens every human who comes into the world, and the character of this origination alone determines the difference between theology and philosophy as a difference between being and thought. The theory of knowledge is a *light*-theory, a theory about *the light as such*, about its nature and meaning in the whole intellectual world; it can only see the light, then, in the light itself, and it therefore also applies here as in all divine knowledge: "*in lumine tuo videbimus lumen* [by your light we will see the light]." But then a second question arises—a question which hits the real center—, namely, whether that [9] light of divinity which is the principle for all knowledge is the peculiar light of religion seen in its *intellectual* activity, or a light from a higher nature *superior* to religion and its authority. Here is asked, what is the *highest* in the human's self-consciousness, indeed what is the human's innermost and original consciousness itself; for most importantly every theory of knowledge must penetrate into that form of consciousness which as the constitutive and proper *dignitate prius* [that which is first because of merit] goes before all the others. Consequently, is it religion or is it speculative thought which must be posited as that highest fundament? Is it religion which must borrow its value and meaning from speculative thought, or is it perhaps speculative thought which needs religion, God's revelation?

Our answer on this is that the real *punctum saliens* [salient point], the most intense and original moment in the God-consciousness, that from which this so to speak draws its power and sustenance, is *the conscience* [*Samvittighed*] in the word's proper meaning (συνείδησις—*Gewissen*). On our view one cannot obtain any true knowledge without considering this co-knowledge. But if one gives this a merely moral meaning as a particular and purely practical concept in ethics, without consideration of theory, either as consciousness of the moral law, as judge of right and wrong, or defining it in other similar ways, then one places all too narrow limits on its concept. For it is a universal and religious concept which with immediate clarity and certainty determines the human's absolute relations, her place in the entire universe, her position in relation to God, and in this way casts light over her entire mode of being and living. This innermost sanctuary of the soul, [10] far from being a vague feeling, is a clear knowledge, and not a merely human knowledge but one that is in equal degree divine and human. Here the human spirit does not move amidst the multiplicity [*Indbegrebet*] of those things and thoughts which stand beneath it in value and meaning because it is itself subject for all these things and ideas that are in themselves *subject*less. Consciousness is by no means sufficient to recognize its precedence over the merely objective world, but in the light of the conscience it knows the very concept of *God's* absolute *knowledge*. However, it does so in such a way that in the most intimate union it separates itself from the latter. By recognizing the validity of this divine knowledge it comes to realize the thought that it does not have its knowledge of God from itself, but *from the knowing* God; it separates this consciousness of God from all others and grants it apriority and superiority. Consequently, since in the light of conscience one arrives at true knowledge of a *source* for all human self-consciousness, we are able to define it more precisely as the light in which the human is revealed as *God's creature*; in this knowledge lies the seed of *all religion and worship of God*. Therefore, the conscience constitutes the rational creature as rational, makes the human human, and in this way must be said to make up his or her essence; it is the *positive* stamp the Creator has impressed on the human, in order that in this the self-conscious creature should have its *character indelebilis* [distinguishing mark]. That is to say, what characterizes the thinking creature as such cannot be an absolute self-consciousness which is perfectly identical with itself, which should stand in relation to itself alone (*I=I*), but must be a consciousness of the absolute *relation* (*I* and Other-*I*). Reason is not the characteristic for the creature as such, but belongs—which we must elucidate more fully [11] in the ✓ following—just as much to every thinking being in-and-for-itself, no less to God than to the creature. But the conscience involves reason, even if the former cannot be deduced from the latter.

All this makes clearly evident, then, the *theoretical* value and meaning of the concept of the conscience, its influence on the theory of knowledge, which in truth it ought to posit as its task, that the laws which underlie the human's *life* are also able to be recognized in the realm of *knowledge*. Since human existence has its roots in the conscience, the human can never break away from it, for no being transgresses its nature unpunished; therefore, every investigation must be contained within the limits of religion and the divine revelation, which here we already have in principle. That is to say, just as in the knowledge of a given object it is an essential requirement that the limit (ὁ ὅρος) be observed, so that thought does not step beyond the matter's own barriers but refrains from every excursion beyond its proper domain, so that in relations that which is *qualitatively* different might not be confused: so there is also placed in us—in that very knowing of our knowledge—this eternal limit, which is to be observed as that which conditions the cultivation of the true concept of our knowledge. This knowledge of our *ground*-relation [*Grundforhold*],[2] which is just as real as ideal (because that knowledge, which the conscience gives the human, [12] is no different from the human's real existence, since it much more is this existence itself), obliges us then to *assign* all our knowledge to God. In this way this knowledge is considered as the secondary knowledge derived from God's primitive knowledge, from whose apriority and superiority human thought obtains all its *meaning*. Consequently, the human cannot arrive at a knowledge of the truth by its own powers, but only by the help of God's enlightening grace (*gratia illuminans*). Consciousness will always stand under the divine authority, it will always need God's assistance, since the human itself is not the truth but has only come to the world in order to know the truth. As we learn the difference between this primitive consciousness of God and the human's secondary consciousness which is derived from this, we learn that precisely here is the limit which may truthfully be called *transcendental*, because it is a barrier human self-consciousness dare not transgress.

---

[2] Cf. Fr. Schlegel's *Philosophical Lectures*, edited by Windischmann (2nd Vol., 88). "*Das Gewissen ist das Vermögen, worin alle Verhältnisse des menschlichen zum göttlichen Bewußtseyn vorkommen. Eine Fühlbarkeit, eine Empfindlichkeit der Verhältnisse zwischen Mensch und Gott;—die Vermittlerin, der Schlußstein alles Bewußtseyns.*" ["Knowledge is the power in which all relationships of the human to divine consciousness take place. A sensibility, a susceptibility of the relations between the human and God;—the mediator, the keystone of all consciousness."]

Despite this relation of contrast between God and the human, the identity of the divine and the human in religious contemplation and speculation is still so intense that one easily grasps the meaning of that old saying of the mystics: "The eye with which I see God is the same eye with which God sees me. My eye and God's eye are one eye."[3] The one moment by no means swallows up the other; the unity, which takes place in such a beholding, is therefore always defined such that there are two who behold and know (γνώσομαι ὡς ἐγὼ ἐγνώσθην [I shall know as I am known] 1 Cor. 13). Although the human's knowledge is consequently only a knowledge by a [13] finite and created spirit, it still does not therefore lose its *absolute* and *infinite* character. That is to say, since the idea of God is granted in religion by God's own revelation, so that we know God *by God*, the very self of God is also effectively given in our consciousness under scientific thinking, under the rational and conceptual development of this idea; God, who is thought by us, consequently thinks Godself in us. And in this certainly consists the true doctrine of the unity of subject and object in speculative thinking, that here takes place not only a relation between the knowing subject and an object which is to be known without itself being known, but between the subject and an object which itself is subject, which consequently is not only to be known but itself knows. The speculative thought of God is therefore not a solitary knowledge but a co-knowledge. The same law, which grounds the unity of God and the creature in religious *love*, is also valid in religious *knowing*, in speculative reflection on God. Just as we, with the apostles, love God because God *first* loved us, so also we know God because God *first* knew us. Just as God's love descends into the human's heart and brings the human's love to rise to God, so is the human's knowledge, which is its free knowledge of God, a reflection of God's absolute knowledge which illuminates the human. God and the creature behold in the same eternal light; they see in the same mirror, in the same Idea, and yet their *qualitative*[4] difference is not sublated. [14]

We thus follow the division of existence John Scotus Eriugena has first put forward as that which comprehends all spheres of life, both theo-

---

[3] Meister Eckhart's Sermons. Cf. *Meister Eckhart: A Study in Speculative Theology.* By the author, 36 [in the original].

[4] Meister Eckhart's Sermons. *"Gottes Wesen mag nicht unser Wesen werden, sondern soll unser Leben seyn; denn wir sind ausgeflossen von den Personen und nicht innebleibend im göttlichen Wesen, sondern wir empfiengen als geschassen ein fremd Wesen, das vom göttlichen Wesen geursprunget ist. Wir werden mit Gott vereinigt in Schauung nich in Wesung."* ["God's essence may not become our essence, but should be our *life;* for we have flowed forth from the persons and do not remain within the divine essence, but we receive as fashioned an alien essence which has originated from the divine essence. We become united with God in *vision* not in *essence.*] Following Franz Baader, *Vorlesungen über religiöse Philosophie,* 1827. And cf. *Mester Eckart,* 35 [in the original].

retical and practical, namely, the creating but not created nature (*natura naturans non naturata*), the created and creating nature (*natura naturata et naturans*), and the created but not creating nature (*natura naturata non naturans*). When this division is applied to the theory of knowledge, we then get: "the nature which thinks, but is not thought (except by itself)," "the thought and thinking nature (the rational creature)," and "the thought but not thinking nature (the physical world)." The thinking but not thought nature enters into another relation to knowledge than does the thought but not thinking nature. This latter (the object, which is to be known without itself knowing) is subordinate to the human as the being who in itself has consciousness of reason and laws. The object of knowledge (which is the thought but not thinking nature) only blindly obeys. The free human can *compel* it to open itself for knowledge, for everything which is a mere object is inferior to the subject and subordinated to the latter. On the other hand, the object which is to be known but which itself is subject (and the absolute subject at that, ὁ μόνος σοφὸς [the only wise]) can only be known by the human in its *free* self-revelation. If with knowledge of the physical world it is the human who makes nature submissive to itself, then in knowledge of God on the contrary thought must subordinate itself to God; this qualitative difference in the various spheres of knowledge must be continually maintained. That is to say, if [15] the relation between subject and object we have here before us is the relation between the finite and Absolute Spirit, between created and uncreated reason; if in addition freedom is a principle for every knowledge, since only through the mediation of *freedom* can the one rational being communicate with the other and live and move within it: then the human must *freely submit* itself to God, in order for the divine Idea really to be able to penetrate into its spirit and be intensely united with its consciousness. In other words, the human must believe in order to understand.

§ 4.

If one would object that this whole development of God's knowledge as that which comprehends and underlies human knowledge, or that the apostle's conviction: "that he is *known* by God" is only a human fiction, a figment of the human imagination, and that never by any convincing argument can one receive full certainty concerning what is actually the case, then to this one must respond that *the most certain thing the human is capable of thinking* cannot possibly be derived from some other thing that is more certain, but is an absolute knowledge *a priori*. All certainty of the object's reality depends, namely, on that it is really present for the thinker, that it enters into her real existence. But the conscience, and the relation between God and the human which is expressed in this, is the human's essential *modus existendi* [mode of existing] and thus also *modus cognoscendi* [mode of knowing]. "*Quicquid cognoscitur per modum cognoscentis cognoscitur* [whatever is known is known through the mode of knowing]."[5] Consequently, God Godself cannot assure the human of the truth in [16] any other way than by placing the truth in connection with God's very innermost nature; and the human cannot grasp any dogma in its truth unless it steps into inner unity with the conscience. On this is grounded— for in passing we will notice this—the indissoluble bond between the anthropological and theological moments in dogmatics. Knowledge of every divine mystery and its relation to the human is mediated by this *most certain truth for the human*; this grounds her entire approach to being and thinking, provides the standpoint for her reflection, and forms so to speak the culmination point from which all speculative outlooks onto the kingdom of the divine are opened (*specula—speculatio* [a look-out— speculation]).

The Autonomy of Human Self-Consciousness as a Principle in Modern Philosophy

§ 5.

Descartes, who may be seen as the founder of modern philosophy, arrived, for reason of wanting to restore science, at the proposition *that one must doubt everything* (*de omnibus dubitandum est*). Only by proceeding from here could one think without taking sides; only through doubt could thought be purified from all presupposed opinions, and a standpoint be achieved where doubt was no longer possible. As in this way in defiance of all external authority he sought the source of certainty, he found by means of his inquiry that the [17] thinking spirit has existence in itself, that thought itself is the spirit's existence (*cogito ergo sum*) [I think, therefore I am]. Consequently, since he had in principle shown the identity of thought and being, he taught that everything which is to have truth and certainty in itself is only to be sought in thinking itself. This doctrine was then taken up and gradually developed further by the philosophers who followed him. That is to say, when thinking involves being, or, in other words, when there is no given reality, no being *outside* of thinking— even if there were something *on the other side of* thought, it would be

---

[5] Cf. Fr. Baader, *Vorlesungen über religiöse Philosophie* and Hegel's *Phänomenologie*. One will also find much for enlightenment on this point in F. C. Sibbern in his book, *Om Erkiendelse og Grandskning*.

impossible to think it—; when further we may say that the *truth's* own concept lies in this identity of thought and being, then *self-consciousness*, which is the absolute for this identity, must be recognized as the source of all truth and certainty; it must be able to decide out of *itself* what is true and false and by this lead the human into all truth. The spirit which thinks or the ideal self-consciousness then sees in objective existence nothing except its own essence—namely, the law of thinking—and is thus itself both true and certain. In this way is formed the concept of self-consciousness's *autarchy* [*autarkie*], or the quality that in an absolute way it is *self-sufficient* and has the ability to *prescribe its law itself (autonomy)*; self-consciousness thus does not stand under any authority because it is itself the highest court of appeal. And in order to exclude all alien interpretations these philosophers have always urged that this autarchy and autonomy do not apply to self-consciousness in its finite and empirical shape but only insofar as it coincides with *reason*. That is to say, reason is self-consciousness comprehended under the categories of *universality* [18] and *necessity*, or self-consciousness "which conceives itself *sub specie aeternitatis*" [under the aspect of eternity].

Although one cannot deny that considered in-and-for-itself all this is true and right, yet the result remains false since the *anthropological* moment has not received its due. The human spirit, which in order to find the truth apart from all presuppositions emancipated itself from authority in every respect, still has the tacit *presupposition*, namely, that it is *self-sufficient* for knowledge of the truth. What applies to self-consciousness as its *abstract* determinations, metaphysically taken, it transfers immediately to the *human* self-consciousness, and obscures by this the qualitative difference between God's primitive knowledge and the creature's secondary knowledge, between the thinking but not thought nature and the thinking but thought nature. This entails a second *presupposition* in this philosophy, which still makes a claim to being perfectly presuppositionless, namely, that the human's ground-relation [*Grundforhold*] is a purely metaphysical relation, although in actuality it is a real and personal relation. Consequently, according to these philosophers the human must be defined as "a being endowed with reason," while according to the true definition the human is a being united with God *in religion*; for this definition contains not merely that abstract character but defines in addition the creature's *specific* character. That is to say, it is not thinking but *religion*—which involves thinking—which constitutes the created and self-conscious nature. Reason forms only the universal *form* of self-consciousness without which no thinking being would exist as thinking; it is the eternal formal side of all thought and being. As such reason is the universal for everything, both for God and for the creature, but precisely on [19] account of this character of universality reason stands under that living and personal actuality which comprises not only the abstract *forms* of life but life itself. The investigation of the nature of self-consciousness must therefore be not merely a *logical* investigation but a *theological* and *anthropological* one; here must be asked not only questions of how self-consciousness is related to being and existence, but how it is related to *life* itself. It is an investigation not only of the relations between the finite and Infinite, but between the *created* and uncreated spirit. Without regarding this *positive* character of the human spirit, the greatest philosophers from Descartes right on down to Hegel—with the lone exception of Leibniz—have followed the onesided metaphysical mode of reflection. ✓

The concept of the human spirit's autarchy and autonomy, which from the beginning was adopted by this movement in philosophy, is presented with the greatest clarity and distinctness in Kant's system. Long since the standpoint of this system has been displaced, at least in philosophy—for in theology it still finds more support—, its autonomic principle still prevails, not only among Kantian philosophers but in the entire literary world as well.[6] [20]

§ 6.

Human self-consciousness, which sees itself in the shape of this spiritual autonomy, prescribes laws not merely for itself but for the universe, for the world of objective things. For on the one hand since it is able to determine what is true and false, good and evil, and does not recognize any *inner* authority, because it is itself all truth and certainty, it must consequently also reject every outer authority. It finds in nature and history, then, only its *own* laws, and what reality is to be conferred on this or that object depends on its rational character or its agreement with the specula-

---

[6] Hegel has drawn pertinent attention to this in his *Encyclop. der philos. Wissensch.*, 2nd ed., 71: "*Die Hauptwirkung, welche die Kantische Philosophie gehabt hat, ist gewesen das Bewußtseyn dieser absoluten Innerlichkeit (der Selbstständigkeit des sich erfassenden Denkens) erweckt zu haben, die, ob sie um ihrer Abstraction willen zwar aus sich zu nichts sich entwickeln und keine Bestimmungen, weder Erkenntnisse noch moralische Gesetze hervorbringen kann, doch schlechthin sich weigert, etwas was den Charakter einer Aeußerlichkeit hat, in sich gewähren und gelten zu lassen. Das Princip der Unabhängigkeit der Vernunft, ihrer absoluten Selbstständigkeit in sich, ist von nun an als allgemeines Princip der Philosophie wie als eines der Vorurtheile der Zeit anzusehen.*" [*Hegel's Logic*, trans. William Wallace (Oxford: Clarendon, 1975, 93: "The main effect of the Kantian philosophy has been to revive the consciousness of reason, or the absolute inwardness of thought. Its abstractness indeed prevented that inwardness from developing into anything, or from originating any special forms, whether cognitive principles or moral laws; but nevertheless it absolutely refused to accept or indulge anything possessing the character of an *externality*. Henceforth the principle of the *independence of reason*, or of its absolute self-subsistence, is made a general principle of philosophy, as well as *a foregone conclusion of the time*."] [Martensen's emphases.]

tive self-consciousness; for this speculative self-consciousness stands as a prototype [*forbillede*] for and as judge over everything and by its authority shall sanction everything which is to have the name of truth. If it seeks *God* in the universe, it can only name *itself* in its absolute development; for the concept of absolute self-*validity* becomes synonymous with the concept of the absolute truth or God, and one then gets, when this is made the leading principle for the human's search for the truth, a God which seeks itself. This thinking will never arrive at a God which differs from thought itself, since the system can never reveal in its conclusion what it has not already had in its beginning. Consequently, if one suspends in principle every *authority*, then by this takes place a tacit denial of the *author* of human self-consciousness. Otherwise it would be inconsistent to *absolve* the human spirit *from all authority* [21] in order to confer absolute self-validity. Therefore, one cannot, without contradicting oneself, both lift up reason's independence and preach faith in a God who has created heaven and earth—something which incidentally is not rare in our time. Still another inconsistency stands in the most intimate connection with this, when one, without giving up the principle of autonomy, nevertheless has hopes of arriving at the idea of a personal God, the source of human self-consciousness. The reason for this delusion lies in a certain mystification, as science indeed promises to lead to God but instead of this *itself* takes on playing God's role.[7] [22]

---

[7] Franz Baader has splendidly portrayed this mystification in his *Vorlesungen über speculative Dogmatik*, 3rd vol., 31; we will communicate to the readers this profound thinker's words, which to a great extent have served to transform and renew modernity's religious knowledge: *"Für eine philosophische Taschenspielerei muß man es darum erklären, wenn man (nach Cartesius) das Erkennen mit dem Ich als einem absolut primitiven anfangen will, oder auch mit einem selbstlosen Nicht-ich, und das Secundaire dieser beeden Ueberzeugungen läugnet, weil doch beede nur mit einer tiefern, ihnen zum Grunde liegenden Ueberzeugung eines Andern oder Ersten, zu welchem Ich oder ein selbstloses Nicht-Ich das Andre ist, nämlich Gottes auftreten, und das Nichtanfangen mit diesem schon dessen Läugnen ist. Mit dieser philosophischen Taschenspielerei fällt aber jene zusammen, gemäß welcher man den Menschen die einfache, primitive oder Grundüberzeugung aus dem Auge rückt, daß sie als erkennend und schauend eben so gut nur ein andres Erkennen und Schauen erkennen und schauen, oder daß dem Erkennen und Schauen eben so wohl nur wieder ein Erkennen und Schauen Objekt ist, als dem Wollen ein Wollen. In der That ruht der forschende Geist nicht, bis er zu solch einem Erkennen eines Erkennenden, d.h. seines Erkanntseyns durchgedrungen ist, oder wie Plato sagt, bis sein Auge einem sein Sehen sehenden Auge begegnet."* ["It must be declared a philosophical sleight of hand, if (according to Descartes) cognition by means of the *I*, or also by means of an outsider not-*I*, are viewed as existing right from the very beginning, and if the secondary nature of either cognition or not-*I* is denied, since both can arise only on the basis of a more fundamental concept of an other or a first, in relation to which the *I* or an outsider not-*I* is the other, namely, God, and *the not beginning with God is already the denial of God*. This philosophical sleight of hand coincides with that one which tries to remove from view of people the simple and fundamental conviction that they must cognize themselves in order to recognize cognition outside of themselves, in other words, that cognition is the object of cog-

Since in the religious understanding there are always two who know, namely, God and the creature, the system of autonomy must consequently dissolve the true concept of religion and fall either into an abstract *separation* or into a *confusion* of these moments God has harmoniously united. As long as self-consciousness has not undergone a speculative development, it limits its autonomy to mere *knowledge,* and does not venture with certainty to indicate any of the *objective* conditions of existence. On the other hand, if self-consciousness realizes that the difference between *rationes cognoscendi* and *rationes essendi* [theories of knowing and theories of being] is only a finite and transitory difference, then it teaches the unity of subject and substance and grasps, so to speak, itself as the spiritual focus of the entire universe. In this way is developed philosophical rationalism both as subjective and as objective. As one holds in contempt God's revelation to the creature in subjective rationalism, the knowledge of God becomes in subjective rationalism merely that of the human, and in objective rationalism only God's own knowledge of Godself. The principle of subjectivity receives its highest expression in Kant's system, the principle of objectivity in Hegel's. What center is to the periphery, these renowned men's systems are for the scientific character of the entire modern era. [23]

The Autonomy of Human Self-Consciousness in Modern Dogmatic Theology

§ 7.

When dogmatic theology obtains autonomy as its principle, it will necessarily appear as a special form, a concrete modification of either one or the other of the systems suggested in the preceding paragraph. Just as these philosophical systems are only the scientific development, either in a subjective or in an objective direction, of the Cartesian principle for the absolute independence of speculative thinking, so also then in dogmatics is everything traced back to this same principle,[8] which, when it is applied to the religious self-consciousness with its positive content, will comprehend the entire world of spirit. Just as in the subjective system of autonomy one sees everything only in relation to the human alone with-

---

nition, like wishing is to wishing. In reality the inquiring mind does not rest until it proceeds to the recognition of a cognizing entity, i.e., one's own state of being cognized; or—as Plato states—until one's eye has met another eye cognizing one's cognition."]

[8] Johann Gottlieb Fichte has properly designated this principle as: *"die in sich verfestigte Selbstgewißheit, (in ihrem Unterschiede von der erfüllenden Gottesgewißheit)* ["the in-itself fortified *self*-certainty (in its difference from the abundant *God*-certainty)]."

out understanding the *objective* nature of things, indeed without even feeling any urge toward investigations of this kind, so the corresponding dogmatic system construes the religious self-consciousness by referring everything to the pious *subject*. It only ascribes value to what is of a *practical* nature, to what can practically contribute either to morality or to religiosity, to what can awaken pious feelings and dispositions, while everything that would cast light on the objective being of God and the universe is expelled from the system. What lies in the [24] principle, namely, that all *knowledge* [*Viden*] is merely subjective, and that only the thinking spirit itself is the sole *certainty*, steps forth here in special form, as it is said that the pious disposition [*Gemyt*] is itself the sole *certainty*, that piety, which appears in the ethical striving or in the soul's movements, is *sufficient in itself*, and that all investigation of God, seen from an objective standpoint, ought to be removed as something irrelevant. To the objective system of autonomy corresponds a dogmatics which in religion certainly understands the *truth's* objective revelation; but since it considers the purely metaphysical concept as the absolute truth, the true loses its character. It posits a contradiction between *concept* and *representation*, and regards the philosophical concept as a higher form of truth than faith, which needs to be liberated from the wrappings of representation.

After having indicated with this provisional investigation the nature and character of autonomic dogmatics, we now proceed to consider its relation to *dogma*. The true relation between God and the human consists in this, that human self-consciousness finds its concept of an *other* self-consciousness, namely, the divine, and receives all truth as a revelation from the latter. Herein lies the qualitative difference between God and the human—a difference, which in theology cannot be urged enough. Consequently, this divine truth of revelation, in which the omnipresent God is really present, is the constitutive principle both for the human's faith and knowledge. As such it is the prototype of the understanding and not only receives the name of dogma but is itself *dogma*. Therefore this contains *what one can know about God* (τὸ γνωστὸν τοῦ θεοῦ) and presents the objective [25] Idea of God and the human as in a pure and spotless mirror; for God cannot deny Godself. But since dogma does not present to us a merely logical truth for thinking but a central truth for *life*, does not present to us the nature of God and the human in bare abstractions but *in positive* shapes, faith is here the solitary organ. That is to say, it lies in the concept of the positive, as that which cannot be produced and construed by mere reasoning, that it must *be received* as it is *delivered*. Therefore, nobody ever settles easily on calling a proposition, which can be demonstrated with mathematical or logical evidence according to the necessary requirements of thinking, a *dogma*. But in an eminent sense the concept of the positive steps forward when, as is here the case, it is applied to what is posited neither according to an abstract necessity nor actuality but from

God's free will. Therefore, the concept of faith here involves the recognition of God's *authority*. Consequently, since dogma contains the concept of the objective truth as that which certainly is to be known by the human but whose knowledge presupposes faith as the necessary medium, it can be defined as a *truth of faith* whose concept bears witness precisely to the indissoluble bond between the anthropological and theological moments. The task of dogmatics, then, is to give a speculative development of that which is contained *implicitly* in dogma ("what one," as we formerly expressed it, "can know about God").

The constitutive meaning which dogma has according to the definitions given here is completely lost when autonomy is made the principle in dogmatics. This is the case in modernity's moral theology and the theology of feeling and in the theology of objective rationalism. The difference between these systems and the principle [26] which we regard as truly *dogmatic* consists principally in this, that dogma is subordinated to self-consciousness, instead of self-consciousness being subordinated to dogma. Thus in the subjective system of autonomy dogma receives its grounding in *piety*, while it is really piety that should be grounded by dogma. The theologians of piety indeed seem to give us a science of the human, but by no means a science of God; they give us what could more appropriately be called an anthropology than a theology. The objective system of autonomy certainly seeks a deeper conception of the truth and teaches that piety is to find its ground in dogma, but since it will allow thought itself to *produce* dogma, it by no means recognizes the meaning of this dogma as such. The latter point is evidenced additionally by the fact that dogma is dissolved in sheerly rational elements and loses completely its *positive* character.

In order for the difference resulting between the two principles to become more conspicuous, it will be necessary to reflect on dogma's own concrete content. The purpose of this investigation is, namely, to unveil as far as possible that radical difference in order with the help of the well-known *opposita juxta se posita* [opposites placed close to each other] to present in a clearer light the problem speculative dogmatics has to solve, and in order to properly grasp the *punctum saliens* [salient point] on which it after all succeeds in a criticism of modernity's dogmatic gnosis. That is to say, according to our conviction the time has come when in theology one must sublate and abandon the principle which quite rightly is characterized as a *solipsism*.[9] [27] The Hegelian philosophy, which though itself

---

[9] Cf. *Die dogmatische Theologie jetziger Zeit, oder die Selbstsucht in der Wissenschaft des Glaubens und seiner Artikel* [*Dogmatic Theology of the Present, or Self-Centeredness in the Science of Faith and its Articles*]. Edited by Dr. Carl Daub. Heidelberg 1833. An excellent writing to which the theologians have not paid enough attention.

is encumbered with the same autonomic error (Cf. § 5), has given a great impulse to going beyond this standpoint. Consequently, as we confine ourselves to the objective content of Christian dogma, we shall attempt to give a detailed development of the point of controversy between that theology which attests to *itself* and that which attests to *God*. The mode of procedure will be this, that we first consider in general the main feature of the dissenting view and next, by a comparison of the most important works belonging to this view, give a more detailed presentation. However, in this special investigation we will give a more elaborate criticism of only the subjective rationalism of moral theology and the theology of feeling and point out its necessary transition into objective rationalism. Such an investigation, which shows this principle's genesis and inner development, seems to us to be sufficient for grounding a true judgment on the principle itself and its relation to dogmatic theology. We scarcely need to draw attention to the fact that when in the following, by investigation and refutation of the very *principle* for this theology, we happen to step up against its famous representatives, then we by no means forget those men's great merits or ignore that in several respects they have enriched theological science. What *relative* worth is due to each of these systems the reader must seek in an *historical* presentation of modernity's dogmatic theology but not in a theological treatise which only out of a dogmatic interest weighs the principle whose essential error lies in this, that it confounds the human's *relative* autonomy and God's absolute autonomy. [28]

§ 8.

Christian dogma has its substantial content in the doctrine of *God*, revealed as Father, Son, and Holy Spirit. This revelation and the appropriation of it by knowledge is realized and perfected in the Creation of the world, the Incarnation of the Word, and the establishment of God's kingdom by the Holy Spirit. Since dogmatics as science seeks to allow knowledge to take possession of this infinite content, the different principles of knowledge will give dogma a peculiar *interpretation* and confer on it a different worth and meaning. Everyone who places the divine process of revelation in all its moments in plain site will see that the Creation and the Incarnation with their reciprocal relation form *the central point in* God's act of revelation, as the ideal beginning—God as God is in Godself in God's eternal essence [*Væsen*], God's absolute ideality—is hereby posited in connection with the ideal end—God's kingdom, where God will be all in all. In these dogmas, which in this way intimate the way and the transition from the still-not-revealed God to God in God's absolute manifestation in God's kingdom, thought consequently has a standpoint from which it can direct attention both forward and backward, with free survey over all the individual parts of the system. In addition, these dogmas contain the original unity and synthesis of the speculative and the historical elements, since they reveal *the most original facts* of religion which precisely give Christianity its entire positive character. We sought a standpoint from which every dogmatic system could be judged (δὸς μοὶ ποῦ στῶ [give me a place to stand), and we have here found the proper *punctum saliens* [salient point]. The same thing will even be able to be shown from another side. That is to say, since the relation between God and the human is theology's [29] subject-matter, and Creation and Incarnation in their reciprocal relation present both the contradiction and the unity between God and the human, they are *instar omnium* [worth all of them] and contain as it were *in nuce* [in brief] the whole theology. In these dogmas lie the most difficult riddle theology has to solve; for if one has first speculatively conceived the mystery of Creation and Incarnation, then everything else in theology will fall into place by itself. According to Plato's view, *wonder* is in fact the beginning of all speculation. But what of the wonderful might lie in this, that there exists a God, a highest and all-perfect Being [*Væsen*]? Indeed, on the contrary, it would be irrational and absurd that the absolute Being not exist. No, what evokes the greatest wonder and causes thinking the greatest difficulty is the question of how anything can exist which is *not* God (*praeter Deum* [beyond God]), since the concept of God's absolute nature seems to demand that only God and *no other thing* [*intet Andet*] exists. The dogma of Creation contains then this doctrine of Not-God (*Non-Deus*), and the being of the world and the human as an existence which is an other than God and different from God; on the other hand, the dogma of the Incarnation contains the doctrine of a God who has become *human*, of the indissoluble bond between the divine nature and the human (not-divine) nature. What in the Creation doctrine is posited as an *other* than God is here seen *within* God in an inner unity with God. Consequently, herein germinates the entire theology, whose task is precisely to maintain these relations of contradiction and unity between God and the human. But then the concrete and specific determination is applied. *How* is this identity and *how* is this contradiction more precisely constituted? For on the very intelligibility of this *how* turns all dogmatic dissent. Consequently, when we seek [30] to bring the principles forth into the light, we believe to hit the heart of the matter by making the dogmas of *the Creation* and *the Incarnation* the object of closer scrutiny.

§ 9.

If we consider the dogma of *Creation* and its scientific development, the conception appears variously as dogmatic *nominalism*—if we are allowed to use this expression—in contrast to *realism*. Dogma, in other words, in the system of autonomy has only *nominal* worth, but no *real* worth. Subjective-autonomic dogmatics (moral theology and the theology of feeling) gives up all speculative investigations and in everything confines itself only to faith and the immediate conviction, since it sustains its ignorance of the divine things revealed to view. *Faith* in God as Creator it grants only a secondary validity, which must *in another way* be seen as *justifying*. But if God is actually the Creator and source of the world and the human, God must also assume the first place in the human's consciousness, so that God is understood as the one who is *really* present within the human, and thought of God becomes the constitutive and all-moving *prius* [prior]. In the opposite case an other who is not God (even if something divine θεῖόν τι) must necessarily assume God's place within human consciousness, since an all-grounding *primum movens* [prime mover] will continuously be manifested in consciousness. In this way, then, in subjective theology the idea of God as the world's Creator is granted only as an hypothesis which is postulated in order to satisfy a practical benefit or also in order to explain one or another feeling of the Infinite; but it can by no means be said to be *primum* [31] *movens* [prime mover] and fundament for the religious self-consciousness. For the idea of God is not derived ✓ exclusively from human self-consciousness—which without taking regard for any authority is itself the highest certainty—, but even so desires the sanction of the latter. Consequently, if the ideal of God first receives validity with practical reason or with the absolute feeling, not conversely, it loses its character of the constitutive, and if one ascribes to it such a meaning, it takes place only nominally; for what constitutes and *determines* everything is after all quite rightly regarded as the *actual* God, the omnipresent deity in consciousness, even if it does not receive the name of God. In this way in moral theology (for which Kant has laid the ground) the law of morality becomes the deity which constitutes consciousness, and in the theology of feeling (here represented by Schleiermacher and de Wette) *the I* in its incomprehensible and infinite feeling state is the supreme judge which has power to determine and *sanction* everything.

The theology of speculative rationalism (which stems from Hegel) is related speculatively to the Creation dogma; but since it does not arrive at knowledge of the existence of a personal God, this dogma receives only a *symbolic* meaning as the designation for the continuous ✓ transition of the Infinite into the finite, of ideality into reality. But the concept of personality is inseparable from the concept of creation; therefore God also becomes in this system a Creator only by name (*nomine*), not in actuality (*non re*), and dogmatic nominalism thus also has a home here. [32]

§ 10.

The same difference which is manifested in the determination of God as that which moves *within* the human also appears when the talk is about the God who steps forth *before* the human, or in the dogma of *the Incarnation*. The idea which lies at the basis of this dogma is the representation of God's *appearance*—a representation which is found in all religions of antiquity. That is to say, the mythical god-figures have no other meaning than that of presenting the gods—who in the human spirit have an internal, ideal existence [*Tilværelse*]—also in a *visible* way, that is, in an external, real presence [*Nærværelse*]. This need for an incarnation or for a visible God, which in mythology merely appears in *shadow-like fashion*, in Christianity as *historically actual*, is so deep-rooted and engrained in the nature of the human race that one can say about God's incarnation in Christ that if it had not actually occurred, humanity itself necessarily would have invented it, which is also confirmed by the entirety of pagan mythology.[10] And in a certain way all dogmatic systems, even those which most push Christ's majesty into the background, are yet said to see in him a visible revelation of *God*. For although they teach that God as the absolute Essence [*Væsen*] can never enter into unity with the imperfect and finite human nature, and consider it a blasphemy to call Christ God, they still behold in Christ a revelation of that which in human consciousness takes God's *place* and in actuality plays God's role; everything divine, which the human spirit must be presumed in truth to be able to possess and grasp, they transfer to him. [33] Thus one can always note a consistent parallelism between God's inner and outer revelation, so that it holds true of every theology (indeed of every human): Tell me which God lives within you, and I shall tell you which God (Christ) you have for yourself; tell me which God you have for yourself, and I shall tell you which God lives within you.

In the dogmatic science, whose history presents precisely the different stages God-consciousness runs through, this parallel can thus be traced such that wherever in the human spirit something divine (θεῖόν τι) is merely acknowledged, there Christ becomes simply the mere appearance of the abstract Idea; but wherever the very self of *God* really lives in human consciousness, there Christ becomes the adequate revelation of God. That is to say, if God's shape in the inner world of the human (*facies Dei interna*) is changed, then Christ or God's shape in the outer world (*facies Dei externa*) is also changed. Therefore moral theology, the theology of feeling, and the theology of objective rationalism each has its peculiar

---

[10] *"S'il n'existeit pas il faudrait l'inventer."* [What does not exist must be invented."]

Christ. They will all have an outer and objective appearance of that God they conceive in their soul's innermost sanctuary; they will all have the Idea substantiated by the actuality of experience. It is the well-known truth *that nothing exists in experience, except that which also exists in the concept* (*nihil est in sensibus, nisi quod fuerit in intellectu* [nothing exists in the senses, except that which has existed in the mind]), which also applies here with respect to Christ's visible appearance. Human consciousness can find nothing in experience, except that for which it already finds *the principle* within itself.

Thus one will be able to see that dogmatic formulas which give Christ predicates such as: God's Son, the God-human, [34] etc., and hereby give the impression of agreeing completely with the church's teaching, still in themselves could readily be to a great extent conflicting with it. In such propositions concerning the *revealed* God the first thing one must ask about is, which God one has *in intellectu* [in the mind] to be posited as the principle of self-consciousness: the Idea of the personal God or the Eternal in its abstract Idea which only first *becomes* personal in the human spirit. For it depends on this whether one shall see in Christ a revelation of the personal God who is the creative ground of human self-consciousness, a revelation of that *Alter-Ego* which human thinking must acknowledge as superior, or whether he shall be only a revelation of the Idea which in him certainly has its absolute representative, but in such a way that he is himself still subordinate to the Idea. Consequently, one must ask whether something is true *because* Christ says it—which no thinker can assert without being convinced that Christ is the *absolute truth-sayer*, who by his assertions impresses on all truth the stamp of truth—, or whether Christ's teaching in itself is truth independent of his self-consciousness. The question is reduced consequently to this, whether Christ's word: "*I am the truth*" shall be taken in a proper or figurative sense. For if Christ is only the *individual* representative for the *universal* self-consciousness of the human race, but not its constitutor, then it is better said that Christ *refers to* the truth than that he *is* the truth; the new creation (ἡ καινὴ κτίσις) then has in him its most outstanding exemplar, but not its true author.

The difference designated here lies not, as the supernaturalists often suppose, exclusively in the acceptance or rejection of the miracles which are done by and with Christ. Surely one could [35] accept all these, and the same difference would nevertheless remain, if he or she explained them as expressions of the natural power which lies in humankind as a race but did not show consideration for God's eternal personality which is the true supernatural principle for the human's existence. The difference must therefore be sought more deeply, not in *factum* [the deed], but in *faciens facti* [the doer of the deed]. It is not a difference exclusively between the historical and ideal Christ; for the historical Christ cannot be thought without the ideal, and the ideal not without the historical. The decisive point, as already indicated, must be sought exclusively in the relation between Christ's self-consciousness and the self-consciousness of the human race. Thus it seems that the autonomic dogmatic has its characteristic in this, that when the human thinks God, it takes place without a consciousness of an *other*, but only of itself.

§ 11.

Concerning the reciprocal relation between the dogma of Creation and the dogma of the Incarnation, moral theology and the theology of feeling certainly refuse all speculative investigation, but yet must necessarily embark upon giving a development of the contrast and the unity between God and the human. The contrast here (since the objective God lies outside the sphere of human self-consciousness) becomes comprehended as a contrast between the empirical *I* and the ideal *I*, between the phenomenon of the human and the Idea of the human, but the Idea itself is again only dealt with as subjective. The purpose of religion's development through the race is to sublate this contrast which lies in the phenomenon's discrepancy with the ideal, in the conflict between πνεῦμα [spirit] and σάρξ [flesh]. The dogma of the Incarnation presents in a unity the [36] moments which originally are separated. In the Christ is given this highest unity of the empirical human and the Idea. As empirical human he—insofar as it is at all possible in the finite world—has revealed absolutely the Idea of the human and therefore is viewed as the *ideal* of the human race.

Objective rationalism urges on the other hand God's *objectivity* and goes to work speculatively in the investigation of everything divine. It solves the riddle of existence (§ 8), i.e., how there can be an *other* than God, how that which is *not* God has come to exist, by placing the *negative* into the very self of God; it grasps *negativity* as a moment in God Godself, as the eternal *Other* through which God mediates God's continuous transition from possibility to actuality. The Creation thus becomes the expression for God's transition into difference, for the transition of the Infinite into the finite; it is God's alteration, from which God wins back unity and restores Godself. *Insofar as the human spirit only reveals the Idea*, it is the point where God returns to Godself, or rather it is the returned-into-itself-God. This eternal Idea of the identity of God and the human is revealed in Christ. It thus appears that in this system also the Incarnation sublates the Creation or God's original *difference*, as both are posited as moments in God's own development whose eternal life consists in this transition into difference and returning to unity.

Christian speculation must necessarily posit with pantheism the negativity *within* God's very self in order to avoid a dualism which cannot exist with monotheism. This also lies already in the old teaching that God has created the world [37] out of *nothing*, that is to say, out of *God's* nothing, consequently out of that in God which is *not* God. It must with the same necessity see in the Incarnation *the perfection* [*Fuldendelsen*] of the Creation; for if the Incarnation is to be motivated by sin alone, then it receives only a relative, not an absolute validity. But the difference between the Christian system and pantheism consists in this, that Christianity conceives the Creation and the Incarnation as one act of God's *free will*, since God is thought as the one who has absolute self-consciousness before the world came into being [*blev til*], and consequently does not first need to gain it through the world and humankind. In pantheism on the other hand God's or the divine Idea's transition into difference is pursuant to a certain blind and fatalistic necessity. In the Christian system the difference is seen to be grounded more in a relation between the human and its Creator than in a relation the human stands in to itself, and the same thing holds for the unity. But to raise the difficulty Christian speculation finds in conceiving the world's existence, and to see its necessity as having gone forth out of God's own Essence [*Væsen*], belongs to the peculiar positive domain of Christian dogmatics. It must here be sufficient to urge that according to the claim of the Christian religion, the Creation has its ground in God's freedom.

Now if we consider in general the debate that appears over the determination of the ground-relation [*Grundforholdet*] between God and the universe, then we have the contrast between pantheism and theism. That is to say, pantheism is the system according to which God only exists *as* the world, *as* human consciousness, where consequently the history of the human race coincides with the history of God and becomes God's own process of development. It might seem strange to designate these systems of subjectivity as pantheistic, when it is well-known enough that they posit [38] God *outside* the world; but just in this, that they posit God outside the world and are not able to grasp God as *the principle within* the world, lies, as one certainly must note, their pantheism. For in religion and science thinking can never dispense with a real working principle; if the truly divine is abandoned, thinking necessarily grabs in place of this one or another worldly principle which is only a *moment within* God but by no means God's very self. In moral theology and the theology of feeling the ideal *I* is constitutor of everything but needs the empirical *I* in order to gain real existence. Since in this way there is in reality no other God in the world than the ideal *I*, and this is elaborated and developed through the empirical self-consciousness whereby God first passes over from possibility to actuality, here the whole history of the human race also becomes God's own history of development, the expression for God's progress from possibility to actuality. Even though the adherents of this theology certainly do not straightforwardly admit this, it yet follows consistently from the principle, for which reason also subjective pantheism or semi-pantheism has dialectically passed over into objective pantheism.

After having given by way of introduction this more general presentation, we proceed to the more special, and make first moral theology and next the theology of feeling the object of consideration. At the conclusion we shall point out the necessary passage of subjective rationalism into objective rationalism. Since in the more precise criticism of the different conceptions of the dogmas of Creation and Incarnation we have not in addition made the systems' different modes of reflection on *sin* a subject of a specific investigation, in spite of the doctrine of sin standing in the closest connection with both dogmas, we must venture the remark that it is our purpose only to present [39] *the ground plan* of the system of autonomy in its difference from the Christian. Moreover, it is our conviction that the eternal truth and its essential types have not undergone any alteration because of sin, so that the *substantial* relation between the Creator and the creature remains the same; and notwithstanding the fact that the Incarnation would have occurred under other conditions (περιζάσεις [circumstances]), one must even urge the proposition: *etiamsi homo non peccasset, Deus tamen incarnatus esset* [even if the human had not sinned, God nevertheless would have become incarnate].[11] Consequently it will not be necessary in a criticism of the general principles of dogmatics to take up the doctrine of sin, since everything in this respect is a straightforward result of what lies in the eternal presuppositions in which the fundamental relation between God and the creation has its ground. [40]

---

[11] This view we share with several Christian theologians in the modern as well as the classical period. Thus Thomas Aquinas (*Summa Theologiæ*, Part III, Question 1, Article 3): *"Ad omnipotentiam divinam pertinet, ut opera sua perficiat et se manifestet per aliquem infinitum actum: sed nulla pura creatura potest dici infinitus effectus, quum sit finita per suam essentiam. In solo autem opere incarnationism videtur præcipue manifestari infinitus effectus divinæ potentiæ, per quam in infinitum distantia coniunguntur, in quantum factum est, quod homo esset deus; in quo etiam opere maxime videtur perfici Universum per hoc, quod ultima creatura sive home primo principio coniungitur, scilicet deo. Ergo etiamsi homo non peccasset, deus incarnatus esset."* ["It belongs to omnipotence that God should complete God's work and so manifest God's power through some infinite effect. But no mere creature can be called an infinite effect, since it is limited by its very nature. The infinite effect of God's power seems to be clearly shown only in the Incarnation, wherein things infinitely distant are joined together: it brought about that a human is God. In this work too the universe seems to be brought to completion, since the final creature, the human, is united to the first principle, God. Therefore, even if the human had not sinned, God would have become incarnate."] *Summa Theologiæ: Latin text and English Translation*, Vol. 48 (New York: Blackfriars in conjunction with McGraw-Hill, 1976), 3a, 1, 3, pp. 16–17. Cf. Mynster, *Om Begrebet Dogmatik*, 44; Molitor, *Philosophie der Geschichte, oder uber die Tradition*, 1ster Th., 98; Fr. Baader, *Ueber den Paulinischen Begriff des Versehenseyns des Menschen im Namen Jesu vor der Welt Schöpfung. (Erstes Sendschreiben an den Herrn Prof. Molitor.* Würzburg 1837.)

Moral Theology

§ 12.

In moral theology, as noted above, religious belief rests on the human's moral self-consciousness, so that the ethical moment becomes the norm according to which all dogmas of religion must be examined to determine whether they are true or false, religious or irreligious, rational or rationally conflictual. This theological system, which in a *general* sense is called rationalism, is looked upon as the fruit of the critical philosophy which appeared toward the end of the eighteenth century with Kant. Kant's moral view of the world spoke to the entire age to such an extent that it exerted nearly as much power and influence in its time as had formerly the ethical-religious anthropology of Augustine, Luther, and Melanchthon, to which incidentally it is diametrically opposed. Therefore, when one wants to point out the principles of moral theology, one need only know Kant's teaching, as it is expressed in his works, namely, in the well-known writing *Religion Within the Limits of Reason Alone* and in his critique of the proofs for the existence of God. For regarding the so-called dogmatic works of the rationalists, they only have life and content from Kantianism; they are so to speak fragile *accidents* in the *substance* of this moral theology.[12] [41]

As he made the Cartesian *cogito ergo sum* [I think, therefore I am] his philosophical motto, Kant advanced three questions which *reason alone* should answer, and wherein he thought that all problems of philosophy, everything that deservedly can lay claim on the human's reflection [*Eftertanke*], is contained. With the help of thinking he endeavored to find out, namely, what the human can know, what one ought to do, and what one dare hope. ("*Was kann ich wissen, was soll ich tun, was darf ich hoffen?*" ["What *can* I know, what *ought* I to do, what *may* I hope?"])[13]

With respect to the first question the critical philosophy declares all theoretical knowledge as empty and meaningless since *the categories*, or our apriositic forms of understanding, in-and-for-themselves are empty and only stand in relation to experience, so that they are useless with respect to everything which lies beyond experience. Therefore this philoso-

---

[12] Rosenkranz, *Theological Encyclopedia*, 320: *"Die Theologen haben in ihren Dogmatiken oft weiter nichts gethan, als den Kern Dieses Buches, (der R. innerh. d. Gr. d. bl. V.), zu vernachlässigen und nur seine negativen, vorzüglich in die unter den Text gesetzen Anmerkungen verstreueten Winke in das Breite auszutreten und zu verseichtigen."* ["In its dogmatics theology has often not dealt with anything more than the kernel of this book (*Religion Within the Limits of Reason Alone*), to the neglect and merely its negative, bringing out and superficializing the excellent suggestions scattered in the verbosity in the remarks typed under the text.]

[13] Immanuel Kant, *Critique of Pure Reason*, trans. Norman Kemp Smith (New York: St. Martin's Press, 1965), 635.

phy asserts that we lack all means for grasping God and the divine things, since our knowledge is encumbered with finite forms which are only able to grasp the finite; they are carried over onto the Infinite when knowledge transgresses its proper limits and grasps metaphysical phantasms instead of the truth. In this way Criticism declares that the human spirit is confined to its finite nature and its finite thoughts. As it continually insists on the *subjectivity* of thinking, it posits principally the paralogism of theoretical reason in the fact that it confuses *being* with *thought*. It constantly enjoins that [42] one cannot infer being from thought (*a cogitare ad esse non valet consequentia*), and it is chiefly with reference to this reasoning [*Raisonnement*] that it declares all proofs for the existence of God as invalid; for as sure as all these proofs are based on the identity of being and thought, the real *nervus* [tendon] in every proof then must be severed. God can certainly *be thought* by humankind, but whether this God which is thought by humankind, also *is* [*er*], one can never know. In a corresponding way one can surely think a golden mountain, but that such a mountain exists in actuality by no means follows from this. The result of Criticism, then, is this, that theoretical reason is totally blind in divine matters; under these circumstances one must therefore always have *Criticism* ready at hand so as to clip the wings of high-flying spirits lest they surpass the boundaries of the human spirit and in metaphysical daydreams grasp *nubes pro Junone* [clouds in place of Juno].

Regarding the second question, since the human finds within itself practical reason, or consciousness of the moral law and the free will, the authority of this is completely independent of theoretical investigations since it is not bound to finite and naked categories of experience but exists in itself without respect to experience with absolute universality and necessity, with immediate and self-sustaining certainty. Practical reason, which is not dependent on any outer object, but has its ground in itself and returns to itself so that one can say about it: *respue quod non es, te non quaesieris extra* [cast off that which you are not, do not seek yourself externally]—thus becomes necessarily *autonomic*, since it itself determines what is good and right, and by itself implements this. Since all theory is destroyed in the human's finite nature, [43] practical reason is the only thing to which the human has to hold itself *unconditionally*; all the human's certainty concerning the Infinite, all its faith has its base of support in this. Although practical reason does not procure the human any knowledge, it still has the same certainty for the human *as if it were* knowledge.

Under the reply to the third question ("wenn ich nun thue was ich *soll*, was darf ich denn hoffen?" ["when I now do what I *ought*, what then may I hope?]) Criticism comes with the idea of the highest Good, which stands as the end of the moral law, to the banishment of God's existence as to a postulate of practical reason. Here is developed then the practical or moral proof, which surely shall not prove God's *existence* but rather the necessity of believing in God, as a necessity which follows from human reason. The proper chief thought in the proof can roughly be determined in the following way.[14]

The moral law commands *categorically*, that is, with absolute necessity and universality, that humankind should obey it; and humankind is not able, if it wants to be consistent, to call into question the necessity of this obedience, or to regard its striving after fulfilling the law as empty and meaningless. One must then accept that the highest Good, whose concept involves a harmony between the human's moral worth and its fate, actually exists. But on the other hand external nature does not seem to permit the actual attainment of such a harmony. For the order of the physical [44] world is subordinate to the law of causality and the law of blind necessity as it follows a law which is not only totally different from but even opposite that of freedom, so that the kingdom of nature and the kingdom of freedom seem to be divided into two different spheres. But now when the moral law *categorically* demands obedience and *eo ipso* [precisely thereby] excludes all doubt about the reality of the striving called forth by itself, it even *postulates* faith in a supreme ruler of the entire universe, which leads to the idea of the highest Good for real existing beings and brings about harmony between the kingdom of nature and the kingdom of freedom; in this faith humankind must consequently live and act. This faith receives the name of *practical*, because its necessity is only conditioned by practical use but does not rest on theoretical and objective grounds.

Thus the *religious* conviction is associated with the human's moral conviction, and this forms in intimate connection with practical reason the basis for the entire theology. The concept of religion is derived from the autonomy of the human. According to its own authority this autonomy determines that all the human's duties must be considered as if they *were* divine precepts.

§ 13.

The kingdom which is here established is not the kingdom of God but the kingdom of the human, since God's will is not the *principle* for the human's moral striving, namely, as practical reason is in every respect itself sufficient. ("*Die Moral, sofern sie auf dem Begriffe des Menschen als eines freien, eben darum aber auch sich selbst durch seine Vernunft an unbedingte Gesetze bindenden Wesens, gegründet ist, bedarf weder der Idee eines andern*

---

[14] A more thorough and superior presentation of this and the other proofs for God's existence Daub has given in his *Theologumena*.

Wesens über ihm, um seine Pflicht zu erkennen, noch einer andern Triebfeder als des Gesetzes selbst, um sie zu [45] beobachten.—Sie bedarf also zum Behuf ihrer selbst (sowohl objektiv was das Wollen, als subjektiv was das Können betrifft) keineswegs der Religion, sondern vermöge der reinen praktischen Vernunft ist sie sich selbst genug."[15] ["So far as morality is based upon the conception of the human as a free agent who, just because *he* is free, binds *himself* through his reason to unconditioned laws, it stands in need neither of the idea of another Being over *him*, for *him* to apprehend *his* duty, nor of an incentive other than the law itself, for *him* to do *his* duty.—Hence for its own sake morality does not need religion at all (whether objectively, as regards willing, or subjectively, as regards ability [to act]); by virtue of pure practical reason it is self-sufficient.])[16] Consequently, the striving of the human does not aim at living in agreement with *God*, doing the good for *God's* sake and avoiding evil and the bad in order not to evoke God's wrath, for all this must be observed exclusively for the law's own sake; but this striving intends that the human by following the law can *act consistently and avoid coming into contradiction with itself.*

For one must surely add the remark that it is *thinking* to which everything in this sphere of practical reason really eventually has to be assigned, so that thought also appears here as the arbitrator in the complications of the practical life and with a decisive voice executes its judgment. For although practical reason is differentiated from the theoretical, it yet contains the theory for all human praxis and must necessarily be thinking. *But hence it cannot do without the logical principles, namely, the principles of contradiction and identity,* and it also maintains these principles to such an extent that everything in the final analysis depends on them. For practical reason realizes that it finds itself in a contradiction when it *thinks* the idea of the highest Good without in addition thinking *God* as existing, and in order to avoid this contradiction God's existence is postulated, so that everything at the end is traced back to thinking; and [46] this is in truth necessary, because—as already *Thomas Aquinas* has rightly realized and drawn attention to—one cannot find any principle which goes before thinking ("*nullum principium cogitatione anterius inveniri potest*" [no principle prior to thinking is able to be found]; although one certainly can find a principle which goes before the principle of contradiction. But if then one examines more carefully this *logic* of practical theology, one will learn that it rejects all *objective* logic, as it teaches that all logical principles, consequently also the principles of identity and of contradiction,

---

[15] Cf. M. H. Bornemann's remark against the onesided self-validity of human reason, especially with respect to moral science. *Alm. Retslaere,* 1st Part, 1st Section, 82.

[16] Immanuel Kant, *Religion Within the Limits of Reason Alone,* trans. Theodore M. Greene and Hoyt H. Hudson (New York: Harper & Row, 1960), 3.

are only the subjective forms of the thinking *I*. Since everything thus is dissolved in *bare* thinking, so that the entire system presents nothing other than the shadowy facsimiles and images of the *I*, then *dogma*, whose concept contains the absolute identity of thought and being, is totally sublated. The result of this theology, then, is that practical reason is the human's self-consciousness of *its own* law and *its own* freedom, that the duties are its *own* practical precepts, and that God is thinking's own postulate. Indeed the very logical principles of identity and of contradiction become by no means the truth's own law but a shadowy facsimile of the *I, which strives to sustain identity with itself!*

The dogma of God, who is the *source of the world* and not only constitutes the human's *existence* but also sanctions its *thinking*, giving it truth and validity, is dissolved in the theology of this subjective idealism in subjective determinations of thought but still retains a *mere appearance* of reality, namely, insofar as it serves to encompass the practical rules with the glory of religion. But since this theology on the one hand is most self-confident that God is only a postulate of human thinking, and on the other hand teaches an [47] absolute dependence on God, the mode of procedure of this self-consciousness deserves quite rightly the name of *dissemblance*.[17] For it behaves as if there were two, where in actuality there is only one. Insofar as this theology grasps itself in its moral shape, the moral precepts proceed from the autonomy of the human; insofar as it acknowledges its dependence on God, they are considered as divine oracles. ("*Wenn die Moral an der Heiligkeit ihres Gesetzes einen Gegenstand der größten Achtung erkennt, so stellt sie auf der Stufe der Religion an der höchsten, jene Gesetze vollziehenden Ursache einen Gegenstand der Anbetung vor, und erscheint in ihrer Majestät.*" ["If morality finds in the holiness of its law an object of the greatest respect, then at the level of religion it presents the ultimate cause, which consummates those laws, as an object of *adoration* and thus appears in its majesty."])[18] "*Nichts ehrt Gott mehr, als das was das Schätzbarste in der Welt ist, die Achtung für sein Gebot, die Beobactung der heiligen Pflicht, die uns sein Gesetz auferlegt, wenn seine herrliche Anstalt dazu kömmt eine solche schöne Ordnung mit angemessener Glückseligkeit zu krönen. Wenn ihn das letztere (auf menschliche Art zu reden, sic!) liebenswürdig macht, so ist er durch das erstere ein Gegenstand der Anbetung.*" ["Nothing glorifies God more than what is the most estimable thing in the world, namely, respect for God's command, the observance of sacred duty which God's law imposes on us, when there is added to this God's glorious plan of crowning such an excellent order with corresponding happiness. If the

---

[17] Hegel, *Phänomenologie des Geistes*, "*Die Verstellung in der moralischen Weltanschauung.*" Daub, *Die dogmatische Theologie jetziger Zeit.*
[18] *Religion within the Limits of Reason Alone*, Preface to the First Edition, 7.

latter, to speak in human terms, makes God worthy of love, by the *former* God is an object of adoration."])[19]

The words sound rather beautiful, but we have seen that this dependence on God in *actuality* is nothing other than the subject's dependence on itself, particularly on *its own* subjective logic together with the principle of contradiction of this logic. The subject really only carries out a doubling of itself, considers itself under a double shape, first as a moral subject and next as an object differentiated from this subject, but does not remember [48] that this object or God is only the subject's own reflex and reflection. If it listens *straightforwardly* to the assertions of ethics, then it hears in these its own voice; if on the other hand it comprehends them indirectly, that is, through that postulate's twofold medium, it *seems* to hear another's voice. In that respect the moral subject can appropriately be compared with a ventriloquist, who also can be said to hear two voices, one straightforwardly natural and one covert, so that there seems to be two persons present, while in actuality there is only one in a double expression.

§ 14.

This theology's solipsistic principle will become more conspicuous when one pays attention to how it handles the doctrine of the attributes to which God is entitled as the Creator of the world. Just as human self-consciousness received the idea of God not from God but from itself, so too the divine attributes which are here revealed are not deduced from God but from the self. Just as God's existence is required only in order to complete humankind's subjective idea of the highest Good, so too the doctrine of God's attributes becomes only a more special division of this general postulate, so that God only receives such attributes as necessarily must *be postulated* for this *practical* purpose. It is thus a necessary requirement that God must be, e.g., *omniscient*, because otherwise God would not be able to judge rightly about the human's moral worth;[20] God's *omnipotence* is necessary in order that [49] the human's conduct should not lack righteous followers, virtue should not lack its reward, vice should not lack its punishment. God must be eternal and omnipresent, for if the moral world's supreme ruler is not elevated over every limitation of time

---

[19] Immanuel Kant, *Critique of Practical Reason*, trans. Lewis White Beck (Indianapolis: Bobbs-Merrill, 1956), 136.

[20] "*Es muß alliwissend sein um mein Verhalten bis zum Innersten meiner Gesinnung in allen möglichen Fällen und in alle Zukunft zu erkennen.*" ["This Being must be omniscient, in order to be able to know my conduct even to the most intimate parts of my intention in all possible cases and in the entire future." *Critique of Practical Reason*, 145.]

and space, God loses God's omnipotence; but this is necessary *for us* in order that the harmony our reason demands between the kingdom of freedom and the kingdom of nature can be brought about.

This practical reason knows very well about all these attributes, that they are not as well suited for God as for *itself*, since it perpetually insists that God's essence [*Væsen*] is inconceivable. That is to say, the human has allowed these attributes to go forth not from God's essence but from *its own* essence, or more precisely from that which the human *ought* to be but *is* not, from what the human *wants* to be but never *can* become. The human feigningly shapes its God as *the ideal* of the perfect moral will, which in one and all things coincides with the moral law, and to whom the empirical human never stands in an adequate relation. Before this God the human prostrates itself, adores, and worships God. But if one considers this worship of God [*Gudsdyrkelse*] more closely, one will find that it annuls itself and is not very far from being idolatry [*Afgudsdyr-kelse*]. For on the one hand the human adores this God and worships God with awe in the knowledge of its absolute dependence on God, praises with fervent devotion God's holiness and omniscience, exalts in every way God's majesty, and raises everywhere temples for its cult of reason, for the believers in pure reason; but on the other hand the human destroys this very cult by teaching that all the attributes, by which God is thought and to which the pious subject refers its feeling of absolute dependence, are credited to God not *in actuality* but are only granted to God [50] by humankind. Consequently it is the human who constructs a self-made God and then deconstructs God; it is the human who dresses and decorates God with the highest and most glorious attributes and then strips and divests God of them. Since no objective idea is found here and all thinking is only purely *human*, this God becomes a necessary composite of sheer *anthropomorphisms*, and while this theology shuns and removes the anthropomorphisms of *representation* it believes to find in positive religion, it yet does nothing other than to insert the anthropomorphisms of *thinking* in their place. Thus, if this God cannot quite be said to be "made by human hands" (χειροποίητος), then it is a God "according to the fabrication of humankind" (ἐνθυμησει ἀνθρώπων, Acts 17) and must in this respect be compared with the mythical gods of paganism who also owe their existence to the *subjectivity*, imagination, and representation of humankind. But in the dreams of the imagination the pagans were ignorant of the fact that their gods were nothing other than the human spirit's own *ideals*; this theology on the contrary knew and knows this as good and in this is not far from irony; and it would in truth act ironically if it clearly realized its contradiction and did not at once forget what it previously had deliberately posited. In the one moment the human's absolute dependence on God is confirmed, in the next moment it is again sublated as one maintains God's absolute dependence on the human. For is it not the greatest dependence one can conceive to receive all its attributes from somewhere else, but not even be able to develop and reveal them out of God's own essence [*Væsen*]? What is more contrary to the nature of truth than that the true should not be that which characterizes itself and its [51] contrast (*index sui et falsi* [an indicator of itself and that which is false]), but that the characterization of both should be given by the *human*? What is more disgraceful for God than to draw the radiance of God's majesty's from humankind, not from Godself, so that God's glory is only a reflection of the light of human reason, that God's decrees are only an echo of the human voice? What finally is more inconsequential than such a divine cult where God and God's pious worshiper are one and the same person?

The duplexity which is here the actual situation is not a difference between God and the human but between the empirical and the ideal human; and the absolute dependence which is talked about here is only the empirical and finite human's dependence on the infinite idea of the human. The human, which is bound to the visible world and its phenomena, is raised to the higher and intelligible world, to the kingdom of freedom, which however does not exist outside the human spirit. Thus the human moves in two worlds, and all religion originates from a mutual relation of these two worlds, with the relation consisting merely of two moments within the human self. The reason why the human in this theology cannot transcend the circle of its own self-consciousness and gain consciousness of an other is this, that from the beginning one has overlooked that *Other* which contains its own true *self*-certification, and by this its self-revelation liberates the human from all solipsism; that Criticism's theory of knowledge from the first overlooks the religious principle and seeks an abstract knowledge but no co-knowledge. When the human spirit is severed from positive reality, from the fullness of life, it cannot transcend its own reflection, but directs the gaze only toward itself and continues in this onesided self-reflection. Consequently, since it has disregarded the conscience, it cannot arrive [52] at knowledge [*Viden*] but only at a thought; for the human self-consciousness is in itself completely formal and empty when it is not filled with God, who is the source of all actuality. Criticism presupposes, on the contrary, that that which is only an *instrument* for knowledge of truth, is the very *principle* of truth. When subjective idealism is consistently developed and completed—such as has happened in Fichte, who was the first who dared to endure the view of this purely unveiled Medusa-head—, it necessarily is annulled by an inner contradiction; since it lacks all inner truth and is only able to present the shadow-images of the thinking *I*, it can do nothing other than strike a *horror vacui* [terror of emptiness] into the thinking subject and bring it to an absolute skepticism, so that it forgets *itself* and seeks the objective truth, realizing that it is only an *image* [*Billede*] of the truth and consequently appoints the truth as lord over itself, but no longer itself as lord over the truth. If modern theologians with Fichte implemented Criticism, they would also thereby get rid of it. Instead of this the vast majority of the modern era's theologians seek more an anthropology than a theology; without really knowing it they still continue to stand by Criticism, as they decorate and obscure with different ornamentations and *panni purpurei* [gleaming garments], but Criticism yet always remains the substance in their dogmatics. Those theologians, who from the standpoint of a more vulgar supernaturalism seek a bibliology instead of a theology, cannot be discussed here.

§ 15.

If we now direct closer attention to the moments through which the object of religion or God is mediated by the religious subject, we find for one thing that [53] the concept of *the conscience* in the religious sense is not at all found in critical theology, namely, since especially according to this viewpoint the conscience is only the immediate judgment of practical reason over the actions' moral worth ("*die sich selbst richtende moralische Urteilskraft*" ["the moral faculty of judgment, passing judgment upon itself"]),[21] which involves the certainty of reason concerning its own reality. As a result the human assumes God's place in the most holy sanctuary of the soul and glorifies itself but not God. It does not respect the holy light of religion by which the human is revealed as God's creature, as the voice of the conscience more than any other makes the case that it is not exclusively the human who *thinks* God but that the human also *is thought* by God, that it is not exclusively the human who judges itself but that the human is also judged by God; this conviction does not depend on the human but is an effect of the very self of God, who thinks Godself and the human. When the creature does not have, or more correctly believes not to have this conviction, and does not know, or behaves as if it did not know that it is God's creature, then this ignorance proves nothing less than that the human has abandoned its original place in the universe and is no longer in its state of integrity. This is here totally revealed, since the creature by its inferences strives to convince itself that it is *one* in its

---

[21] *Religion Within the Limits of Reason Alone*, 273.

thought and action; and even when it comprehends the idea of holiness, it classifies this not with God but with itself, as it says: "I am," while it ought to say: "I am not" (John 1:20).

Subjective idealism's fundamental error in general can be assigned to this, that as it seeks a knowledge *about* religion it completely overlooks God's knowledge *in* religion, this knowledge, namely, which in a more restricted sense we [54] call *conscience*, insofar as it draws attention to the creature's submission to the Creator, and which in a more general sense receives the name of *co-knowledge*, insofar as it signifies the creature's participation in knowledge of the divine essence [*det guddommelige Væsens Erkendelse*]. For not only with the same right as Kant asserted that the moral law rules in the human's soul with absolute universality and necessity, without regard for the human's well-being and without asking about the human's true state, but with an even greater and absolute right we assert that in the human's spirit there resides a primitive knowledge of *God*, independent of the feeling of pleasure and pain, for these soul-states, insofar as they fall under the concept of religion, are only forms of revelation of this idea and depend completely on the relation in which the human and its entire life stand to this idea revealed by the very self of God. This primitive knowledge of God is the basis for all religious cultus and for all theology. Certainly it can be denied and can be eclipsed, but in actuality it is really always granted, so that the Middle Ages' *doctor angelicus* [the angelic doctor] quite rightly could say: *Deus non creditur sed scitur* [God is not believed but known]; (when he here excludes belief, he is thinking of voluntary belief [*frivillige Tro*], namely, in order to indicate the absolute independence of this knowledge or *necessary* belief from the human's feeling and will; therefore he shows that it is not from a psychological nor a anthropological origin but from a theological origin, that it proceeds from God alone, whose revelation the human under every condition, either with or against its will, must recognize). In fitting harmony with this the Holy Scriptures also teach "that the demons believe and tremble," where then the "believing" contains nothing other than the concept of God, combined with *the recognition* [*Anerkjendelsen*] of the *reality* of this concept. If this primitive concept of God [55] did not live in the creature, the apostle Paul could not, as when he teaches that the pagan are without excuse (ἀναπολόγητοι), demand faith (the voluntary) of humankind as a *duty*. Consequently, since from God's standpoint the conscience is the eternal eye, then from the creature's standpoint it is the necessary beholding of this eternal eye and constitutes this necessary knowledge in the creature, that it always is seen, as the psalmist says: "Where shall I flee before your *countenance* O Lord! If I rush up to the heaven, you are there, and if I step down in the abyss, you are there," and in another place: "I wonder if the one who planted the ear should not itself hear, I wonder if the one who formed the eye should not itself see?"

§ 16.

Just as critical theology completely lacks the concept of the conscience, so does the same thing apply to the concept of *faith*. *Nemo credit nisi volens* [No one believes without willing], says Augustine, and by this he means that it depends on the human's free will whether or not it will give this primitive knowledge of God its free witness. Since this knowledge of God is by God, it is a revelation of God's freedom, so that faith (in a higher sense) is the free submission of the human will to the divine will—a submission which entails a personal relation. But since practical reason does not know any other revelation than *its own*, it can only put confidence in itself, and instead of believing [*at troe*] in God it believes in itself alone. This onesided, self-entrusting human reason (*solitaria ratio hominis sibi derelicti* [the solitary reason of a human being abandoned to itself]) appears particularly in this theology's conception of the mystery of *prayer*, which indeed reveals life's highest communion with God, [56] the most intense union between the personal God and the creature, God's *real* presence in the religious subject. But since the human here, reduced to itself alone, does not dare to trust in God, the real presence is only the subject's own, which expresses its pious desires *for itself*. Here the human calls the idea of God to help merely in order by it to inflame its moral feeling, to be confirmed in good intentions, etc.; but regarding God's real presence in prayer and praying to God as to a God who, actually being present [*tilstedeværende*], hears and sees, is for this theology a superstitious absurdity which must be denounced as reprehensible devotion. ("*Im ersteren Sinn [als einem Wunsche zur Belebung seiner Gesinnungen vermittelst der Idee von Gott] kann ein Gebet mit voller Aufrichtigkeit statt finden, wenn gleich der Mensch sich nicht anmaßt das Dasein Gottes als völlig gewiß betheuern zu können [sic!]; in der zweiten Form als Anrede nimmit er diesen Gegenstand als persönlich gegenwärtig an, oder stellt sich wenigstens [selbst innerlich] so, als ob er von seiner Gegenwart überführt sei, in der Meinung, daß wenn es auch nicht so wäre, es wenigstens nicht schaden, vielmehr ihm Gunst verschaffen könne; mithin kann in dem letzteren [buchstäblichen] Gebet die Aufrichtigkeit nicht so volkommen angetroffen werden, wie im ersteren [dem bloßen Geiste desselben].*" ["In the first sense (as a wish for the quickening of his disposition by means of the idea of God), a prayer can be offered with perfect sincerity even though the person praying does not presume to be able to affirm that the existence of God is wholly certain; in its second form, as an *address*, he supposes this Supreme Being to be present in person, or at least he adopts an attitude (even inwardly) as though he were convinced of God's presence, with the idea that, even if this be not so, his acting thus can at least do him no harm and is more likely to get his favor. Hence such complete sincerity cannot be found in the latter (verbal) prayer as it can in the former (the pure spirit of prayer)])."[22]

According to everything cited here it seems obvious to us that the dogma of Creation and the mutual relation between God and the creature is totally undermined, so that God and the creature remain as mere names, and that in this way this system can deservedly be designated as theological nominalism. The true concept of religion, which has its roots in the human's [57] fundamental relation, is overturned. For we have shown that the object of religion—God—is here *deduced from the thinking subject itself*; and that the subjective moments in religion, by which the object of religion is mediated with the subject, that is to say, the conscience, faith, and prayer, *do not have any object and only stand in an empty and contentless relation to the thinking subject.* Consequently, do we not have full justification in characterizing such an idealism as solipsism?

§ 17.

We proceed from this to presenting *the dogma of the Incarnation*, and ask first about the eternal idea of God's Son, in which the *possibility* of the Incarnation is grounded. Instead of a speculative and objective knowledge of this idea, such as has found its expression, for example, in the Nicene-Constantinople Creed, we find here a *moral* interpretation of it, and instead of the absolute and real consubstantiality, we get only a moral and subjective consubstantiality. One learns here that the idea of God's Son is no different from the idea of the human race. ("*Das was allein eine Welt zum Gegenstand des göttlichen Ratschlusses und zum Zweck der Schöpfung machen kann ist die Menschheit [das vernünftige Weltwesen überhaupt] in ihrer moralischen ganzen Vollkommenheit.—Dieser allein Gott wohlgefällige Mensch ist in ihm von Ewigkeit her; die Idee desselben geht von seinem Wesen aus; er ist kein erschaffen Ding, sondern sein ewiger Sohn [ifr. Symbolum Nicænum: "deus ex deo, genitus non factus"]; das Wort [das Werde!] durch welches alle Dinge sind und ohne das das nichts existirt, was gemacht ist, denn um seiner, das ist, um des vernünftigen Wesens in der Welt willen, so wie es [58] seiner moralischen Bestimmung nach gedacht werden kann, ist alles gemacht.*" ["Humankind (rational earthly existence in general) *in its complete moral perfection* is that which alone can render a world the object of a divine decree and the end of creation.—The human so conceived, alone pleasing to God, 'is in God

---

[22] *Religion within the Limits of Reason Alone,* 183.

through eternity'; the idea of him proceeds from God's very being; hence he is no created thing but his only-begotten Son (cf. the Nicene Creed: "God of God, begotten not made"); "the *Word* (the *Fiat!*) through which all other things are, and without which nothing is in existence that is made' (since for him, that is, for rational existence in the world, so far as he may be regarded in the light of his moral destiny, all things were made.")[23]

The formerly mentioned contradiction and difference is also resumed here. Practical reason appeared from the beginning with absolute autonomy, next it postulated a God different from itself, i.e., the ruler of the moral order of the world (God the Father); then it returns again to itself, declares itself as God's Son and derives its eternal origin from him. But the proper relation is completely turned around, since everyone easily sees that the Son here is not begotten by the Father, but the Father is begotten by the Son, or in other words, practical reason posits first the moral ideal, whose principle it itself is, *outside* itself and gives it the name of the Father who is the Creator and Sustainer of the world; but thereon it pretends as if that ideal which resides in the human race has descended from heaven to human nature, although in actuality nothing has taken place other than that practical reason has gone out of itself and therein returned to itself in order through this roundabout way to arrive at conceiving itself in the shape of *God*. Instead of God's *objective descent*, by which God for ever and ever has been united with the human race, we have here the human's *subjective ascent* to heaven; here it is not God who has become human, but the human who has become God.

§ 18.

Our next question applies to the incarnation of this Idea (which here is determined exclusively as the moral), and this coincides with the question of whether the idea can enter into unity with a human individual so that this [59] individual's nature is absolutely determined by it, so that in one and all things it becomes a revelation of the idea and does not have any particular existence outside of this. Here we hear that such a revelation of the idea in the world of experience certainly is *possible*, but that the idea's reality is not dependent on the outer appearance but is true in itself. ("*Diese Idee hat ihre Realität in practischer Beziehung vollständig in sich selbst; denn sie liegt in unserer moralisch gesetzgebenden Vernunft. Wir sollen ihr gemäß sein und müssen es daher auch können.*" ["From the practical point

---

[23] Compare the further development of this doctrine in *Religion within the Limits of Reason Alone*, 54.

of view this idea is completely real in its own right, for it resides in our morally-legislative reason. We *ought* to conform to it; consequently we must *be able* to do so."])[24] Kant concluded from the necessary nexus between *ought* and *could* to the possibility that this Idea could appear inside the circle of experience.

When it here is said that the revelation of God's Son is not true in itself but receives its validity from the Idea, then this is certainly formally correct, insofar as the outer does not exist [*ikke er*] without the inner. But the question remains what kind of an idea this is. If it is the Idea of the *absolute personality* and freedom, then the revelation of this Idea exceeds the idea of the human *race*. That is to say, it follows from the concept of *the race* that the race does not have any existence outside the species and the individuals, but that species and individual are absorbed in the race, and that thus nothing falls outside it. The hypostasis of the one disappears in the hypostasis of the other. But the Idea of personality transcends all these abstract categories. It embraces them, is in them—for otherwise it would not be in all respects an *absolute* idea; but it exists *in itself*, as it overcomes and subordinates all those determinations to itself. God, who is the *principle* of human nature, is not absorbed by it; for in the latter case God would only be the human race, considered in its ideality, that is to say, in its universality and necessity. But every category, every law, and every necessity [60] stands under absolute freedom and winds up in it.

Consequently, if the true idea of God is the Idea of the absolute personality, then there appears also that historical individual with whom the Idea has entered into a perfect union, with absolute authority, so that, liberated from all *particular* subjectivity, it shall only reveal the Idea. That is to say, since the Idea he reveals is the ideal of *personality*, and since further the unity into which he has entered with the Idea is a *personal* unity, then his revelation of the absolute idea is not a revelation differing from his own person, but as he reveals the Idea he reveals *himself*, so that his person is a revelation of the divine mystery itself. But in this way the entire human race, in order to be personalized, must be subordinated to him, for as a God-human he is not one individual among the many but is the absolute individual, the central monad. Since the absolute freedom which stands not only over all universal and abstract determinations, but also over all finite monads, constitutes his *essence* [*Væsen*], he not only reveals the principle of the human race but is this very principle.

In Kant on the other hand the concept of God's Son is a concept of the race [*Slægtbegreb*], a general concept, which is tied completely to the human spirit and does not have any objective reality outside this, but more precisely is the very human spirit itself construed in the shape of

---

[24] *Religion within the Limits of Reason Alone*, 55.

universality. The category in which thinking here moves is the category of the race. (Race, Species, Individual). Christ is subsumed under the human race as one individual among the many, even if one grants that he is the most outstanding exemplar in the race. Humankind sees in him an image of *its own* eternal essence, but not of God's essence. He remains *primus inter pares* [first among equals]. All rationalists and [61] all who see in Christ the most outstanding flower of the human race—however, as in merely a figurative and symbolic sense but not on the contrary in actuality—are able to know him as a God-human, acquiesce under their aspiration after the truth in this category (the concept of the race), and embrace everything under this schema.[25] But precisely by this is denied the reality of absolute freedom and its revelation *within* the human race. For then all individuals stand *under* universal necessity, whether this is the moral or the logical law, and Christ becomes not qualitatively but only quantitatively different from the remaining humans. When Christ is classified under the human race, his history becomes placed under the principle of causality, while conversely the human race should be subordinated to him, "in whom and to whom everything is created." Christ's history should not have the universe's causal nexus or a certain *relative* freedom as its principle, but absolute freedom, as it is not confined to a relative necessity but places under *itself the very principle of causality.*

§ 19.

"Tell me which God lives in you, and I shall tell you which Christ you have for yourself." The God who here in actuality lives in the human is the moral ideal; the Christ the human here has for itself is an appearance of this idea. But if one looks more closely at the nature of this revelation, one finds that an incarnation of the Idea [62] certainly is possible, but that one by no means can state with certainty that it has actually taken place. For one cannot with perfect certainty conclude from experience, from external life, to the inner life of the human, to the motives for his or her actions. (*"Der Idee ist kein Beispiel in der äußeren Erfahrung adäquat, als welche das Innere der Gesinnung nicht aufdeckt, sondern darauf, obzwar nicht mit strenger Gewißheit, nur schließen läßt."* ["No example in outer experience is adequate to the idea; for outer experience does not disclose the inner nature of the disposition but merely allows of an inference about it though not one of strict certainty."])[26] This has its truth, namely, since the

---

[25] The history of Christ moves in the same schema in the well-known work, *Das Leben Jesu,* by Strauss. The author has implicitly presupposed that this category is human thinking's *"non plus ultra* [that beyond which one can go no further]."

[26] *Religion within the Limits of Reason Alone,* 56–57.

Idea here is totally subjective, from which nothing objective is able to be derived with certainty. Yet, if human reason had not concluded from itself but from the eternal personality's nature to the possibility of Christ's Incarnation, then it would have also realized Christ's historical reality. On the other hand, then, we get instead of the objective Incarnation only a subjective revelation of God. Thus the Idea is revealed more in Christ as he is construed by *our representation* than in Christ as he actually existed in history. Since all reality is grounded in the Idea, this Idea does not apply to the historical Christ but to the ideal Christ, and it does not settle the matter of the extent to which what is narrated about him are actual occurrences. Consequently, in the Gospels one reads not an actual history but a narrative which according to the old saying *"mutato nomine de te narratur fabula"* ["with a mere change of name, the story applies to you"] shall be applicable to us. Here we have the principle and the seed of that modern Gnosticism which separates the Idea from history, the ideal Christ from the historical, and gives the gospel a mythical and symbolic interpretation.[27] Therefore it is said [63] in general that one shall not seek a temporal but an eternal history, not a special but a universal history. Also here one has tacitly presupposed the referred-to concept of the race, in which everything is grounded as in the general principle. But those who in defiance of history state that one shall remain standing by the Idea, reject *eo ipso* [precisely thereby] the idea of absolute freedom and the idea of the central-individual and the central-monad. For freedom, which not only involves an ideal but also a real existence, demands a real revelation in life and not merely an ideal appearance in the mirror of representation.

§ 20.

According to what is developed here one will see with what right we have given this theology the name of pantheism, even though on first glance it seems to be tremendously different from the same. As pantheism insists on the idea of God's substantiality and universality, it determines with respect to the relation between God and the world, God as the inner reality, the world as the outer reality, God as the essence, the world as the phenomenon, God as substance, the world as accident, God as the absolute cause, the world as the absolute effect. It is a correct determination that God is the world's *principle*, and—what is a result of this—that the world is a moment in God's own existence; but it is on the other hand an error when it is said that God is only in *the world* but not *in Godself*. It only

---

[27] Among the theologians of subjective rationalism de Wette in particular has taught this view.

knows what God is *outside* Godself, but not what God is *in* Godself. It only knows the exoteric but not the esoteric God, that is to say, it does not know the divine freedom which alone is the innermost mystery in the heavenly kingdom, so that all who do not grasp this quite rightly could be [64] said to be οἱ ἔξω [those outside].

But how then can this pantheistic view be ascribed to Criticism, which removes God far away from the world, as with the greatest modesty it admits that knowledge of God surpasses the limits of the human spirit, and thus, by positing God over and outside the world, declares itself as a mortal enemy of all pantheism? We respond that because it is in absolute contrast to pantheism, by the fact that it denies that God is the immanent principle in the world, *precisely therefore* is it pantheism. What in pantheism is objective and universal, here becomes subjective and is placed inside the sphere of self-consciousness. When God is removed from the world, human self-consciousness which is the highest form of the world's existence becomes the *very* principle for all things; as Criticism urges the subjectivity of thinking and only acknowledges God as a postulate of thinking, it precisely corroborates the proposition *that God does not have any actual existence outside of the human's self-consciousness.* This agrees completely with the doctrine of pantheism *that the human spirit is God's own existence.* The abstract separation of God and the creation involves a pantheistic confusion. The common error must be sought in the principle of autonomy, which claims for the human a dignity that is due only to God, or the thinking but not thought nature. (Cf. § 3).

Insofar as pantheism is manifested in history, it sees in this only a mediation of the universal self-consciousness with the single and individual, a mediation of the infinite self-consciousness with the finite and empirical self-consciousness which is bound to the phenomena. This would be completely in order if it were a mediation of the absolute personality [65] with the human self-consciousness. But since universal self-consciousness is here a mere possibility which only arrives at actuality in the human, then history contains only the development of the idea of the human race—a development which coincides with God's own development, and its goal is that the particular human can become a general and universal human, that the individual can absorb the totality into itself. The most excellent exemplar of the identity of the race and the individual is beheld then in Christ.—What is here manifested in an objective and universal sense, critical theology teaches subjectively and in the particular sphere of ethics. History is considered as the mediation of the self-consciousness of the human race (seen in its ideal generality) and the self-consciousness of the particular and individual human. It strives to guide the empirical human to knowledge of its eternal essence (practical reason), to live in harmony with the eternal human (the moral ideal). Christ also becomes here *primus inter pares* [first among equals]. The principles for this conception of history, particularly of the history of religions, the reader will find developed in Kant's writing on religion that we have referred to. The contrast which is introduced here between the principle of good and the principle of evil is dissolved into a contrast between the idea of the human and the empirical condition of the human, and this contrast is then mediated in the religion of practical reason.

§ 21.

The reader could perhaps demand that after having presented the principles for this theology we should enter more detailedly into the dogmatic works in which the theologians have given these principles a wider development. But since our intention has only been to present the principles and fundamental motifs of the teaching, we will not [66] enter into the individual relevant works. We merely draw attention to the fact that "where there is theology, there also are theologians, where there is nationalism, there also are nationalists"; still applicable here is the proposition: *mutato nomine de te narratur fabula* [with a mere change of name, the story applies to yourself], and: *hæc tibi dicta esse puta* [imagine that these things have been said to you]. One can in general observe that the theologians to a great extent, in forgetfulness of Kant's theoretical philosophy, substitute "sound reason," which is an empirical thinking, in the place of his critical reason, which is confined strictly to the categories of universality, and that they are inconsistent in insisting on the subjectivity of thinking. Thus Wegscheider says in the doctrine of the proofs for God's existence (Instit. ed. 3. p. 155): "*quæ Kantius ad refutanda illa argumenta, præter alias quasdam minoris momenti obiectiones, contra causalitatis legem eiusque vim et ambitum monet, tantum abest ut sanam rationem in fingenda et assumenda primaria et absolute perfecta causa erroris convincant, ut ei contraria sententia, progressus nimirum causarum sine initio et fine ceu flumen sine fonte et ostio appareat.*" [The things, apart from certain other objections of less importance, which Kant presents against the law of causality and its force and influence, in order to refute those arguments, are so far from demonstrating sound reason by devising and adopting a first-rate and fully-developed cause for the error that an opinion contrary to it appears, of course, to be a progression of causes without a beginning or end like a river without a source and mouth."] This Kant has never wanted to deny, but he asserted that one dare not conclude from this the objective use of this concept, whose necessity for *the human* he admitted.—But on the other hand Wegscheider follows Criticism, when he teaches: "*solam rationem practicam bene excultam suppeditare ideam sanctitatis* [that only practical reason which has been well developed provides an idea of sanctity]"; and in the section on God's attributes (p. 167): "*Ceterum recte observatum est, distinctionibus istis differentiam in numine ipso non realem, quippe quum mens nostra non veram numinis essentiam, sed nostras tantum de ea notiones describere valout, sed formalem s. nominalem significari; licet respectu habito ad subiectum, differntia* [67] *illa vere realis dici possit.*" [Moreover it has been rightly observed, based on those distinctions, that the differentiation in the divine nature itself is not considered to be real but formal or nominal, since indeed our mind is not able to describe the true essence of the divine nature but only our ideas about it; although, after having considered the matter subjectively, that differentiation can be said to be real indeed.] How then in the knowledge of God's essence this nominalism can exist alongside of realism in the certification of God's existence, must remain the peculiar matter of a person.—In Christology the category of *the race* plays the most important role. Christ is subordinated to the human race.

With respect to the mode of treatment of Christian dogmatics in general—which has passed from the Kantian dogmatics into the so-called rationalism and into the theology of feeling (in the following we shall show in particular that this is not only a higher form of Criticism)—it can be classified into two moments, namely, *theology's distinction from philosophy* and, closely connected with this, a *historical-critical method*. That is to say, since the speculative idea *in* religion itself has entered into a shadow, seeing that all theory has received its place *outside* of religion, and religion itself is confined to praxis alone, Christian dogmatics retains no other object than the religious-practical self-consciousness which as known under various modifications is called "the immediate religious consciousness," or—insofar as it is presented specifically as a modification of the Christian religion—"the immediate Christian consciousness." This dogmatic science develops or more properly describes the religious consciousness in such a way that dogmatics becomes an explicative and descriptive science but not a speculative science. However, if the immediate self-consciousness were to dispense with the objective Idea which implicitly contains the whole speculative system, it would become emaciated and empty. Therefore, the dogmatician asks history and the premodern dogmatic works for assistance in order not to languish from lack of content; it sets forth criticism of the church's symbolic [68] doctrine and the Holy Scriptures themselves; it develops the previous generation's meaning with great historical learning and thorough philological ἀκρίβεια [accuracy] and separates out to the end everything from the domain of religion and theology that belongs to the theoretical sphere. This critical method is never different from the *dialectical* method of speculative theology, which also criticizes premodern dogmatic science, however not merely negatively but also positively, so that the historical

development of every Christian dogma is known as a *moment in* the
speculative Idea. Consequently, speculative dogmatics sees in history the
Idea's different rays and gathers them into one focal point in order ideally
to construe and preserve the entire history. But the critical method only
takes history up into itself in order right away again to cast it from itself. In dogmatics it presents the history of speculative dogma in order to
show that these dogmas, insofar as they are speculative, simply do not
belong in Christian dogmatics. In this way all attempts at explaining
the mystery of creation, original sin, etc., receive a place outside of theology, for it belongs to theology only to describe the human's dependence
on God, and to present the human in its present, sinful condition. For lay
people this is surely sufficient, but it is still a question whether theology
should not go further. The church's dogmas of the Trinity, of Christ's natures, and other similar ones, are presented with much historical learning
in order to show that such fall completely outside of the sphere of religion and theology, that these dogmas do not have religious and practical
meaning, that the older theologians have confused the spheres of theology and theoretical philosophy, and that such questions consequently
must be referred to the forum of theoretical reason. But we have seen how
Kant [69] judged theoretical reason. And the theologians—by the fact
that without philosophically appropriating Criticism's standpoint they
separate theology from philosophy—have really upheld the contrast between practical and theoretical reason. Although they do not go critically
to work against theoretical reason, like Kant did, they still have as good as
no confidence in it. But *the principle* for this separation between the theoretical and the practical, the objective and the subjective, the speculative
and the religious, the theological and the anthropological moment is to be
sought in Criticism, however differently the principle is modified.—Even
in the Holy Scriptures, in both the sayings and history of Christ, one distinguishes that which has a religious-practical meaning from that which
falls under theoretical questions, as the essential from the accidental. If
this theology is going to be consistent, it does not dare a bit to deny the
reality of such things; for if it did that, it would necessarily get an objective knowledge of God, and the negation would necessarily result in
a speculative affirmation of God's nature, but such things fall outside
of theology. On the other hand it asserts, as it relies on its religious self-
consciousness, that such investigations are by no means essential, that
they have no religious value, and that human salvation is not dependent
on them. As a matter of fact it mentions them generally with the greatest modesty—a modesty of which Kant has provided a good example.
We will quote a passage which gives as it were a type for this mode
of treatment of dogma which many theologians have followed and still
follow.

"Es mag sein, daß die Person des Lehrers der alleinigen für alle Welten gülti-
gen Religion ein Geheimniß, daß seine Erscheinung auf Erden, so wie seine En-
trückung von [70] derselben, daß sein thatenvolles Leben und Leiden lauter
Wunder, ja gar daß die Geschichte, welche die Erzählung aller jener Wunder be-
glaubigung soll, selbst auch ein Wunder (übernatürliche Offenbarung) sey: so
können wir sie insgesammt auf ihrem Werthe beruhen lassen, ja auch die Hülle
noch ehren, welche gedient hat, eine Lehre, deren Beglaubigung auf einer Ur-
kunde beruht, die unauslöschlich in jeder Seele aufbehalten ist, öffentlich in Gang
zu bringen; wenn wir nur den Gebrauch dieser critischen Nachrichten betreffend,
es nicht zum Religionsstücke machen daß das Wissen, Glauben und Bekennen
derselben für sich etwas sey, wodurch wir uns Gott wohlgefällig machen können."
["The person of the teacher of the one and only religion, valid for all
worlds, may indeed be a mystery; his appearance on earth, his translation
thence, and his eventful life and his suffering may all be nothing but miracles; no, the historical record, which is to authenticate the account of
all these miracles, may itself be a miracle (a supersensible revelation).
We need not call into question any of these miracles and indeed may
honor the trappings which have served to bring into public currency a
doctrine whose authenticity rests upon a record indelibly registered in
every soul and which stands in need of no miracle. But it is essential that,
in the use of these historical records, we do not make it a tenet of religion
that the knowing, believing, and professing of them are themselves means
whereby we can render ourselves well-pleasing to God."][28] [71]

Theology of Feeling

§ 22.

The theology of feeling finds its highest expression in the famous work:
"The Christian Faith according to the Fundamentals of the Evangelical
Church in Systematic Interrelation presented by Dr. Fr. Schleiermacher."
The autonomy of self-consciousness is here raised to a higher form. No
doubt many will be surprised over the fact that we ascribe the principle
of autonomy to a dogmatic system which has Anselm's *"credam ut intel-*
ligam [I believe in order that I might understand]" as a motto, and which,
disregarding all the wisdom of "this world," does not contain anything
other than the peculiar pronouncements of the Christian disposition,
which will know nothing other than Christ. But one must add the remark
that this system is inaugurated by a *general* concept of religion which is
of constitutive significance for the construal and interpretation of dogma;
consequently one must penetrate into this more closely.

---

[28] *Religion within the Limits of Reason Alone*, 79–80. Cf. Lessing's *Nathan the Wise*.

With respect to this general concept of religion which is the *principle* of the system, we believe then to be able to assert with justice that its genesis must be derived from Criticism. For if one knows on the one hand that the *absolute* meaning of religion has been destroyed in the practical principle of Criticism because this includes only a single sphere of human existence, namely, the moral sphere, but not the whole of life; and on the other hand if one maintains Criticism's teaching *that all theoretical determinations must be removed from religion*, then religion, if its absolute character is to be vindicated and restored, receives no other seat than *feeling*. Religion [72] here obtains a greater significance than in Criticism; it includes the whole of life and is not a mediated postulate of moral self-consciousness but is allowed *immediately* in the human's spirit. In this way it looks in part as if religion were reinstated in its absolute majesty, and in part as if one now could avoid every scientific objection against it, by the fact that the speculative element is removed from its province and relegated to the theoretical sphere.

The essence of religion is determined then neither as theoretical nor as practical, but as that which precedes all theory and praxis. Feeling, which is the *principle* of religion, goes forth not from knowledge; on the contrary one must say that all knowledge, insofar as it is *religious* (not merely theoretical), has its origin in feeling. Knowledge is so to speak the visible image of feeling, yet in such a way that feeling remains the prototype (τὸ ἀρχέτυπον), knowledge the ectype (τὸ ἔκτυπον); feeling is *primus motor* [the prime mover] and mainspring for all religious (not merely moral) praxis. How this feeling, which is the principle of religion, shall then be determined will be evident from the peculiar nature of feeling. All feeling is namely an immediate consciousness of itself, the *I*'s consciousness of *its* state. Feeling, considered in-and-for-itself, contains only the soul-state of the sentient subject; the subject, which feels, insofar as it expresses a real feeling, can only talk about itself as affected in a certain way but not about the objective character of things. With respect to the egoity of this feeling, the correct observation has been made that the human has feeling in common with the animals especially at the lower stages. For the lower animal classes—e.g., worms, insects, etc.—grasp from the whole universe only themselves and what they immediately are able to refer to their own existence; whereas those which exist at a higher stage grasp much of the objective environs without respect to themselves. But one must still always remember that when feeling is here talked about, one is then thinking of the spiritual and infinite feeling.

How then will the subject, which feels itself affected not in a relative way, not by the finite, by the world and the worldly, describe its state? It can only characterize it as the feeling of absolute *dependence*. For if one determined it as the feeling of *freedom* or in other ways, this would presuppose a distinction between subject and object, and the feeling would then not be a primitive feeling but one derived from a higher principle. But here, where not the idea but feeling is *principle*, is demanded precisely a *real* feeling (*sensus purus* [pure sensation]), which in itself is the immediate unity of subject and object. The pure feeling is absolute receptivity; but absolute receptivity, which excludes all spiritual reaction, can contain nothing other than the absolute dependence of the subject. Consequently, the feeling of absolute dependence is the expression for feeling in its abstraction from all self-activity, all spiritual self-determination. Schleiermacher, as he scientifically develops his dogmatic system out of this principle, has not presented a single form of the theology of feeling but the theology of feeling *itself*; this renowned man's system, which is permeated with much genius and art, may be considered as a pattern *instar omnium* [worth all of them] in this theology.

Rather than Criticism's absolute dependence on a particular and finite principle as the moral law, we here have dependence on—what in truth is not easy to say, since one does not have to do with any objective idea, and feeling can only talk about itself—on that which fills us with [74] a feeling of absolute dependence, what consequently one can call absolute causality, the infinite, eternal, *God*. This religious principle lies *according to its possibility* in the human race, but it only becomes *actual* by being united with the finite and empirical consciousness of the human, by comprehending and underlying this. Consequently, according to this system the true religion is found where that absolute feeling enters into unity with the entire finite sphere of spirit, where human life and the human soul with all its interactions receive their backbone and basis by this feeling. The history of religions contains the development of the religious feeling, but first in Christianity, where the *subjective* union of the *finite* and the *Infinite is* absolutely revealed, has this principle obtained its victorious influence on actual life.

§ 23.

It is self-evident that the center in this theology is not God in God's absolute independence and freedom, but the human, reflected into itself and fixed in the feeling of absolute dependence. The theology which is constructed on this principle consequently develops not the word of *God* but only the pronouncement of the *pious soul*; it describes not the revelation of God but the different forms and *modi* [modes] whereupon the *substantial* feeling is revealed, the various modifications of the substantial fundamental feeling. This will perhaps become even more clear for the reader if one looks to Spinoza's teaching on *substance* and the worldly existent beings as its *modi* [modes]. For what in Spinoza is *objective* and universal, is here seen *subjectively* and in the sphere of the religious self-consciousness. On account of this system's subjective character Schleiermacher has [75] always naturally disavowed the accusation of Spinozism. Spinoza has presented the objective idea of God, namely, the universal Substance in whose very depths the thinking subject is destroyed. Here on the contrary all objectivity is removed, or more correctly disappears in the depth of feeling. Only the sentient *I* returns and plays the role of substance. The substantial feeling is consequently theology's center, and the various modes in which this is revealed are the radii. The system is thus the opposite pole from Spinozism and on account of the subjective character closely related to Criticism. There can only be talk about *God* in this system, insofar as the subject, which *thinks* over its feeling states, must necessarily trace them back to absolute causality. (*"Wenn der Ausdruck Gott eine Vorstellung voraussetzt: so soll nur gesagt werden, daß diese, welche nicht anders ist, als nur das Aussprechen des schlechthinigen Abhängigkeitsgefühls, die unmittelbarste Reflexion über dasselbe, die ursprünglichste Vorstellung sey, mit welcher wir es hier zu thun haben, ganz unabhängig von dem eigentlichen Wissen und nur bedingt durch unser schlechthiniges Abhängigkeitsgefühl, so daß Gott uns zunächst nur das bedeutet was in diesem Gefühl das Mitbestimmende ist, und worauf wir dieses unser Sosein zurückschieben."* ["If the term 'God' presupposes a representation, then we shall simply say that this representation, which is nothing more than the expression of the feeling of absolute dependence, is the most direct reflection upon it and the most original idea with which we are here concerned, and is quite independent of that original knowledge (properly so called), and conditioned only by our feeling of absolute dependence. So that in the first instance God signifies for us simply that which is the co-determinant in this feeling and to which we trace our being in such a state."])[29]

There can only be talk about *the world* and the universe insofar as our pious feelings are mediated by this. (*"Die dogmatische Sätze werden Aussagen über Beschaffenheiten der Welt, nämlich nur für das schlechthinige Abhängigkeitsgefühl und in Beziehung auf dasselbe."* ["The dogmatic propositions become utterances regarding the constitution of the world, but only for the feeling of absolute dependence and with reference to it."])[30] Thus everything objective is absorbed in the pious subject. The immediate states of *the pious soul* are *modi principales* [primary modes]. (*"Wir müssen die Beschreibung* [76] *menschlicher Zustände für die dogmatische Grundform erklären, Sätze aber, welche Begriffe von göttlichen Eigenschaften und Handlungsweisen oder Aussagen über Beschaffenheiten der Welt enthalten, nur für zulässig,*

---

[29] Friedrich Schleiermacher, *The Christian Faith*, trans. of 2nd ed. H. R. Mackintosh and J. S. Stewart (Edinburgh: T. & T. Clark, 1968), 17.

[30] Ibid., 125–126.

sofern sie sich aus Sätzen der ersteren Form entwickeln lassen; denn nur unter
dieser Bedingung können sie mit Sicherheit für Ausdrücke frommer Gemüthser-
regungen gelten." ["We must declare the description of the human states as
the fundamental dogmatic form, propositions, however, which contain
concepts of divine attributes and ways of acting or assertions concerning
the qualities of the world, as permissible only insofar as they can be developed out of propositions of the first form; for only on this condition can
they be really authenticated as expressions of religious emotions."])[31] These
modi principales [primary modes] are two, the one is the state in which the
human's life is still not grounded by that substantial feeling, consequently
where the difference and contrast between the finite and infinite take place
(the sinful state); the second is the state in which the substantial religious
feeling prevails and subjugates human life (the state of grace).

One asserts that all this can and shall be developed *outside* of philosophy. But one still makes use of thinking and that even a systematic form
of thinking; one talks in logical categories and makes dialectical use of
them; by the help of thinking is developed the intelligible and inner connections [*indre Nexus*] in everything which the human maintains by faith.
Consequently, if one is to be able to grasp the meaning of the proposition that theology should be separated from philosophy, one seems to be
allowed to take refuge in Criticism's distinction between *theoretical* and
practical philosophy.

§ 24.

We have seen how Kant appointed practical reason as the principle of
theology and derived everything from this, so that the doctrine of God,
God's attributes and what stands in connection with this, came forth as
postulates of the practical reason; insofar as practical reason is entitled to
any reality, [77] one must also admit the validity of its postulates. Consequently, these postulates stepped forth on the one hand with universality
and necessity, because the human, who is bound to absolute dependence
on the moral law, with necessity must think them because they are necessary moments in the development of moral dependence, they are, so to
speak, the necessary complements to the full concept of this dependence.
But on the other hand their truth and validity were only hypothetical
because they were supported on the authority of practical reason, not on
their own authority. In this way then Schleiermacher also appoints the
feeling of absolute dependence as the basis for his theology and derives
all dogmas from this feeling, as he regards them as true only if they either

---

[31] Ibid., 126.

lie immediately in this feeling or are necessarily postulated by it. Consequently, if that feeling contains the truth, which is his argument, then everything which can be derived from it also has truth.[32]

In Kant's view, although the human stands under the authority of practical reason, it can only be granted a human validity, since every objective idea, every revelation of God *in-and-by-itself* is completely removed from the system. It is for this reason that Kant also continually enjoins that those theological postulates may only be conceived practically, for practical employment, that is, merely subjectively, but that one by no means may allow them any theoretical validity. In parallel fashion, if Schleiermacher's feeling of absolute dependence, which is not grounded in any objective idea [78] but rather displaces every objective idea, receives only a subjective validity, then everything which is taught in dogmatics as a *postulate* of this feeling may be construed only subjectively. This view insists that it shall only be construed in the interest of piety, not theoretically. The interest in piety in the theology of feeling corresponds perfectly to the practical interest in moral theology.

Moreover, just as Kant could not claim for practical reason an immediate authority, independent of all theory, without allowing theoretical philosophy to take precedence, so that practical reason's *immediate* authority appears by a *theoretical mediation*, so also Schleiermacher called on various propositions borrowed from different disciplines to help, before he could claim for feeling an immediate authority and implement the contrast between faith and knowledge. For from faith, as it is in its original purity, this opposition and polemical contrast to science cannot originate. This feeling's immediate authority, then, is not in truth immediate but a truth *artificially [konstigt] invented by thinking*.

Kant consequently distinguished theoretical reason from practical reason and appointed *practical reason* as theology's principle of knowledge; Schleiermacher set the contrast between speculative science and religion, excluded the objective idea from religion, and appointed *feeling* as the principle of knowledge. But thus in both systems human *self-consciousness* becomes judge and *constitutor* in everything, and the theology of feeling is declared with as much legitimacy as moral theology as *autonomic*, since it does not know the divine truth out of God but out of itself. With as much legitimacy as moral theology does the theology of feeling also receive the name [79] of *rationalism*, for thinking here has not God but the human subject as its principle, so that here also Descartes' proposition *cogito ergo sum* plays the most important role. But in order that one shall not be prejudiced in the objection that the system which

---

[32] Cf. F. C. Sibbern, *Philos. Archives and Repertorium. 3 Bidrag til Besvarelse af det Spørgsmaal: Hvad er Dogmatik.* Initiated by a critique of Schleiermacher's concept of this.

teaches the human's absolute dependence on God can hardly be seriously accused of solipsism, it must be maintained that solipsism does not lie in the fact that it is a teaching about human dependence on God but in the fact that this dependence *is tied to feeling*, with the exclusion of all objective knowledge of what God is, a knowledge which only becomes possible by God's own revelation. Rather than the human's absolute dependence on God we here have the human's dependence on itself, for the human continuously moves in the circle of *its own* self-consciousness and cannot arrive at knowledge of a divine reality in its independence from the human spirit. If self-consciousness acknowledged such a knowledge, it would necessarily transcend the bounds of feeling and not acquiesce in the description of its own piety but forget itself in order to lose itself in the consideration of God and God's revelation.

§ 25.

From this one can see in which sense Schleiermacher wants the Anselmian words he places at the top of his system to be understood. The view of faith and knowledge of Anselm and Schleiermacher could be considered as *opposita juxta se posita* [opposites placed close to each other]. Regarding faith, Anselm's *credam* or his subjective faith is in the innermost unity with *credo* or the objective faith; the theology of feeling expresses its *credam* [subjective faith] without any *credo* [objective faith]. For insofar as it addresses itself to the church's [80] objective faith, this receives only a purely subjective interpretation. In Anselm subjective faith receives all authority from objective faith; in Schleiermacher objective faith is grounded in subjective piety. There piety reposes in an objective content, in *God's* revelation; here on the contrary it lacks all objectivity and moves within itself. And then concerning *knowledge*, Anselm strives to conceive God; he feels no peace until he has arrived at rest in the Lord and God's mystery. The theology of feeling on the contrary does not seek to grasp God or the human according to their *essence* [*Væsen*]— for how can the innermost depths of the human heart be searched without God?—but it is enough for it to describe the *phenomena* of the pious soul. Just as in Anselm God in God's eternal personality is the object of knowledge, and the same God is the principle of knowledge, so in the theology of feeling, where the human is the object of knowledge, the human spirit becomes the principle of knowledge.

In this way *dogma*, or the objective truth of faith, is totally annulled. Instead of dogma one encounters only the assertions of the pious soul together with the exposition of these. In Anselm dogma *is* the *principle* of the pious soul, here pious feeling becomes the principle of dogma. Can one really think of a greater contrast? And is it not the greatest injustice that a system which posits feeling as a principle for theology appoints Anselm's word as its own? Anselm's theology by no means excludes pious feeling, but the difference between the newer and old theology, between modernity's piety and that time's old faith, is this, that God, the True, the Good in that time was the first and the human the second. It is this which Augustine and Anselm, Luther and the church's other Reformers [81] have wanted, namely, that *dogma*, the objective truth of faith, should be the constitutive principle which sanctions all human thinking, feeling, and willing. They knew that the general character of the creature is its *need for God*, that consequently the human neither in a theoretical nor in a practical respect is sufficient unto itself.

When in modernity one often hears talk of the subjective principle of Protestantism, then the true meaning of this can only be that the human by its thought and action ought to *appropriate to itself* the objective truth and not blindly subordinate itself to it as a purely external authority—for which to a great extent Catholicism can be blamed. Consequently in Protestantism everything outer is in indissoluble unity with the inner. But if the principle of subjectivity receives the explanation that the human subject is the principle of *knowledge*, that human reason is autonomic, then the idea of divine revelation is annulled, and Protestantism transcends the limits of the Christian religion, whose principle is precisely *God's* revelation by *Godself*.

§ 26.

As regards then the dogma of God, Creator of heaven and earth, nothing at all can be said about this in this system. That is to say, the creation can only be thought of as an act of freedom of God; according to the concept of creation God is thought of as self-conscious, as that which with self-consciousness and absolute freedom creates the world as its other. But if the human is to be able to grasp this concept, if one wants to be able to think of God as that which exists *in itself*, different from the world, then the boundaries of feeling must necessarily be transgressed and the objective idea be grasped by thought. [82] Hereby thinking becomes recognized as the constitutive element of religion, as that primitive knowledge in religion by which the human grasps itself as God's creature, as dependence is derived not from an unknown God but from absolute freedom. This runs completely contrary to the principle of the theology of feeling. For since the feeling of piety is here sufficient unto itself, theology is also satisfied by such a development of the dogma of Creation as is provoked by piety's interest to explain the existence of this feeling. But feeling can say nothing about the objective character of things. It feels no appeal to trace *primordia rerum* [the origins of things], or what God is *in Godself*; it does not exceed the human's present and immediate state. Therefore Schleiermacher from the beginning also dissolves the dogma of Creation in the dogma of Preservation, which better finds its application in the human's immediate present state. (*"Die Lehre von der Schöpfung ist vorzüglich in der Hinsicht zu entwickeln, daß Fremdartiges abgewehrt werde, damit nicht aus der Art wie die Frage nach dem Entstehen anderwärts beantwortet wird, etwas in unser Gebiet einschleiche, was mit dem reinen Ausdruck des schlechthinigen Abhängigkeitsgefühls in Widerspruch steht. Die Lehre von der Erhaltung aber vorzüglich um daran jenes Grundgefühl selbst vollkommen darzustellen."* ["The doctrine of Creation is to be elucidated pre-eminently with a view to the exclusion of every alien element, lest from the way in which the question of origin is answered elsewhere anything steal into our province which stands in contradiction to the pure expression of the feeling of absolute dependence. But the doctrine of Preservation is preeminently to be elucidated so as to bring out this fundamental feeling itself in the fullest way."])[33] Everything speculative is differentiated from this doctrine, one makes a critical attack on the old dogmatics because it has not [83] confined itself to the precincts of pious feeling—this system's transcendental limit—, and the result of the entire investigation, *the ground-relation between God and the world* becomes reduced to this, that on the one hand everything is absolutely dependent on God, and that on the other hand the individual is conditioned and determined by the mutual relations of the whole. (*"Das fromme Selbstbewußtsein, vermöge dessen wir alles, was uns erregt und auf uns einwirkt, in die schlechthinige Abhängigkeit von Gott stellen, fällt ganz zusammen mit der Einsicht, daß eben dieses Alles durch den Naturzusammenhang bedingt und bestimmt ist."* ["The religious self-consciousness, by means of which we place all that affects or influences us in absolute dependence on God, coincides entirely with the view that all such things are conditioned and determined by the interdependence of nature."])[34]

However, the result of this can indeed only be this, that the world is a system which has God as its principle, a total organism in which the individual moments are conditioned and determined by their mutual interrelation, but that the whole is still dependent on one and the same

---

[33] Ibid., 148. Cf.: *"Dem Bedürfniß der practischen Vernunft gemäß, ist der Glaube an Gott, als den alleinigen Schöpfer Himmels und Erden, d. i., moralisch als heiligen Gesetzgeber."* [Cf. Kant, *Religion within the Limits of Reason Alone*, 231. "Conformable to the requirement of practical reason is the belief in God as the omnipotent Creator of heaven and earth, i.e., morally as holy Legislator."]

[34] Ibid., 170.

principle. Yet, since concerning this principle or God nothing is said about what God *is in Godself*; since God is only determined insofar as God *is the principle of the world* and receives no other predicates than those to which God is entitled with respect to the world; since God can receive no other determination than this, that God is that *on which all existing beings of the world depend absolutely*, on which they all have their relative existence, then it is in truth not difficult to say what God is, or at least, how God is thought of in this system. God is thought of, namely, as *Substance*, a concept which is well-known from Spinoza's teaching. Substance is indeed the universal principle on which all things are absolutely dependent, since they are only its *modi* [modes] and the very existing beings of Substance. Therefore when Schleiermacher asserts that we are not able to *know* what God is in Godself, then he is completely [84] entitled to this, namely, since Substance or pantheism's God *exists* not in itself but only in its *modi*, in the world. He certainly asserts that the objective difference between pantheism and theism belongs among the theoretical questions, not to Christian dogmatics, and in this way has sought to avoid the accusation of Spinozism. But it is factual that a development which is given only for the sake of subjective and religious application contains no other concept of God than Substance, and as a consequence of this he must state that at least in Christian dogmatics on behalf of piety one must acquiesce in this concept. For although the word "Substance" is not used in his system, we have no doubt that everyone who thinks logically—and theologians still have at least the logical principles in common with philosophy—must admit that the relation between God and the world, where God is posited as the principle for everything but cannot find its determination except in that whose principle God is, coincides with the relation which takes place between Substance and its *modi*. Rather than the almighty God, Creator of heaven and earth, we consequently get Spinoza's Substance, carried through in the subjective domain.

§ 27.

If we now offer a critique of the concept of this absolute dependence in which the world harmonizes with God, such as it is presented in this system, then it will appear that it is encumbered with the contradiction that neither the dependence on the human's side nor the independence on God's side is in truth *absolute*.

Regarding the human, its dependence on Substance, which subordinates everything to itself, cannot in actuality receive [85] the name of absolute dependence because the concept of the absolute must not be determined merely quantitatively but *qualitatively*.[35] In other words it is not sufficient for constituting the concept of absolute dependence to teach that everything must be classified under God as the principle for all things, that nothing falls outside God's power; for this gives a purely quantitative concept which only determines the divine power according to its *size* but not according to its *inner* character. For not all creatures are dependent on God in the same way, and quantitative dependence, which is here taught, should be called an external rather than an internal dependence, a natural rather than a spiritual dependence. The dependence of nature and the physical world on God can quite rightly be called an *external* dependence, namely, because the physical existing beings are not able to exist *in themselves* but only in Substance. In the same way Substance itself can be called external, because it cannot exist *in itself* but only in its *modi* [modes]. Therefore pantheism, as it defines its God as that which does not have existence in itself but only in the other, worships an external, an exoteric, but no esoteric God. For that which cannot exist in itself but only in the other is to be called an *external reality*, and that which exists not only in the other but also in itself receives quite rightly the name of an *internal reality*. Nature may be called God's outer kingdom, while God in God's spirit lives in God's inner kingdom. For only the spirit whose essence is freedom can be called inner, since it can exist both in itself and in the other; while nature can only exist in the other (as Substance in its *modi*, and as *modi* in Substance). But Substance [86] never has any being [*Væren*] in itself, but only in its *modi*, just as its *modi* never exist in themselves but only in Substance. The unity is here an immediate one and precisely therefore no true unity; for true unity takes place only where two, which are also able to *exist* independently *each for itself*, are joined.

Consequently where the human's dependence on God is to be able to be called in truth absolute and infinite (not only in a quantitative but also in a qualitative respect), there must it necessarily be determined as *inner*, that is to say, as *free*; it is a necessary requirement that the human with freedom shall certify its dependence on God. But she would not be able to give it her free witness if she could not in addition *negate* it, that is, if she could not in addition be in itself, if she could not exclude God from her soul's innermost sanctuary, from her kingdom of freedom and thus even live *outside* God. In other words, the human's dependence on God cannot be thought of without in addition positing the human's relative independence. Consequently only by *negating* its own independence can the

---

[35] Concerning the bad [*slette*] confusion of quantity and quality, which pantheism follows in the determination of God, cf. Schlüter, *Die Lehre des Spinoza*. Münster 1836 (5th Supplement).

human certify its dependence on God. And this dependence, which as the negation of the negation bears the mark of spirituality, must be called in truth an absolute and infinite dependence. But where thought is bound to the category of substantiality, where it is said that everything depends on God in like fashion, there the dependence which applies in the kingdom of nature is carried over to the kingdom of grace, necessity is confused with freedom, God's outer kingdom with God's inner, the quantity of dependence with its quality.

And now with respect to God, God's independence is not presented as in truth an absolute independence, as this theology only thinks of God as Substance. But since such [87] a God's existence is tied completely to the world and the human spirit, God becomes *absolutely dependent* on the world and the human. We surely admit that God or Christianity's principles in a certain way can be said to be dependent on the world, namely, insofar as the human can impede just as well as advance the development of God's kingdom. But one may always remark however that God with freedom has decided this its dependence on the world, that God with free resolve has so to speak descended from God's eternal majesty and independence to this sphere of interaction. But in this theology the very self of God becomes only a moment in the world, namely, the *universal* moment. God is Substance, the world God's *modi*; God is Essence, the world existence; God is the inner, the world the outer. With the same justice as the world can be said to depend on God, God can be said to depend absolutely on the world; but this is totally contrary to the concept of God as the one who is in possession of an absolute self-validity and independence. Thus this religious cultus annuls itself. On the one hand the human declares itself totally dependent on God, but on the other hand it is still aware that God's existence is absolutely dependent on the human, that in order to gain existence God needs the human in every respect— a view which comes very close to irony. The concept of such an independence is annulled by an inner contradiction and passes into its negation; for God's true independence can just as little as the human's true dependence be maintained and defended without the idea of personality and freedom. [88]

§ 28.

God's absolute dependence on the human, such as it is contained in this system which gives the impression of teaching the human's absolute dependence on God, will become more conspicuous when we remember that everything which here is taught about God must not be construed objectively, as in Spinoza, but subjectively, as in Kant. One sees this most pointedly in the doctrine of God's *attributes*. Just as in Kant God does not reveal God's attributes Godself but receives these from humankind; just as these attributes are only those of the human spirit but not the divine essence's own reflexes, so also Schleiermacher teaches that all God's attributes are a *reflection* of the human's piety—not conversely. The attributes present nothing other than the different ways in which the pious feelings stand in relation to absolute causality; but they by no means reveal to us anything of the divine essence, so that we also here have "a God, who is formed according to the fabrication of humankind" (ἐνθυμήσει ἀνθρώπων). The difference between Kant and Schleiermacher is only this, that Schleiermacher has posited pious feeling in place of Kant's practical reason, substantial dependence in the place of the absolute dependence of the moral law. Incidentally, the entire mode of argumentation, the polemic against the objective, that is, the true knowledge of God and the autonomy of the thinking *I*, are derived completely from Criticism. The following arranged schema, which gives several parallels by which the inner bond of kinship between the theology of feeling and Criticism is made obvious and raised above all doubt, will perfectly substantiate the truth of this. [89]

KANT.

Es liegt uns nicht sowohl daran zu wissen, was Gott an sich selbst (seine Natur) sei, sondern was er für uns als moralische Wesen sey. [It concerns us not so much to know what God is in Godself (God's nature) as what God is for us as moral beings.][36]

SCHLEIERMACHER.

Alle Eigenschaften, welche wir Gott beilegen, sollen nicht etwas besonderes in Gott bezeichnen, sondern nur etwas besonderes in der Art das schlechthinige Abhängigkeitsgefühl auf ihn zu beziehen. [All attributes which we ascribe to God are to be taken as denoting not something special in God, but only something special in the manner in which the feeling of absolute dependence is to be related to God.][37]

KANT.

Zum Behuf dieser Beziehung müßen wir die göttliche Naturbeschaffenheit so denken und annehmen als es zu diesem Verhältnisse in der ganzen zur Ausführung seines Willens erforderlichen Vollkommenheit nötig ist (z.B. als eines unveränderlichen, allwissenden, allmächtigen Wesens) und ohne diese Beziehung nichts an ihm erkennen können. [To know what God is for us as moral

---

[36] *Religion within the Limits of Reason Alone*, 130.
[37] *The Christian Faith*, 194.

beings we must conceive and comprehend all the attributes of the divine nature (for instance, the unchangeableness, omniscience, omnipotence, etc. of such a Being) which, in their totality, are requisite to the carrying out of the divine will in this regard. Apart from this context we can know nothing about God.][38]

SCHLEIERMACHER.

Wir haben hier keine andere Vollständigkeit anzustreben, als daß wir keines von den verschiedenen Momenten des frommen Selbstbewußtseins vorbeigehen lassen, ohne die ihnen entsprechenden göttlichen Eigenschaften aufzusuchen. Und bei diesem Verfahren ergiebt sich auch die Classifikation von selbst, indem bei jeder Abtheilung nur die dahin gehörigen Eigenschaften zur Darstellung kommen. [We have here to strive after that completeness alone which guards against letting any of the different moments of the religious self-consciousness pass without asking what are the divine attributes corresponding to them. And with this procedure the classification emerges of its own accord, because in each division only the attributes belonging there can be subjects of exposition.[39]] [90]

KANT.

Wird nun aber unsere Erkenntniß auf solche Weise durch reine practische Vernunft wirklich erweitert? Allerdings, aber nur in practischer Rücksicht. Denn wir erkennen zwar dadurch weder unserer Seele Natur noch die intelligibele Welt noch das höchste Wesen nach dem was sie an sich selber sind, sondern haben nur die Begriffe von ihnen im practischen Begriff des höchsten Guts vereinigt—aber nur vermittelst des moralischen Gesetzes und nur in Beziehung auf dasselbe. [Is our knowledge really widened in such a way by pure practical reason, and is that which was transcendent for speculative reason immanent in practical reason? Certainly, but only from a practical point of view. For we thereby know neither the nature of our soul, nor the intelligible world, nor the Supreme Being as they are in themselves, but have only united the concepts of them in a practical concept of the highest Good—but we have so united them only by means of the moral law and merely in relation to it.].[40]

SCHLEIERMACHER.

Wir müssen hier gleich bevorworten, daß in sofern aus der göttlichen Ursächlichkeit mehrere Eigenschaften entwickelt werden, die Verschiedenheiten derselben ebenfalls nichts reelles in Gott sind, ja, daß sie weder einzeln noch zusammen

---

[38] *Religion within the Limits of Reason Alone,* 130–131.
[39] *The Christian Faith,* 196–197.
[40] *Critique of Practical Reason,* 133.

genommen das Wesen Gottes ausdrücken. [We must at this point state that insofar as a plurality of attributes is developed out of the idea of the divine causality, this differentiation can correspond to nothing real in God; indeed, that neither in isolation nor taken together do the attributes express the Being of God in itself.][41]

KANT.

Also bleibt nur ein einziges Verfahren für die Vernunft übrig, daß sie nemlich als reine Vernunft von dem obersten Princip ihres reinen practischen Gebrauchs ausgehend ihr Object bestimmt.—Der Begriff von Gott ist also ein ursprünglich nicht für die spekulative Vernunft sondern zur Moral gehöriger Begriff. [Thus there remains to reason only one single procedure, namely, that as pure reason it must determine its object by starting from the supreme principle of its pure practical use.—Therefore, the concept of God belongs originally not to speculative reason but to morals.][42]

SCHLEIERMACHER.

Daher ist noch immer nöthig zu bevorworten, daß ohne spekulative Ansprüche zu machen aber auch ohne spekulative Hülfsmittel in Anwendung zu bringen, wir uns ganz innerhalb der Grenze des rein dogmatischen [!] Verfahrens halten. [It is still therefore always necessary to premise that, without making any speculative demands but at the same time without bringing in any speculative aids, we keep ourselves altogether within the limits of purely dogmatic procedure.[43]] [91]

§ 29.

Just as in Kant so also here we miss the true concept of the conscience. It is surely said that the conscience must be referred to God's holiness, since it contains the eternal law and with this also the knowledge of sin and the need for reconciliation with God.[44] But if one looks more closely it will become apparent that this relation to God's holiness is a purely nominal one. That is to say, if one raises the question of what God's holiness is, then one gets in the first place not its determination from God but from the human's sin; and next we have indeed seen that none of God's attributes must be thought of objectively, so that this theology dare not guarantee that God in actuality is holy but only that it necessarily must

---

[41] *The Christian Faith*, 198.
[42] *Critique of Practical Reason*, 144, 145.
[43] *The Christian Faith*, 195.
[44] Ibid., 341.

appear to us in this way. However, since the idea of holiness does not belong to God but only to our thinking, the concept of the conscience also becomes merely subjective, and in it the human grasps not a *will* which is different from the human itself, just as was the case in Kant, but only an abstract law whose subject is the human self; for should the human know a will different from itself, this will would necessarily reveal *itself* and be known as the ideal of the personal God.

In a similar way one undermines the concept of *prayer*. For although in agreement with the Christian religion it is said that one should pray in Jesus' name,[45] and that such a prayer will always be granted, so with this nothing is really said other than that the pious wishes and prayers of humankind, which aim at the true and highest Good, and likewise [92] their fulfillment, or *the realization* of the highest Good, are advanced with eternal necessity, since both the subjective moment (the human's striving), and the objective moment (the highest Good) depend on God to a similar degree. But since the concept of personality is here lacking, one must make the remark, firstly, that there cannot be talk about the fulfillment of prayer as a *gift* of God, which after all is its true concept, but only talk about the substantial necessity; secondly, such a prayer is heard only by the human, namely, since the human certainly knows that all the attributes, predicates, and names under which the human thinks of and speaks to God by no means correspond to the divine essence [*Væsen*], so that God does not have real presence in God's name. E.g., when a person prays: "Our Father, who art in heaven," that person is surely aware that God is not in actuality Father, but that God is only called such by the human, that this name is only a symbolic designation for that *obscure principle* on which everything is dependent to a degree, that indeed from the human's side all spiritual reaction is excluded.

If this is the case, then we with justice are able to state the same thing about the theology of feeling as before about moral theology, namely, that the dogma of God, *Creator* of heaven and earth, and the mutual relation in which God stands to the creature have been totally destroyed in the autonomy of human self-consciousness entrusted exclusively to itself.

§ 30.

According to what has been worked out above this theology cannot have any doctrine of *God's Son* who from eternity is begotten of the Father, since this teaching completely transcends that immediate [93] *self-consciousness*; therefore one only refers critically to this doctrine in order

---

[45] Ibid., 671.

to annul it. But what kind of a Christ, then, does this system portray for us? Is it not in the highest degree incorrect to assert that the principle of autonomy is also here the prevailing one, since all true piety, the truly religious life, and the human's liberation from sin are derived exclusively from Christ; since it is said that Christ is the life-principle in the religious life of the human race, so that only by him does one manage to come into unity with God; since the assertion is made that the aim of life is that the human shall no more live unto itself alone, but that the Christ shall live in the human? We gladly admit that the image of Christ the genial Schleiermacher has presented is in truth beautiful. It is a painting which not merely is artfully laid out but even breathes and lives. But nevertheless it is our conviction that the same principle also lies at the bottom of this, and that that *theory* of Christ is to be derived completely from Criticism.

Kant portrays in his Christology the ideal of the moral human, of such a human whose will is so perfectly in harmony with the moral law that his entire life only reveals the moral idea and at every point is penetrated by it, however, such that the reality of the idea does not depend on the reality of this person, but belongs to the human spirit as such. This human is presented as an *ideal*, that is, an individual in whom the universal idea is perfectly taken up, between whose individuality and the universality of the idea no difference takes place, which in itself is, if we may so say, the absolute synthesis of individuality and universality. If we keep this in mind, and if on this we posit the subjective idea of religion instead of the moral idea; if we represent for ourselves instead of [94] a human, who in his life and his person reveals the absolute dependence of the moral law, a human who in an absolute way is so penetrated and filled by the feeling of dependence, the principle of religion, that in every moment of life it is the moving principle; consequently, if we paint for ourselves a human who has perfectly united that universal and constitutive element of all religious life with his individuality, so that by revealing his individuality he reveals religion itself, is at once a single individual and yet a general and universal human, at once one among the many humans and yet the only one, *instar omnium* [worth all of them]: then we have, if we are not mistaken, sketched the image of Christ which the famous author's system presents. ("*Der Erlöser mußte als geschichtliches Einzelwesen zugleich urbildlich sein, d. h. das urbildliche mußte in ihm vollkommen geschichtlich werden und jeder geschichtliche Moment desselben zugleich das Urbildliche in sich tragen.*" ["As an historical individual the Redeemer must have been at the same time ideal (i.e., the ideal must have become completely historical in him), and each historical moment of his experience must at the same time have borne within it the ideal."])[46] ("*Er ist sonach allen Menschen gleich*

---

[46] *The Christian Faith*, 377.

vermöge der Selbigkeit der menschlichen Natur, von allen aber unterschieden durch die stetige Kräftigkeit seines Gottesbewußtseins, welche ein eigentliches Sein Gottes in ihm war." [The Redeemer is like all men in virtue of the identity of human nature, but distinguished from them all by the constant potency of His God-consciousness, which was a veritable existence of God in him."])[47]

Thus what is here taught about the synthesis of the universal and the individual, about God's *being* [*Væren*] in Christ, is only formally true and right; those definitions are, so to speak, only heuristic, that is, they contain the formal types according to which Christ must always be described, the condition without which he cannot be thought. That human, on whose authority everything is dependent and who with justice of all other humans requires faith in his person, must necessarily be thought of such that by his self-revelation he immediately reveals the absolute. [95] But one cannot remain standing by this formalism and by such a heuristic definition. One must enter into the inner and qualitative content, one must ask about what that absolute is, which and of what sort this idea is which is united with the individuality by an absolute synthesis. One cannot remain standing by God's being in Christ, but must investigate the *essence* [*Væsen*], whose being [*Væren*] it is this teaching presents. And here then the above-stated complaint returns; namely, since the concept of *God* right away at the beginning of the system is undermined, the concept of Christ is also undermined. In this system God is Substance, comprehended from the subjective side. Therefore the Christ can only become the most outstanding flower of the subjectively revealed Substance; he cannot step forth as the absolute, objective truth, but only as that of pious feeling, the hero of human piety. That is to say, when that substantial feeling becomes the principle of religion, when God has no other revelation than in feeling, then the significance of Christ can only be posited in feeling, and in this respect alone can he be called the absolute ideal of religion. Consequently, the ideal in this theology is, when one investigates its inner content more closely, just as in moral theology only a subjective and finite ideal, namely, because the God of whom the ideal is a visible appearance is not any true God but only a finite essence [*Væsen*]. As the Father is, so also is the Son.

§ 31.

However, this Christology is in a way different from the Kantian, as Kant taught that Christ's *historical* existence was only hypothetical, and on the

---

[47] *The Christian Faith,* 385.

contrary it is here regarded as historically certain, just as here also is asserted that all true piety in the human [96] stems from Christ's historical appearance. This view, which agrees so little with the system's principle, can be called according to our view its *eclecticism*. For in the first place, we ask how does one know that this ideal has actually appeared in history, since neither historical nor speculative grounds but only the so-called inner experience here has truly evidential weight? How can one from this experience, which is confined to feeling alone, conclude with certainty to *the character* of the causality which has produced this effect in feeling? It is certainly said that this effect cannot come forth except by an individual who has lived in history. But, then we ask, why can it not as in all mythical religions be a product of the idealizing imagination? For feeling is indeed, as noted above, totally ignorant concerning the objective nature of things. It can only talk about itself in this or that mood and refer this to a determined causality, about whose objective character it dare express nothing except this alone, that it has called forth that determined effect. But here, where the authority of self-consciousness has been utterly vindicated, and feeling posited as a principle, one can and ought with the same justice as in Kant assert that that *real* ideal is in the human's spirit and does not depend on any outer experience.[48] [97]

But even if we will concede that Schleiermacher in accordance with the system's principle has vindicated the historical existence of his Christ, then we yet assert that this theology's Christ is not the one who is presented to us in the Holy Scriptures and the ecclesial tradition. That history of Christ, as it is given us in the Holy Scriptures, is here only considered as the material he has employed and further developed in the same way as the poets treat an historical subject, when they often with a certain *licentia poetical* [poetic license] omit or add, according as their plan requires this. That this is the case here one will not possibly be able to deny, when one merely pays attention to the doctrine of the Lord's resurrection and ascension and also his second coming for judgment. That is to say, this theology only requires such a Savior who is himself the hero of pious feeling and in addition can enable this feeling to pass into others. But his life and death are in every respect sufficient to reveal the feeling of absolute dependence on God. In the resurrection and the ascension, on the con-

---

[48] Kant, *Billig sollte ein jeder Mensch ein Beispiel zu dieser Idee an sich abgeben, wozu das Urbild immer nur in der Vernunft bleibt, weil ihr kein Beilspiel in der äußeren Erfahrung adäquat ist, als welche das Innere der Gesinnung nicht ausdeckt.* [Kant, *Religion within the Limits of Reason Alone,* 56. According to the law, each person ought really to furnish an example of this idea in his or her own person; to this end does the archetype reside always in the reason: and this, just because no example in outer experience is adequate to it; for outer experience does not disclose the inner nature of the disposition.] Cf. Baur, *Chr. Gnosis,* 664; Rosenkranz, *Kritik d. Schl. Glaubenslehre,* 74; Strauss, *Leben Jesu,* 2nd Volume, Appendix.

trary, the Lord is revealed not as a creature who is *absolutely dependent* on God but as the one who is reinstated in God's own glory. His personality arises out of the embryo of individuality. He, who in actuality has descended from heaven, rises in actuality to heaven. He returns in order to judge the living and the dead and is revealed as Lord over everything, not in a certain relative way in a purely ethical respect, but in an absolute way in a universal and cosmical respect, that is, he is revealed as true God and true human, under whom is placed the entire created nature. But all this, which shows the absolute significance of the Savior, cannot find any place in this theology that only accompanies the Lord—which is to say, a human, who in an absolute way has *felt* [98] the absolute dependence on God and expressed it in his life—to his death, where the flower of the pious dependence first blossoms.

According to the same mode of procedure which Kant pointed out (§ 22), namely, that one should exclude that which does not coincide with the system, Schleiermacher teaches here, that those dogmas do not pertain to the essence of the Christian religion. ("*Die Thatsachen der Auferstehung und der Himmelfahrt Christi, so wie die Vorhersagung von seiner Wiederkunft zum Gericht können nicht als eigentliche Vestandtheile der Lehre von seiner Person aufgestellt werden.*" ["The facts of the resurrection and ascension of Christ, and the prediction of his return to judgment, cannot be laid down as properly constituent parts of the doctrine of his person."])[49]. Even though their historical reality is not denied, yet that which is the most important is denied, namely, their religious reality.[50] And here appears especially the autarchy of this piety which appoints itself as the Lord of Lords, puts its own idea into history, relies on itself and is sufficient unto itself. The system asserts that it only wants to develop the universal consciousness of the Christian religion, the general faith of the church. But in relying on its own authority it really asserts that the dogma which is central in apostolic preaching and central in the Christian cultus—for the Sunday and Easter celebration stands and falls completely with the dogma of the resurrection—is not part of the substance of the faith. The apostle Paul says: "If Christ is not risen from the dead, then our faith is in vain." Schleiermacher asserts on the contrary that faith by no means needs this foundation. Does not this theology's *credam* [subjective

---

[49] Ibid., 417.

[50] Kant, "*Die als Anhang hinzugefügte geheimere bloß vor den Augen seiner Vertrauten vorgegangene Geschichte seiner Auserstehung und Himmelfahrt kann ihrer historischen Würdigung unbeschadet zur Religion innerhalb der bloßen Vernunft nicht gerechnet werden.*" [Kant, *Religion within the Limits of Reason Alone*, 119. "The more secret records, added as a sequel, of his resurrection and ascension, which took place before the eyes only of his intimates, cannot be used in the interest of religion within the limits of reason alone without doing violence to their historical validation."]

faith] then taste of a onesided arbitrariness, which appoints itself [99] as Lord over the church's *credo* [objective faith] and the apostolic tradition, and which introduces not its own dependence on Christ but Christ's dependence on the autonomy of the human? Although we could mention several examples of the same mark, we will merely confine ourselves to this, which compensates for all others and pointedly shows that Christ does not constitute the human's self-consciousness but that this constitutes Christ and shapes him according to its own image.

§ 32.

This will become even more evident when we turn from Christ's *history* to his *teaching* and investigate what significance one confers on his words. It is surely said that his words contain the highest truth which will not be surpassed in all posterity. ("*Weder kann außerhalb des Gebietes in welchem Christus schon anerkannt ist, eine Darstellung unseres Verhältnisses zu Gott entstehen, welche nicht hinter jener Offenbarung zurückbliebe, noch kann auch alle Fortschreitung innerhalb der christlichen Kirche jemals dahin führen, in der Lehre Christi selbst etwas unvollkommnes zu erkennen, an dessen Stelle man besseres zu setzen hätte, noch auch etwas zum Verständniß des Menschen von seinem Verhältniß zu Gott, geistiger, tiefer und vollkommner aufzufassen, als Christus es gethan.*" ["No presentation of our relationship to God can arise outside the sphere in which Christ is recognized, which would not fall short of that revelation; nor can any possible advance within the Christian church ever bring us to the point either of perceiving anything imperfect in the teaching of Christ himself, for which we could substitute something better, or of conceiving anything, which aids the human's understanding of its relation to God more spiritually, more profoundly, or more perfectly than Christ has done."])[51] But what kind of a *truth* is it about which this theology talks? It is only *feeling* itself. The word, or the expression of this feeling, has its reality then not from the objective and universal truth, but from feeling, whose *expression* it is. According to the system's principle the meaning of the passage cited can only be that in his teaching and preaching Christ has given a perfectly adequate expression of his feeling of absolute dependence; and since this feeling resides in him in an absolute way, [100] his words must also present the absolute type for the description of this feeling. But *Christ thereby himself becomes restricted by the limits of the in-itself-reflected-subjectivity*, and those meaningful words: "I am the truth" therefore receive not an absolute but a relative meaning, since the truth here cannot be conceived objectively but merely with

---

[51] *The Christian Faith*, 445.

respect to the truth of feeling, which is subjective. The entire religious worldview articulated by Christ is the view of the human and not of God, not an objective mirror of God and the universe but the clothing of pious feeling; it is not an image of the eternal truth, the very *revelation* of the light, but only an image of piety which lacks objective knowledge or the true light. "The Word," which rightly demands the first place in God's kingdom since it not only is no different from the very revelation of God but in fact is God's revelation itself, receives here only a secondary and derived meaning.

And yet the *Word* alone can enable the human's individuality to be fulfilled and be permeated by true universality, because "the Word," which is the utterance of God or the most universal Essence [*Væsen*], only expresses the universal, or such *individualia* [particularities] which are also *universalia* [universals]. Therefore only by entering into human nature can the eternal Word, ὁ λόγος [the Word], ground the true Christ and liberate his knowledge from every particularity. For this reason only, that λόγος [Word] is in Christ and constitutes his nature, can he with justice demand faith in *his person*. For one cannot in truth really *trust* in one who has no *knowledge*. To believe in one who lacks knowledge and insight into the divine is simply contrary to reason. Consequently, if it is in earnest and not for the sake of appearance that faith in Christ is impressed on the [101] human race, then the human race must necessarily be thought of as ignorant [*uvidende*], devoid of true knowledge [*Viden*], but to the contrary Christ in whom it believes must be thought of as the absolutely *knowing* [*vidende*]. From this it follows on the one hand that knowledge belongs essentially to faith, since faith is precisely on the verge of *taking up into itself* God's or Christ's absolute knowledge. Faith, whose content is *the truth* about God and the human, can therefore also be called an absolute knowledge and therein is barely different from Christ's knowledge, except that this knowledge is the original (ἀρχέτυπος) [archetype], that of faith on the contrary the derived (ἔκτυπος) [ectype]. Thus, Christ, although he is in the human race and belongs to it, yet is higher than the human race and the creation and constitutes its knowledge; he possesses by nature what the rest only have by grace and must receive as a spiritual gift of grace (χάρισμα πνευματικόν). But wherever Christ, as is here the case, although in many respects different from other humans, yet like the human race is ignorant of the truth as it is in itself, and is only the most outstanding hero for pious feeling, which according to real possibility lies in the whole human race, there the human race cannot hear in Christ the voice of an other but only its own voice, only an expression of the principle which lies in the nature of the human race.

What is said here about *faith*, which according to our view cannot take place where one does not see in Christ the objective truth, a revelation of the eternal personality, applies also to *love*. For when Christ—as here has occurred—is only presented as the most outstanding flower of the human race, in loving him the race only loves itself in the same way as it can love itself in other distinguished individuals. But [102] it is necessary that in every love there must be two, who, even though they are each able to be for itself, and although there is a real difference between them, yet enter into union. But in this universal love, where not one or several individuals but *the human race itself* is thought of as a subject which seeks an object for its love, it is necessarily demanded that the object also be a *subject* and in reality be different not only from the single individuals [*de enkelte Individer*] but from the whole race. For only the loving subject can in actuality be loved, only the knowing subject in truth be known, only the thinking subject in truth be thought. Consequently, if Christ's personality, which is the object of love of the human race, is not presented as differing in actuality from this race, then the love lacks its true object, becomes empty, and revolves around itself alone. This is the common error in all pantheism, which does not really differentiate God from the world, Christ from the human race, and which therefore never arrives at a true identity of subject and object. That is to say, it is required that the object, whether that of faith or love, shall also be a subject from which it is separated in actuality. For *real* unity can only be thought of as the sublation of the *real* difference. Inside the limits of the human race every love is only to be called particular, since it is only a love between two or several individuals, which as *individuals* enter reciprocally into a real contrast to each other. But when the human race itself is presented as an individual which seeks an object for its universal love, then this can only be thought of as an absolute individual who differs in actuality from the race. [103]

§ 33.

Concerning the question of the reciprocal relation between the race and the Incarnation, this is described in agreement with the Christian religion as two moments in the same idea, the first and the second creation (καινὴ κτίσις). We encounter here the universal mode of reflecting on the history of the human race. Insofar as the human race carried on a life before Christ, or rather *outside* of fellowship with him, outside the sphere of true religion, it is presented as the first Adam (χοϊκός); but insofar as the human race has taken up life's fellowship with Christ, insofar as it has become the body and he himself its head, it is viewed as the second Adam (πνευματικός [spiritual one]). But since everything is absolutely dependent on God, the first creation is regulated by the second, which as possibility already lies in the former. ("*Kam gleich bei der ersten Schöpfung des Menschengeschlechts nur der unvollkommne Zustand der menschlichen Natur zur Erscheinung: so war doch das Erscheinen des Erlösers ihr auf unzeitliche Weise eingepflanzt."* ["For although at the first creation of the human race only the imperfect state of human nature was manifested, yet eternally the appearance of the Redeemer was already involved in that."])[52] This can surely be said, since Christ's historical revelation, even if humankind had not sinned, yet would have been necessary in order that God could obtain the unity with the creature (cf. the previous quote in Thomas Aquinas § 11), which from the beginning is the goal of the creature. But one must remark that the concept of the creation appears here only nominally, since—as is sufficiently pointed out above—the concept of God's freedom and personality is missing. But where God's freedom is not found, there cannot be talk of a creation but of an origin and birth. For all *creation* goes forth by freedom, all emergence [*Opstaaen*] and *birth* on the contrary by the principle which, just as by [104] the seed, is developed according to a certain inner necessity. On the basis of this we with justice posit the concept of a *birth*, an *evolution* instead of the concept of creation. The two moments through which the entire history of the human race is completed are not moments in God's free revelation but in the development of the human race. Instead of the Creation of the human race we get its birth, instead of God's Providence and Governance we get the necessary development of the human spirit.

This development runs through three stages. The first is that where human self-consciousness has still not awakened to knowledge of sin, where the difference between that which it immediately is and that which it ought to be, between its empirical state and its idea, has still not arisen for consciousness. The second stage is the state of sin, where this consciousness together with the need for reconciliation is awakened in the human. The third is the state of grace or communion with Christ, the Perfecter of the human race, the unity of the finite and the Infinite. These are the necessary forms through which the substantial feeling is developed. The entire history of religions—paganism, Judaism, and Christianity—presents to us the history of this feeling and forms the necessary moments in its development.

Consequently, with the first creation the human steps forth as that which deviates and degenerates from the eternal ideal which constitutes its nature; with the so-called "second creation" the opposites are united, the difference is sublated, and the entire development becomes the self-mediation of the human spirit, the process whereby it becomes self-conscious of its substantial content, whereby that which lies dormant

---

[52] *The Christian Faith*, 368.

as possible becomes actual, whereby the human's eternal essence gains existence. But since everything must here be conceived [105] *subjectively*, so that that development does not become God's own development but that of the human race, we also find here a parallel to Criticism, namely, to Kant's teaching on the reconciliation of the empirical human with the eternal human. There is no thought about any God outside of this process; self-consciousness is mediated not by a God who is different from itself but only by itself. History presents to us the way of the human race but not God's own eternal way.

Transition to the Autonomy of Human Self-Consciousness in the Form of the Absolute Spirit.

§ 34.

Autonomy as understood by the theology of feeling rejects on the one hand all objective authority, as it even appoints *itself* as lord over everything; and on the other hand it admits that *it lacks* absolute knowledge. It teaches that its propositions have universal validity and necessity; but on the other hand this universal validity and necessity is dependent on human particularity, on the pious feeling in the individual. The self-entrusted, pious soul lacks *the revelation of God*, who gives human religion its truth, and such a religion which is tied to the human's [106] individuality cannot receive the name of truly catholic and universal. Thus this autonomy contains its own sublation. For if universal validity and necessity are to be properly deserving of this name, then they must also be posited in a universal and necessary *form*, that is, free of all particularity, as that which reveals only *itself*. It is demanded that these shall be conceived in the form of thought and the concept, by which alone the human is liberated from the particularity of feeling and is raised to the sphere of truth.[53] But when this autonomy, this freedom of the human spirit which does not submit to any objective authority, admits that it does not know

---

[53] Hegel, *Religionsph.*, 1:114 "*Auf dem subjectiven Standpuncte ist die Einheit des Endlichen und Unendlichen noch in die Einseitgleit geseßt, daß sie vom Endlichen selbst geseßt, noch unter der Bestimmung des Endlichen ist, ich, dieser Endliche, bin das Unendliche. Somit ist diese Unendlichkeit selbst die Endlichkeit. Von dieser Affirmation, von dieser Unendlichkeit ist noch zu trennen diese Einzelnhelt meines endlichen Seins, meine unmittelbare Ichheit.*" "From the subjective standpoint the unity of the finite and the Infinite is still posited in onesidedness, for it is posited by the finite itself, still under the determination of the finite; I, this finite, am the Infinite. *Consequently, this infinitude is itself the finitude.* From this affirmation, from this infinitude has yet to be separated this finitude of my finite being, *my immediate I-ness.*"]

anything about God's objective nature which lies beyond the human's self-consciousness, that it is restricted by limits which have not posited themselves, then *eo ipso* [precisely thereby] *the concept of autonomy is sublated*; for this concept is no different from the concept of spontaneity, of that in-every-respect-perfect freedom which does not have anything outside itself that can restrict its power. Autonomy cannot be thought of in its truth except as God's *own* autonomy. Consequently, insofar as self-consciousness is to vindicate its autonomy, this can only happen by the sublating of all human particularity, and the grasping of the human spirit's necessary development as God's *own* development. [107]

Consequently, there takes place a reversal. The thinking [*tænkende*] *I* no longer plays the primary role, but on the contrary this role is played by the *eternal thinking* [*Tænkning*] in its independence from the human spirit, the absolute Idea, which is no different from God, and which unfolds everything from itself as its moments. God passes over into God's other—becomes nature and finite spirit; God returns to Godself in the human spirit under its absolute thought—God becomes the Absolute Spirit. God is threefoldly in the beginning, the middle, and the end, but in a *different shape*. Incidentally, if one comprehends the eternal process, God experiences (through God's alteration from the sphere of the phenomena, from God's being outside Godself, to the return to Godself) the same stages as we have already seen in subjective theology, namely: the natural and immediate standpoint, the standpoint of reflection which involves the sin of finite spirit, and finally the spiritual standpoint. These moments are historically presented in paganism, Judaism, and Christianity. But the difference lies in this, that the history of religions is not so much the history of the human as that of God, the self-mediation of the Absolute Spirit, more God's way than the human's way. Religion is conceived as God's own consciousness of Godself. The finite religions present the idea of God in its own negativity—God in the shape of the finite; the Christian religion presents God revealed as God—God in the shape of the Infinite. This return of God to Godself takes place in the human spirit, under its speculative thought. Here all particularity vanishes in the divine Idea. The human spirit, which is conceived in the shape of the eternal, is not outside the divine Idea, but is the mirror of the divine clarity, or is rather the divine clarity itself. [108]

Since it is not our purpose here to enter further into this system, the remark may be sufficient that neither is this form of autonomy the true. Certainly it thereby has to a great extent advantages over the above-considered subjective theology, that it attributes autonomy to *God* and does not vindicate human reason's authority but the authority of divine reason. But absolute knowledge, which is here talked about, cannot with truth be called God's own knowledge; it cannot be thought of as the primary and original but only as the secondary and derived. This shines forth in the following way: the concept of absolute autonomy coincides with the concept of absolute freedom, which produces everything out of itself. But absolute knowledge—the identity of the absolute Idea and the thinking *I*—such as here finds its expression, cannot be called a *productive* knowledge in an eminent sense, since, although in the universe it only finds its own laws, yet it is different from the *power* which has called forth this universe, and which thus is not any real unity of power and knowledge. The universe originates from the eternal Idea *which is not self-conscious*—the *implicit* God; God first in the human spirit grasps Godself in the shape of absolute knowledge—the *explicit* God. But in this way God's wisdom and omnipotence fall apart from each other. Where power is, there is no knowledge, and where knowledge is, there is no power; it is a blind power and an impotent knowledge. This autonomy is not in actuality entitled to the concept of *aseity*, since that which is the basis for the spirit's *existence*—namely, nature and the outer universe—is not produced by it. But thus neither does this *self*-consciousness actually have itself in its power, since it has not itself posited the basis which is the condition for its [109] *existence*. But then it is precisely the criterion of *the creature* not to have itself posited its own basis ("where were you, when I formed the earth?"), and thus we conclude that that speculative knowledge, even though it contains eternal truths, is yet only the knowledge of the created spirit but not that of the Absolute Spirit, that it is derived from God's absolute knowledge where *power and knowledge go into one (ubi potentia et scientia in unum coincidunt)*. All autonomy which is predicated on a knowledge that is different from omnipotence is only an invented autonomy; just as on the other hand one may also say that the omnipotence which is posited as a knowledge differing from the infinite knowledge is not any true omnipotence, since it does not have itself in its power and operates only blindly. On only *the Creator* alone, who has an absolutely productive knowledge and is absolutely self-conscious of this productivity, can one confer autonomy and autarchy.

We have sought to substantiate that when one vindicates the autonomy of the human spirit, the idea of the Creator is sublated, a pantheism is introduced, which confuses the *homoousia* of God and the world with the *homoousia* of God the Father and God the Son, which instead of the Creation of the world teaches a *cosmogony* and instead of the Incarnation of God's Son teaches a *theogony*. We trust the fundamental features in moral theology and the theology of feeling have here been pointed out. If by this investigation we have succeeded to make a contribution to the elucidation of the position of dogmatic theology in modernity, to clarify the contrast which takes place between the general theological principle in our time and the principle of the Christian religion; to realize that the dogma of God, who is the *author* of human self-consciousness, is the foundation for the true theory of knowledge, and that by this the [110] necessary nexus between theological knowledge and the authority of dogma, the indissoluble bond between knowledge and co-knowledge, is brought about, then perhaps we dare believe ourselves to have undertaken a not unprofitable work.

Mester Eckart.

Et Bidrag

til at oplyse Middelalderens Mystik.

Af

Dr. H. Martensen

Lector i Theologien ved Kjøbenhavns Universitet.

Kjøbenhavn.

Paa Universitetsboghandler Reitzels Forlag.

Trykt hos Directeur Jens Hostrup Schultz,

Kongelig og Universitets = Bogtrykker.

1840.

MEISTER ECKHART

A Study in Speculative Theology

By

Dr. H. Martensen

Lector in Theology at the University of Copenhagen

Copenhagen

At Reitzel's University Book Publishers
Printed under the Direction of Jens Holstrup Schultz
Royal and University Publishers

1840

Preface

The present writing was originally destined to be published as a treatise for the theological doctorate degree at the University of Copenhagen's festival on the occasion of the crowning of Their Majesties King *Christian the Eighth* and Queen *Caroline Amalie*. His Majesty the king had most graciously allowed that the treatise could be written in the Danish language, on the condition that the oral disputation should be held in Latin over Latin theses. In the meantime the theological faculty in Kiel showed me the unanticipated honor of conferring on me the doctorate degree, and it thus became superfluous for me to dispute at the University of Copenhagen. The treatise is hereby given over for the benevolent consideration of scientific readers.

Copenhagen
June 24, 1840

Contents

Introduction

There are few concepts whose representations are at once both so controversial and yet so indeterminate as the concept of mysticism. In the view of the eighteenth century, mysticism is synonymous with irrationality and fanaticism. At a later period something holy was sensed in mysticism, but as something ineffable and beyond reason which conceptual thought could not approach without profanation. The irrational and the suprarational are the categories set against one another here; and yet the opposing parties who employ these concepts have one thing in common: that neither of them explains mysticism or is able to say what it is in actuality and in its ground. If such a thing can be articulated at all, then it will only be as a result of an investigation in which the mystical spirit [*Aand*] is obliged to speak for and give an account of itself, and in this way to answer the question of science and reveal its secret. That this is not as impossible as it may seem is based on the fact that mysticism is more closely related to science, and in particular to philosophy, than the latter has often been willing to admit. Christian mysticism—and this is what specifically is under discussion—is not just [2] a rather remarkable form of piety, not just a peculiar *religious* shoot having its deep roots in disposition [*Gemyt*] and feeling, but is itself a form of speculative theology. Far from being in its intrinsic nature contrary to reason [*Fornuft*], mysticism instead occupies a significant place in the history of religious speculation itself.

The present treatise has as its goal to set forth the spirit of mysticism in one of its major forms: *German mysticism in the fourteenth and fifteenth centuries*. In a religious and philosophical sense this is the richest and most fully developed form of Christian mysticism. It is the first form in which German philosophy appears in history; and it is the first, immediate, yet bold, attempt to sublate the contrast within reflection between faith and knowledge, thereby procuring for spirit an absolute reconciliation and satisfaction. The highest speculative Idea is present here, but only as if its light were just able to break through the window panes of the Middle Age

152

monastery. Philosophical thought is born out of the depths of the religious disposition, but is not yet cut loose to an independent existence in the world. Speculation is still one with religion. They are twins. The one is, immediately, also the other.

In the following, as we subject this remarkable phenomenon of consciousness to a scientific examination, it will of course be neither in order to laud it nor to find fault with it, but simply in order to understand it. Mysticism affords important points of comparison with recent philosophy and theology. It goes without saying, moreover, that what stirred in those times is not simply to be relegated to dead and bygone things, but rather to eternal and present matters of spirit. I [3] have entitled the treatise *Meister Eckhart* not because he is the exclusive object of this study, but because he is the most brilliant figure among the German mystics and the master for the whole school. Mysticism appears in him with the most powerful originality and the others seem to be especially influenced by him. Meister Eckhart is the patriarch of German mysticism. It is therefore no wonder that Hegel, who seems only to have been acquainted with a few of his thoughts, has to such a high degree been attracted by these.

The interest in and appreciation for mysticism has recently been revived from two sides: partly on account of romanticism, and partly on account of philosophy. The romantics were inspired by the flowering of religious contemplation, whose aroma wafted in the crystal clear nights of the Middle Ages. They absorbed an ethereal nourishment from the mystical buoyancy and the inwardness of the cloister and consequently forgot the worldly essence of the present. They felt themselves attracted to those quiet souls for whom God's Spirit was revealed, not in storms and earthquakes, but in the gentle breeze of holy feelings. Such mystical sympathies have often been expressed by poets. Tieck, for example, has quite recently used Tauler in a short story. Also from the standpoint of romanticism, Görres has given a scientific examination of mysticism in his introduction to the Diepenbrock edition of the German mystic Suso.[1] He has depicted mysticism with great historical acumen as that which, in its manifold ramifications, was interwoven throughout the whole of the Middle Ages. However, his elegant, poetic presentation, though it possesses all the merits [4] his standpoint allows, also suffers from its defects. The concept [*Begrebet*] is hidden under a mass of representations [*Forestillinger*] in the obscure twilight of feeling. Görres stands in the service of the Middle Ages and is himself gripped, indeed prejudiced, in favor of mysticism, and therefore he lacks the free, clear vision of philosophical thought. The philosophical element is grasped only superficially in his

---

[1] *Susos Leben und Schriften*, with introduction by J. Görres, Diepenbrock, Regensburg, 1837.

examination and consequently the organizing theme becomes the ecstasies, visions, apparitions and revelations.[2] Such a point of view remains onesiddly partial to a single aspect of mystical conscious life, i.e., its sensuous-spiritual condition.

Above all, romanticism is committed to gazing at mysticism merely as a mysterious phenomenon. The flight of the heavenly Psyche, who moves in enigmatic regions, cannot be comprehended by the concept—its delicate wingdust does not tolerate the touch of thought. She is an object only for quiet wonder and love. Yet if it were actually the case that beauty could not bear to be seen by the light of philosophical thought, then perhaps this would be a merely mortal Psyche. One could then comfort oneself with the thought that, though the perishable part may have been destroyed, nevertheless the better and imperishable half will have been saved. Yet this is not the case. The concept does not stand at enmity with finitude when this is an individual reflection of thought. The concept conserves the individuality whole, without any dispersal or dismemberment, because individuality as such [5] is the characteristic, indispensable form of the Idea. Thus, if it is the endeavor of philosophical thought to secure for every actual spirit eternal immortality, then this applies also to mysticism, because in the mystical psyche philosophical thought recognizes itself as a child. Schelling and Hegel have born this in mind and demanded that philosophical thought rejuvenate itself in the immediate knowledge of God and divine things found in mysticism.

If mysticism is seen as a link in the development of philosophy, then the fourteenth and fifteenth centuries must be seen as the most important period of the Middle Ages. In his review of the new edition of Suso,[3] Rosenkranz has succinctly and aptly characterized this period as the first epoch of German philosophy. He calls this epoch 'mysticism' because it makes knowledge of truth dependent upon an immediate intuition [*Anskuelse*]. Rosenkranz says: "Though the mystics sometimes diverge from one another in particular places when they state what the truth is, they nevertheless agree upon the same path by which they arrive at their *certainty*: practical resignation and self-denial, which mediate theoretical freedom. Theoretical freedom, i.e., conceptual knowledge of God, is essentially *a knowledge by means of God, God's own self, in the one knowing*."[4] Though this quotation provides a merely orientating preconception, it nevertheless contains, in a formal sense, what is correct: namely, that mystical vision is always conditioned by a determinate type of the religious life. [6]

---

[2] This tendency is seen especially in his larger work on mysticism, which is a large catalogue of mystical states; cf. his *Die Christliche Mystik*, Regensburg, 1836–43.

[3] This can be found inserted in his text, *Zur Geschichte der deutschen Litteratur*, Königsberg 1836, under the title "Die Deutsche Mystik."

[4] Ibid., 39.

progressive development

Mysticism does not exist in the form of a philosophical system, but expresses itself only in sermons and edifying treatises. It is an edifying philosophy: a popular religious philosophy in the best sense of the word. Not that, in mysticism, the reflective understanding [*Forstand*] comments upon Christian representations whose central content it is unable to express; no, the edifying contains a speculative point at its core. The addresses are full of penetrating statements which, in a manner just as naive as paradoxical, express the Idea. Paradox—a form also found in the Bible—appears here as an immediate form of the speculative; it strikingly expresses truth's contrast to everyday consciousness, and by means of a divine foolishness it liberates the understanding from its false wisdom. There is no progressive scientific development. Not uncommonly the speculative appears by means of a spiritual explosion in which the soul is immediately illuminated and unknown regions are opened up. Because no genuine development occurs, mystical contemplation has no great variation. There are only a few substantial thoughts which are continually born anew in the soul; but these are so intensive and fruitful that they may well be considered first principles—στοιχεῖα—for a philosophical system.

Concerning the external history of these mystics only a little is known. Their lives were hidden in God. Görres calls Eckhart an almost Christian-mythical, fog-enshrouded figure; and not inappropriately. For only his inner life is known, while his actual historical life is enveloped in darkness. His sayings are often quoted by his disciples with deep respect. He seems to stand before them like a hero of contemplation [7] and he reveals himself to them sometimes even in visions. The year of his birth, just as the year of his death, is unknown. We do know, however, that he lived at the end of the thirteenth and the beginning of the fourteenth century. He was a Dominican, was supposed to have studied in Paris, and under Pope Boniface VIII received his doctorate in Rome. It is reported that for a time he was the provincial of an order in Saxony and later the general vicar in Bohemia; moreover, that he was distinguished by his strict morality and observance of discipline. His activity as a mystic seems especially to have been in Strassburg and Cologne, in the latter of which he probably lived out his final days. After his death his teachings were condemned by the Avignon Pope John XXII (died, 1329).[5] According to the papal bull, Eckhart before his death was supposed to have retracted his teachings and returned to the Catholic faith. Later we shall discuss this point. The suspicion of heresy which rested upon Eckhart seems to have had the effect that he was pushed into the background behind his disciple,

---

[5] Concerning this report cf. The Dominican Annals of Eckhart and Quetis' *Scriptores ordinis prædicatorum* Par., 1719, fol. T. I page 507; also see Carl Schmidt's investigation in *Allmanns und Umbreits theologische Studien und Critiken*, 1839, 3rd edition.

the Dominican Johannes Tauler, renowned preacher in Strassburg (died 1361). Normally one considers Tauler to be the school's greatest figure. Another disciple of Eckhart was the Dominican Henry Suso (died 1365) from Schwaben who had been named Amandus on account of his burning love for eternal wisdom. Spiritually akin to these is Johannes Ruysbroock (died 1381), [8] prior in Grünthal near Brussells. The unknown author of the *Theologia Germanica* of the fifteenth century seems to stand in a relationship to Eckhart through Tauler. These men are to us the most distinguished representatives of German mysticism. Though different individuals, they reflect the same spirit; their writings are but different representations of the same system (if it is even appropriate here to use that word).[6]

The condition of those times was such that, in many ways, spiritual persons were forced to retire into themselves. The old system had begun to tremble in its foundations. In the political as in the ecclesiastical realm a great confusion reigned. The Babylonian exile of the papacy and its scandalous controversies with state powers is evidence that Catholicism had culminated. Dante (died 1321) held judgment day over Catholicism in his *Divine Comedy*. Reforming tendencies, protest and opposition were felt everywhere, even though nobody knew what they wanted, nor could they espy an exit from the confusion. An indeterminate longing for freedom resonated through the whole period. Nations began to assert their spiritual individuality, native languages were revived, national characters began to express themselves in their own tongue. The mystics had a tremendous importance in the development of language, in this liberation from the dominance of Latin, which was abstract and levelling of all individuality. The [9] deepest root words of German appeared in their discourses and writings. Justly are the mystics called the poets of prose.

Their contemplative spiritual outlook must have been powerfully advanced because of the times. The old order had begun to collapse, but history's rebirth was still distant. What belonged to spiritual persons was only the past and the unknown future; they lacked an actual present time, an actual *præsens*, because everything actual was merely fermenting transition. It was appropriate, then, that these contemplative natures, in order to free themselves from the stress and historical strain of the times, sought to transform time to eternity, to annihilate the dispersed moments of the age in the 'now' of contemplation and so produce an actual presence. Under this generalized tottering they sought in the Idea that harmony

---

[6] The few biographical notes, in and of themselves insignificant, can be looked up in the introduction to the new Frankfurter edition of Tauler's Sermons (1826), in Diepenbrock's recountings in Suso's *Leben und Schriften,* and in Engelhardt's *Richard von St. Victor und Johannes Ruysbroock* (Erlangen, 1838).

and reconciliation which they did not find in actuality. The artistic endeavors of the age in architecture and painting, which in part bloomed in those regions where the mystics had their most important headquarters, i.e., the Rhine valley, especially Cologne and Strassburg, can also be seen in this connection. Spirit seeks to conjure in the world of the imagination what has vanished from life.

The age's lack of satisfaction in actuality, its longing after spiritual reality, manifested itself in its dogmatic problems—which attracted great interest. They concerned the vision of God which occurs in the state of eternal blessedness [*Salighed*]. When eschatological questions and investigations into the life to come are conducted with anxious intensity, it is a sign that the fullness of life has flown from the present. Under Pope John XXII a great dispute arose as to whether the saints who were exempted from purgatory came immediately after their temporal death to view God [10] face to face, or whether this complete vision first took place after the resurrection of the body and the last judgment. The Pope confirmed the latter, but the spirit of the times longed impatiently for complete vision and tried to compel him to the opposite declaration.[7] This succeeded under Benedict XII, his successor, who expressly declared himself to be of the opposite opinion as his predecessor. Many sought to transform these dogmatic problems on the future life into a present certitude. They anticipated future blessedness and identity with God in contemplation. The question of the identity of *thought* with God was thus set in motion. One questioned whether God was merely the object of the beatific vision, or was rather also the beatific vision itself in such a way that the knower became one in essence with the thing known.[8]

Characteristic of this period (and a phenomenon not without connection to mysticism) were the many sects who sought emancipation from the tradition and external cultus of the church. They were filled with a fervent, fanatical enthusiasm for freedom, by a spirituality that aimed at rending external forms and by an unbounded craving after unity with God. For this they came into conflict with the doctrines of the church. The fermenting speculative element came to breakthrough in pantheistic visions. The reigning church could perceive these errors, but could not comprehend their significance. Already in the beginning of [11] the thirteenth century the Parisian theologians Almaric of Bena and David of Dinanto, apparently adherents of John Scotus Eriugena's system, were condemned by the Council of Paris (1209) because they taught that God was all, and all was God, that God was the essence of creatures, and that everything

---

[7] *Münscher Dogmengeschichte*, 3rd edition, 309.

[8] Gerson deals with this question in detail in his *epistola ad fratrem Bartholomeum Carthusiensem*.

ought to return to God and remain in God as one single individual. The principle of their system was indicated by the following: "*Quod deus sit Esse Formale omnium* [that God is the formal Essence of everything]." They were charged with not having ascribed to Christ the appellation 'God-human' [*Gud-Menneske*] in any other sense than one would ascribe it to every person, for every spiritual person was a God-human. Concerning holy communion they taught that the presence of Christ in the bread and wine did not first occur by means of the consecration, but that Christ was no less present in all bread and wine than he was in the Eucharist. They interpreted the dogma of transubstantiation as an emblem of the divine presence in the whole of nature. For God could only be seen in creation, and creation and God were one.[9] The Council of Paris charged them further with forsaking faith and hope and bragging that their knowledge was enough for them. They asserted that knowledge was itself Paradise. They interpreted the doctrine of the resurrection of the dead not as something futural, but considered themselves to be resurrected ones.[10] The kingdom of the Father had [12] been in the first world epoch; this was supplanted by the kingdom of the Son, which superseded the Mosaic law and introduced a more spiritual law; the kingdom of the Spirit, they thought, had appeared with them and their adherents. Every external law and cultus was to be abolished; the sacraments were declared to be superfluous, for the Spirit alone was to rule.

A similar construction of world history appeared in the apocalyptic visions expressed in the same century by the Franciscan's "Eternal Gospel." In this a new order of things was heralded—and a stinging polemic was conducted against the pope and the condition of the church. Almaric's school could count many disciples. The persecutions levelled against this sect only contributed to its further spread, and in the course of the thirteenth century pantheistic currents could be noticed throughout Christendom. The adherents of this sect, who gradually became more learned and moderated, are normally called the 'Brothers and Sisters of the Free Spirit.' Toward the close of the thirteenth century they were supposed to have concentrated in large number along the Rhine—hence, at the same time and in the same region that Eckhart lived. In several places in the writings of the mystics we encounter references to them. Their pantheistic spiritualism seemed to many to have manifested itself in a false antinomianism which not only placed itself beyond the church's precepts, but also beyond the moral law [*Sædelighedsloven*]. Religious genius pro-

---

[9] Cf. Gieseler's *Kirchengeschichte*, vol. 2, 409; Möhler's *Neue Untersuchungen der Lehrgegensäße zwischen den Katolischen und Protestanten*, excursis on Almaric of Bena, 435.

[10] 'Ceaser haisterbach' in Möhler, *Neue Untersuchungen*, 443.

claimed the emancipation of the flesh, because spirit was not bound by anything external.[11]

Meister Eckhart is often brought into connection with this sect. Pope John XXII, who [13] was embroiled not only in political but also in theological and religious controversies his whole life, and who did not avoid the charge of heresy himself, issued a bull of condemnation against the Brothers of the Free Spirit in 1330.[12] The year before he had condemned twenty-six propositions of Eckhart. Since the teachings which he condemned from the Brothers of Free Spirit can almost be correlated with those he condemned from Eckhart,[13] it seems he considered them from the same point of view. Historians have followed his opinion and combined Eckhart with this sect,[14] but a closer familiarity with Eckhart himself shows this to have been unwarranted. He ought to be placed together with Tauler.[15] If we compare the papal bull with what we know of Eckhart's writings, we certainly find many of the pantheistic propositions which the pope ascribes to him,[16] but no trace of the [14] immoral antinomianism which the papal bull alleged against him. Moreover, the indicated pantheistic propositions are torn out of the whole context in which they can be seen to have originated in a *unique* way of thinking and spiritual tendency—the same one we encounter in those mystics not accused of sectarianism. Since the experience of modernity shows adequately enough how labels like 'pantheism,' 'nationalism,' 'liberalism,' etc., are used popularly to cram the most differentiated things in under the same rubric without regard for *essential differences*—i.e., a thing's genuine nature—it occurs to me that it is not improbable that the appellation, 'Brothers of the Free Spirit,' was used regularly in those times as a generic name with which one could paint the most differentiated phenomena with a single brush (the same way 'idealist' and 'pantheist' are used today). None will find it unreasonable that the pope, whose concern was not to initiate himself into unusual spiritual differentiations and who

---

[11] Gieseler, 627. Cf. ME, 80.

[12] Ibid., 629.

[13] The bull against Eckhart is quoted in *Raynaldus ad annum*, 1329; the most important parts are reported in Gieseler and Schmidt. [Cf. also ME, 71f.]

[14] Cf. Müncher, Gieseler.

[15] The most recent contribution by Schmidt acknowledges this, even though the treatise is ambiguous and indecisive since it allows the possibility that Eckhart at least *secretly* belonged to the sect. Cf. *Stud. u. Crit.* 1839, 667.

[16] Of these we set forth only article 26: *Omnes creaturæ sunt unum purum nihil; non dico quod sint quid modicum vel aliquid, sed quod sint unum purum nihil.* [All creatures are one pure nothing; I do not say that they are a little something or anything, but that they are pure nothing]; and article 22: *Pater generat me suum filium, quiequid deus operatur hoc est unum, propter hoc generat ipse me suum filium sine omni distinctione.* [The Father gives birth to me his son; everything that God performs is one; therefore he gives birth to me, his son, without any distinction.]

stuck to individual "results," did not see anything different in Eckhart than he had seen in the above mentioned sect. But science cannot remain content with this papal opinion.

Certainly Eckhart and his spiritual kin were idealists, 'Sons of the Free Spirit'; and naturally they were not unmoved by the spiritual movements around them. But Eckhart's mysticism must be thought in terms of its own independent category, because it is a new, original point of development. It is not the pantheism of Almaric, fashioned after Eriugena; nor does it contain his opposition to the ecclesiastical cultus. There is no apocalyptic, religious-political polemic against the established state of things—as, for example, in the spiritualistic Franciscans. Just as little is [15] there an immoral, fanatical antinomianism which blends together flesh and spirit. Eckhart's antinomianism and pantheism require their own standard of measure. However many obscurities rest upon the sects of this time and their multiple ramifications, they all seem to have had it in common that they formally broke from the established church; they had an outwardly directed activity which more or less had as its goal the introduction of a new state of affairs. Their presence was not uncommonly oppositional, tumultuous, and offensive. Yet such a tendency to opposition, such a combative appearance on the stage of actuality, lies outside the nature of authentic mysticism, which retires into the inward regions and lives a quiet life in the spirit. It lies in its nature to be absolutely satisfied within itself, to produce the presence of reconciliation which is not dependent upon any external power or condition; to be the point of blessedness in the midst of confusion. It does not place itself in a polemical relationship to the established church and its teachings, but seeks rather the spiritual comprehension and appropriation of them. To the extent that it comes into conflict with the church—which it undeniably does—this is unconscious. It is only from this standpoint that we can account for the fact that, shortly before his death, Eckhart was supposed to have retracted his teachings. Since he did not want to remove himself from the church, he very likely retracted those propositions only in the sense in which they could be set in a hostile relation towards the church. But it is inconceivable that, in his inmost being, he could ever have relinquished the convictions which had absorbed his whole spiritual life; [16] or that he himself did not think his teachings could be aligned with the doctrines of the church. However improbable this latter may seem in-and-of-itself, a closer familiarity with mystical consciousness (see below) will render this altogether explicable.

The writings of Eckhart known to us are sermons, some of which were given to the people, some of which were given as lectures in the monastery. [However], the bearing of the mystics is such that a large number of texts are not required in order to discern their whole conception [*Anskuelse*]. They have their system *in nuce* [in brief] and express the whole thing all at once. Each time the mystic appears in the discourse or in the text it is *omnia sua secum portans* [everything delivered with the single one]. Even if much has been lost, one can be certain nothing is lacking. [18]

In order to lead the reader into the heart of the matter, I have excerpted some selections from Eckhart's sermons, which are only now beginning to be recalled from the obscurity in which they have so long lain.[17] An initial familiarity with the fundamental tone of mysticism, with its diction and manner of expression—here more than elsewhere inseparable from its thought—will also serve as an appropriate transition to the main goal of this treatise: the presentation of the mystical tendency as a whole, developed through its different moments. What is excerpted here from the mystical master are only thoughts and aphorisms whose internal coherence is not made explicit, even though it is everywhere present. I have striven to combine selection and presentation in such a way that the thoughtful reader will be able to discover a deeper coherence and to discern in these quotations something more than scattered and random thoughts. The quotations which contradict the ones found here will be evaluated in what follows.

The objection which must be feared—not so much against this brief resume of Eckhart, which I have simply translated and arranged, but against the whole following explication—is that the object, by being thematized in the service of a definite philosophical interest, [19] will not be grasped in its purity; that a subjective consideration necessarily imposes itself here; that a great deal of meaning will be added to the text which it does not possess in-and-of-itself, but rather belongs to the presenter's own system, etc. This can always be said whenever what matters is to achieve a spiritual outlook on whatever object. And to this it must always be answered: the matter of the text of course cannot show itself differently than it is seen. There are two ways one can go about thematizing a historical object: one can limit oneself to taking it as a bare fact, to gathering

---

[17] [*Trans. note:* I have excised a page of text in which Martensen comments on the now obsolete volume from which he has excerpted the quotations from Eckhart's sermons to follow. Not only did Martensen not have access to a critical edition of Eckhart's sermons, but, due to the shadow of heresy which still clung to Eckhart's name, his only access to Eckhart's sermons was from a 1521 Basel edition of *Johannes Tauler's* sermons. Martensen notes that, at the time of his writing, the Eckhart selections found in the Basel edition had disappeared from the more recent editions of Tauler's works. Fortunately, he writes, the volume containing Eckhart's sermons could be had at the Royal Library in Copenhagen.

The critical edition of Eckhart's writings and sermons was begun in 1934 by the *Deutsche Forschungsgemeinschaft* under the direction of Josef Quint (German works) and Joseph Koch (Latin works).]

and sifting the material, but in such a way that one refrains from all actual spiritual contact with it in order better to conserve it as a fact. This is useful preliminary work. Its results are correct, but they lack truth. Truth, or the essence of the object, is nothing factical. It is not immediately manifest in empirical data, for the historical material is not the matter itself. Essence is thought and it manifests itself only for a thinking conception in which the object ceases to be something material. The question then becomes whether the philosophical method followed and the way in which it is employed is such that, by means of a knowledge of the truth, one does not place oneself in a skewed *relation* to the object. Empirical history can only have a voice to the extent that it can point out factual inaccuracies. But even the refutation of a philosophical comprehension of a historical object can only take place by means of a different kind of philosophical comprehension: one which develops itself out of the center point of a system and validates an opposite fundamental intuition. [20] Whether this comprehension, already indirectly present in the presentation and arrangement of these quotations, is the true one, this can only be tested by the subsequent development of the *concept* of mysticism.

Excerpts from Meister Eckhart's Sermons[18]

When I preach, I am accustomed to speak about detachment from the world and how a human being can become independent of himself or herself and all things. Also, how we ought to be formed according to the one simple good and rightly consider the soul's great nobility and the unspeakable clarity of the divine nature.[19]

―――――――――

Everything rests only in its origin, from which it is born. Throw a stone into the air and it will not rest until it has again returned to the earth. Why? The earth is its native land; in the air it is a foreigner. The place where I am born is the Godhead [*Guddommen*]. The Godhead is the land of my birth. Do I have a father in the Godhead? Not only do I have a father there, but there I have myself. Before I became I, I was born in the Godhead.[20]

―――――――――

The closer a thing is to its origin, the younger it is; the further from its origin, the older it is. Therefore everything temporal must grow old and

―――――――――

[18] [*Trans. note:* All of the excerpts to follow have been translated by Martensen from the Middle High German into Danish, from which I have translated them. This requires some comment. The quotations Martensen renders are not strict citations from the Middle High German. Most are collages of texts from disparate sermons—occasionally, for example, Martensen draws from *three* different sermons to weave together a single short excerpt. The quotations are carefully selected and meant to illuminate each other. Martensen explains his rationale for selection and translation in this way: "In order to avoid tiresome tautologies I have sometimes had to combine scattered quotations which reciprocally explain each other since they express the same thought from different sides. In the translation of the Middle High German text I have stayed as close as possible to the original wording. Yet it lies in the nature of translation that, in order to render the thought with greater fidelity, I have sometimes had to choose a different expression." Should the reader desire to check the quotations against the Middle High German, I have made reference whenever possible to the critical edition of Eckhart's sermons (*Meister Eckhart: Werke I, II*; Bibliothek des Mittelalters, vols. 20, 21; edited and translated into German by Nicholas Largier, Deutsche Klassiker Verlag, 1993; these volumes are based on Quint's text). I have also made reference to any existing English translations.]

[19] Sermon 53; *Werke* I, 564f; ME, 203.

[20] Sermon 60; *Werke* I, 636f.

die. According to my temporal birth I shall die; according to my eternal birth I shall live eternally. The child in the womb is [21] old enough to die; but I will be saddened if tomorrow I have not grown younger than I am today.[21]

What is truth? Truth is so noble that if God were to turn away from the truth, then I would remain with the truth and let go God. For God is the truth, and everything in time, everything which God has once created, is not the truth.[22]

What is eternity? Eternity is a present now which knows nothing of time. A day which passed one thousand years ago is no further from eternity than this hour in which I am standing here; a day one thousand years in the future is no further from eternity than the hour in which I am now speaking. When the will looks away from itself and from everything created and turns toward its origin, then it stands in the present now of eternity; and in this moment a person can recover all the time they have wasted and lost in the world.[23]

In the fullness of time God sends the son into the soul. What is the fullness of time? It is where time is not. Whoever, in the midst of time, has set their heart on the eternal, in him or her is the fullness of time.[24]

What is freedom? Free is that which is not bound by another. God is not bound by anything; God hovers within Godself and is free from all things. Freedom also belongs to lordship, that one possesses many and beautiful things. [22] Now God is the good in all things. Therefore God possesses God's own self in all things. For all that God has, God *is*.[25]

None is good but one, that is God. What is good? That which makes itself common and communicates its essence to others. We call a good person one who is useful and who has something to communicate to

[21] Sermons 42, 43; *Werke* I, 453, 463.
[22] Sermon 26; *Werke* I, 294.
[23] Sermon 26; *Werke* I, 294.
[24] Sermon 4: *Werke* I, 56; EPT, 251.
[25] Possibly from Sermon 44: *Werke* I, 468f.

others. God is the most *common* [*Almindeligste*] essence which communicates itself to all things. Other things do not give themselves. The sun gives its rays but remains where it is. God gives Godself in all God's gifts. If God did not communicate Godself, nor make Godself common, then God would not be God. In everything created there is something of God, but in the soul God is divine.[26]

All things in time have a *why*. But if one were to ask a good person, why do you love God? he or she would answer: 'for God's sake.' Why do you love the truth? 'For the truth's sake.' Why do you love justice? 'For justice's sake.' Why do you live? 'That I don't know, but I like to live!'[27]

If you are to seek God in truth, you must be without all *why*. If you seek God for your own use or for the sake of your salvation, then you are not seeking God in truth. Some people want to see God with the same eyes as they see a cow (which they love for the sake of the milk and the cheese and for its use to them). In this way such people love God for [23] the sake of outward wealth and inward comfort; they do not love God with the right love and seek only themselves and their own profit.[28]

If you seek God and something else besides God, then you will not find God; but if you seek God *alone*, then you will find God and the whole world along with God.[29]

Simple people think that they should see God in such a way that God stands yonder, while they stand here. It isn't like that. God and I are one in an act of knowing. God's essence is God's act of knowing. It is God who causes me to know; therefore God's knowing is my knowing.[30]

People often say to me: 'Pray to God for me!' Then I think: why are you coming out? Why do you not stay in yourself and hold on to your own good? After all, you carry all truth essentially within you![31]

---

[26] Sermon 9: *Werke* I, 108; EPT 257; Sermon 73: *Werke* II, 94.
[27] Sermon 26: *Werke* I, 296.
[28] Ibid.; Sermon 16b: *Werke* I, 194; EPT, 278.
[29] Sermon 26: *Werke* I, 296.
[30] Sermon 76: *Werke* II, 130; EPT, 328.
[31] Sermon 5b: *Werke* I, 74; ME, 184.

Where nature ends, there God begins. God desires nothing more of you than that you should leave yourself according to your creatureliness and let God be God in you. The smallest created image which forms itself in your soul is as great as God. Why? It comes between you and the whole of God. When the image comes in, God departs with all God's divinity. But when the image leaves, then God enters. God desires for you to go out of yourself according to your creatureliness so much that it is as if God's own [24] blessedness [*Salighed*] depended on it. Dear person! What does it harm you to allow God to be God in you?[32]

If someone should ask me finally to say what the Creator meant by creating all things, I would answer: rest. If someone asked me a second time what all creatures seek in their natural inclination and desire, I would again answer: rest. If someone asked me a third time what the soul seeks in all of its paths, I would again answer: rest. The vision of the divine nature draws the whole power and desire of the soul to itself. God savors this so well, it is so pleasant for God, that the whole divine nature is turned towards it. In the same degree to which the soul rests in God, to that same degree God rests in the soul. If the soul rests only partly in God, then God rests only partly in the soul. If the soul rests completely in God, then God rests completely in the soul. In the pure soul God finds a perfect reflection of God's own self—there God rests in the soul, and the soul in God. Whoever wants to bring God to rest in the soul wants to strip God of God's divinity; for God seeks rest in all things, and the divine nature is rest.[33]

Every going-forth is for the sake of the return. Every beginning is for the sake of the end. God does not seek rest where God is the beginning of essences, but where God is the goal and end of all essences. Not that these essences should become nothing, but that they should be perfected according to their highest perfection. What is the last end and goal? [25] It is the hidden darkness of the eternal divinity. This is unknown and will never be known.[34]

All creatures strive after becoming like God. If God were not in all things, nature would have neither activity nor desire. But nature secretly

[32] Sermon 5b: *Werke* I, 72; ME, 184.
[33] Sermon 60: *Werke* I, 636.
[34] Sermon 22: *Werke* I, 264; ME, 196.

seeks God. Whether it will or no, whether it knows it or not, it always intends only God in all its desiring. No matter how thirsty a person would be, he or she would not desire something to drink if there wasn't something of God in it.[35]

My outward person tastes all creatures as creatures: wine as wine, bread as bread. My inward person tastes all as God's gifts. But in all God's gifts God gives only Godself.[36]

God loves Godself, God's essence and God's divinity. In the love with which God loves God's own self, God loves all creatures; not as creatures, but as God. Now I ask that you pay attention. I will speak in a way I have never spoken: God enjoys Godself, and in this enjoyment God enjoys all creatures—not as creatures, but creatures as God.[37]

God loves nothing outside of Godself. God consumes all God's love within God's own self. None should be dismayed that I am [26] speaking this way. It is the best thing for us; and our highest blessedness lies in this.[38]

Saint Paul says: 'God's love is shed abroad in our hearts.' Since God has given us God's love, God has also given us the Holy Spirit. Thus we love with the divine love with which God loves God's own self. If there were not such love, there would not be the Holy Spirit.[39]

Insofar as a person denies himself or herself for the sake of God and becomes one with God, that person is more God than creature. When the person is freed from himself or herself and lives entirely in God alone, that person is the same by grace what God is by nature; and God knows that there is no difference between God's own self and this person. I have

---

[35] Sermon 69: *Werke* II, 68; EPT, 313.

[36] [*Trans. note:* The authenticity of this sermon is uncertain. Cf. Joseph Quint's *Neue Handschriftenfunde Meister Eckharts* (Kolhammer, 1940); also, *Meister Eckhart: A Modern Translation*, by Raymond Bernard Blakney, Harper Collins, 1941, 224f.]

[37] Ibid.

[38] Sermon 73: *Werke* II, 96.

[39] Sermon 27: *Werke* I, 310.

said: by grace. For God is, and this person is. Thus God is good by nature, the person is good by grace.[40]

I tell you on account of the eternal and everlasting truth that in every person who has annihilated himself or herself before God, God must pour out Godself so richly, so completely and thoroughly, that in God's life and essence, in God's nature and divinity, nothing is kept back. God must with great fecundity pour out everything.[41]

It is a certain truth that it is so necessary for God to seek us, that God's own divinity depends on this. God [27] can as little avoid us as we can avoid God. If we can turn from God, God is nevertheless unable to turn from us. Therefore I will not pray to God that God shall give me something, nor shall I give thanks for what God has already given me, but I will pray to God for God to make me worthy to receive God; and I will praise God because God's nature is such that God *must* give good gifts.[42]

Leibnitz

I do not thank God because God loves me; for God cannot do otherwise, whether God will it or no. I thank God that it is impossible for God to forsake God's goodness.[43]

* * *

With great fecundity the Father speaks forth his own nature in the eternal Word. But the Word is not a work of his will or purpose. Whether he will it or not, he must incessantly speak forth and give birth to this Word. In this the Father speaks forth my soul and your soul. The Father gives birth to the Son in the soul in the same way as he births him in eternity—not differently. The Father gives birth to the Son incessantly, and I say more: the Father gives birth to me as his son. Indeed, in the innermost ground he gives birth to me as his essence and nature; I well-up in the Holy Spirit. There is there one life, one essence and one deed.[44]

---

[40] Possibly sermon 41: *Werke* I, 436f.
[41] Sermon 48: *Werke* I, 504; ME, 197.
[42] Sermon 26: *Werke* I, 302.
[43] Sermon 73: *Werke* II, 96.
[44] Sermon 6: *Werke* I, 82; ME, 187.

It is the Father's essence to give birth to the Son; it is the Son's essence to be born and *that I am born in him*. Likewise, it is the Spirit's essence that I am burned up in it and transformed into pure love.[45] [28]

When the will is unified in such a way that it has become a singular one, then the heavenly Father gives birth to the Son both in himself and in me. Why in himself and in me? Because I am one with him; he is not able to exclude me. And therefore the Holy Spirit proceeds just as much from me as from God. Why? I am in God. If the Holy Spirit does not proceed from me, then neither does it proceed from God.[46]

An authority says: God has become human, therefore the human race has obtained an exalted worth and we ought to rejoice that Christ, our brother, has ascended over the choirs of angels and sits at the right hand of the Father. This authority has spoken well, and yet I don't think much of it. What would it help me if I had a brother who was a rich man if I were a poor man? What would it help me if I had a brother who was a wise man if I were a fool? I will say something which goes deeper: God has not simply become human, but has taken on human *nature*.[47]

The authorities normally say that all persons are just as noble according to nature. But I say that all the good which Mary and the saints and Christ had according to their humanity belongs to me in the selfsame nature. Now you could ask: if in this nature I possess everything which Christ was able to achieve according to his humanity, then why do we listen to and appraise Christ as our God? This is because he has been God's tidings to us and has shown us the way to our blessedness. But the same blessedness which he brought to us belonged to us and was our own.[48] [29]

Our Lord said: 'Everything which I have heard from my Father, I reveal to you.' Now I am astonished that some, who are supposed to be great masters, here allow themselves to be satisfied with so little. They explain it in this way: that he has, along the way, revealed just as much as

---

[45] Sermon 39: *Werke* I, 426; EPT, 298.
[46] Sermon 25: *Werke* I, 288.
[47] Sermon 5b: *Werke* I, 66; ME, 182.
[48] Sermon 5b: *Werke* I, 66; ME, 182.

is necessary for our salvation. I don't think this is true. Everything the Father has and is, the abyss of his essence and his nature, he pours out in the Son. This is what the Son hears from the Father; and he reveals to us that *we* are the very same Son. God has become a human being so that I can become God. God has died so that I can die away from the world and everything created.[49]

Human nature [*Menneskeheden*] and the human person [*Menneske*] are not the same. Human nature is in itself so noble that it is like the angels and is related to divinity. The highest unity with the Father which Christ ever possessed would be possible for me to acquire if I could lay aside my separateness and put on human nature.[50]

The Father gives birth to his Son in the just person. The whole virtue of justice and all the works which originate in justice are nothing other than the Son being born of the Father. The Father does not rest until the Son is born in me; he drives and compels me incessantly to birth him the Son. Enlightened people ought to know this, simple people ought to believe it.[51] [30]

A just person serves neither God nor creatures; he or she is free. And the closer he or she is to justice, the more he or she is freedom itself. Everything created is unfree. Only the person who has destroyed everything created is just, for there is nothing of truth in the created.[52]

An authority says: The soul which loves God loves God under the form of goodness. But I say that essence is more than goodness. For if there were no essence, there would be no goodness; and it is only to the degree that goodness has essence in it that it is good. Moreover, essence is purer than goodness. That God is good does not make me blessed; and I would never desire for God to make me blessed by means of God's goodness. For perhaps God does not desire for me to be blessed. I am only

---

[49] Sermon 29: *Werke* I, 332.
[50] Sermon 25: *Werke* I, 290.
[51] Sermon 39: *Werke* I, 422.
[52] Sermon 28: *Werke* I, 320.

blessed because God is a rational essence [*fornuftigt Væsen*] and because I know this.[53]

God has many names, but the most outstanding name for God is "essence." Everything fragile and transitory is a scrap of essence. To the extent that our life is an essence it is in God. Any life, be it ever so sick or feeble, to the extent that you take it as essence is more noble than anything which has ever lived. If you consider a flower according to its essence in God, then this flower is more noble than the whole world.[54]

The will can rest content with God's goodness, but reason [*Fornuft*] finds rest neither in goodness nor in wisdom nor in truth nor in God's own self—to the extent that God is God. [31] It wants God as the marrow from which goodness flows forth, as the seed from which goodness springs forth, as the root from which goodness blossoms. Reason penetrates to the ground from which truth and goodness break forth and takes them originarily (*in principio*), before they even have received their names. Reason desires only the pure God as God is in Godself, when goodness and all names are cast off like robes. Therefore reason does not rest content with Father, Son and Holy Spirit; it penetrates into the Godhead's most inward depths—to the root from which the Son proceeds and the Holy Spirit blossoms forth.[55]

There is a point in the soul which is above its created essence. It is in itself one and simple. It is above all names and knowing; it is a pure nothing. If you could for a moment annihilate yourself, then you would have everything which this is in itself. But as long as you tarry with yourself as with some thing, you no more know what this is than my mouth knows what color is, nor my eye, what taste is. Concerning this I have often spoken in my sermons. Sometimes I have called it a power, sometimes a light, and sometimes a divine spark. It is free from all names and forms, as God is free in God's own self. It is above knowledge and love, and above grace, for grace is bound up with creatureliness. In this power God blossoms forth in all God's divinity and the Spirit blossoms forth in God. In this power the Father gives birth to his only begotten Son as

---

[53] Sermon 9: *Werke* I, 110.
[54] Sermon 8: *Werke* I, 98.
[55] Sermon 69: *Werke* II, 52f.

essentially as he gives birth to him in himself. In this light the Holy Spirit originates.[56] [32]

Saint Paul says: "I am what I am by God's grace." These words are true, and yet grace was not in him. For grace has made it possible for essence to come—and then grace accomplishes its work. But when grace had accomplished its work, then Saint Paul became what he originarily was. There all difference and dissimilarity between God and the human being is laid aside. Therefore I pray to God, that God will free me from God, for *essence* is above God and above all difference.[57]

The more a person turns from himself or herself and from everything created, the more he or she is perfected in the soul's pure light which is above all time and place. This light wants to transcend all creatureliness and desires only the pure God as God is in Godself. Indeed, it is content neither with the Father nor the Son nor the Holy Spirit, nor with the three persons to the extent that each of them subsists in their separate qualities. I will say something which sounds even stranger. I tell you by the eternal and everlasting truth and by my soul, this light rests content only with the superessential essence. It wants to enter the eternal ground from which the persons break forth, the quiet desert where none are home, the silent unity, in which nothing is distinct, the simple stillness, which is immovable in itself, but by which all things are moved.[58]

When I stood in my first cause I had as yet no God. Then I belonged to myself, I wanted nothing, I desired nothing, for I was pure being and conformed [33] myself to the divine truth. What I wanted, I was, and what I was, I wanted. I was free from God and all things. But when I departed from my freedom and took on my created essence, then I got a God. Because before creatures were, God was not God. God was only what God was. When creatures came into being and received their created essence, then God was not God in Godself, but God in creatures. Now we say: to the extent God is God, God is not a perfect final goal for creatures. For if a fly had reason [*Fornuft*] and if this rational creature could seek the abyss of the divine essence, then we must say that God as God would not be enough for a fly. Therefore I ask God that God would lead me out beyond

---

[56] Sermons 28, 2, 48: *Werke* I, 322, 28, 506; ME, 178, 198.
[57] Sermon 52: *Werke* I, 560; ME, 202.
[58] Sermon 48: *Werke* I, 508; ME, 198.

God so that I must take truth and use eternity—where I stood when I wanted what I was and I was what I wanted. When I penetrate into this, then I and God are one. There I neither increase nor decrease; there I am the immovable which moves all.[59]

When I stood in the Godhead's ground and the Godhead's depths and the Godhead's circle and the Godhead's source, none asked me about my will or my doing. When I flowed forth I heard all creatures speaking about God. They asked me: Brother Eckhart, when did you leave home? Then I was home, though I was outside. Why were they speaking only about God and not the Godhead? All that is within the Godhead is one and cannot be spoken of. God and Godhead are not the same. God works and creates; the Godhead works nothing, it is quiet and immovable within itself. When I return to the point I departed from, [34] my entrance is better than my departure, for I bring all creatures with me in my reason. When I enter into the ground and deep and circle and source of the Godhead none question from where I have come, or where I have been—and none have missed me. Here all becoming is laid aside.[60]

* * *

Many learned people could not suffer one to place the soul so near the divine essence and appropriate to it so much likeness to the divinity. This is because they do not know (the soul's fundamental nobility;) for if they knew it in a fundamental way, at several points they would not know where they ought to place the distinction between the soul and God. For my part, I am astonished at and have meditated long upon the marvel whereby it has come about that the soul is not able to utter as powerful a word as the heavenly Father. Some masters say it stems from the fact that what is in God is in God essentially, but is in the soul only by image [*billedligt*]—and therefore the soul can resemble God in its acts. I do not think this saying is true. For if one lays aside everything which is added to the soul, then it is essentially formed after God. Other masters say: what God is, God has from Godself; but what the soul has, it has received—therefore it cannot resemble God in its acts. I oppose this also. For the Son has also received what he is from the Father and works with the same power as the Father, for he and the Father pour out the Holy Spirit with the same power and perfection. This [the reception of what it has from God], cannot be a hindrance to the soul. The soul is hindered for another

---

[59] Sermon 52: *Werke* I, 554, 562; ME, 200, 203.
[60] [Unable to locate reference—trans.]

reason, [35] and with saying this I am more or less content. That is, that the Son has flowed forth from the Father's person and has remained one with him in essence; therefore he is personally and essentially able to do what the Father is able to do. But the soul has flowed forth from the persons and has not remained one with them in essence. Indeed, it has accepted a foreign, another essence which has its origin in the divine essence.[61]

As you love, so you are. You are transformed in what you love. If you love the Earth, then you are earthly; if you love God, then you are divine. Thus, if I love God, then am I God? I do not say that, but I point you to the scriptures where God says: "You are gods and children of the most high."[62]

How ought we to be essentially united with God? This ought to occur in vision, not in essence itself. God's essence cannot become our essence, but ought to be our lives. Therefore Christ says: "To know you, Father, is eternal life"; he does not say, "eternal essence."[63]

The soul is a blessed mirror. Now one will ask whether the essence of the image is most properly in the mirror or in the object from which the image comes? Answer: as long as the mirror stands in front of the object, the image is there. But if the mirror is shattered, then the image disappears.[64] [36]

The eye with which I see God is the same eye with which God sees me. My eye and God's eye are one eye, and there is only one vision, one knowledge, and one love.[65]

When I was coming here today I considered how I would preach sensibly to you in such a way that you could understand me. I thought up a parable, and if you can understand this, you can understand all my preaching. The parable is taken from my eyes and a piece of wood. If I open my eye, it is an eye, if I close my eye, it is still the same eye; and my seeing

---

[61] [Unable to locate reference—trans.]
[62] Sermon 39: *Werke* I, 246f.
[63] Sermon 6: *Werke* I, 84.
[64] Sermon 9: *Werke* I, 112; EPT, 258.
[65] Sermon 12: *Werke* I, 148; EPT, 270.

the wood makes no difference for the wood. Now understand me. If I open my eye and fashion my glance upon the wood then each remains as it is—but in the *actuality of vision* they become one in such a way that one will have to say, in truth, that in the actuality of vision the wood and my eye consist of one essence. If this is true of bodily things, how much more is it true of spiritual things?[66]

I take a basin of water and place a mirror in it and set it in the sun. The sun shines its rays of light into the mirror and yet does not perish. The mirror's reflection is sun in the sun, and yet the mirror remains what it is. Thus it is with God. God in the soul with God's essence and nature and Godhead is still not the soul. The soul's reflection is God in God, and yet the soul remains what it is.[67] [37]

Whoever has understood this sermon, I wish him well. If no one has understood this sermon, I might as well have preached it to the offering box. Whoever has not understood this, let them not worry their hearts over it. As long as a person is not himself or herself like the truth, it is impossible to understand it. For this is a truth not merely thought up, but one which has come from the heart of God without intermediaries.[68]

The Mystical Consciousness

If the reader has received a general and immediate impression from the preceding excerpts of the fundamental tone struck by the mysticism of Meister Eckhart, then this will serve as a point of departure for a more comprehensive examination in which we will draw upon a larger circle of mystical writings. Insofar as we shall not remain stationary with the above quotations, though we ought always to keep these in mind, we shall from now on view Meister Eckhart within the larger connection of the development of mystical consciousness. We shall not merely report on certain individuals, but rather on the form of the mystical consciousness itself which has been awakened and called forth in Eckhart to the largest degree. In this presentation I pay special attention not only to Eckhart but also to Tauler, Suso, and the author of the *Theologia Germanica*. Even though Ruysbroock belongs essentially to this same category, I pay no

---

[66] Sermon 48: *Werke* I, 504f; ME, 197.
[67] [Unable to locate reference—trans.]
[68] Sermon 52: *Werke* I, 562.

special attention to him. The reason for this is his abstruse, often turgid and fantastical mode of presentation. [38] As far as I understand him, he offers no new perspectives, and in purity of expression he is far surpassed by the others.

Since we shall present the mystical consciousness according to its moments it is necessary also that we try to penetrate into the essence of all mysticism and assign German mysticism its place in mysticism's general development.

I. MYSTERY

Acosmism and Atheism
Acosmism and atheism articulate the thought [*Forestilling*] which in reading Meister Eckhart most nearly and immediately presents itself: namely, pantheism. Even though the attentive reader of Eckhart's teachings will easily see, on closer scrutiny, that *here* there is more than there is in Spinoza, I do not doubt that what is most noticeable and dubious about these sermons, in the first instance for the pope, will be so as well for the present reader. However, it is just this dubiousness which separates these sermons from the usual run of edifying writings and secures for Eckhart a place in the theological and philosophical literature. Indeed, this dubiousness is, in a religious sense, the condition for the sermons' more profound worth. It also constitutes the possibility of a deeper insight into the mysteries of Christianity, which are everywhere present in his texts. [39]

Pantheism is the first and immediate form in which the Idea shows itself for thought, i.e., thought which has turned away from traditional ways of thinking and set foot upon speculative ground. It is to be considered the generally speculative in all speculation, philosophy's pure universal which circulates at every point of the philosophical view of life. The spirits of pantheism are, as it were, the fleeting spiritual elements which must coarse through and rejuvenate life's organic forms. Philosophical thought is shipwrecked upon the rock of finitude, it stagnates in the prosaic, unless the refreshing air of pantheism, which is the continuous negation of the prosaic, flows through the system. Pantheism is not just the normal living element of philosophy, but also of religion. If it is true that God is not just figurally, but essentially and actually present in the soul, then there must be a pantheistic element in all religion. A religious devotion and enthusiasm which lacks this element lacks the proper immediacy. For God's immediate presence in the soul is not different from God's substantial presence in which all immediate religious consciousness and certainty has its ground; and God's all-permeating substantiality is the characteristic idea of pantheism. From the fresh well of this speculative and religious enthusiasm the old mystics have drunk deeply. In particular, Eckhart is absolutely engorged and saturated by the thought that it is in the Godhead [*Guddommen*] that we live, move, and have our being. He is not merely ardent over this thought, but has drunk from its well so deeply that one can say about him [40] what is said about Spinoza, yet with even more significance: he was a God-intoxicated man.

Pantheism, we said, is the first thought speculation must state if it is not simply to content itself with representing God's essence, but with actually thinking it. Pantheism is the thought: only God is, an *other* than God does not exist (*præter deum nihil*). God would not be God, that is, the Absolute, if there were an other which limited God. According to the idea of God, God must be one and all; however, this would not be the case if there were something different from God's own self or if there existed something which was, not merely in appearance, but actually, other than God. God cannot stand in relation to something outside of Godself, but only in a relation to God's *own self*.

Filled with the thought of God's absolute substantiality, speculation conceives the bold thought of doing away with the world in order to make a place for God. Thought is not able to step outside of the eternal circle of the divine and must therefore deny the existence of the world in order to assert God's existence. This process of annihilation of the finite is what characterizes pantheism as acosmic and world-denying. Thought shows the reality of the world to be an appearance reality, something which in truth is non-being: a merely phenomenal existence which, by continually disappearing, must itself testify to its own illusory actuality. The existing things of the cosmos are only transitory and accidental. They are the contingent points of departure into the one Substance, merely the necessary appearances without which essence cannot be revealed *as* essence. But the more the finitude and contingency of the world becomes known, the more knowledge absolves itself from every worldly content, [41] the more it is filled with the one permanent reality; the whole world disappears from sight and its colorful lights are extinguished, one after another, by the undimmed clarity of the one eternal light.

From the completed negation of the finite results the absolute evidence of the reality of the Infinite. This is the true meaning of the *via negationis* [way of negation] through which the older theologians wanted to raise thought to the knowledge of God's essence. From the knowledge that all is transitory comes forth the imperturbable certainty concerning the one thing which is not transitory. This *via negationis* is the introduction to all speculative theology; it is the pre-school in which consciousness is weaned in order to contemplate life *sub specie æterni*. Here it is forced to lay aside that vulgar way of thinking which cannot conceive God except in terms of finite and cosmic relations, thereby ignoring God's pure, relation-free being in-and-for-itself. Acosmism is thus the general expres-

\sion for spirit's philosophical and religious liberation from the finite, the first stroke of its wings and its first breath in the ether of the eternal.

The *via negationis* and the acosmism which it contains is the typical foundation for the knowledge of God in mystical theology. This appears with the greatest energy in Meister Eckhart and his spiritual heirs. Mystical theology's most important name for God is Essence [*Væsen*], and an essential intuition [*væsenskue*] is the highest goal of this theology (however, there is only a single Essence which encloses and encompasses everything within itself). Whatever is outside of God's essence is mere appearance and contingency.[69] Here it is not a matter of grasping essence with "images" [*Billeder*], since all images are taken from the creaturely realm, but rather of grasping it by means of pure [42] intelligence. From the manifold [*mangfoldige*], therefore, contemplation must lift itself to the "simple" [*eenfoldige*]; from the imperfectly "fragmented," in which it is sundered in the finite, it must raise itself to the "undivided" and "perfect."

A second category in which mystical theology grasps God is the pure "Nothing." "*Das Nichts*" [nothing] is the opposite of "*Das Ichts*" (*etwas*) [something]. Everything which can be considered "something" is thus finite, limited, has an other outside of itself. Such fragmentariness is called created being. Created being can never be adequate to itself because every "something" correlates with a limit, a cage, a prison. The divine nothing is for the mystics identical with infinite '*Freedom*.' For what is free is that which is not dependent upon an other, what hovers in itself and stands in a relation only to its own self. Thus essence, imagelessness, freedom and pure nothingness are the categories to which the mystics return again and again.

Acosmism therefore forms a complete contrast to a theological thinking which remains at a merely cosmic and human standpoint. For 'cosmic theology,' which thinks only in terms of finite relations, God is the highest object, and yet only one object amongst all other objects—which also can be thought. God is the highest thought, and yet only one thought amongst all the other thoughts which move in the realm of the human *I*. For mystical theology, on the other hand, there exists only one actual object and they know of only one true thought: "Whoever takes the whole world in addition to God," says Meister Eckhart, "takes thereby nothing more than if he had taken God alone; for all creatures are a pure nothing, not a divine nothing, but a creaturely nothing."[70] This acosmism [43] is not the abstract negation of the finite, but its referral to the Infinite. It denies the world to the extent that it is life as finite and temporal exis-

---

[69] Cf. ThG, ch. 1.
[70] Cf. Eckhart, sermon 4: *Werke* I, 46f.

tence, but it validates the world insofar as it is an essence in God: "Whoever forsakes things where they are divided and sundered, finds them again where they are unified and perfected." For all earthly existences are preserved in God as idealities even while they disappear as finite realities. All things are in this nothing in their beginning and their end. This nothing is therefore not abstract, but an infinite fullness of essence, the power of ideality over *everything*. That it is called "Nothing" is only to be understood in relation to every "something" as we ascribe it in a creaturely manner. For that to which one ascribes in this manner, i.e., as a "something," is always in a certain way false and its denial true.[71] Insofar as this theology sees in everything only the One and considers everything *as* the One, it never ventures outside of the eternal circle of the Godhead [*Guddommen*].

The theology which takes finitude as its standpoint asks only what God is in reference to the world; or, more specifically, what God means in a practical sense for the human *I*. It knows the divine essence only in its reflection in worldly things, but not the divine essence itself. It knows of a divine revelation and world governance which [44] does not have God, Godself as its purpose, but only that which is not God. From this standpoint the divine qualities indicate only finite relations through which God can be grasped by the human spirit, but not the eternal Essence's own determinations. All such [finite] standpoints are extinguished in mystical seeing. For mystical contemplation the world places itself as a dark, impenetrable point between thought and God, who is known without any "*intermediaries*."[72] It is only from a lower standpoint of consideration that the world, as a speck of dust in the earthly eye, hinders true vision.

To see God in creaturely things and in God's works is the poorest form of knowledge; it must be called "evening knowledge," since only reflections of light are grasped, while the eternal sun itself is hidden behind the mountains. To see creaturely things in God is a higher form of knowing; it must be called "morning knowledge" because the dark creaturely forms are transfigured and taken up in the dawn breaking forth. But when the divine essence is seen in-and-for-itself without creaturely reflection, then

---

[71] "*Das ist zu verstehen nach allem dem Wesen und Icht, das wir ihm nach creatürlicher Weise zulegen mögen. Denn, was man ihm deß in solcher Weise zulegt, das ist alles in etlicher Weise falsch, und seine Läugnung ist wahr. Und aus dem so möchte man ihm sprechen ein ewiges Nicht.*" ["This is to be understood in relation to all essence and isness we could attribute to God in a creaturely way. For whatever a person could attribute to God in this manner is, in a sense, false, and its negation is true. And thus one could call God an eternal Nothing."] *Susos Leben und Schriften*, 289; cf. also HS, 309.

[72] "*Alle unsere Ledigkeit liegt daran, daß wir Gott erkennen und lieben ohne Mittel der Creaturen.*" ["Indeed, our entire blessedness rests in this, that we know and love God without the mediation of creatures."] Cf. BPS, 185.

thought stands in the absolute identity [with divine Essence], or the "bright noon-day."[73] It is only the human *I* itself which hinders this perfect knowledge. Human beings must therefore die away [*afdøe*] from the *I*, i.e., from their creaturely nothingness. The soul must divest itself of all images, for the smallest creaturely image positioning itself between God and the soul hinders union. The soul must not seek God with reference [45] to this or that, for its own use or for the sake of its salvation [*Salighed*], but must be without a why. Knowledge of the divine Essence must therefore be free from all affect, purely detached. "If you will seek God in truth," Meister Eckhart says, "then you must put aside all joy, all fear, all confidence and all hope. For all of these things are creaturely and hinder the true union. While your thought is turned upon these things, it is not turned towards God."[74] The normal expression for this condition, in which the absolute identity between subject and object, soul and God, can occur, is perfect "poverty," for poverty fastens onto nothing. As the absolute negation of the manifoldness of the creaturely world, perfect poverty is one with perfect independence and "freedom"; but as absolute freedom, the soul is one with the divine "nothing."[75]

Even though it may seem that the mystical standpoint has suspended all relations, and even though its pronouncement on God indicates the highest theoretical interest, mysticism has as its most inward root a *subjective and practical interest*. And even though it downplays the practical standpoint which asks only what God is for human beings, it nevertheless itself asks essentially the same question, but in [46] an infinite way. Mystical theory is mediated by a practical and subjective interest; and it is this which gives mysticism its specific character and establishes its difference from theoretical pantheism. This practical interest is more particularly the individual's concern for his or her salvation [*Salighed*]. This is, as it were, the secret thread which leads the soul along its way through the labyrinth of contemplative thought. Knowledge for the true mystic is not a matter of science but a matter of salvation. Even though the mystic does not seek God for the sake of salvation, but purely for God's own sake, the subjective concern does not vanish. For what is known is simply this: that the soul can find its blessedness only in *absolute identity*, i.e., in a relation

---

[73] Cf. Eckhart, sermon 8: *Werke I*, 96f.

[74] Cf. Eckhart, sermon 69: *Werke II*, 42f.

[75] *"Armuth is eine Gleichheit Gottes. Was ist Gott? Gott ist ein abgeschieden Wesen von allen Creaturen. Ein frei Vermögen. Ein Lauter Würken. Also ist Armuth ein abgeschieden Wesen von allen Creaturen. Was ist abgeschieden? Das an nichts haftet. Armuth haftet an nichts und nichts an ihm."* ["Spiritual poverty is God-likeness. What is God? God is a being detached from all creatures. A free power. A pure act. In the same way spiritual poverty is an essence detached from all creatures. And what is detachment? That which clings to nothing. Spiritual poverty clings to nothing and nothing to it."] Cf. BPS, 53.

between God and humanity, which is essentially an infinite relation between the Godhead and itself.

If one therefore wants to characterize the typical features and essence
of mysticism, one can indicate the following: it is an instruction in the
blessed life; and not just instruction toward this, but its actual praxis and
real enjoyment. Fichte's *Anweisung zum seligen Leben*[76] is perhaps the work
in the most recent literature which, in spirit, physiognomy, and language
has most in common with the old mystics.

Mysticism's historical point of departure is asceticism and the monastic life. The religious disposition [*Gemyt*], dissatisfied with the objective
condition of the world where it sees only sheer vanity, wants to seek
for salvation itself when it does not find the normal ways adequate. Such
a disposition accomplishes a practical acosmism and lays upon itself
poverty, chastity, and obedience; it withdraws itself into its own depths,
there to find the eternal and the holy, which in vain is sought in the
world. But [47] insofar as the soul in quiet loneliness seeks God as the
highest Good, contemplative thought is purified through various stages in
its knowledge of the nature of the good. It is known that the good is not
different from the true and the all-substantial, which is not anything singular, empirical, or concrete. It is known, to speak in mysticism's own language, that the perfect good which the human being shall love, is neither
this nor that, neither *I* nor you, but only the One, which is above all *I*
and you, above every here or there. In this one good every good which
can be mentioned is loved. One can say: all in one and one in all. For what
is either here or there is not on every side; and what is either today or
tomorrow is not always and above all time; and what is something is
not everything. If God were something, then God would not be the Perfect but only something fragmentary.[77] However, this intellectual love
for God cannot be realized by means of some empirical activity in actual
life, which always has this or that as its goal. It can be realized only as an
infinite vision and blissful enjoyment in the quiet kingdom of eternity.
"One hour of contemplative vision," all the mystics repeat since Dionysius the Aereopagite, "is worth more than all the good works that holy
Christianity performs in a thousand years."

The highest Good is consequently the infinite identity of God and the
soul. Now since the religious individual removes himself or herself from
actuality and, as it were, tears himself or herself out of the context of the
life of the world, his or her striving for perfection, or the praxis to which
he or she subjects himself or herself in order to attain the ideal, cannot be

---

[76] [Cf J.G. Fichte, *The Way towards the Blessed Life*, University Publications of America,
1977.]

[77] ThG, ch. 30.

an acting in the actual ethical [48] realm, which has lost its reality for mystical consciousness. On the contrary, the religious individual strives for the goal of perfection through a series of *absolute* activities: penance and devotional practices, a continuous ritual life. Through such deeds the empirical individuality was to be purified and, so to speak, undergo a transubstantiation through which the limited would be transformed to the unlimited, the temporal to the eternal. The mystical process moves through all of the levels between the individual's immediate naturalness and sinfulness and its perfected ascension into God. Mysticism is like Jacob's ladder, which binds together heaven and earth, and on account of which the soul can lift itself to unity.

Only when the soul, by means of a continual negation of individuality, has put behind itself all the stages, can a perfected acosmism make its appearance. Here it seems the process must end with the complete dissolution of the individuality and its disappearance in the Godhead. However, we shall see in what follows how Christian mysticism, when it speaks about the destruction of the individual, nevertheless corrects itself again and restores the individual. As a consequence of the nature of mysticism it cannot finally deny the soul's individual immortality. More specifically: the infinite self-concern which constitutes the beginning of mysticism also constitutes its real end. The soul which has achieved the highest perfection and has sunk into the abyss of the Godhead is not forfeited, for it knows the Godhead as its own *self*, as its infinite freedom; it knows *itself* as the infinite point of identity. If the mystic at certain times seems to desire an annihilation of his or her I, then the I here is merely a phenomenal thing, a definite form or a subordinated potency [*potents*] of consciousness from which he or she desires to liberate himself or herself; [49] for freedom does not die but reproduces itself ever again in a higher potency. The religious psyche, out of love, burns itself up as a sacrifice. Yet it is not merely an eternal dying away and vanishing, but also an eternal rebirth; it is that blessed point in which the divine never ceases to pulsate.

This is then the closer specification of mystical acosmism. However, the authentically mystical element in acosmism will first become clear if we consider it as atheism. Atheism is just acosmism considered from a different standpoint. Naturally we are not thinking here of an atheism which denies the existence of God and the Idea pure and simple. Such an atheism posits only matter as real and is consequently the most crass divinization of the world. The atheism about which we are speaking involves acosmism: to the extent that it denies God, to that very extent it denies the world. Since mysticism repudiates every single determination of finitude, it cannot find repose in God as *God*, i.e., insofar as God is set in relation to the world, but rather seeks God as *Godhead*, i.e., as that which is itself the divine personality's ground and possibility. This is a high, authentically speculative thought. The true mystic seeking the most inward mystery abolishes both God and the world in order to arrive at that *third* [*det Tredie*] which was before God and the world were. The true mystic can find repose only in that which is the most originary, the beginning for everything. Therefore Meister Eckhart prays to God that God make him free from God so that he will no longer take God as Creator, nor place God under any other category which merely expresses a relation, but take God as *reason itself*. For Eckhart, therefore, the concrete determinations 'Father,' 'Son,' and 'Holy Spirit' are not adequate; he wants to grasp these determinations in a radical way and in terms of their origin. For this reason [50] he longs after his first cause, where he was from eternity, where there was neither God nor world, but only a pure nothingness. He will not be stilled by God's goodness nor by God's forbearance, but seeks the marrow in goodness and in every divine quality, the essential, the authentic kernel in every husk: that which makes even God divine.

Meister Eckhart articulates this thought concerning the metaphysical ground of God's existence in his sermons with a logical enthusiasm and with the full force of pure thinking—so much so that one is often spontaneously reminded of Hegel, whose logical idea is precisely this All-Substantial Reality, which is, in itself, an enshrouded Godhead before it constitutes itself as God in a world.

It is at this point where consciousness shows its mystical nature; for this pure depth of thought, this originary ground [*Urgrund*], is not explicated in terms of a logical idea as it is in more recent philosophy. Rather, the originary ground is represented only as an infinite pleroma, an ungrounded sea of light in which all colors and determinacies are abolished. In addition, and in just this lies the mystical element, this *immediate* mystery, which has not yet developed itself to the point of being a revelation, is posited as the *true* mystery, and the identity with this *deus implicitus* [the implicit God] is posited as the highest Good. In this esoteric stillness mystical consciousness, with its holy silence, merges with the ineffable and the inexpressible which transcend all sense and understanding. It is this religious mystery which maintains, following the example of Dionysius the Areopagite, that God must be stripped of all names, since these contain only finite determinations. Therefore mystical theology will be much more a *theologia* ἀποφατικη [apophatic theology], which thinks God purely predicatelessly, than a *theologia* [51] καταφατική [kataphatic theology], which expresses the essence of God in definite predicates. This is what Meister Eckhart means when he somewhere says that the more one praises God, the more one denies God, and that one should rather be silent than give name to God. Moreover, the mystery of the originary ground is what mystical consciousness has before its eyes when it teaches God's incomprehensibility and when it affirms that God cannot even comprehend God's own self. For all comprehending establishes finitude, negation, limit, all of which must be held at a distance from the Godhead.

The soul first comes into the mystery of the originary ground through *ecstasy.* Not only sight and hearing but also all articulated thought passes out of consciousness; it perishes in the contemplation of pure light, or in what is identical to pure light, pure darkness, because just as much is seen in the one as in the other. For both expressions—pure light and pure darkness—occur continually in mystical writings and indicate the same thing. Nevertheless, mystical consciousness finds no static repose here. At the heart of the infinite pleroma mystical consciousness longs again after *determinate* content, and in order to find this it must give itself over to the kingdom of finite relations. For the Christian mystics, this is the sphere of the Trinity which includes God's revelation in the world and God's coming to the salvation of humanity. Nevertheless, just as mystical consciousness arrives in the sphere of *revelation*, it once again longs for mystery; it runs once again through the entire *via negationis* in order to penetrate the pure nothing, and so forth. The soul continuously oscillates between the hidden God and the revealed God, and with this the 'claire-obscure' of such consciousness comes to the fore, the proper element of the mystic.

Mystical consciousness moves, without knowing it, in a dialectical contradiction: it moves between two moments [52] which it allows to remain outside of each other instead of bringing them together. Its contradiction consists in the fact that it seeks the Godhead outside of God, the esoteric behind the exoteric, that it wants to grasp the mystery behind and outside of the revelation. Mystical consciousness hypostasizes the abstract, pure essence, which ought to be only a vanishing dialectical moment in speculative thinking, as a self-subsisting sphere.

Specifically: just as content only becomes actual in form, just as essence is only true essence in its phenomenon, just as substance must develop itself to concept in order to gain subsistence, so also must mystery open itself to revelation in order to be true mystery. Mystery or the idea of the Godhead in its substantial fullness of essence is the ground for all actual existence; it is life's invisible root and secret and all religious and speculative interests aim at living in this and raising this up into consciousness. Mysticism is thus not mistaken in supposing that human beings can penetrate into the mystery of the Godhead, but insofar as it supposes the *immediate* mystery and the immediate identity [of the soul with the Godhead] to be the highest. Only the expanded and developed mystery, i.e., revelation, is the truth.

Revelation contains the difference, negation, and contrast which are the conditions for all consciousness and knowledge, but it contains unity just as much. Revelation is system, articulated logos, infinite *concept* [*Begreb*], for which the deepest expression is self-consciousness, personality. The concepts mystery and revelation are not true outside of each other, but only within one another. Just as that which has mystery within itself, i.e., what stands in an *immediate* relation of identity to the Idea, has something to [53] reveal, so also, on the other hand, mystery is actual only when it is *life* and *spirit*—the concrete, revealed Idea which is based upon the development of immediacy through the negative. If there were neither negativity nor finitude within the absolute Idea, then life could not gain form, nor could there be any consciousness or will, any creaturely exis-tence, any pain or happiness. In such a case there would only be a deso-late quiet in which no spirit stirred, where there was neither God nor humanity. However, so that the whole multiplicity of God and human beings and creatures might be, the divine essence must develop negation, separate itself from itself. Its mystery can then render itself into per-sonality. Only the personal God, i.e., the God who reveals the divine es-sence both to God's own self and also to God's creation, is the *true* God. A mystery without spirit and revelation is a contradiction [*Modsigelse*], an invisible beauty, an ineffective good, an unknown truth, a light without eyes. The eternal essentialities lie dormant in the immediate mystery; yet the contradiction, in which they are encumbered, has its ground in their immediacy, that they are not reflected back in the knowing spirit.

Insofar as mystery becomes revealed it liberates itself from its contra-diction and is developed to *concept*. Spirit is the mystery itself in which truth and the knowledge of the truth cannot be distinguished. Divine *knowledge* is truth itself; the divine *will* is the good itself. Even as mystery and revelation are eternally united in the divine Spirit, they must *become* thus in human spirit, because human spirit has been set as a locus of di-vine revelation. For no mystery would be able to enthrall a human being with its elusive and secretive [54] power unless the person had some inti-mation that in this mystery human spirit would find also itself. Just as spirit involuntarily is drawn towards the mysteries of religion and phi-losophy and cannot find rest outside of these, so also these mysteries wait upon spirit, therein to become revealed. This is accomplished only on account of the energetic striving of self-consciousness; only thought and freedom, which seek and find the hidden Idea, can liberate it from its mysterious obscurity and give it definite form and shape.

Precisely here, where mystical consciousness achieves its highest goal and posits itself as mystical, it forfeits its determination as religious con-sciousness. For mystical consciousness, the mystical union neutralizes God and the human being into an absolute indifference; this is different from holding that the human being and God shall be one in God's *reve-lation*. The union established by revelation contains all qualitative dif-ferences, and consequently also the most essential difference of all, the difference between God and the created spirit. Every created existing thing, even the most insignificant, appears here in its relative independence, meaning and distinction. Pantheism dissolves and attenuates [relative differences] to pure accidentalities and modifications. In the system of revelation, on the other hand, the *principium individuationis* [principle of individuation] rules. But insofar as all creaturely existents, whether unconscious or self-conscious, subsist as merely relative loci for the revelation of the absolute personality; insofar, that is, as all creaturely existents are suffused by the one divine Substance and all maintain an either direct or indirect rapport with the absolute Subject, the isolated independence of the individuality is sublated [*ophævet*] into an infinite mediation.

It is thus mediation, or the concept, which mysticism lacks. Its praxis strives [55] for freedom by tearing itself out of the relations of worldly life and by transforming the temporal into the eternal in an act of immediate transubstantiation rather than gaining the eternal through the temporal. Its theory strives to gain the Absolute by abstracting from the finite determinations of thought rather than transposing them into the concept. Mysticism's negation of finitude cannot be a consistent negation because it relates itself to it in an indeterminate and 'hovering' way. It perpetually means the opposite of what it says. In the mystical consciousness there is a continual play of day and night; sometimes it moves in the regions of the hidden God, sometimes in the illuminated regions of revelation. With regard to the latter it articulates the deepest knowledge of the system of revelation and brings to bear conceptually rich mediations on the highest problems of Christian speculation. What a surprise, then, that such consciousness, which has seen the truth and managed to articulate it, nevertheless once again seeks the Absolute behind the absolute. For us these glimpses of revelation can stand as eternal truths, as guiding lights. For mystical consciousness itself these truths are enveloped once again in darkness. For even though it views the fundamental feature of the concept, it does not think the concept *as* concept; it is not the master of itself and not in possession of its own ideas. Thus it expresses in the same breath the purist acosmism and the Christian conviction of the reality of finitude and creation. In the above excerpts from the sermons of Meister Eckhart, the reader will have met with such antinomies, whose two sides he often expresses in the same sermon without resolving or even noticing the antinomy. Properly speaking, therefore, mysticism should be considered a standpoint in the phenomenology of the religious spirit. [56]

If we would now, after generally setting forth the moments in the mystical consciousness, lead these back to their ground and transpose them into the concept, then the following can be said: mystical consciousness is the *immediate, subjective* unity of religion and philosophy. Herein lies its unique worth—what is interesting and attractive about it—but herein also lies its untruth. The unity of religion and philosophy is the highest, but their true union comes forth only in and through their separation and division, when speculative thought and religious disposition undergo a *free* reconciliation. The speculative is always present in religion and to that extent one can say that philosophy is always *implicite* [implicitly] present in religious consciousness. But mysticism is more than religion, for the philosophical urge is so strongly present here that the speculative makes a breakthrough *as such*. On the other hand, it is not speculative science: its thinking is worship, its investigations are cultic, and thought is, as it were, bound to the religious subject and its pious condition. Religion and speculation, these two, are immediately at one in the mystical subject; therefore for the mystical subject religion cannot effectively become an *object* for speculation, just as little as speculation can become an object to itself. For speculation to become an object to itself presupposes the separation and division of religion and speculation and in such a case consciousness would no longer be mystical; for its mysticism hinges precisely on the fact that it cannot in actuality objectify itself and its infinite content—in which case it would be revealed. The speculative element is present here only within religion's powerfully developing drive, which, according to its nature, seeks to posit what religion originarily *is*, i.e., the reconciliation and [57] identity of life's contrasts; specifically, the identity of God and human beings.

As we have seen, the first, immediate form of this speculative identity is the idea of *pantheism*. This idea wells-up in the religious disposition as a bubbling spring which overflows religion's positive content. The religious subject is not powerful enough to master and guide this stream but is continually close to drowning in it because he or she cannot remove himself or herself from the stream, that is, cannot render the pantheistic idea into an *object* for thought. This would require that philosophy and religion actually were separated, that the philosophical *I* split itself off from the religious *I*. But from the standpoint of mystical consciousness this is impossible; its consciousness perishes in its own spiritual wealth because it cannot make this into an object for itself—it cannot unload its treasure, and so its contents remain elusive to it. This is unfree mysticism. No matter how much mysticism speaks about self-examination and self-contemplation, it never comes to see itself, because it lacks the requisite *doubleness*, the internal self-differentiation. In its substantial identity with itself mystical consciousness is an ineffable secret, a silent mystery. Thus Eckhart says that he has stood in the Godhead's depths and in the Godhead's source. This is to be understood not merely as the soul's ideal preexistence, but also as a description of the mystical condition itself. For when consciousness envelops itself in its basic substantial ground, then it stands in the Godhead's depths, where it neither knows anything nor wills anything, because every object and every relation between subject and object is transcended [*ophævet*].

Yet the mystical [58] consciousness develops itself out of the consciousness of revelation, which is its indispensable *alterum* [other]; and with this the previously developed reflexive relationship between mystery and revelation reappears. When, however, in the sphere of revelation, the true identity of subject and object is articulated by the mystics, the identity cannot be stabilized. This is because in the stream of thought the mystical consciousness is not able to stabilize itself. It cannot stabilize the *objects* of revelation, because it cannot become an object for itself; it is invisible to itself, and when invisibility is its own nature, it aims at leading revelation back to this point. We find also that the history of revelation, on this account, perpetually ceases to be an actual history, object and fact, and is transformed into an inward one, to a pure essentiality which is enclosed and sealed in the soul's silent identity. Mystical consciousness posits the dualism between mystery and revelation, within which it moves, but without knowing that it posits it even within the divine essence. It thus ends by making revelation into an ineffable secret.

The much-disputed question about God's incomprehensibility is illuminated from an important side by a consideration of mysticism. Specifically, the manifold forms under which this teaching has appeared in various times are reducible to two main forms: one teaches God's incomprehensibility in an objective sense, the other in a subjective sense. The objective standpoint teaches that God in Godself is an incomprehensible essence and thereby makes incomprehensibility into a divine quality. This is the mystical standpoint. God is in Godself incomprehensible because comprehension presupposes finiteness; but God is the one, [59] undifferentiated Essence. In this sense philosophy must be willing to admit God's incomprehensibility, for the immediate mystery is, of course, incomprehensible; only what is in itself developed can be an object for concept. To the extent that God is considered as an immediate mystery, God dwells in light which no one can approach. And no one has ever seen God. The Godhead's most inward depths are unknown and will always remain unknown. It is here that the Godhead is unknown to its own self, for it has not separated itself into subject and object. But just as much the contradiction which the immediate mystery contains slumbering within itself must be pointed out and developed to concept.

The subjective standpoint is the rationalistic one. It teaches that God is comprehensible for Godself, but incomprehensible for human beings because all human concepts are only finite. According to this standpoint human beings can never transcend their subjective and limited horizon.

This way of thinking found its highest expression in eighteenth-century philosophy. If mysticism posits an abstract division between mystery and revelation, considered in-and-for-itself, rationalism posits an abstract division between divine revelation and human self-consciousness, thereby separating what God has put together.

All doctrines of God's incomprehensibility can be reduced to these two theories; they are merely modifications of the mystical or rationalistic standpoint or a combination of both (for example, supernaturalism). For questions such as these—whether we can partake partially in this life in the knowledge of God or only first in the future life, whether human science [60] has already attained to the highest knowledge possible for human beings in this existence, or whether we can expect a diversity of philosophical evolutions, etc.—all of these more relative and special questions on the doctrine of incomprehensibility can only be answered or demonstrated when the eternal possibility or impossibility of an absolute knowledge of God has been established. But the purely metaphysical grounds from which God's incomprehensibility can be argued are given in the above two standpoints.

Because all mysticism is entangled in the dialectical contradiction between mystery and revelation, Christian mysticism only achieves its specific, distinctive character on account of the specific revelation which it strives to transcend. In the mystical night which lies on the far side beyond the border of revelation, no difference between Christian and non-Christian mysticism can be marked. It is only on account of the journey's point of departure and along the way that they can be divided by the light of revelation. It is clear that the mystic who moves amidst the richest content of revelation will bear the richest fullness of thought. The mystical 'nothing' achieves its particular significance from the 'something,' i.e., the revelation, which precedes it.

The sphere of revelation comprising the Christian mystic's presupposition is the following: Trinity, Creation, Incarnation, Sin and Redemption. With these a conception of *finitude* is rendered which sharply separates itself from acosmism. Finitude is not nothing but something. It is an actual, essentially distinct existence from God, a life which stirs outside of God; it is a creaturely ego, a thought, a will, which is an *other* with respect to the almighty [61] God's ego, thought, and will. Sin is the wretchedness of human beings—earthly life's entire empirical distress. The lament over the world's vanity is no mere illusion, but deep seriousness. Redemption from these negative powers is not simply the liberation of thought from illusion, but the restoration of *existence* to its true ground-relation [*Grundforhold*]. God's Incarnation for the salvation of the race is no image of thought [*Tankebillede*]; Christ has not put on any mythical-illusory body and is no mythical appearance or theophany. In *history* God has become a human being and entered into empirical finitude and has taken the *cross* upon God's own self in its full actuality.

The consideration of finitude is the heart of the matter in all religion; similarly, finitude is the proper cross of philosophy. The Christian gospel, as it is expressed in an old mystical symbol, shows to human beings the rose in the cross and the cross in the rose. This gospel must necessarily have been a scandal to the Jews and a foolishness to the Greeks, because it was at one and the same time the opposite of paganism's esthetic acosmism, which idealizes away and ignores the sting of finitude, and Judaism's abstract monotheism, which grasps finitude only in its prosaic, God-abandoned nakedness. Moreover, the pantheistic conception sees in the world only God and nothing but ideal splendors. An abstract theism sees in the world only the prosaic cross, but does not notice eternity's rose in its middle.

It is the conception of finitude indicated here which gives Christian mysticism its unique color and separates it from both Oriental and Neoplatonic mysticism, which are the two world-historical forms of mysticism which preceded Christian mysticism. The *via negationis* [62] which the Christian mystic shall go through takes its point of departure from a creation which is encumbered by sin, i.e., from the knowledge of sin and the infinite pain over sin. It moves through a process of conversion and rebirth as it moves through the Christian order of salvation. Oriental and Neoplatonic mysticism, on the contrary, lack this deep *ethical* moment. They strive merely after the abstract liberation from finitude, not from finitude as sinful and *guilty*. The brand of pantheism which is expressed by the Islamic poets is of an authentically mystical nature: the fundamental theme in these poems is the soul's love for God and its salvation by giving up its finite *I*.[78] However, this salvation is not fought for through the soul's deep distress and suffering. The cares of finitude float merely as light, dreamy clouds in the poetic sky. Contemplation is more extensive than intensive: it sees the Godhead in the stars, the ocean, in dewdrops, flowers and clouds, in nature's quantitative infinity (which is painted with the whole luxuriousness of the Eastern imagination.) It never tires of letting the whole splendor of nature perish in the one divine Substance; and since the *I* sympathizes with every object of nature, it is itself content to disappear as a dewdrop in the sun. The instruction in the blessed life which this poetic mysticism gives is the immediate joy of life, the blissful intoxication in the universal and eternal. It does not cost the *I* any difficult struggle and resignation to give itself up, for the human [63] personality in this form of mysticism does not have an infinite importance

---

[78] Cf. Hegel's *Aesthetics: Lectures on Fine Art*, T. M. Knox trans., Oxford (1974); and Tholuck's *Bluttensammlung zur Orientalishen Mystik*.

in itself as it does in Christendom, since it has not yet been clearly separated from nature.

Neoplatonic mysticism returns to the life-view of the ancient Orient and asserts an ascetic cleansing through the annihilation of the material world; the flame of ideality has consumed all consideration of nature. Here sin-consciousness is not grasped and there is no real relation of contrast between God and the world (which is merely a docetic illusion). *Christian* mysticism, by contrast, proceeds from a fallen world. In the whole of the created world there is only a single point to which contemplative thinking is attached: the human *I*. And in all of the visible world there is but one image to which this mysticism constantly returns: the image of the Savior. Nature is profane; and the soul, which is dominated by the natural, is sinful. One feeling permeates the soul: the split between its actuality and its eternal essence; or, the feeling of its creatureliness, an infinite hunger and thirst after God. The soul desires to be freed not merely from sin, but also from its naked creatureliness, whose extension it desires to have clothed with the uncreated, inviolate essence. The soul must become divinized [*gudforvandlet*] and united with God [*gudforenet*]; the creature must be glorified, the human deified. The human person's union with God is mediated only by Christ, who is the mediator between God and humanity. Therefore the human person can be deified only by becoming christified [*christificeret*]. The task of the Christian mystic, then, achieves its fullest expression only when it is specified as the *imitation of Christ*. This is by no means just a moral imitation of the example of Christ merely preserved in one's memory, but a real, inward, and essential *process of Christification* [*Christificationsprocess*]. [64]

Closer consideration thus shows that a double view of finitude appears within Christian mysticism, [i.e., non-absoluteness and sin], and also that the contradictions between these two often stand unmediated, side by side one another. They remain unmediated partly as a necessary consequence of mysticism's concept, partly as a consequence of the peculiar nature and condition of the Middle Ages. For even though the outward form of the Middle Ages was Christian, a multiplicity of pagan elements remained undigested inside of it. The Christian principle was not yet strong enough to consume and assimilate these elements. Thus the entire intelligence of the Middle Ages had to base itself upon pagan philosophy; but it did so without managing to accomplish that process of transformation required for making pagan philosophy a handmaiden of the Christian spirit. The same holds true concerning the relation between Christian mysticism and its relation to Neoplatonism, whose pantheism extends itself across the whole of the Middle Ages.

The Neoplatonic view of finitude manifests itself in its purest and most accomplished form in Dionysius the Areopagite, the mystic of the Greek church. The Greek church stands closest to the Orient. The direction of its speculative spirit lies almost exclusively in reference to the Godhead's essence and its inward determinations. By contrast, the anthropological moment and an interest in the human remains in the background. Orthodox dogmatics is comprised essentially by the doctrine of the Trinity. Yet this doctrine is taken to be not so much about the triune God as revealed in the world, but as a doctrine about God's internal being in itself. This preponderant interest in the divine, along with its marginalization of the human, repeats itself also in the mysticism of the Eastern church. Certainly the above-mentioned [65] double view of finitude is present in Dionysius, since he has Christian dogma as his presupposition; but the contradiction is superficial here because the immanental side of revelation, i.e., its most conceptually negative points (sin, redemption, Christ's human nature), have no actual root in consciousness. They shine in, as it were, only from the outside of consciousness. What inspires Dionysius is simply the intelligible world, the heaven of ideas which lies on the far side of human actuality, the divine light and the society of pure, suprahuman spirits into which we are supposed to be raised by continual purification, and for which we are supposed to be prepared by the mystical symbols in the life of the church.[79] But this consciousness does not presuppose the full actuality of the Christian revelation. The anthropological side of Christendom is not squarely faced. This is what distinguishes the mysticism of the Greek church from that of the Western church. The latter's presupposition and foundation is the completely developed content of revelation. The mystics of the Occident articulate the words 'soul' and 'human being' with a completely different and deeply resonant tone which one does not find in the Dionysian conception. For here the soul has had a look into the abyss of its own human nature, which it can no longer forget. The Greeks had but a distant intimation of this. It was Augustine's profound conception of human nature which made sin and redemption the foundation for the Western life-view. This has also contributed toward giving Western mysticism its unique [66] stamp. This stamp is found not only in German mysticism but also in Roman mysticism (mysticism's second epoch), whose most important representatives are Bernard, St. Francis, and Bonaventure. We could designate Dionysian contemplation as the objective side of Christian mysticism, Occidental mysticism as its subjective side.

If we could indicate the unique quality of Occidental mysticism with a single word, that word would be '*Gemyt*' [disposition]. With a closer consideration of this word we can also designate the difference between Roman and German mysticism. *Gemyt* is the soul collected into itself; it is the life and stirrings of the soul's internal infinity, the human person's esoteric personality. It is not one or the other of the soul's powers, but

---

[79] This applies also to his work on the *Celestial Heirarchy*. Cf. also Englehardt, "Die angeblichen Schriften des Areopagiten Dionysius."

their undivided unity in an internal focal point. It contains the totality of spiritual life as the individual's internal estate. The religious *Gemyt* is the ideal fusion of the absolute truth, not just with the abstract, thinking *I*, but with the *empirical I*. This unification makes it so that the *Gemyt* feels itself at home in truth; and so that truth itself assumes individual human nature, informs itself palpably, guides the person through life's most insignificant relations: in a word, *Gemyt* makes truth capable of being *experienced*. Just as it is true that Christianity first produced the idea of the religious personality, it is also certain that on account of this the religious *Gemyt*-life was also actually awakened. Christianity contains an infinite unification not just of God and the generally human, but of God and the empirical, individually human. God has become a *particular* [67] *human being* [*et enkelt Menneske*]. This comprehensive truth contains also what the religious *Gemyt* seeks and what it, ideally conceived, is: the Absolute concentrated into a single empirical point; the infinite truth, God's own self, as a particular object of experience.

Thus even though the *Gemyt* belongs as an aspect of all Christian consciousness, we assert that it first gains historical and theological significance in the development of the Western church. For the ideas concerning redemption and the appropriation of Christ are here for the first time epoch-making. In contrast to the Scholastics, who sunder this profound content in an atomistic dialectic, the mystics strive to preserve the content's totality and its undivided fullness of life. The mystics set for themselves the daily task of spiritually reproducing and re-experiencing the unification of God and humanity, something objectively seen in the story of Christ. Just as God let Godself be born in a manger in the East, so also God is born anew in the lonely cloister-cell of the West. The Western church first determines the mystic's task as that of the imitation of Christ. It was not just the great interest in anthropology stemming from Augustine which worked to create this inwardness, but also the natural proclivities of the people and the development of the romantic principle. In the West every thought, even the most abstract, is spiritually disposed [*gemytlig*], because it always contains the reflection of individuality. The interest in individuality can be traced even into regions where thought has lost its way, even into the most remote regions of the divine Essence. The bold pantheism of this interest is only seen in its proper significance when it is seen as originating in the rich *Gemyt*, which not only loses itself, but also continually finds itself again. For [68] whether thought flies up to heaven or sinks down into the divine abyss, it discovers at length that the divine nature is not alone, but always has human nature with it; and if thought wanders out into the lonely desert of the divine Essence, it finds there human tracks. The mysticism of the Greek church knows only of the soul's going-forth from itself, but not its return to itself as an entering and immersion into its own interiority.

If we posit the Christian *Gemyt*, in the indicated sense, as the common foundation for both Roman and German mysticism, then we can also say, from another side, that this establishes the difference between both. Namely, the difference lies in the degree of the intensity and depth of their respective developments of the concept *Gemyt*. This can be further illuminated by considering their relation to Scholasticism. Scholasticism is a philosophy with an empirical concern; it is a conceptual formalism without a connection to life and actuality. Religious dogma stands in relation to the scholastic as a foreign, impenetrable positivity which is entangled in the artful net of a metaphysics of the understanding [*Forstandsmetaphysik*]. This net, which floats in the air, is merely the internal form in which the precious yield is hidden, which no one dare touch, nor has anyone even been able to see. The scholastics prove everything, but comprehend nothing. In contrast to this merely immediate knowledge, the religious *Gemyt* seeks a knowledge not from books or human artfulness, but a knowledge from experience. It does not want to relate itself to the subject matter [*Sagen*] through any foreign medium, but seeks to experience the thing itself [*Sagen selv*]. But if the religious *Gemyt* actually will gain the thing itself, it must be able to develop itself to thought, or must be able to develop the Idea out of its experience. Scholasticism attempts in vain to grasp [69] the Idea through its unending string of conclusions.

This is where the difference between German and Roman mysticism manifests itself: in Roman mysticism the *Gemyt* is encumbered by a barrier which it cannot break through. It is bound to forms of representation [*Forestilling*] and feeling; thought cannot achieve a breakthrough *as such*. Roman mysticism holds only to a religious *Gemyt*, not a speculative one, and therefore produces only a half-way mysticism. Here *Gemyt* does not manage to give its experience a speculative imprint, because it has not hit the appropriate depth from which pure thought can well-up from it as from a living spring. For this reason, such mysticism does not come into opposition with Scholasticism (as, for example, in Saint Bernard's struggle with Abelard). It desires only a thinking contemplation and does not develop thought as its *own*, i.e., out of its own free interiority; therefore it must unite itself with Scholasticism and from there fetch its means for thinking. We see this especially in the Victorines and Bonaventure. Only the "person with deep yearnings" was set for contemplation; reading was not to have been without anointing, speculation without devotion, investigating without wonder, knowledge without love, intelligence without humility, study without divine grace.[80] This ladder of pious affections

---

[80] Cf. Bonaventure's *Journey of the Mind to God*, trans. Philotheus Boehner, Hackett (1993), introduction.

runs parallel with a refined scholastic *raisonnement*. By contrast, in real [German] mysticism, feeling gives birth to thought from out of itself without the help of the categories of reflection found in the School.

In this way it is understandable how Scholasticism and mysticism could be united in one and the same individual. Mysticism here is not fully accomplished. It is merely a pious asceticism making [70] Scholasticism edifying and giving it a greater anointing. It is not one and all. The unification of Scholasticism and mysticism happens by producing an *æquale temperamentum* [balanced temperament] of both. Scholasticism's metaphysical speculations were meant to be tempered by mystical feeling and presented in their edifying aspect. On the other hand, clear *raisonnement* was meant to regulate mystical feeling and swear off any outbreaks of pantheism. Even though such a unification of religion and philosophy may avoid the onesidedness contained in true mysticism's *immediate* and primitive union of religion and speculation, nevertheless it is far below the latter in a speculative sense, since it lacks actual immanence and freedom. In the fifteenth century Gerson's work on mystical theology did away with the fundamental features of such a prudent [*forstandig*], that is to say, non-actual, speculative mysticism. *The Mystical Theology* is characteristic both of Roman mysticism and Gerson himself. The famous *juste milieu* of the Middle Ages which sought in all directions to temper the various contrasts of the time and to bring about a reasonable equilibrium was not able to produce any actual reconciliation, either in life or in thought.

We could call the second epoch of mysticism *prudently reflecting*, whereas the first and third epochs (the Greek and Germanic), are speculative, that is, actual mysticism [*virkelig Mystik*]. The reflecting mystic is captured in the contrast between *faith and knowledge*. In particular this is seen in the struggle between Bernard and Abelard, where Bernard asserted, against the latter, the faith of the church and declared human thinking incompetent to comprehend it. This opposition is not present in speculative mysticism. Its knowledge extends just as far as its faith. [71] As long as it believes 'something,' it is satisfied with a determinate knowing [*Viden*]. Where its knowledge slips, faith also is lost in the ineffable. Its dialectical contradiction is only that between mystery and revelation. This contradiction is perhaps also found in reflecting mysticism, but without speculative yield, for the dialectic drives it only to a pantheism in feeling, but not in thought. Therefore this half-way, merely upbuilding mysticism can be compared with Protestant pietism and ought rather to be called pietism than mysticism. For pietism is a Christian-religious empiricism which cannot develop itself into the Idea. It relates itself negatively to thought and is constantly plagued with scruples over whether science has offended faith. However, the parallelism between this form of mysticism and pietism ought not to be extended too far: for a mystic such as Saint Bernard and his spiritual kin have, partly on account of their interior greatness, partly on account of the age and circumstances, an enthusiastic and romantic tinge, an idealized coloration, which Protestant pietism lacks.

Of the mystics from the Netherlands, Thomas à Kempis is merely an ascetic, Johan Wessel is a reflexive unity of Scholasticism and mysticism, and Ruysbroock belongs to the speculative mystics.

German mysticism is the West's retrieval of the speculation of Dionysius the Areopagite. The Christian *Gemyt* [disposition] is liberated from the opposition between feeling and thought. The Idea flows unrestrained from the limits of reflection and the reconciliation between the divine and the human, for which the preceding epoch had only a pious longing, these mystics in all seriousness strive to carry out. Divine *thought* breaks through here in worship as self-consciousness' own essence. Eckhart articulates this thought in a way most nearly approaching metaphysical [72] purity, while with Suso it is proclaimed through the balladeer's imaginative meditations. Not as logical as Eckhart, nor as image-rich as Suso, is Tauler: with the internal harmony of his *Gemyt*, and the tranquility of his meditations, he forms a connecting middle between Eckhart and Suso. In the *Theologia Germanica* there are already traces of that striving to form thought into a kind of systematic ground-plan. German mysticism did not require the help of Scholasticism, whose power was already on the wane: it had enough to do with its own acquired thought. *Human nature's union with the divine* comes to consciousness here as nowhere else in the Middle Ages. It is especially in this sense that its ideas are to be considered as anticipations of the more recent speculative philosophy. It has Scholasticism behind it, but it is not able to raise itself to a free philosophical science. This in-between position makes it a mysticism which desires the unity of religion and philosophy; and here is where the above-mentioned contradiction plays itself out. We have considered the nameless mystery, acosmism and atheism, but this consideration first gains significance only when we follow consciousness through the domain of revelation, where it steps forth in its full distinctiveness. [73]

II. REVELATION

Creation and God's Incarnation
"God's essence cannot become our essence, but ought to be our life. The Son has gone forth from the Father and remained one with God in essence. But in our created being we have taken on a foreign, an other, essence, which has its origin in the divine essence. We should be united with God in contemplation, but not in essence." We have already cited

this quotation from Eckhart. In another place, where he enthusiastically exalts the nature of the soul and its union with the divine essence, he ends by saying: "now I don't dare add anything more to the soul; for if I add more, then it will become God."[81]

With these and other similar citations from Eckhart our consideration is placed within the sphere of revelation, where the fundamental *difference* between God and humanity is asserted. Those who consider Eckhart exclusively pantheistic overlook the fact that he lives and moves in the revealed God just as deeply as he is buried in the hidden God. In such as the above citations, Christian speculation can only recognize its own deepest truths. When Eckhart says that the word '*sum*,' I am, cannot be pronounced by any creature but only by God about God's own self, because it pertains to the creature to give witness about itself only by saying, '*non sum*'—just as John the Baptist, when he was asked whether he was the Christ, replied with humility, '*non sum*'—and further when he says, 'what in God is an effecting, in me shall be a suffering; what in God is speech, in me shall be a listening; what in God is [74] an image, in me shall be a vision,'[82] then this must be seen as a pure expression of *Christian* acosmism, which necessarily deprives humanity of its autonomy and being in itself and of itself, which belongs only to God. The soul shall be thoroughly saturated by God, but this shall be as the full moon, which gains its light from the sun. The soul is a word of God: not an individual dissonant [*selvlydende*] word, but a consonant word [*medlydende*]. In the beginning was the eternal Word, which is God's Son and God's own self. To this major Word the soul is a supplemental word: where God's own self is blissful, the soul becomes blissful.[83] And Meister Eckhart prays to the Father, the Word, and the Holy Spirit to help us so that we may ever be a supplemental word to the eternal Word.[84] In the soul's union with God it is drawn into the divine essence to such an extent that it seems, but only seems, to be one essence with God; however, they are *two* essences.

Eckhart's disciples, especially Suso and Tauler, often return to these pure ideas of revelation. They speak often about how profitable it is for a person who would lead a divine life and accomplish divine contemplation to know the proper and rational *difference* between things. What is indicated in Eckhart one finds more fully developed in these others; and because of their more practical natures and their greater interest in the life of the church, [75] there appears in them a more determinate consciousness of revelation and an intimation of the unity of mystery and

---

[81] [Unable to locate reference—trans.]

[82] Cf. Eckhart, sermon 60; *Werke I*, 636f.

[83] Cf. Eckhart, sermon 73: *Werke II*, 90f.

[84] Ibid.

revelation. The contradiction is not here resolved, because they do not manage to supersede [*ophæve*] the mystical principle, but they continually rupture it. The doctrine of the fundamental difference is developed in detail in Suso's book on the *Eternal Wisdom*: Wisdom (the Idea), in a conversation with his disciple, illuminates him on the way of truth.

This remarkable text contains the typical benchmarks of mysticism which already have been reported on above: the doctrine of the eternal nothing; that only the human person finds himself or herself as a blessed essence which is not hindered on account of difference, and for whom all things have become one. Before examining its expressions on the fundamental difference, we desire first to test its mystical character, which contains, besides, an interesting connection between the mystical and the logical reminding one of Eckhart.

The disciple, who remains dependent upon sensible images, cannot raise himself to the mystical essential intuition [*Væsenskue*] which Wisdom requires of him. For, he says, 'I do indeed see mountains and valleys, air and water and all kinds of creatures, how then can it be said that all is one?' Wisdom then answers: 'except that human beings learn to grasp two contraries, that is, two contradicting things, in one, one cannot talk with him about spiritual things. If he can grasp this, then he is already half-way to salvation [*Salighed*].' Therefore the disciple is admonished to place together the unbegotten and the begotten, the eternal and the temporal (the Infinite and the finite) in one. 'Eternal wisdom,' cries the disciple, 'to posit two contraries in one, this flies in the face of the art of logic!' Wisdom reproves him, because he [76] speaks only according to human truths and thoughts and what relates to such things; as, for example, that two people cannot be at one and the same place at the same time, or that the one path swings to the right, the other to the left. 'These things,' Wisdom says, 'must be understood in a way which transcends all the senses.'[85] 'If you therefore would know the truth, you must give the slip to your natural knowledge and become without senses, for truth is beyond all sense.' This logical conversation now produces a purely metaphysical result in the disciple: for it is reported that, after this time, such a change happened to him that he often became enraptured from all of his senses, often for ten weeks (sometimes more, sometimes less), both in the presence of the people and when no one saw him, so

---

[85] "*Ich und du bekommen einander nicht auf einem Zweige oder auf einem Platze; du gehst einen Weg, und ich einen andern. Deine Fragen gehen aus menschlichen Sinnen, und ich antworte aus den Sinnen, die da sind über alles menschliche Gemerk.*" ["You and I do not meet on one branch or in one place; you go one way, and I go the other. Your questions arise from human thinking and I answer from an awareness which is far beyond all human comprehension."] *Susos Leben und Schriften*, 300; cf. also HS, 318.

that everything became one for him, and he saw only the One without multiplicity.[86]

Just as this teaches the mystical union, where consciousness loses its object, other passages teach the union of revelation in a real and fundamental difference. For Wisdom teaches that so long as creatures have from eternity been in God, they are the same, one divine life and essence, the only one, with God; but after their *issuing forth* from God they receive a differentiated essence and a differentiated form.[87] In this [77] issuing forth from God they for the first time become creatures and must lay aside the evidence of their almighty Creator. The form gives to each creature its differentiated essence and its independent movement: with this creatures are both separated from God and self-related. If now creatures are considered according to their eternal being in God, then they are not creaturely, but one and the same divine life and essence; but each thing's creatureliness is still nobler and more useful for it since it has been in God from eternity. For in the general essence, where all is one, the human person is not different from a stone. However, considered according to its formed essence, the human person is the pinnacle of creation.[88]

The revelation-consciousness in these Christian mystics throws light especially upon the explicit polemics they conduct, in several places, against pantheism, that is, against the pantheistic sects (the Brothers of the Free Spirit) and the practical errors which guided them. Pantheism is continually posited as the basic error; namely, that they suspend [*ophæve*] the fundamental difference between God and creation, Christ and human beings, and so blend them together. They vanquish pantheism in a few victorious encounters, but because they carry the pantheistic principle in the nature of their mysticism, it returns; and without themselves knowing it they give themselves over to the force of its substance. In order to show their sharp and perceptive thoughts on pantheism and how they from a spiritual perspective fought against it so as not to allow the precious jewel of revelation to be taken away, we shall cite a few examples. The most remarkable are found in Suso. [78] For example:

---

[86] Ibid.

[87] "*Nach dem Ausschlag, da sie ihr eigen Wesen nehmen, da hat ein jegliches sein besonder Wesen ausgeschiedentlich mit seiner eigenen Form, die ihm natürlich Wesen giebt. Denn Form giebt gesondert Wesen und geschieden, beede von dem göttlichen Wesen und von allen andern.*" ["After their issuing forth, when they receive their own essence, each has its own particular essence distinguished by its own form from which its natural being derives. For form gives separate essence and distinction, both from the divine essence and from all others."] *Susos Leben und Schriften*, 292; cf also HS, 311.

[88] Ibid.

One time, it is reported, when Wisdom's disciple sat deeply sunk in contemplation on a clear summer day, in the depths of his *Gemyt* he came upon a clever image, who was terribly subtle in his words, but unpracticed in works, and had a haughty and boasting appearance. The disciple took note of this and asked: 'Where are you from?'

The image answered: 'I am from nowhere.'

He said: 'What are you then?'

It answered: 'I am not.'

He said: 'What do you want?'

It answered: 'I want nothing.'

He continued: 'That's strange. Tell me, what is your name?'

And it said: 'I am called the nameless wild one.'

He replied: 'You certainly must be called the wild one, for your words and answers are so wild. Listen to me: what are you getting at, what is your point?'

It answered: 'a pure and perfect freedom!'[89]

In response to the disciple's closer questioning, the image, quite in keeping with the fundamental principles of the Brothers of the Free Spirit, explains that in which perfect freedom consists: pure freedom is such that every person lives according to their own inclinations and discretions without limit and negativity. It is a freedom which pays no attention to anything, but repudiates all differences and sets itself above them. For when a person has been annihilated in the eternal nothing, he or she is perfected and has nothing to say about differences; he or she looks only to the ground, where all is one. To this the disciple answers that perhaps all is one in the ground, but things cannot be taken simply as they are in [79] the ground, but also according to what they are in themselves outside of the ground. It is one thing to be separated from the ground and the one essence, another thing to be different from this. There is nothing which is *separated* from the one essence, but everything is different from it.[90] Thus the difference constitutes true freedom, for true freedom is well-ordered freedom; but where there is order, there is also difference. A disorderly freedom, which posits itself above difference, is no different from sin and evil.

The central point in the theory of unbridled freedom is of course the pantheistic union of God and humanity. In order to maintain this theory

---

[89] *Susos Leben und Schriften,* 310; HS, 326.

[90] *"Also versteh ich, daß in der Wahrheit nichts ist, das Geschiedenheit haben möge von dem einfältigen Wesen, weil es allen Wesen Wesen giebt; wohl aber Unterschiedenheit, also, daß das göttliche Wesen nicht ist des Steines Wesen, noch des Steines Wesen das göttliche Wesen, noch keine Kreatur der anderen."* ["Thus I maintain that nothing truly is which can be separate from the simple essence, because this gives essence to all essences; yet with regard to distinctness, the divine essence is not the stone's essence, nor is the stone's essence the divine essence, nor is one creature the other."] *Susos Leben und Schriften,* 312; HS, 328.

against the disciple's objections, the appeal is made to the fact that Christ is God's only begotten Son: what is now given to Christ, is given also to human beings. And just as Christ did not need to be reborn, so also human beings do not need rebirth, but are immediately one with God and effect whatever Christ effects. The disciple in this also perceives the wild, disorderly reason [*Fornuft*], which has much in common with the true light, and yet is false, because it does not distinguish between nature and grace. For what Christ is by nature, human beings can only become by grace. By means of such thorough answers the wild apparition is forced to retreat. 'You and your kind,' the disciple says at its leaving, 'are above all to be corrected with the knowledge [80] of the correct rational difference, without which one cannot come into a blessed life.'[91]

In another place Suso discusses the fact that a person, when he or she has with joy begun to advance beyond time and space, comes to a point which, spiritually speaking, can be compared to a deep sea, in which many drown. For when a person's eyes begin to be opened up and when he or she has cast a glance into eternity's presencing now, when the created reason [*Fornuft*] begins to notice the uncreated reason both within itself and in all things, then the person finds that he or she has up to this point been distant from God, yes without God, ignorant and blind. And now the person attacks the matter with an altogether too great vehemence and untimeliness and thinks that he or she has already grasped it. In this joy it seems to them that they are full of God, and that God and all things are one and the same. Their *Gemyt* [disposition] becomes like a fermenting cider which has not yet clarified itself, where everything is wildly churning with everything else. Such a person pays no heed to heaven nor to hell, neither to devils nor to angels, but will know of nothing other than God. He or she even forsakes the suffering humanity of Christ, seeking nothing other than God in these sufferings. Such a person is like bees when for the first time they come out of the hive into the fresh air: they swarm wildly and disorderly around and are completely crazed. Some of them fly away and perish, but most of them turn back orderly to the hive.[92]

The *Theologia Germanica* also speaks of a false light which deceives concerning its likeness to the divine. Its falseness consists in the fact that it wants to be God, even though it is only nature. The false light says: "since God is above all things, free, immutable, [81] the one who needs nothing; and since God is above all law and conscience, and everything God does is rightly done, I also want to be this way! The more likeness to God, the better. Therefore I will be like God and myself be God." This light claims

---

[91] Ibid., 310f; HS, 326.
[92] Ibid., 139; HS, 177.

for itself everything which pertains to God; not so much what pertains to God according to God's human nature, or as a just person, but insofar as God is God from eternity. Such a person requires that all creatures be submissive to it and does not want to know about the cross or suffering: indeed, it desires to fly up over our Lord Christ's earthly life and be celestial and supernatural, just as Christ was after the resurrection—and other such things this false and fanatical teaching says.[93]

Tauler fights against the same error. He speaks about *"die falschen, Gottschauenden Menschen"* [the false persons who see God] who describe freedom by saying that spirit must perish according to its created essence and become a pure nothing. If this were possible, he says, then human beings could no more be holy nor blessed than a stone or a piece of wood could be. Without our own love and knowledge we cannot become blessed; but God is and becomes blessed, as God has been from eternity. This helps us only a little towards our improvement if we do not love God. Even though the false spirits, who aim at such a freedom, are so subtle that one cannot conquer them, their freedom is but a delusion, and they themselves are not unlike the condemned spirits. For they have neither desire nor love nor knowledge, neither [82] worship nor thanksgiving nor praise, but are eternally condemned.[94]

Now were it enough, as it usually is, to know the basic error in a system in order thereby effectively to surpass it throughout the whole application and completion of its thought, then Christian mysticism would be altogether clean of pantheism—in other words, it would no longer be mysticism. But the fight with pantheism is here more a fight *ad extra* [externally] than *ad intra* [internally]. Pantheism is fought to the extent that it appears *outside* of the mystical subject. Its forbidding consequences are seen, but in the mystic's own hand its secret root is not advanced. This is a phenomenon which repeats itself in all regions of human spiritual knowledge: a onesided principle can be opposed with the sharpest and most fortuitous weapons, as a matter even of life and death, so long as it presents itself as an object outside of us, if its whole shadowside plainly exposes itself to the day. But in our inner thought-world we give ourselves over not uncommonly to its invisible inspirations, secure in the thought that we have certainly fought against its images outside of us. This unconscious contradiction, which so easily insinuates itself even in the most purely scientific consciousness, is for mysticism not something contingent, as it is for science, but a necessary consequence of its own nature.

This is the perspective from which one should judge the controversy which broke out after Ruysbroock's death concerning the purity of his

---

[93] ThG, ch. 38.

[94] *Taulers Predigten*, Frankfurt (1826), 1 B 293.

teachings. From his writings on the spiritual wedding garments Gerson, the Parisian counselor, cited a number of plainly pantheistic texts, on which basis he refers to him as a heretic. Ruysbroock's apologist, Johan von [83] Schonhofen, sets forth a series of passages which plainly contain a refutation of pantheism. Mysticism has, as it were, two handles with which it can be grasped. Ruysbroock himself in many places engages in a forceful critique of pantheism. He speaks of that heresy which says: "when I stood in my eternal ground, then I had no God; what I desired, that I was, and what I was, I desired. I hoped not, loved not, believed not. I neither prayed nor adored, for I ascribed to God no advantage over and above me. There is no difference of persons in God, neither Father, Son, nor Holy Spirit. There is only one God, and with him I am one, the same One, which God's own self is. With God I have created all things; without me God is nothing."[95] Because several of these sentences, which Ruysbroock ascribes to heretical sects, are found in Eckhart in almost the same exact words, it could seem as though Eckhart and Ruysbroock were fundamentally different and that Eckhart at bottom belonged to the Free Brothers sect, whereas Ruysbroock was authentically within the church. However, above we cited passages from Eckhart which contained the opposite of this heresy and, consequently, have shown that Eckhart himself distinguishes his teaching from pantheism. On the other hand it is easy to show passages from Ruysbroock which teach that the human personality loses itself in the abyss of the divine essence in such a way that it no longer can be found, because in this abyss there is neither beginning nor end, neither way nor path; and the soul according to its uncreated being is itself one with the divine abyss. For just this reason [84] Gerson suspected Ruysbroock of belonging to the sect of free spirits.

We now proceed with our consideration of mysticism's revelation-consciousness and its anticipations of more recent speculative ideas. If we turn to their understanding of Christian dogma, we find mysticism initiating a higher evaluation of theological knowledge. This forward step and turning point in the process of the development of dogma can be characterized, according to what was said above, in the following way: here the *immanental* understanding of dogma is made pertinent in contrast to scholastic supernaturalism, in which dogma stands as a foreign, impenetrable positivity. The thought of God's immanence, which led to pantheism in its separation from revelation, in the sphere of revelation must lead to a contemplation in which the smallest seeds are given for a more profound, speculative understanding of God's *personality* as that which contains human personality within itself as one of its own moments.

---

[95] Cf. Englehardt, *Richard von St. Victor und Johannes Ruysbroock*, Erlangen (1838), 226.

Thus if we consider the dogma of creation to be the first dogma of revelation and inquire into creation's ground and wherefore, the church-
consciousness' typical answer is the following: that what has brought
forth the world is not some blind necessity, but only God's free love
and goodness; and that the human being, as rational creation, is this
love's authentic object and creation's final goal (*causa finalis creationis*).
This thought about the human being as the central point of the universe is
also the center point in mystical theology's doctrine of creation. It is a
natural consequence of the [85] principle of subjectivity which belongs to
the mystical character. The personalism entailed by the love relation is
powerfully articulated: love is posited as both the Creator's and the creature's life-element. Human beings gain true personality only when they
lose their life in order to gain it. Moreover, love's process is considered as
a process of annihilation and the burning up of all the 'material-like' elements in a person, i.e., the dark and egoistic elements.

When mysticism thus teaches, in correspondence with the church's theology, that the world is sustained and brought forth by God's goodness
and love, it thereby positions itself in such a way that, in contrast to the
church's theology, it does not continue to think of God's love and goodness as limited to an arbitrary and formal freedom, but as the necessity of the divine essence. It thinks the Godhead's relation to the world
not merely within the category of causality, but within the category of
substantiality. More exactly: for mysticism, creation and the relation
this establishes between God and creation is not merely for the sake of
human beings, but for God's own sake, inseparable from the divine life-
process itself; and God can do without human beings just as little as
human beings can do without God. As long as the idea of personality and
love is seriously held fast, this latter point leads the way through which
mysticism enters into the Christian speculative Idea and sublates [*ophæver*] traditional theology's exoteric conception of the God-creation
relation. Whoever would accuse this of pantheism must look for it in
another place, not here. For if goodness is not merely an external, contingent determination of [86] God, but God's own being; and further if
it is the concept of goodness and of love to be *communicativum sui* [self-
communicating], to communicate themselves to that which is other than
themselves, then neither can God be without a world. It is then not necessarily a pantheistic idea, but equally a Christian idea, when it is said:
without a world God is not God.

It is from this perspective that several of the above citations from Eckhart must be considered. It is also as inspired by this substantial, actual
and necessary love that Angelus Silesius exclaims:

Ich weiß, daß ohne mich Gott nicht ein Nun kan leben,
Werd ich zu nicht, er muß von Noth den Geist aufgeben.

[I know that without me God could not for an instant live,
Were I to perish, God must necessarily give up the ghost.]

If love and goodness are thus taken not merely in a onesided moral
sense, but in a metaphysical sense as the divine essence's own necessary life-movement which in itself contains the negative, then these rich
categories must be led back to the more typical expression that more
determinately indicates the inner life-movement within the Godhead:
the concept *revelation*. In the concept of God's revelation mystical theology finds the authentic ground for God's creation. The world only exists
so that God can be revealed. This idea appears in a way most nearly
approaching speculative-scientific categories in the *Theologia Germanica*.
Where the truth works and wills, there its willing and working are for
no other reason than that the truth can become revealed and known.[96]
Yet the One or the Best cannot become revealed except in relation to its
opposite, from which it can be known. The essence of the creature [87]
consists in the fact that, through it, God can become revealed and known.
The eternal will is originally and essentially in God without all works and
actuality. But since it is the will's essence to will and effect something,
and this cannot happen without the creature, so God wills and effects
what God wills in and with creatures.[97] Herein the author of the *Theologia
Germanica* finds the answer to the question as to why has God created
the free will: namely, so that the uncreated will shall be revealed in it. The
One only *can* become revealed in the manifold, the Infinite in the finite.
This concept of revelation can be pantheistic; and it is quite in order that
we find certain passages which say that God first in the human *I* comes
to actual thought and will. A comparison can be made here with Fichte.
Fichte deprived God of self-consciousness because self-consciousness
involves reflection and finitude, which he could not harmonize with the
divine essence in-and-for-itself. Therefore as a direct consequence of his
teaching, if there were to be talk about a divine self-consciousness, then
this could only be found in the human moral and religious *I*; for here
the divine essence has appeared within the limitations of reflection and
determinateness. This is thus the same thought lying at the base of the
relevant pantheistic passages in the mystics. In like manner the author of
the *Theologia Germanica* poses himself the question about whether affects,
such as sorrow, suffering, aversion, distress, etc., can be ascribed to God.
But here one must take note: insofar as God is God, there can neither be
suffering nor affliction in God, and yet God does sorrow over human sin.
Since this now cannot happen in God without creation, then it must [88]
happen to the extent that God is human, i.e., *in the divinized human (in*

---

[96] ThG, ch. 24.
[97] Ibid., ch. 44.

einem vergottenen Menschen). *There* is the place, then, where God sorrows over sin; and sin causes God such violent afflictions that the divine self would suffer and die a bodily death in order to remove humankind's sin. The secret sufferings of Christ, about which no one knows except Christ himself, came also from this sorrow over sin. It is in truth God who sorrows, and sorrow over sin is the quality of God; for it does not belong to human beings and human beings cannot manage it of themselves.[98] We shall not here enter in to a more special commentary on this passage. Its *relative* validity for the concerns of Christianity, and particularly of Christology, or for that matter for any Christian thinking, cannot be denied.

In other places the *Christian* idea of revelation appears in a more determinate way. It belongs to God to open Godself, to know and love Godself, to reveal God to God's own self. Now this revelation and knowing are still within Godself without creation.[99] In this revelation arises personal difference (the difference of persons within the Trinity). However, this revelation is only in terms of essence and not actual deed. For that which is in God originarily and essentially God desires to have carried out and executed so that it can become formed and actual. [89] It exists in God only in order to be made actual and molded—and since this cannot happen without creation, creation must and shall be. Indeed, were there to be no informing or actuality or any such thing at all, then of what use would God be? Or what would God be? One gets no further than this.[100]

This aperçu contains at one and the same time what is, for theology, an especially important distinction: that between God's self-revelation and God's revelation in the world (*manifestio ad intra and ad extra*) [internal and external manifestation]; and also the latter's necessity and inseparability from the first. The external revelation is the evolution of the internal. But the external revelation is also involved in the internal revelation and is led back to the divine personality's central point, through which [the divine's] own exteriorization becomes actually inward to itself. God's revelation in and for the world is a moment in God's self-revelation. Whoever then, presupposing a flat theism, would deny the truth of this idea and carve through the eternal copula uniting God's inner and outer revelation, must themselves be careful about how they will be able to jus-

---

[98] Ibid., ch. 35.

[99] "*Gott als Gott gehöret zu, daß er sich selbst eröffne, bekenne und liebe, und sich selbst ihm selber offenbare, und dieß noch alles in Gott und noch Alles als ein Wesen und nicht als ein Würken, dieweil es ohne Creatur ist, und in dieser Offenbarung wird der persönliche Unterscheid (oder der Unterscheid der Personen.)*" ["It belongs to God as God to open Godself, to know and love Godself, and to reveal God to God's own self; and all this is still in God, still as an essence and not as a working; because God is still without creatures. And in this revelation the distinction between persons, or the distinction of persons, arises."] Cf. ThG, ch. 29.

[100] Ibid.

tify faith in an inessential, unnecessary, and thereby untrue revelation. Such a revelation would not belong to the actuality of God's own existence and knowing. God first becomes actually objective for Godself, as an other than Godself, through the world with which God knows Godself to be identical. If this is to be possible there must exist in the world, as the negative and the not-God, a point which, in spite of its creaturely nature, can be identical with God. God, who seeks Godself, can actually at this point find, view, know, love and have the divine self [90] in the other. This infinite focal point of revelation is the *soul* according to the mystic's unanimous teaching.

As Eckhart says: those who want properly to consider the soul's essence must at certain points know not to posit difference between the soul and God. The soul is that point where the created and the uncreated become one and through which the finite world, which is only fragmentary, can again return to its originary source. The entire universe cannot contain God. Only in the soul can God be God. There is no created thing whose concept is wide enough for God to be able to install God's whole essence so perfectly as in the soul.[101] The reason for the gloriousness of the soul lies in the ideal nature of self-consciousness and freedom, in *thinking*, which is the soul's substance. In knowledge the soul is made participatory in God's nature. For God's knowledge, in which also human beings know, is God's substance and essence; and when God's substance is my substance, then I am God's son.[102] In order to possess their own glory, human beings must themselves know and will this glory. This knowing and willing is itself the glory and indeed the authentic focal point of the human being's life. God [91] is much closer to human beings, says Tauler, than human beings are to themselves. But even if I were a king and yet did not know this, I would be no king. All our blessedness [*Salighed*] consists in the fact that we know and acknowledge the highest Good on heaven and upon the earth, which is God's own self. God is also present in stones, trees, and other creatures, but they know it not. If they did know it, they would be just as blessed as human beings and the angels.

---

[101] *Taulers Predigten:* 1, 97.

[102] "*Gott macht uns sich selber bekennende, und sein Wesen ist sein bekennen, und es ist dasselb, das er mich macht bekennen, und das ich bekenn, und darum ist sein bekennen mein. Und wann dann sein kennen mein ist, und wann sein substanz sein bekennen ist und sein Natur und sein wesen, und darum volget, das wesen sein Substanz mein ist, und wenn dann sein substanz und wesen und natur mein ist, so bin ich der sun gottes.*" ["God causes us to know God; and God's being is God's knowing and it is the same thing that God causes me to know and that I know. Thus, God's knowing is mine—just as what the master teaches and what the disciple learn are one. And because God's substance is God's knowing, nature and essence, it follows that God's essence and substance is mine. And because God's substance and essence and nature is mine, I am God's son."] Cf. Eckhart, sermon 76: *Werke* II, 75; EPT, 328–9.

God stages a blessed banquet for the soul in which the noblest delicacy for it is knowledge. For the more God reveals Godself to the soul, the more it hungers after God; and the more it hungers, the more it desires that God fill its empty ground. This is an infinite circle in which knowledge hungers in its fullness, and is filled in its hunger.[103]

This infinite process of self-objectification, a circle turning back into itself, is both God's life and the creature's life. God makes God's own essence creaturely, but the creature's issuing forth from God is only for the sake of the return. As revelation, seen from one side, is creation, i.e., insofar as God posits what is different from God's self, so also, from another side, revelation can be considered reconciliation. This is so to the extent that in reconciliation the difference is dissolved in union and the soul in knowledge and love leads finitude back to its ideal perfection in God.

Creation and reconciliation in mystical theology can thus be considered as the divine Love's play with itself. This idea *need not* be pantheistic. For, as mysticism often repeats: God does not love Godself as God; but as *the highest Good*, [92] i.e., not in God's abstract, self-identical *I*-ness [*Jeghed*], but in God's kingdom, into which God has poured out the divine essence. Or in other words: God wills Godself and God's existence to the extent that God also wills the world's and, more specifically, the soul's existence. God's self-revelation consequently involves God's revelation to the other and its relative subsistence.

In diametrical opposition [*Modsigelse*] to its teaching on God as the nameless and differenceless unity, mysticism thus posits an internal relation of opposition in Godself and thinks God's personality as a mediation of this opposition. With internal necessity this leads to the *doctrine of the Trinity*. This doctrine is the thought concerning the metaphysical opposition and reconciliation within God's own essence; it is this which necessitates the determination of the divine personality as a trinity. In like manner, the church's doctrine of the Trinity can only rationally be thought when it is grasped as a construction of the different moments in the divine self-consciousness; or, as the theogonic process through which God eternally brings forth God's self. The question about the extent to which the Christian idea of God is validated in the mystic's doctrine of the Trinity turns on a closer determination of the relation between God's Son and the world. This is the point on whose determination the *Christian* character of every doctrine of the Trinity turns.

If one in this respect gets no further than the above-reported consideration and determines the other, the θεως δευτερος [second God], in which God becomes objective to Godself, immediately as the world, then one

---

[103] Cf. *Medulla animæ*, ch. 12, in *Des Hocherleuchteten und theuren Lehrers D. Joh. Tauleri Predigten* (Franfurt, 1720), 359f.

identifies the world (more specifically human spirit) with the idea of the Son. This opposes the church's doctrine which has at all times sharply distinguished between the Son as the Father's uncreated essence-image [*Væsensbillede*], and the world, [93] which is created out of nothing. However, even as the identification of the Son with the world is unorthodox, it does not satisfy the requirements of thinking either, because the required act of self-objectification is not actually present here. The objectified God, in particular, cannot be nature; for according to its concept nature is the not-divine because it is *subjectless*. In nature God seeks in vain for God's other *self*, God's alter-ego. It seems, then, that it must be the world of finite spirits, the kingdom of self-conscious monads, where God can be known and willed. From these innumerable points it seems God can shine back into Godself.

Thus if the finite world is *immediately* determined as the Son, then God's self-objectification is not consummated. In particular: each of the finite spirits is considered in itself as only a relative revelation of God which must be completed by all the other relative moments in order to reveal the whole God. If these relative moments, which are, as it were, individual fulgurations of the divine Essence, are now heaped together into a totality, then such a totality would lack the authentic *punctum saliens* [distinguishing mark]: *the Absolute Self*, the central personality in the system of finite spirits. In the act of self-objectification it is certainly not simply the divine Substance which shall become the object for the divine vision; it is above all the Absolute *I*, which seeks *itself* as its own object. But even if the entire manifold of fragmentary points of revelation were set together into a unity, what would be viewed in such a revelation of the world would be only something fragmentary, not a whole God. Such a unity, then, would be simply the substantial unity of the *race*; God would find Godself merely as the spirit of the world parceled out into the system, but not as the eternal Logos *reflected into itself*. The latter's non-rounded-off [94] knowledge and will is the subjective point of unity for every finite spirit because it is the medium through which all see God. Only when God, who seeks God's own self in this revelation, can reflect Godself in the eternal eyes of the Son, only then has God actually found God's self-revelation. Likewise: God can find God's object in the human spirit only to the extent that God finds the divine self there not simply as the substantial life of that spirit, but as the subjective, personal focal point; as the soul within the soul. Consequently, in the self-objectification process it is above all the subject which must reduplicate itself and as object not cease to be the subject.

If then the existence of the world is necessary for God's revelation, then this necessity cannot be any kind of *immediate* necessity; it can only be a mediated or secondary necessity. Or in other words: the world cannot be thought as the *first* negativity in God's self-revelation. The first negativity in the divine essence is the Son, who is himself God. The world can be thought only as the Son's other (*alterum dei filii*), as a negation contained within the Son presupposing the Son as its positive *prius* [prior element]. Only through the Son does God stand in relation to the world. Likewise, God loves the human soul only in that love with which God loves the Son. But insofar as the world's existence is thus posited as mediated by the Son, it must also, on the other hand and just as much, be said that the Son's revelation is mediated by the world. The consideration which says that without the world God would not be God here must find its necessary validity. Creation and the Son's eternal Incarnation cannot fall outside of the trinitarian process, just as certainly as that God's manifestation *ad extra* [externally] and *ad intra* [internally] are two sides of the same concept. [95] The thesis that without the world God is not God acquires Christian significance when it gets articulated from the standpoint of the Trinity and its meaning is the following: without the world God's Son would not correspond with the concept of the Son as the self-opposition within the divine essence. If indeed this opposition is to be real the Son must, in his unity of essence with the Father, also be essentially different from him. That is, he must at one and the same time have a divine and non-divine, i.e., cosmic, nature. He cannot simply be the Father's only-begotten, but must also be the first-born of all creation. He must be not simply God, but also human. Without this *the difference* would not gain its full rights, and God's self-objectification would not acquire its true actuality.

As θεως δευτερος [second God] the Son can only be revealed through the negation of his divine nature. A creaturely world must be posited which is the Son's negation; but precisely because it is the Son's negation it belongs to the Son's principle. Consequently: what from one point of view is considered Creation, the bringing forth of the world, is from another point of view considered the Son's eternal Incarnation. In human nature, which is *capax dei* [fit for God], the Son can be revealed as the *world's personal soul*, as the universe's most interior self, its reconciler and mediator. And as the Son in his worldly nature does not cease to have the divine nature, which is owed to him as the Father's eternal essence-image, he is the true personal not-*I* which the Father seeks. The Father's love for the Son can be thought as a real love only when the Father loves in the Son not his own divine nature, but also an other nature, i.e., when he loves him as the [96] first born of all creation and loves in him the whole world (or what in him is the inclusive [*indesluttede*] system of created spirits). It is a significant incident in Dante's *Paridiso* when the vision of the Trinity appears to the blessed. In the middle of the Trinity's radiant circle there is seen a smaller image (when their glance comes into focus):

it is made out to be the image of humankind. The triune God cannot do without human beings. God cannot accomplish the thought of the divine *I* without thereby also accomplishing the thought of the human being as the negative, finite point. The human must be in God's objectification so that this can be a serious, an actual, alterity [*Alteritet*].

Thus there are two onesided elements in the determination of the Son's relation to the world which must be conquered by Christian speculation. The first is the pantheistic mixing together of the world and the Son. The second is the abstract supernaturalistic conception which excludes the world from the Son's eternal nature and does not know of any eternal Incarnation, but only a historical one; it does so not considering that the two natures must belong to the Son from eternity, and that the idea of the human race as the Son's kingdom is inseparable from the idea of the Son.

How does mysticism stand in relation to this? It is part of its nature that it frequently falls into the pantheistic mixing together of the Son and the world. However, the *difference* is *also* honored. When Eckhart says that the Son departs from the Father's nature and yet remains one with the Father in essence, whereas we [human beings] have departed from the persons—consequently from the Trinity which has being in itself—and have assumed an *other* essence, then this articulates the truth. Mysticism presents the difference of persons quite in keeping with Scholasticism's familiar [97] development of this theme. The Son originates in the root of the Father and this is not a work of God's will or intention, but the necessity of God's nature. For in God's seeing-through the abyss of God's essence, God must speak forth Godself in God's self-knowledge and this self-knowledge is the Son's birth from eternity. God knows Godself in the Son, but that which is known is one with the knower.

Insofar as the Father issues forth from himself in the Son, he returns again into himself on account of the Holy Spirit. There is an eternal issuing forth and an eternal returning. God sees and loves God's nature, and in so doing becomes an object for Godself. This is, as it were, an eternal play in God. The interplay of the Father and the Son is the Holy Spirit.[104] Suso's development of the Trinity proceeds from, and adds imaginative considerations to, the words of an old master: that God is a ring whose center point is everywhere and whose circumference is nowhere. If all the oceans of the world were mirror-still and one threw a stone into the middle of them with such force as to move the whole, then an enormous ring would be formed in the water: the first ring signifies the Father, the second the Son, both together bring forth the third ring, which signifies the Spirit of both; and from the great triune ring of the divinity an infinite number of small rings—souls—flow forth. Suso conducts this imaginative

---

[104] Cf. *Taulers Predigten:* 1, 91; *Susos Leben und Schriften*, 159; HS, 193.

discourse on that which transcends all sense only in order to come to the aid of our fragile senses, and with these images to chase away other, poorer images. But one must know that from the Father's essence originates the Word, who is in person different from the Father, yet in essence one with him, [98] even as he assumed human nature.[105] The Father loves the Son and the Son loves the Father; the bond between lover and beloved is the Holy Spirit. And within the Godhead's triune ring, from the most interior abyss of the Son's heart, there originates a similarly formed image whose nature is a continual staring-back and turning-back to its origin: this is the soul, created in God's image. Just as in the Godhead's ring the end joins up with the beginning, so also shall the soul turn back to its origin.[106]

Moreover, mysticism's development of the difference of persons has nothing special viz. a viz. Scholasticism; the latter rather distinguishes itself by its much greater multiplicity of subtle distinctions. Mysticism's distinctive characteristic in its consideration of the dogma of the Trinity is to have anticipated the knowledge that Creation and God's eternal Incarnation are moments in the trinitarian process and that there is no idea of the Son apart from the idea of the world. *God's Son and the human soul* are always viewed together at once. It is the Father's essence to give birth to the Son; it is the Son's essence to be born, and also that *I am born in him*; it is the Spirit's essence that I am burned up in it and transformed into pure love.[107] The negativity [of the human soul] is thus necessary for the Son's and the Spirit's manifestation. In his eternal Word the Father speaks forth all creatures and therein speaks forth both my soul and your soul. The Son is born [99] in the same way in the soul, not in a different way, as he is born in eternity and God's own essence depends upon the Son being born in the soul. Therefore God compels and drives us so that we might birth him the Son.[108] It is not enough that God's Son was born of Mary, but daily God is born and shall be born in every believing soul.[109]

Consequently, it is the determination of human beings to be "the other" in which the Son shall be revealed. For this reason mysticism places as the highest practical task, the deepest obligation for human beings, to let

---

[105] *"In diesem tiefen Abgrund ist die göttliche Natur in dem Vater sprechend und gebärend das Wort heraus nach persönlichkeit, innebleibend nach Wesenheit, das an sich nahm die natürliche Menschheit."* ["In this deep abyss the divine nature is present in the Father speaking and giving birth to the Word: externally according to personality, internally according to essence—which in itself takes on human nature."] Cf. *Susos Leben und Schriften*, 169; HS, 201.

[106] Ibid.

[107] Cf. Eckhart, sermon 39: *Werke* I, 420f; EPT, 296f.

[108] Ibid.

[109] This last expression continuously appears in Tauler, especially in his Christmas sermons.

the Son be born in them and to give God space in the soul so as not to hinder the Son's Incarnation. Because the Son cannot exist without human nature, Eckhart can make the further claim that the Holy Spirit just as much proceeds from human beings as from God; for since the complete Idea of the Son is the Idea of the eternal God-human, the Spirit's procession from the Son must just as much be a procession from human nature as from divine nature.

It is a natural consequence of the subjective character of German mysticism that an elaborated development of the doctrines of Creation and Trinity do not become, *as such*, the central concern. It is essential to the mystic to make his or her life only in God, to enter into the divine unity. There is here no interest in a theoretical construction of the universe, of nature and history, wherein the doctrine of the Trinity could become the key—as, specifically, when world history is comprehended as a moment in God's own history. Only the idea of the Son's eternal Incarnation [100] has continuing interest for our mystics' *subjective* consciousness. The idea of the eternal unity of the divine and human natures becomes the central point of contemplation for the soul, whose poetic aspirations extend only to practically actualizing this unity and itself experiencing it. The mystic's spirit, indeed his or her whole individuality, is as it were impregnated with this idea; every other dogmatic category stands, in relation to this, as an ulterior motive which acquires its significance only by reference to this. For if a mystic tarries on another thought, the concern for the idea of humanity's deification (*die Vergottung*) will almost certainly lie in the background, and the consideration will suddenly break-off in order to return to this.

The most characteristically dogmatic elements of the mystical theology we must therefore expect to find in *Christology*. Since the unity of the divine and human natures is a result of every mystical consideration of the soul's nature and essence, the difficulties in a strict supernaturalistic conception of the doctrine of Christ disappear. The idea of Christ now becomes the most natural thing of all for the human; for ideally every human being is Christ. However, insofar as this thought is expressed, it opens up an opposition and turning point for the church's Christology. Church dogmatics, to the extent it appears partly as symbols, partly in the elaborations of the scholastics, posits the unity of the divine and human nature only as an isolated point in history, in a discrete individual. In mystical theology this unity is articulated as an eternal unity which is present at all points. Christ's appearance in history stands for the church as an absolute miracle; the church-body's consciousness is [101] permeated by the feeling of its infinite distance and difference from the God-human [*Gud-Menneske*]. But here nothing is seen in Christ which does not straightforwardly follow from the concept of human nature; and rather

than representing Christ's infinite majesty and difference from all, the
ruling thought becomes that Christ is *our brother*. What is epoch-making
in mystical Christology is to have made the human being's essential unity
with Christ the central concern for Christological considerations.

According to our earthly and temporal birth, says Tauler, we human
beings are perhaps different from one another; but in the eternal birth
there is only one Son of God. For in God there is only one origin, one beginning, and therefore there are not two births, but only one birth, not
two sons, but only one Son. If therefore we are not to be many sons, but
only one son with Christ, then it is in truth required that we also with
Christ have a birth from the Father.[110]

The identity of the human being's eternal birth with Christ is specified
more closely in terms of its common human nature considered in its
purity and generality. For in spite of all individual differences human
beings are one in the one human nature, which according to its concept is
in an indissoluble union with the divine. *Essentially* considered, Christ has
no other human nature than the poorest and most wretched human
being. According to Tauler:

> All human beings are just as close to one another in nature, the smallest and
> the greatest, the most foolish and the wisest, the emperor and the pope.
> Nature is just as noble and perfected in them all, though the persons are dif-
> ferent. So also the nobility of human nature is just as near to me as to our
> Lord Christ; indeed everything that Christ has in his human nature belongs
> [102] also to me in the same nature. But woe unto me if I am close to him in
> nature, but personally I am myself closer to self-will and self-love. Therefore
> there is a difference between the human and human nature. Human nature
> is more dear to me than the human which I myself am. When the eternal
> Son in the fullness of time took upon himself human nature, he took it upon
> himself not as it was in this or that particular human being, but in its uni-
> versality [*Almindelighed*], without any contingency, in-and-for-itself. If we
> then would become God's children, we must isolate and separate from us
> that which is particular and distinct. As when one mentions a person such
> as Peter or Paul, then one considers the contingent difference of nature. But
> you shall look at yourself as you are in your human nature in-and-for-itself,
> apart from all contingent difference; and you shall so little concern yourself
> about your own person as you concern yourself about the Sultan who lives
> on the far side of the ocean. When you behold yourself in this universal
> nature, then you will have become divine; and when you by means of love
> are united with God, then you will have become one son with Christ. Were
> my soul only so prepared as our Lord Christ's soul, the Father would work
> in me as in his only-begotten son and not differently. I perhaps have nature

---

[110] *Taulers Predigten*: 1, 56.

in common with our Lord Christ, but not his person; but when I with my own person stand back, what can he do about that?[111]

During the mystical submersion in the soul the transcendence associated with the church's teaching vanishes: Christ *in us* becomes the dominant thought and the religious a priori (*ab interiori*) steps forth against the church's a posteriori (*ab exteriori*). This [103] describes not simply mysticism's relation to Scholasticism, but also its relation to the ruling Catholicism. How, more specifically, to solve the highest task of the Catholic church: to maintain the savior's presence in spite of his sensible departure? How is Christ spiritually present in his spiritual communion? Plainly the Catholic church wants not simply to maintain the spiritual presence of Christ, but also in a sensible manner to make the church into a sensible reflection and bodily presence of Christ on earth. But the form in which the idea is present in its sensible exteriority is art; and Catholicism becomes in its cultic life the art-religion of Christendom. Christ is exteriorized for the believer in images and sounds. His body and blood are offered in the holy Eucharist as immediate, sensible realities. In the mass he is offered up continually anew for human sin. However, the believing *Gemyt* [disposition] is only an observer and listener and not a co-worker in this process wherein Christ is brought to presence. Christ is set forth and presented to consciousness only for beholding and he remains an external thing; an impermeable barrier is securely placed between Christ and the believer.

In contrast to this exoteric cultus, the mystics form a quiet, esoteric spiritual choir which turns away from the composite world of images and seeks Christ's imageless essence in human nature itself. When the crusaders, driven by the exoteric orientation of Catholicism, went forth to regain the Holy Land as Christendom's most cherished relic; when the pious pilgrims found comfort by setting foot on that land where the Lord had walked, because they thought that in those places they could more authentically experience the Lord's presence than anywhere else; so here in mysticism the soul knew in the infinite certainty of its inner experience that it itself was [104] the only place where Christ was to be sought—that Christ was either here or nowhere. The mystic's *intinerarium mentis* [journey of the mind] is the opposing image to the journeys of the crusaders to the Holy Land. The mystical journey is not a going forth, but a continual entering in by means of the annihilation of time and space. When the mystics strive to reproduce the various moments in Christ's life in their own individualities by the imitation of Christ, then in this they become a spiritual counterpart to the church's martyrs. For the martyrs step forth

---

[111] *Taulers Predigten:* 1, 56; 2, 21; cf. also Eckhart, sermon 25: *Werke* I 284f.

into the limelight of actuality and in an external struggle against the world they reproduce Christ's suffering in an external manner by bodily suffering and actual death. The mystic's main goal is to reproduce Christ in a non-sensuous way. The story of Christ becomes the Idea; particularly, the story of Christ's suffering is repeated spiritually as an invisible purification, as the soul's dying away from sinfulness and its naturality and the world of images.

Thus, an opposition between an esoteric and an exoteric consideration of Christ came into formation. The theological antinomy between the empirical and the Idea, between the historical Christ and the ideal Christ, which is so sharply expressed in our own day, already surfaced in those days. If we are more fully to elaborate this antinomy we shall again enjoin the following: that our mystics do not position themselves in a consciously polemical relation to the dogma of the church; on the contrary, they always *presuppose* the doctrine of the church and want only to bring about a *practical appropriation* of the doctrine.[112] However, [105] through the practical, subjective appropriation the religious and speculative a priori comes to develop itself, and the tradition must yield to the Idea.

The first step towards the development of the ideal Christ is finding in the holy dispensation itself the separation between the esoteric and exoteric consideration of the Savior. The mystics are drawn with a secret power to the Gospel of John, with its purely spiritual, more eternal than historical understanding of the Savior, where the thought about life in God and communion with Christ—Christ in us and we in him—is continually returned to by the contemplative vision. It cannot fail to be appreciated that a significant point of contact with mystical contemplation is found in this Gospel. Also, in this Gospel the soul's union with God and the Savior are the central concern. Here there are only a few basic ideas which are seen in their immediacy and again and again repeated without any kind of development or variation; and consciousness is not sated in these repetitions because it is in the grip of the hidden fullness of the content. The impression this has made on the mystics shows itself in the

---

[112] *"Kinder, ihr sollt nicht nach grossen hohen Künsten fragen. Gehet einfältig in euern Grund inwendig, und lernet euch selber im Geist und in Natur erkennen, und fragt nicht nach der Verborgenheit Gottes, von seinem Ausfliessen und Einfliessen von dem Icht in das Nicht, und dem Funken der Seele in der Istigkeit, denn Christus hat gesprochen: Euch ist nicht Noth zu wissen von der Heimlichkeit Gottes. Darum sollen wir einen wahren, ganzen, einfältigen Glauben halten."* [Children, you ought not to inquire into great and high questions. Simply turn inward into your ground and learn to know for yourself in the Spirit and in Nature; and do not ask about the hiddenness of God, about God's going forth and return from that which is to that which is not; nor about the spark of the soul in its essential being. For Christ has said: "It is not necessary for you to know the secrets of God." Concerning these we are to have a true, complete and simple faith.] Cf. *Taulers Predigten,* 2 B 73.

Johannine form and tone which often breaks forth in their discourse on the divine. The Gospel of John has set in tune all the mystical spirits in Christianity. In the contemplative attunement which does not seek God in the world's bustle, but desires to see God in the light of eternity as God reveals Godself to those who love God, [106] the mystics go further. There are moments in the events of the Gospel in which the distinction between the esoteric and exoteric elements expressively comes forth in the factical itself. Thus, the form of Christ is different before the resurrection than after the resurrection. After the resurrection his form is transfigured, but in this way he is not revealed for the crowd but only for the disciples; similarly, he ascends to heaven only for their eyes. A second feature is the transfiguration on the mountain for the disciples. Only to those who have left all in order to follow him does he show himself in his eternal glory; for the crowd, which is dispersed in its worldly business, he veils his essence. Therefore we also ought to forsake the world and ascend the mountain of *contemplation*, the spiritual Tabor, if we are to see him not merely in his sensate robes but as he is.

Christ himself makes a distinction between those who are outside and can only grasp his teaching in parables and those who are within, to whom it is given to understand the mysteries of the kingdom of heaven without parables. A perfected person knows the truth without any natural images, and he perceives inwardly what God and creatures are, what time and eternity are, what sin and virtue are.[113] The ancient opposition between πιστις [faith] and γνωσις [knowledge] and the modern opposition between representation and concept comes forth in its own way in mysticism as the opposition between *image* and *essence*. The allegorical interpretation of Scripture is tied in with this. Words and events are understood not in their immediate, historical significance, but are considered only as images. If you desire to have the kernel, then you must break the shell; [107] if you will find the pure essence, then you must smash in two all parables.[114] In this manner the religious a priori properly comes forth.

The allegorical interpretation desires to suspend every barrier between itself and the content of Scripture; it desires to know everything as an eternal presence. But its onesided subjectivity shows itself in the fact that it does not actually expound [*udlægge*] the positive given of the text but installs [*inlægge*] its own contents into the text. It becomes a *docetic* treatment of the text in which the text's empirical content and actual meaning are transformed into an illusion. The content of the allegorical interpretation is only that which is the normal property of spirit independent of external history. For this reason the result of the interpretation is always

---

[113] Cf. BPS: 85f, 100f.
[114] Cf. Eckhart, sermon 51; *Werke* I, 538f.

predetermined. Thus, the mystic sees in everything only reflections of the mystical process.

When Tauler, for example, preaches on Jesus in the temple, he develops on the basis of this how we ought to seek our spiritual birth, Christ in us. Jesus' parents sought for him in vain among their acquaintances and friends: they found him only in his Father's house. In this way we also must forsake all human beings and turn back to our eternal source. We should forsake everything of our own: our own thoughts, our own understanding and will. These are the many acquaintances which scatter us.[115] Eckhart preaches on the Samaritan woman. Christ tells her that she has had five husbands and that the one she now has is not her husband. The woman signifies the soul! Who are the five men? They are the five senses! With these the woman has sinned, and therefore they are dead: "the man you have now is not yours!" It is the free will which does not belong to the woman, for it is bound in the thralldom of sin. "Bring to me your man!" That is, give me [108] your will![116] Christ awakens the widow's son from Nain. The widow is the soul; the dead son is reason [*Fornuften*]. "Young man stand up!" says Christ. The human person's awakening and spiritual resurrection is the theme of the sermon.[117] On the feast of Mary Magdalene he preaches about her meeting with Christ in the garden after his resurrection. "Do not touch me", says Christ, "for I have not yet ascended to my Father!" Why does he say, 'I have not yet ascended', since he in fact never left the Father? He means to say: "do not touch me, for I am not yet resurrected in *you*![118] In the story of the conversion of Paul, Eckhart follows the Vulgate translation of Acts 9:8: "But Paul stood up from the earth and with open eyes he saw *nothing*." What kind of light was it which shone around him on the road to Damascus? It was God's own self which shone around Paul's soul. God dwells in unapproachable light; if a person therefore would know God, then God Godself must be the light in the soul. What then was the 'nothing' which Paul saw? It was the pure mystical nothing. Paul saw God as the divine nothing and creatures as a creaturely nothing; and in all creatures Paul saw nothing but God.[119]

Since the mystics thus reflect themselves into the Scriptures, and their own images confront them on every page, the question asserts itself: how then was the personality of Christ comprehended? A denial of the historical Christ one must not expect to find here. On the contrary, our mystics

---

[115] *Taulers Predigten:* 1, 53.
[116] Cf. Eckhart, sermon 66: *Werke* II, 10f.
[117] Cf. Eckhart, sermon 5A: *Werke* I, 58f.
[118] Cf. Eckhart, sermon 55: *Werke* I, 594f.
[119] Cf. Eckhart, sermon 71: *Werke* II, 64f.

seek to be the church's true sons. But if we ask what *inspired* them, then it is plainly that in Christ which, as it were, was the reflection of the ideal of the God-human which they themselves bore in their [109] interiority. In Christ, Tauler says, there are two kinds of works. The one belongs to Christ's divinity [*Guddom*], as his walking on the water, performing signs, fasting for forty days, and all such things. These works we cannot imitate, for they are God's. The other works which were in Christ belong to his humanity, as being poor and destitute, being despised, suffering hunger and thirst; and finally all the virtues of Christ—being humble, patient, gentle. In all of these we are to be one with Christ.[120] The latter is what actually inspires the mystics, because they see in these that which constitutes the reality of their own consciousness. Their standpoint is practical, ethical, and one can with full right call this Christ a *moral* Christ. This is, of course, by no means to be understand in the manner of Kant and the eighteenth century. However, the mystics and Kant hold one thing in common: the practical standpoint is the dominant one in their Christology so that they only have an interest in the 'purely human' in Christ, only look upon him as the ideal of *freedom*. Yet on the other hand there is this great difference between Kant and the mystics: Kant thinks of this morality as God-abandoned [*gudforladt*]; the mystics think of it as God-fulfilled [*gudopfyldt*], so that the 'purely human' is *eo ipso* [precisely thereby] the *God*-human [*Gudmenneskelige*]. The divine nature is given in the concept of the second Adam or the perfected human nature:

> Everything which has been destroyed and died in (the first) Adam has been raised up again and made living in Christ; and everything which was raised up in Adam, has died in Christ. But what is this and what was this? I say: it is true obedience and disobedience. With reference to this one should note the following: disobedience is that the human holds on to itself and thinks that it knows and is capable of something; it is that the human seeks its own. But obedience is that the human is without selfhood and egoity [*Jeghed*], [110] that it considers itself and all things as nothing and only sees, grasps, and loves God in all things. In this way the true human nature is in Christ. It does not consider itself or any other thing, but is nothing other than a house and domicile for God; and it is this that makes the self not to be something of itself. In the obedience of Christ there was neither fear for hell nor hope of an eternal reward; but this is the highest Good in the service of a free love. Christ spoke his words and did his works not for the sake of any advantage. Rather, it is as if one were to ask the sun, why do you shine? It would answer: I can do no other; it is my nature and quality. Just this way was Christ. He was filled with a profound and essential humility which knew that essence, life, knowledge, and ability belong only to the highest Good. Before Christ everyone was turned toward themselves,

---

[120] Cf. BPS, 121.

everyone desired to possess, none wanted to be poor but everyone sought riches. But when Christ came he brought us again the true poverty both internal and external. Hence, where there is selfhood and egoity, there is the old person, disobedience and Adam; but where the old person dies, there is the new person, obedience, and Christ. Where God and the human being are so united that there is only one—true, perfect God and true, perfect humanity—and the human is so devoted to the divine that *God Godself is the person* and works and does everything, *there is seen the true Christ and nowhere else.*[121] [111]

This passage, whose concerns are the most typical and frequently met with, clearly contains only a description of the God-human which the mystics themselves strive to realize. The historical Christ is presupposed and the outward Christ is not held apart from the inward Christ. Moreover, whether the image of Christ here represented is actually outside of us, or only forms itself within the soul's own ground, i.e., whether we have to do with a person or only an idea, is a continually hovering and indeterminate matter.

The consideration always returns to the story of Christ's suffering and death. Just as the rose most gloriously reveals itself in its aroma, so also the essence of Christ reveals itself in his sufferings and death. If a person would be free of all worldly defect, if all worldly vanity and contingency were to lose their power over him or her, then he or she must submerge himself or herself in the suffering of the Lord. That which sets itself between God and the human is destroyed and annihilated in this suffering—which is, as it were, a consuming fire in which all *unlikeness* vanishes.[122] This fire which Christ brought to the earth is the flame of love. In this, true lovers give up all bodily things on account of God; indeed, they give up their own life for life in God. Their disposition [*Gemyt*] is lifted above all created things, breaks through to the uncreated Good, which is itself God, and loses itself in the [112] unknown God's hidden darkness.[123]

---

[121] [*This quotation once again weaves together disparate passages*—trans.] Cf. ThG, chs. 13, 10, 33; BPS 100; ThG, 22: "*Und doch der Mensch Gott so gar ergeben, daß Gott da selbst ist der Mensch, und Gott ist auch daselbst und würket stets daselbst, thut und lasset ohn alles Ich, Mein, Mir (das ist ohn allen eigenen Willen, Liebe und Eigenthum) siehe da ist warhaftig Christus und sonst nirgend.*" [And yet the person is so resigned to God that God is there Godself, as that person, and also there as God; and God continually works, acts, and lets be without all I, Mine, and Me (i.e., without all self-will, self-love, and self-possession). There is seen the true Christ and nowhere else.]

[122] *Es ist kein Mittel so groß, so es getragen würde in das Leiden unsers herrn, es muß vergehen und zu nichte werden. Denn es ist ein brennend Feuer in dem alle Ungleichheit verschwindet und verbrennet.* [There is nothing so great that it does not pass away and become nothing if it is brought into the passion of our Lord. For this is a burning fire in which all dissimilarity disappears and is consumed.] Cf. BPS, 165.

[123] BPS, 165; 128.

Consequently, in Christ's free suffering and death are beheld the culmination of humanity's union with God. For since this death contains the giving-up of every worldly reality, the crucifixion of egoity and the annihilation of the world of naturality and images, the soul's unlikeness to the divine becomes thoroughly sublated [*grundig ophævet*] by the uncreated essence. Reconciliation here is not understood as in Scholasticism, i.e., as something which happens external to human nature, but as a universal, internal process which must repeat itself everywhere the finite shall be united with the Infinite. Alongside this conception of reconciliation, according to which Christ has suffered death only for others and where this has significance only *ad extra* [externally], a consideration presents itself from a speculative-ethical standpoint: that suffering and death are immanent determinations in Christ and just as necessary for his own perfection.

A scriptural passage which the mystics have hidden deep in their hearts and which is often repeated in this connection is John 12:24: "Truly I tell you, unless a kernel of wheat falls into the earth and dies, it remains just a single grain; but if it dies it bears much fruit." The kernel of wheat is our Lord Christ's noble soul, the fruitful field is his human nature (considered in its universality [*Almindelighed*]). The singular human being must, as it were, let himself or herself be buried into the universally human [*almindelig Menneske*]; the individuality must give up his or her immediacy, must put his or her life at risk in order to gain it. This is expressed in the following passage: "This death in Christ was both spiritual and bodily: bodily, insofar as his soul partook of all bodily sufferings—hunger, thirst, the cold of winter, hail and snow, [113] pain and that bitter death—and he gladly brought all this to God as a sacrifice; spiritual, insofar as his soul, in spite of its being-together with his body, nevertheless died away [*afdøde*] from this and was outside of the body in a continual vision of the divine essence. In his deepest sufferings on the cross Christ beheld the highest Good uninterruptedly. No deprivation or pain could intrude into this vision; and when the body died on the cross, his spirit lived in the presence of the highest Good. This is the fruit which grows in the fruitful fields of his human nature, and into these noble fields you shall cast your soul as a kernel of wheat so that it can die and bear fruit."[124]

Another passage, not infrequently remembered by the mystics, are the words of Christ: "'Why do you call me good? None is good except one, who is God.' If then a human being is called good, it is only because this person is more God than creature."[125] In this connection belongs the thought that the glorification of the creature only happens by means of a continual dying away [*Afdøen*]. The application to Christ lies close at

---

[124] Cf. Eckhart, sermon 49: *Werke* I, 528f.
[125] Cf. Eckhart, sermon 41: *Werke* I, 436f.

hand: although he is without sin, he is not good (in a metaphysical sense) until he has realized his determination, i.e., until he has forsaken the world of finitude and fragmentariness. He becomes good only on account of first falling into the earth and dying like the kernel of wheat.

The Christmas sermon always contains the thought that God's Son is not merely born of Mary, but daily is born in every believing soul; and that Mary must first birth Christ spiritually before she can birth him physically; and that she is much more blessed on account of the spiritual birth than the physical birth. In the same manner the Easter sermon is a rich discourse [114] on the kernel of wheat and an echo of the Lord's words: 'it is a benefit to you that I am going away' (i.e., so that I can raise up in you). Even our Lord Jesus Christ's beloved image and his fatherly, fertile presence were harmful and hindered them in their salvation [*Salighed*], for the disciples loved him as a merely mortal human being. Unless the soul is raised up over all created things, the Holy Spirit cannot come into it, for all of the divine works, which God effects, God effects not in *time and space*, but in spirit.[126] The contrast between the image of Christ and the essence of Christ comes into focus here, and the believing soul poses itself the question whether it is not better to bear in mind its savior's life and suffering without images, than to consider them with images.

Tauler says:

> What is better, that I give up all my thoughts and works and hold myself free from all multiplicity and all creaturely forms, or that I think about our Lord's suffering, about his life and image and the fact that God has created me, born my sin, and granted me eternal life? All this is good and must by rights awaken great love and gratitude in you. But where these images intrude and acquire a place, there other images could also acquire a place. Therefore we must hold ourselves free from all images so that the essence of Truth can shine in us in its nakedness. This is not to say that one should disdain the Lord's image and his pain, but rather that, out of great love and gratitude, everyone who is able should consider these without images. It is like when someone who owes me five shillings gives me five marks, he will not have [115] sinned. Many good people are hindered in their perfection because they are, with too great a desire, fastened onto Christ's humanity. Yet even if we *see* the divine truth in Christ, who is the way to the Father, we are still not on this account perfectly blessed; for as long as we still fasten onto this vision we are still not one with that which we see; and as long as we still consider and understand something, we are not one in the One. One cannot see God except in blindness and one cannot know God except in ignorance.[127]

---

[126] Cf. *Taulers Predigten*: 3, 94.

[127] Cf. *Taulers Predigten*: 1, 202; 2,78: "*So wir nun in den Weg der Wahrheit kommen, der Christus ist, so sind wir dennoch nicht vollkommen selig, wiewohl wir doch die göttliche Wahrheit*

The mystical identity which transcends vision and the imagistic Christ once again comes into conflict here with the concept of revelation. The true identity of the subject and the object in faith, knowledge, and love certainly demands that what is believed, known, and loved is inwardly present to and dwelling in the soul; but with this internal existence these latter also do not cease to be independent *objects* for the soul and must to this extent remain something external for it. Thus, when representation [*Forestilling*] and image are correctly led back to thought and essence, so that the external content can become an internal one, then this ought not to be thought as the annihilation [116] of vision, but only as its explanation. With the annihilation of vision the object's own actuality is annihilated. The object and the subject merge chaotically in the indeterminate universality of essence. They become merged rather than becoming one. For just as thought in its universality can be considered an expression for the thing's interior presence to and essential unity with self-consciousness, so also is *representation* the expression for the thing's independence from self-consciousness, or its independent actuality as *object*. The internal and the external, the immanent and the transcendent, thought and representation, essence and image, concept and vision, presuppose and mutually corroborate one another in the actual identity. In the true consideration of Christ, therefore, the essence must be seen in the image, the image in the essence.

Just as it is true that this image shall become, indeed originally must have been, essence in us, it is also no less true that the universal divine-human ought to gain form and *'character'* in us. But character is gained only by being formed according to Christ's image [*Billede*]. It is the imagistic [*billedlige*] (i.e., historical) Christ which makes it so that the essential [*væsentlige*] Christ can step forth from the mystery of the human soul, forsake the esoteric depths of possibility along with the obscure kingdom of intimation and feeling, and stand up into *actual* consciousness. The mystical consciousness which abstracts from the revelation of Christ wants to fuse itself with the soul's internally hidden Christ, which as such can neither become an object for love nor knowledge. The same thing which we have shown in the previous section to take place in the general relation between mystery and revelation, the hidden God and the revealed God, now [117] repeats itself here in the domain of Christology. When the image of Christ disappears from view and consciousness grasps only the characterless essence, then consciousness notices that it is getting to be evening in it and around it and it longs to return to the clear day of

---

anschauen, denn dieweil wir an der Schauung sind, so sind wir nicht Eins mit dem, was wir schauen, denn dieweil Etwas in unserm Gemerk ist oder Verstand, so sind wir nicht Eins in dem Sinen; denn wo nichts als Eins ist, da siehet man nichts als Eins; denn man kann Gott nicht sehen, als mit Blindheit, und nicht bekennen als mit Unbekenntniß." [Translation above in quotation—trans.]

revelation from this realm of shadows, to where the Word has become flesh. And when consciousness has once again found the *object* of its love, when it stands by the Incarnation, by the God visible, then it thinks that God dwells only in pure light, and it hunts again after the imageless identity. It consummates its *via negationis* [way of negation] and makes acosmism pertinent once again.

An important determination which often appears where Christ's historical actuality and his only-begotten personhood are to be maintained and secured, is the following: Christ is by *nature* what everyone else by *grace* must become. But this important dogmatic idea, which in the mystic's writings continually shows up in passing as a corrective, does not get developed. This is because it is not set in relation to the thought which first casts the proper light on it, namely, the thought that Christ is the head of the church, the personal point of unity in whom both the race and the individual are perfected. This Christ, revealed for the whole spiritual communion [*Menigheden*], who is the All for everyone—and only through everyone does he stand in relation to each one—communicates himself to the single individual [*den Enkelte*] only through social life as his spiritual body and organism; this Christ remains in the shadows in mysticism. The mystic, who is at least partially removed from the life of society, imagines his or her Christ [118] according to his or her own likeness as the lonely, subjective God-human, whose glory does not suffer to manifest itself before the eyes of the crowd, but enters only into a secretive rapport with the single soul.

Because the historical personality of Christ thus lacks the proper posture and basis, it cannot be held fast, but immediately assumes a purely esoteric physiognomy. The mystical shows itself again in the fact that the revelation of Christ is sought outside of Christ's spiritual communion. Yet outside of the spiritual communion Christ is hidden. For revelation is Spirit's appearance for spirit, its life and actuality for consciousness. The revelation of Truth, as the revelation of Spirit, is not in the most exact sense for the single individual, but for *universal* consciousness [*almindelige Bevidsthed*]. And Christ, as personal truth, can only be revealed to the spiritual communion. Only the social consciousness [*Samfundsbevidstheden*] is the proper organ for understanding him. Therefore only the Christ of the spiritual communion is the true Christ, and he only is to the extent that he lets himself appear to the spiritual communion. For just as every light only is for the corresponding eye, so also the 'light of the world' only is for the 'social eye,' or for spirit in the spiritual communion. To say that the Christ of the spiritual communion is not the true Christ is to say that he has not been revealed at all; for a revelation to an esoteric circle of particular individuals who do not have the power to become universal and exoteric would, *eo ipso* [precisely thereby], not be the true revelation, but only an abstract, subjective side of it. Here mysticism often coincides with Gnostic systems of thought which also seek the true Christ outside of the spiritual communion, thereby pulling him out of the circle of revelation, more hiding him than setting him in the true light. In such systems the personal Christ is made [119] unknowable and transformed into an indeterminate, foggy, and, so to say, disguised character who perpetually mystifies the contemplator. But all gnosis is true only by the criterion that it has developed itself out of social consciousness and can again return to this, i.e., can give back what it has received from the fullness of social consciousness.

Since the mystical Christ is outside of the spiritual communion, consciousness also steps into relation with him without this being mediated through the spiritual communion and the means of grace in social life. In the preceding this principle has shown itself in the idea concerning the Father's flight into a colorless pleroma and in the idea that the Son's personality and Incarnation are dissolved into the 'essence' of Christ. The mystical principle manifests itself in the doctrine of spirit in the following way: that the imitation of Christ is undertaken independently of social life, that Spirit's rich, disseminated life in the spiritual communion vanishes into a subjective being and a movement within the individual, where it exercises its immediate works.

The mystical appropriation of the divine and blessed life, the soul's practical way to perfection, now becomes the task for our presentation. Only after this can the whole picture be made complete for us.

III. THE HIGHEST GOOD AND VIRTUE

Nature, Grace, and Essentiality
The principle and foundation for the morality of mysticism has already been given in the preceding. The task is determined as the imitation of Christ, which is not simply to adopt an external [120] relation to Christ, but to relate to Christ in such a way that the same practical task which was accomplished in the life of Christ is accomplished in that of the true mystic. None is good except one, who is God. The highest Good is God, Godself. But since God does not desire to be without human beings, because God in human beings beholds the divine self, God has posited human nature as the means for the eternal revelation of the Son.[128] Thus, it is the destination of human nature to reveal the Son and to realize the union of the divine and human natures. The Father incessantly incites humanity to birth him the Son. The necessity of God's own divine nature

---

[128] Cf. above, 212–213.

leads God to the human. However, just as the revelation of the divine nature cannot be consummated without the free will of the human being, the free will itself comes into its repose only in God. The highest Good, as the infinite goal [*Formaal*] of the will for human beings, is thus the person's union with the divine Essence. The necessity, which is just as human as divine, for the will to strive after its object, is duty. This practical striving itself, the actualizing of the ideal, is virtue.

Clearly the moral ideal here has quite a different significance than in many of the moral systems operative not so long ago. These systems set forth the moral ideal as an eternally unachievable goal which continually recedes further with every approach. The content of such morality is an empty concept concerning God's will which expresses itself in a system of abstract commandments. Here, on the contrary, the divine as well as human nature require that the ideal become actual, that the content is not merely God's will, but God's essence, which is [121] one with human essence. The thesis that 'the human being shall do the good,' is the same as the thesis, 'the human being shall realize God, bring God's essence into existing actuality.' This is the knowledge at the heart of all religious and speculative morality. The mystics coincide on this point with the most penetrating moral philosophers, with Spinoza just as with Fichte. In Spinoza's *Ethics* the divine Substance is the only object of moral striving. His notion of intellectual love of God is the unity of the thinking will with the divine Essence and constitutes a part of the infinite love with which God loves God's own self. Similarly, in Fichte's moral conception of the world God is placed as the authentic task for human activity. To realize God, which here only means the moral order of the world, is the human being's all-comprehensive duty.

However, if speculative mysticism changes over into pantheism it falls into the same practical onesidedness as the above-mentioned systems and it can just as easily be grouped together with Spinozism as Fichteanism. God is then actual only *actu* [in act], insofar as God's essence comes to a breakthrough in the soul. If, on the other hand, speculative mysticism rests in the Christian conception of the divine personality, it expresses the true principle for Christian morality. God is not, in this case, *merely* the moral ideal. As ideal God only *is* to the extent that God's revelation is continually *brought forth* by freedom; but in God's eternal self-revelation God is just as much a being-in-and-for-itself. God wants to unfold the riches of God's essence through human beings in a new revelation and therefore God *fashions* Godself into the ideal of human nature. Eckhart expresses this [122] in the following way: God requires God's Son from every human being; every human being is consequently duty-bound to render to God a form for the revelation of the Son. The concept of duty remains without reality when the command of duty is not recognized as the expression for God's *essential* will, that is, when every determination of duty [*Pligtbestemmelse*] is not conceived in the final instance as a divine determination of essence [*Væsensbestemmelse*] expressed under the form of an absolute requirement for human nature.

A lack in the fulfillment of duty thus hinders not just the human being in achieving its determination, but has a restraining effect on the divine Essence itself. Self-will [*Egenvillien*] becomes a barrier for God's revelation in that the truth, as the Apostle says, is kept in unrighteousness (Rom. 1:18). The concept of *duty as over against God*, which is so important for Christian morality, cannot be accomplished unless God enters into an actual relationship of reciprocity with human beings. Yet insofar as God fashions Godself into the practical ideal of human nature, God places Godself in a relation of dependence upon the subjective will.[129] According to the mystic's profound conception, God is Godself that which God commands. God commands love, God is love; God commands goodness, righteousness, mercy, etc. But all of this is God, Godself. It is God's Substance. God's own self is the content of every command of duty. As regards all of the concrete duties which are laid upon human beings, their true meaning is only this: that the divine personality [123] itself desires to come forth in the human being.

When the mystics thus paid homage to the fact that God's own happiness depended upon this coming forth, they realized (to the extent they remained within the sphere of revelation) that, at least in principle, they satisfied the requirement which must be made of every profound morality: that the Good should be practiced for its own sake, not simply in reference to the individual's ultimate happiness or salvation. For just as, I dare say, the soul which has been set aflame in love finds its inspiring ideal and thereby its own blessedness [*Salighed*] in God, so also, on the other hand, the ideal is the object of its deepest and purest *obligation*. The good is done, in the most significant sense of the word, for God's sake. God has, as it were, laid God's own blessedness in human hands. And what does it harm you, O human being, that you wish God to be God in you!

It is illuminating that the line which here lies between the purest resigned love and a fanatical spiritual arrogance can be compared with a fine, almost invisible hair; similarly, that the mystics, especially Eckhart, have often stepped over this line (even though in certain holy moments they have remained within its limits). But on the other hand, it ought not

---

[129] "It is clear that, for as many human beings as there are who close their hearts or their spirits to the eternal, for just so many individuals God's existence gets crowded out; on the other hand, everyone who lives for ideas thereby opens their minds to the divine existence and contribute to its extension." J. L. Heiberg, *Perseus*, 1 B, 19.

to be forgotten that every line in these regions is fine and more difficult to observe than the precepts of everyday morality. For the perceptive reader, both the similarities and differences with Spinoza, who did not require God's reciprocating love, but desired to love God for God's own sake alone, will be evident.

However, even though in their best moments the mystics articulated the true *principle* of morality, this nevertheless remained *only* a principle rather than expanding itself to revelation in a worldly, ethical life. The high and purifying element in [124] this conception lies (just as in Spinoza) in the moral acosmism which annihilates the small details of duty and allows the multiplicity of empirical goals to be destroyed in the one, absolute duty. However, this high ideal becomes ineffective as long as it high-mindedly disdains to descend into those details and exempts itself from the mediation of finitude. Certainly in accordance with this the infinitude of the ideal is circumscribed. But precisely here the ideal is brought into that form whereby the universal [*almindelig*] Christian consciousness properly can be recognized. It is a duty for the human being in his or her life to realize the unity of the divine and human natures. However— as both the church [*Kirken*] and science must urge—the realization of this unity is not possible *immediately*, but only on account of Christ as the mediator between God and human beings. The abstract-infinite require- ment that the individual ought to realize the ideal of a God-human [*Gud- Menneske*] now is reduced to the concrete duty to *believe* in Christ and put on Christ.

Similarly, when speculative thought unites with the representation of the spiritual communion, it becomes for the first time true. This is also ac- knowledged when the goal is determined as the imitation of Christ. Thus, when the historical Christ, as so often happens, vanishes in the face of mystical contemplation, the requirement just as often disappears into that abstract infinity wherein the mystical individual ought to make him- self or herself into Christ. Moreover, the imitation of Christ itself becomes an abstract ideal for the Christian consciousness when it is not mediated through social life and its variegated, definite, and finite ends. For it is in these ends that the single individual [*enkelte Individuum*] acquires its allot- ted portion, in accordance with its proper spiritual gifts. The ideal does not disappear in this mediation but no longer steps forth in its pure uni- versality. It has here descended from the ethereal [125] heaven of thought and assumed actual human form. The mystical principle, by contrast, de- mands that the ideal's *essence* be grasped apart from its *phenomenon*.

The same must be said about virtue. In this connection the antinomy between the one virtue and the many virtues comes to the fore: the one virtue is supposed to be grasped outside of the many virtues. We are sup- posed to set aside the images of virtue so that we are able to achieve its essence; we are not supposed to have virtue in multiplicity, but in unity.[130] However, the one virtue is only the *mystery* of virtue; its *revelation* is the many virtues and the actual deeds. "The virtuous one ought to be without all why, he or she ought not to do something for the sake of benefit." But benefit is the necessary moment of finitude in all effectual acting. Virtue in its pure, blank universality is an impressive looking bank note, but in actual life one cannot spend it without first converting it to usable currency. The mystical ethical discourses could in this sense be compared with the Stoics and with Kant's high discourses concerning pure duty as an end in itself.

The condition in which human beings live in the one virtue can, of course, only be brought about by means of a detachment: partly from nature as a limitation upon freedom simply speaking, partly from the actual and active life in which the *many* virtues have their home, and where the essence of virtue only steps forth in the *image*. The moral abstraction through which the infinitude of freedom is won is described by means of three stages (*die Staffeln des geistlichen Lebens*) [the stages of the spiritual life]: the stage of nature, the stage of grace, and the stage of essentiality. The last, which is the expression for perfection and completion, Eckhart (in particular) denotes the stage of *justice* [*Retfærdighed*]. Within these three stages, there are still [126] a multiplicity of levels which perhaps ought to be conceptualized as nuances and adumbrations in feeling rather than held fast and expressed by means of some category of thought.

The outward nature is subjected to contingency and restlessness. Solicitousness for it is a hindrance to true perfection. Mystical spirit relates itself negatively almost everywhere with respect to nature. Tauler praises the example of a monk who, walking in the month of May through the monastery gardens, pulled his cape over his eyes in order not to be disturbed in his meditation by the contingent forms of the flowers. To the extent that spirit is not in the position to detach itself from the beauty of nature and enter into a positive relationship with it, nature must there be won to the Christian side: it must immediately be transfigured in grace. Its beauty is perceived *only* with the religious organ, the only organ with which the mystic senses. The emerging spring in forest and glade only makes an impression upon the mystic when church bells ring out over the fields and the fragrance of flowers blends with a religious aroma.

The poetic Suso, compatriot of the balladeers, often expresses such a feeling for nature. He greets the new-born May, but plants the cross as a spiritual sapling because the fruit of eternal salvation sprouts forth from this. For every red rose he offers his savior a heartfelt love; for every small violet an inward humility; for all white lilies a pure embrace; for all the

---

[130] Cf. BPS, 55.

flowers of the field a spiritual kiss; but for every small bird his heart breaks forth in a perpetual song of praise.[131] This *immediate* reflection of grace in nature is the only [127] condition under which meditation upon nature appears here. (Incidentally, meditation upon nature occurs more frequently in the Roman mystics than in the German mystics. St. Francis of Assisi's hymns to the sun and his sermons to the birds are examples of this mystical nature poetry which has sprung forth from the profound feeling of creation's movement in God. However, this also sets in motion the religious explanation of nature in a naive, immediate manner).

However, it is above all the naturally human itself which is to be trans-figured in grace. The effects of grace manifest themselves in the fact that human beings acknowledge their sin and nature's defect, and that a long-ing for the recursion to God is awakened in their hearts. The first stage of grace is *active* virtue. The human being strives to maintain God's com-mand and the precepts of the church, to show pure and holy manners, to practice good works. But to active virtue adheres contingency. It moves amidst temporal things. It always seeks to effect '*something*' and is thus conditioned by external objects. Contingency is: that which can be at one moment, and then not be at another moment. Active virtue only is as it happens to be.[132] Essential virtue is not dependent upon objects and there-fore eternal and imperturbable.[133]

Yet in order that human beings can arrive at essential virtue, grace leads them from the active life to the contemplative life. [128] The essence of virtue, however, exists in the contemplative life only to the extent that contemplation arises from a perfect spiritual poverty. The person must not simply be poor in virtue and works, but also in knowledge and love; indeed, he or she must be poor in grace. Grace is only a point of passage into essence. Grace is encumbered by creatureliness, for what is known and effected in grace is still altogether in creaturely forms.[134] At the stage of essence, the person does not *have* virtue, he or she *is* virtue.

Belonging here is the distinction between active and passive reason. Active reason [*virkende Fornuft*] is the expression of grace; it prepares place

---

[131] Cf. Suso's *The Exemplar*, ch. 12; HS, 83.

[132] "*Was ist Zufall? Das ist das nun ist und nicht ist. Und also wirket er nun Tugend und nur als es ihm vorgehet oder kommet.*" ["What is accident? It is that which now is and then is not. And thus it works virtue, but only as it appears or seems to one."] Cf. BPS, 56.

[133] "*Das (der Mensch) nicht vermögens hat zu wirken einige Tugend mit den Materien, denn allein mit einem einfeltigen Willen.*" ["The person does not have the power to perform various virtues with material reality, but only with a simplified will."] Cf. BPS, 56.

[134] "*So die Seel erhaben ist über alle Leiblichkeit, über Zeit und über all Mannigfaltigkeit - so wird Gnade gewandelt in Gott, daß denn Gott die Seele nicht mehr ziehet creatürlicher Weise, sondern er führet sie mit ihm selbst in göttlicher Weise.*" ["Thus the soul is elevated above all bodiliness, above time and above all manifoldness . . . Grace is so changed into God that God no longer draws the soul after a creaturely manner, but leads the soul with Godself in a divine manner."] Cf. BPS, 55.

for essentiality and passive reason [*lidende Fornuft*]. Active reason annihilates all forms, working in such a way that the creature is recognized in its nullity; God becomes the only master craftsperson. Active reason is what we may call negative-dialectical.[135] It effects its own destruction in passive reason. Passive reason suffers what God alone effects: all unlikeness disappears; the passive reason becomes a *mother* of God, giving birth to the eternal Son.[136] This is the stage of essence and the mystical identity with the Good.

Normally the mystic's life hovered between active virtue and essential virtue, between a life for the spiritual communion [*Menigheden*] and [129] a life for the abstract ideal. In striving for the abstract ideal, mystical self-consciousness turns itself with contempt away from social life and the contingency of the external world. When, however, essential virtue is not merely hidden in God but tied to an *empirical* personality who must step forth into the external world—while yet revealing pure essence without finitude—then there appears a phenomenon, which, within the circle of Christendom, is the same as what the wise person was in antiquity: an *idealized* personality who contains all moral perfection. The practical philosopher who sought to represent the wise person as an empirical personality attempted to transform himself or herself into something morally abstract. In particular, it is the Stoic wise person who appears reborn on the Christian stage having switched a philosophical toga for a monk's gown. As everywhere, this abstraction appears most strongly in Eckhart. The "exemplary form of a perfect human being" is described in the following way:

> There was once a learned man who for at least eight years had desired for God to show him a person who could instruct him in the way of truth. At length [130] God's voice rang out to him: "Go hence to the door of the church, there you will find a person who can show you that for which you seek!" So he went thence and found a poor man, whose feet were torn to shreds and full of dust and whose clothes were not worth two cents. He greeted him and said: "God grant you a good morning!" The poor man answered: "I have never yet had a bad morning!" The man continued: "Then God grant you fortune!" To which he responded: "I have never had bad fortune!" Again the man said: "Then God grant you eternal blessedness [*Salighed*]—how will you answer to this?" The poor man replied: "I have never not been blessed!" "Explain all this to me," said the man, "for I do not comprehend your meaning." The poor man answered: "You wished me a good morning. I have never had a bad morning, for when I am hungry, I praise God; when I am cold, when it hails, snows, whether the weather is

---

[135] *"Sie heist eine würkende Vernunft, denn sie würket alle Dinge ab."* ["This is called the active reason, for it strips away all things."] Cf. BPS, 243.

[136] *"Da liegt sie im Kindbett und gebiert den Sohn in der Gottheit."* ["(The soul) lies on the maternal bed and gives birth to the Son in his divinity."] Cf. BPS, 244.

lousy or good, I praise God. If I am wretched and forsaken, I praise God, and for that reason I have never had a bad morning. You wished that God would grant me good fortune. I have never had bad fortune, for I have learned to live with God; and whatever God allots to me, whether good or ill, I receive as the best. Therefore I have never had bad fortune. You wished that God would make me blessed [*salig*]. I have never been without blessedness, for I have given over my will to God's will in such a way that what God wants, I also want. And therefore I am always blessed."

The learned man objected: "And if God wanted to cast you into hell, what would you do then?" "Throw me into hell," the poor man answered, "that God cannot do; God's goodness prevents God from this. And yet if God would cast me into [131] hell, I have two arms with which to grab God. The first arm is true humility. With this I unite myself with God's sacred humanity. The other arm is love. With this I unite myself with God's divinity [*Guddom*] and cling to God so firmly that God would have to come with me into hell: and I would rather be in hell with God than in heaven without God!" Then the learned man understood that humility and poverty were the closest way to God.

The learned man inquired further: "From where have you come?" The poor man answered: "From God!" And again: "Where have you found God?" "When I forsook all creaturely things!" "Where do you have God?" "In a pure heart and in good people." And the learned man continued: "What kind of a man are you?" "I am a king!" "Where is your kingdom?" "In my soul, for I can rule over all my inner and outer senses, and all my faculties and desires are subordinated to my soul! My kingdom is greater than any kingdom upon the Earth." The learned man continued, "What has brought you to such perfection?" And he answered, "My quiet contemplation, my elevated thoughts, and my union with God. I could not rest in anything that was less than God, and now I have found God."[137]

Whoever wishes to compare the Stoical tales of the wise person, who is a solitary king, free though in chains, detached from affects, etc., will without a doubt recognize the same principle here (in accordance with the necessary changes accompanying a new world). Moreover, in the outward poverty and the tattered clothes one can without difficulty recognize the Cynics.

However, this ataraxia, freedom's repose in its own [132] inward infinity, cannot, from the standpoint of Christianity, be realized. This is because the flesh never ceases to desire contrary to the spirit; and virtue, in its loneliness, gets toppled over by the non-Christian forces of nature. A

---

[137] Besides other places, I have found this quotation in the Frankfurter edition of Tauler (1720) as an appendix to *Medulla Animæ*. For internal reasons this quotation seems as though it ought to be ascribed to Eckhart. This also applies to the preceding chapter which contained several short table talks by Eckhart under the title: *Meister Eckharts Wirtschaft von wahrhafter Armuth des Geistes*.

continual ascesis is necessary in order to mortify the flesh and freedom turns into the worst kind of dependence. The idealized personality unceasingly collides with the actual personality and can establish its royal monarchy only in the most despotic way: by imposing upon the actual person a servile obedience to the law which, for the most part, consists of self-torments. Thus, it is reported concerning Suso's life that he wore an undergarment with pointed tacks, turned inward towards his body; another time, that he carried a wooden cross fastened to his back with nails; or again, that in order to mortify the flesh he let his body be infested with vermin, etc. The subject cannot achieve repose for a speculative intuition of essence [*Væsenskue*], because it is disturbed by the vermin of reflection.

Relating also to the conflict between the spiritual and the bodily are the dreams and visions of the mystics, i.e., their ecstatic states. Görres is full of praise and tribute regarding these ecstatic states, and views them with approximately the same eyes as the mystics themselves when they reflected back upon them: namely, as visible proofs of divine grace which have elevated the soul above the life of reason and set it into a rapport with the transcendent reality. We have already mentioned that Görres, in his large work on mysticism throughout the centuries,[138] has compiled an enormous number of such ecstasies, visions, and revelations; and in this higher empiricism he posits the principle essence and glory of mysticism.

For us the important thing is to realize that, along with these visions, there appears a new *contradiction* in the mystical consciousness. Free spirit, [133] which has elevated itself above all images and torn itself lose from nature, sinks involuntarily into a dream-world and pure intelligence is imprisoned in a somnambulistic state. The same consciousness which, by means of its intellectual power, transforms the external world and its experiences (specifically, the historical facts of religion) to a pure interiority, now takes that which can *only* be an interiority as a real experiential externality. It annihilates an actual object and gets an illusory one instead. Often these visions have a lovely, poetic hue; but the content is most often insignificant and turns on the empirical individuality as its center point. An odd contrast to that point in the mystical theory where the immortality of the individual seems to be wiped away occurs when Eckhart, after his death, revealed himself to Suso and reported to him that he had now completely crossed over into God.[139] When Suso desired a more approximate description of this condition, he learned it was ineffable.

Mary, the virgin mother, plays a large role in most of the visions. When Suso, after having mortified his body with fasts and water-drinking for

---

[138] Görres, *Die Christliche Mystik.*
[139] Cf. Suso's *The Exemplar*, 75. [Modern scholarship thinks it probable that the 'Eckhart' of Suso's vision referred to another Eckhart, not the Meister. Cf. ME, 18f.—trans.]

many days, was appeared to by Mary, she allowed him to enjoy some drops of wine. Another time she brought him a basket of delightful fruits. The fact that the *natural* is so often the content of the visions is easily explained by spirit's ceaseless struggle against nature. Sensuality is slain in the actual world, but it returns in the ideal [134] world and with a magical spell-binding power it paints its objects so they acquire the full presence of actuality.

These conflicts belong to essential virtue. However, the mystics do not live a life simply outside of society, in themselves and for themselves, but also a life *for the spiritual communion;* they think not only of their own salvation, but also of the salvation of others. When they step forth into life from the lonely cell, their preaching sounds a purifying note for a consciousness lost in a spiritless exteriority. Once in a while their preaching descends to the relationships of actual life, but normally it is pure virtue and the ideals of the highest Good which they, from the mountain-top of contemplation, represent to the spiritual communion standing below in the valley. The life about which they discourse is the monastic ideal. But it is precisely this abstraction which is cathartic for the crassly Catholic consciousness of the spiritual communion.

Here we come to the question of the extent to which the mystics can be considered predecessors of the *Reformation.* Some of their thoughts are necessarily preparatory for the Protestant doctrine of faith: in particular, the idea that virtue is creaturely and frail when considered according to the external deed, but is divine when considered in view of the fact that God accepts the pure will in place of the external deed. The idealistic conception of the will, so often articulated in the sermons of these mystics, must have had a liberating effect on the people's consciousness, imprisoned as it was in quasi-mythological representations: for example, understanding the concepts of good and evil as external facts, and imagining punishment and reward as sensate objects. Eckhart is especially great at expressing the will's independence from all exterior things, i.e., the will's ideality as its only actuality. He says, "The one who gives one hundred gold marks for a spiritual use has done a great deed; [135] but I tell you, if I have the will [*Villie*] to give one hundred marks, then I have paid God. God shall vouch for me as if I had paid God the hundred marks. I say more: had I the will to give God the whole world, God would vouch for me that I had given the whole world. And if the Pope was slain by my own hand, and it happened without my will, I would not even present myself before the altar and read the Mass."[140] Such discourses must have worked toward the emancipation of a consciousness ensnared by such representations as *opus operatum*, indulgences, the church's tax on good

---

[140] Cf. Eckhart, sermon 25: *Werke* I, 284f.

deeds, and a consciousness anguished by fear over a sensate purgatory and hell. For example: what burns in hell? It is only self-will [*Egenvillien*] which burns in hell.

The spiritual freedom which announced itself here as a Christian *antinomianism* has many features in common with the picture Luther sketched in his essay "On the Freedom of the Christian." Moreover, it is akin to the joviality [*Gemytlighed*] and expressive inwardness which has evolved in such rich measure in the Protestant, especially Lutheran, church. Religion is an experiential matter; every thought is edifying; every cognition blends together with the personality. A wonderful example of this rich disposition [*Gemyt*] is preserved for us in Tauler's biography (found in most editions of his works). This poem, or as Tieck has recently called it, this theological novella, contains Tauler's inner history. It relates the way in which the highly learned doctor Tauler, who was widely esteemed for his great artistry in preaching, was converted in Strassburg by a simple lay person. It tells how this man [136], with simple speech rendered by God's Spirit, convinced him that, though he had imagined himself to be a Christian preacher, he was nothing but a Pharisee because he lacked true humility and spiritual poverty; that with his Christian discourses he sought only his own honor and was much too puffed up over his scholarly sagacity. Further, it narrates how the highly learned doctor came to radical humility and self-denial through many inward strains and outward derisions, thenceforth to learn to preach in true Christian simplicity.

That in this story a lay person reproves a priest is an indication that the *external* difference between the clergy and the laity is of no account. It is the principle of subjectivity which is in movement here. The disposition requires its due and will not ascribe the Christian proclamation any worth if the person is not grasped by the truth. Such proclamation of the word by a person who is deeply moved—one could say, impregnated— by the subject matter belongs to what is characteristic of mystical preaching. If one adds to this the fact that these homilies were preached in the mother tongue, which through these preachers resounded with a hitherto unknown wealth of deep and beautiful forms in which the folk-consciousness could feel itself at home and recognize its own thoughts, then it is comprehensible that they must have produced an enormous effect, and in several senses prepared the way for the Reformation.

The immediate religious fervor animating the mystics shows itself also in that they set the living word above the scriptural text. Every person, according to the preface to Suso's book on eternal wisdom, ought to know this: that the words which are received with and sung from pure grace and which stream forth [137] from a living mouth and a living heart (especially in the German language), versus the same words when they are inscribed on the dead parchment, are as unlike each other as hearing a line of music is different from hearing talk about it. Such words stiffen from the cold and fade like the cut rose. However, a diligent person will learn to consider these (written) words in relation to their source, in their original deliciousness and first beauty; then the person will feel the influence of the presence of grace, in which the dead heart is solaced. Whoever considers them in such a way will be unable to pour over this without his or her heart being inwardly moved to a fervent love, to new light, to distress before God and sorrow over sin, or to one or another holy desire with which his or her soul can be renewed in grace.

While this freedom and inwardness may be considered the announcement and heralding of the spirit which eventuated in the cleansing and rebirth of Christianity, nevertheless, more closely scrutinized, it was merely a moment of the principle of reformation which circulated in mysticism, rather than the principle itself in its deepest and complete truth, because the dogmatic kernel of mysticism is qualitatively different from that of the Reformation.

This point can be illuminated with reference to the concept *unio mystica* [mystical union] which is an important moment in the Protestant *ordo salutis* [order of salvation]. It is developed with great relish especially by the Lutheran theologians. The different renderings of this concept will most easily lead us to see the point on which the dogmatic difference hinges. The difference does not lie in that Lutheran theology wanted to deny an essential, substantial and real identity of the human person and God. Lutheran theology elaborates the principle that there is a double *unio mystica*: a general one, in which [138] all persons participate, both believers and non-believers, insofar as they all live, move, and have their being in God just as the birds in the air and the fish in the sea; and a special one, in which only believers participate. In this latter the believer's substance becomes united with the Trinity's substance and with the human nature of Christ.[141] Luther supposes the human person's identity with Christ is so real that he says: "You shall be so merged with Christ that out of you and him there shall become, as it were, one person. So much so that you with confidence will say, 'I am Christ, that is, the righteousness, victory, and life of Christ are mine.' And Christ likewise will say, 'I am this sinner, that is, his sins, death, etc. are mine.' The *Formula of Concord* expressly condemns the proposition that it is not God, Godself, who dwells in a believer, but only God's gifts.[142] Therefore the difference does not consist in Lutheran theology's wanting to limit itself to a merely moral, or religious, identity, and not accept a speculative and substantial identity.

---

[141] Cf. for example, the explication in Hollaz, *de gratia inhabitante*.

[142] *Quod non dues ipse, sed dona dei duntaxat in credentibus habitent*. Cf. the *Formula of Concord*, article 3, antithesis 6; *The Book of Concord*, trans. Theodore Tappert, Fortress (1959), 475.

However, the Lutheran *unio mystica* stems from the Reformation's fundamental idea, *justification by faith*, which appears only dimly in the mystics. In justificatory faith the historical Christ is appropriated through the word and sacraments, and through the spiritual communion [*Menigheden*], whose head he is. The *unio mystica* is only an expression for the fact that this faith [*Tro*] is not merely a historical belief [*historisk Tro*], not a subjective moral or religious conviction, but rather contains within itself divine substantiality and essentiality; or, in other words, that it [139] is the *true* point of identity between God and the sinful human person. Christ's essence, as the mystics discuss it, is therefore contained in the Lutheran *unio mystica*, but this becomes inseparable from the objective, historical reconciliation of Christ. Indeed, justification by faith must be thought, in principle, as preceding the *unio mystica*. By placing the *unio mystica* in this indissoluble relation to *fides justificans* [justifying faith], Lutheran theology in principle excludes any onesided, pantheistic unity of God and human beings. For the mystical, substantial unity with Christ *presupposes* his historical actuality as a sinful human race's objective righteousness before God. In our mystics, on the other hand, there is not so much talk about faith; at least, it is not set forth as justifying. There is talk only about virtue, spiritual poverty, transformation in God and Christ, all of which proceed immediately to the *unio mystica*, rather than that this exists only in the Lutheran church, '*mediante fide, verbo evangelii & sacramentorum usu accensa*' ['mediating faith, the word of the gospel and the orderly use of the sacraments'].

A closer scrutiny of this contrast shows that mysticism, though having disconnected itself from Catholicism in many ways, yet coheres with its deepest root. A spiritualized Catholicism is therefore not yet authentic Protestantism. It is perhaps necessary only to indicate the Catholic difference from Protestantism on the doctrine of the order of salvation by noting the differing emphases justification and sanctification receive in both systems. In particular, if the question is raised concerning human justification or reconciliation with God, or the way in which the finite, sinful person can become the object of God's recognition and love, then it is the evangelical church's idea that the human person cannot do this on his or her own account, not even by means of a [140] Christian *striving*, which is always relative and piecemeal, beset by lack and limitation, but only by means of faith alone. For by faith Christ is appropriated. And God does not see humanity in its naked, sinful finitude, nor with respect to its (always relative) virtue and sanctity; but sees humanity only in Christ as the restored Adam, the one in whom human nature's originary righteousness, its idea, is *objectively* realized. The believer thus knows himself or herself to be righteous not according to their empirical actuality, but only according to the ideal obtained in Christ. But the *unio mystica* indicates that the human person, by faith, is taken up in the righteousness of Christ not merely verbally, but in truth.

The same is expressed in the representation of the spiritual communion as the mystical body of the Lord, which means: the substance of Christ, his divine-human nature, is the soul of the community of believers. It is only on the basis of this existing reconciliation that sanctification, or its successive empirical actualizations in the person's life and activity, proceeds. The Catholic system, on the contrary, as is known, is permeated by the subjective, Pelagian tendency which, by marginalizing the righteousness of Christ, allows reconciliation successively to be brought forth by moral striving and continual progress in virtue and sanctity. In this respect the mystics have only sublimated Catholicism, but not vanquished it. It may have annihilated Catholicism's focus on the external sanctity of works with a spiritualized morality; but morality, sanctification, is all and everything; the *unio mystica* is supposed to be the *product* of the human striving after the ideal. Mysticism itself acknowledges the unsatisfactoriness of such a piecemeal reconciliation, which is only a continual approach and therefore, to that extent, *not* a reconciliation. The individual, [141] therefore, makes an end of its anxious craving by bringing itself as a sacrifice of reconciliation, and Pelagianism then changes into pantheism and nihilism. This fault stems from the idea that the subject himself or herself is to accomplish reconciliation rather than, in faith, appropriating to themselves the existing reconciliation accomplished independently of frail human striving. Justification by faith rests upon the rock of objectivity; mysticism holds merely a subjective concept of reconciliation.

As is known, in his youth Luther studied Tauler and the *Theologia Germanica* with great enthusiasm. Certainly, on account of this study, his consciousness must have undergone a tremendous catharsis. This was a contributing moment making possible the breakthrough of a new worldview in him. But Luther did not come to know justification by faith, the soul of his Reformation activity, from these writings. Nor did he find there his conception of original sin. In part, the mystical conception of sinful human nature hovers between an Augustinian and a Neoplatonic interpretation, the latter of which conceives sin as a lack or limitation; in part, the attention to the *individual* is so predominant that mysticism never comes to any fundamental reflection on the sin of the race. Luther's universal conception of sin, the inseparable unity in which he posited the individual's sin-consciousness along with consciousness of the race, is altogether contrary to the individual's atomistic appearance in the morality of the cloisters. Where the individual appropriates to himself or herself the sin of the race, he or she consequently finds salvation and justification only in the midst of the race. Sanctification thus occurs not as a lonely, private occupation, but in society, in the ethical world-order of actuality. [142]

It is precisely on account of its moral atomism that mysticism is bound so intimately together with the Middle Ages and the Catholic principle. Generally, one is accustomed to think of the Middle Ages and Catholicism as the system of onesided objectivity, i.e., as the system which establishes the absolutism of the *universal* [*det Almindelige*]. But saying this one has only indicated one side of Catholicism, for it belongs to it just as much to allow the *single individual* [*det Enkelte*] to appear with an isolated, one-sided independence. The unresolved dualism between the objective and the subjective, the universal and the singular, realism and nominalism, is the Middle Ages' concept. On the one side stands the church in its all dominating catholicity; the view of the church is *realistic*, for only the Catholic, the universal, is actual. The independence of individuals was a nullity; they were, so to speak, only exemplars on which the one, saving church stamped its impression of unity and universality. It is the church in which all live and move and have their being; the church, which knows and desires individuals to be its instruments; the church, which works all in all. But parallel to this—and without noticing the contradiction—is the nominalist, Pelagian view of the individual's independence, its free will and personal competence. In the realm of morality this manifested itself in such a way that, outside of the circle of normal societal duties, there was a realm of subjective ideals, the attainment of which was a special, self-subsistent task, pursued *alongside* the universal. The one individual tried to outdo the other, not just by fulfilling the church's requirements or benefitting society, but by acquiring for himself or herself an exclusive, personal excellence, honor, and blessedness, with which they could [143] lift themselves above the universal. Since this could not be achieved by fulfilling the normal societal duties, they sought adventures in good deeds. The figure of the knight and the monk are the most noticeable phenomena of this moral atomism, this cleaving of the moment of discretion from continuity. Such a morality and religiosity, which at the same time presupposes its absolute dependence upon the church, and yet along side this posits a sphere for the freedom and spiritual autarchy of the individuality, also comprises mysticism. With this antinomy, and its implicit Pelagianism, Catholicism has impressed its stamp upon mysticism. The Reformation's principle, on the contrary, is the reconciliation of the universal and the singular, of society and the individual.

Appendix:
Mysticism's Relation to Jacob Böhme's Theosophy

After the Reformation a trend appeared in the evangelical church which was related to mysticism. It was natural that this came forth in the Lutheran church which, of all the confessions, was most deeply permeated by the actual presence of the divine in the human. The religious life was on the point of being annihilated by the sectarians; theology had become spiritless and degenerated into a sterile Scholasticism. Then the aforementioned trend appeared as a powerful spiritual fermentation. Jacob Böhme (died 1624), its foremost representative, lived in a time when terrible factional polemics raged from the pulpit and in the cathedrals and spilled out into the literary world by means of thick volumes and innumerable masses of pamphlets. Religious controversy, in those days, found the same level of general participation as a political controversy does in our day. Politics itself was in the service of dogmatics, and the [144] theological debates played out with word and pen would also be conducted with the sword in the horrors of the Thirty Years War. In the midst of this confusion, the simple layman finds he has nothing to gain from sects; he can live amidst sects, even appear at their worship services, but he does not belong to any of them. In the theological Babel there were quarrels only over the opinions of schools and the letter; the highly learned viewed religion only as history, as something which once had been. The Spirit of God was not in their historical repertoire. The true Christian has only one science, Christ, who is in her or him; and true knowledge is the revelation of God's Spirit through the eternal wisdom, the heavenly Idea.

When Böhme heard the name of this Idea for the first time, he broke out in a state of rapture: "I see the heavenly virgin!" This Idea wedded itself to his soul and in his spirit a youthful dawn broke, a heavenly Aurora, in which all mysteries were revealed. He testified concerning himself: 'It is not me who knows and understands all of this, it is God's Spirit who searches out God's own depths within me.' Thus, we see here again that it is contemplation which grants the spirit peace and reconciliation in a stormy and agitated time. While everything surrounding Böhme testifies to a paradise lost, it is rewon in his religious disposition [*Gemyt*] and in his inward visions.

This is not the place for a detailed exposition of Böhme's teaching and its relation to the Lutheran church. We shall limit ourselves here to indicating its relation to the mysticism of the Middle Ages. Often one proposes a correspondence between them in such a way that the difference is thereby overlooked. Böhme's contemplation could only appear on the basis of Protestantism and is [145] saturated by the Reformation's principle. It is more often remarked that the Reformation opened up the human sense for the universe, while the Middle Ages held the human spirit magnetically bound in a onesided orientation toward heaven. Heaven and earth, which in the view of the Middle Ages were dualistic contrasts, were welded together in the Reformation. The Reformation's comprehensive striving repeats itself in Böhme, for the whole universe, nature and history, are the content of his contemplation. The soul's onesided ascetic self-preoccupation, which forgets all else in the world over its own purification, has disappeared. For Böhme, the main thing is the objective intuition [*Anskuelse*] of the Idea in all of its cosmic forms. In the great unfolding of the world the individual is but a relative moment, or, as Böhme says, a trace. Böhme's predecessor, the world-renowned natural philosopher Medicus Theophrastus Paracelsus, though Catholic according to confession, nevertheless shows the same Protestant spirit; for he, by the light of religion, sought thoroughly to investigate *nature*. He thought of the human person as a microcosm, that is, as a quintessence, a synopsis, of the entire, great universe. Therefore human beings could search out the secrets of nature; for all intelligibility, spread abroad in the whole of nature, in the four elements, in the stars, in plant and animal life, lay compressed within the human being. Hence, nothing can be hidden from a person when God should arouse them. Paracelsus founded a speculative medicine, positing physics, astronomy, alchemy and theology as the four fundamental pillars. But the entire building rested upon Christ as the true cornerstone.

This natural philosophy was taken up and transfigured in Böhme's philosophy of spirit. Here again there was an ascetic separation from worldly consciousness, [146] but a reconciliation of the whole of worldly consciousness with the God-consciousness: seeing all things in God; no wrenching away [*Bortrykkelse*] from the world, but a blissful ecstasy [*Henrykkelse*] at seeing the whole of it in a magical reflection. Böhme knew that God is Spirit, that the Trinity is God's circuit and life. Yet Böhme was not content with this, but desired to know all created things in the image and likeness of the Trinity. He saw its reflection in every creature, even in grass and stones, but above all in the human religious disposition. He meditated upon reconciliation and God's Incarnation. Just like the Middle Age mystics he knew that it was egoity [*Jeghed*] which removes the human being from God. But he considered this from its universal, cosmic aspect and expressed his conception as a representation of Lucifer's falling away from and struggle against God. The unfolding of this struggle, the light's gathering triumph over the darkness, is world history. This universal and objective tendency in Böhme's conception is indicated by the fact that it is called *theosophy*, a denomination which nicely expresses its peculiar difference from Middle Age mysticism.

We have previously pointed out that the mystical principle in more recent times has recurred in the subjective-practical idealism of Fichte. It is expressed in his *Anweisung zum seligen Leben*, a work which he wrote during his last period in which he was strongly inspired by Christianity. Jacob Böhme on the other hand, has found his modern repetition in Schelling; in particular, in his famous treatise on human freedom. And also Baader's thoughtful reflections concerning "life's great coherence" are of a theosophic nature.

The separation between mystery and revelation is sublated in Böhme's theosophy. The Neoplatonic conception [147] of finitude has altogether disappeared. The negative appears in its full power and the finite is established in its properly Christian significance. Böhme is thoroughly clear and consistent in his view that God cannot remain an originary ground, but that God's essence is *will*, and this will is simply the will for revelation, for God's own revelation, in order that God may become understandable and comprehensible. From out of this Böhme develops the doctrines of the Trinity, Creation and Incarnation. God's holiness and love would not be revealed if there were nothing which required grace and love, nothing which was the opposite of God. The negative principle is the finite *I*, which is simultaneously understood as life's pain and agony, but also as the source of blessedness [*Salighed*]. Precursors to the knowledge of the significance of the negative were found already in the mystics, especially in the *Theologia Germanica* (cf. above); but Böhme remains steady in his perception that all things subsist in "yes" and "no," and that their reconciliation or mediation—which contemporary philosophy calls it in order to express the sublation of immediacy—is the actual, is life and spirit itself. Theosophic vision thus does not lack mediation *per se*, but only its development and consummation in the concept.

The preference owed to theosophy over mysticism stems from the fact that the mystical unity of religion and philosophy is subjective-practical, whereas the theosophic is objective-theoretical. The Idea has worked itself loose from its immediate connection with the atomistic *I* and won actual independence, whereby *intuition* comes into its own. Intuition seeks to render everything into form; it does not rest content with mystery, but craves revelation. But theosophic [148] intuition is still only an immediate unity of religion and philosophy: although everything elaborates itself as revelation, it does not come to develop itself into a philosophical system; it arranges itself only as a *philosophical apocalypse*. And since philosophical thought never detaches itself from religious intuition, whereby all rational reflection becomes impossible, it remains indeterminate whether the forms standing before intuition are internal or external. The rational historical consciousness concerning the facts of the Christian religion disappear and one does not know whether the biblical names (for example, Adam and Christ) are types for universal ideas, or whether they betoken historical personages.

In this way theosophy is related to mysticism. Yet because of its predominantly theoretical character, one must, with Baur, place theosophy in the ranks of the genuinely *gnostic* systems. The consideration of mysticism and theosophy teaches us to realize the great significance of critical reflection in the scientific study of religion as a necessary point of transition towards the true conceptual unity of religion and philosophy. Every more recent attempt which has been made immediately to reconcile these two by leaping over critique and reflection has only been a falling back to the standpoint of mysticism and theosophy. To a large extent this is true of Schelling and his school.[143]

---

[143] [Martensen concludes his study by appending Eckhart's sermon *Noli timere eos* in its entirety in the Middle High German. See *Meister Eckhart: A Modern Translation*, op. cit., 224f. See also footnote 36, page 167–trans.]

Grundrids

til

Moralphilosophiens System.

Udgivet

til Brug

ved academiske Forelæsninger

af

Dr. H. Martensen,

Professor i Theologien ved Kjøbenhavns Universitet.

Kjøbenhavn, 1841.

Paa Universitets-Boghandler C. A. Reitzels Forlag.

Trykt hos Directeur Jens Hostrup Schultz,

Kongelig og Universitets-Bogtrykker.

Outline

To a System of

Moral Philosophy

Published
for Use
with Academic Lectures

By

Dr. H. Martensen

Copenhagen
C.A. Reitzel Publishers
1841

Preface

The lectures in moral philosophy which I have held for the younger students of the University under a vacancy in the philosophical faculty have most immediately occasioned the preparation and publication of this writing. Although primarily intended for the philosophical course, it will additionally, I hope, be able to be employed temporarily by my theological students until I am in a position to put before them a textbook worked out on a grander scale regarding particularly the theological moments of ethics. Since my theological ethics is the positive elaboration of the general scheme presented here, and since accordingly the system's general structure and the relative position of the fundamental concepts to each other are the same, I will hereby be able to excuse both my students and myself from at least part of the both fatiguing and time-wasting dictation. Also, it will essentially be my theological lectures in which I will now be able to make use of this guide. For in the philosophical course it is only in the present semester, thus both for the first and last time, that I will be able to use it, seeing that the vacant philosophical chair at this very time is being [iv] filled, and in the future moral philosophy will be taught by the other philosophical professor.

Having hereby indicated this writing's external occasion and purpose, I must still add a provisional scientific explanation.

It has not infrequently been remarked that in our day an extraordinary disparity takes place between the interest which is shown ethics and the interest which is shown other branches of science. While the most outstanding talents devote their powers to purely metaphysical and logical investigations, while the problems of dogmatics and esthetics, politics and natural science occupy the most gifted thinkers of the age, the science of the moral [*Videnskaben om det Sædelige*] finds only scant participation. In many this remark is combined with a complaint against modern philosophy. The now prevailing philosophy, it is said, makes thought and the metaphysical concept into everything, contains no practical impulses, and aims more at cultivating scholastic theorists, idle spectators of the necessity of the world's development, than powerfully-willing and energetically-acting humans. The present devotees of science have thus gone astray in the labyrinth of theoretical thinking, having lost the instrument for the practical investigations of ethics. However [v] much this generation prides itself on its speculative progress beyond Kant and Fichte, however much it prides itself on its knowledge of God and knowledge of the world, still in one primary area it stands far behind that time, namely, in moral self-knowledge. The present literature also lacks the stamp of that virile, firm earnestness, that inspiring and purifying moral enthusiasm with which those thinkers electrified their contemporaries!

Although these complaints can be put forward with an appearance of legitimacy, so long as one considers only externally the phenomena of the literature, they still by no means strike the essence of the present science. It is so far from the case that the ethical interest in-and-for-itself should be alien to modern speculative science that an actual ethic has only become possible by the sweeping reformation of metaphysics which was effected by "the great thinker," as our age with justice calls him. Nothing can be more groundless than to assert that a metaphysics, which posits as its highest task to penetrate living actuality and which determines true actuality as the unity of the theoretical and the practical Idea, should be related indifferently to ethics, or lack practical [vi] impulses. Even if Hegel's moral enthusiasm is conspicuously less significant than Kant's and Fichte's, it is not therefore completely insignificant. At the same time it can be obviously seen that Hegel has not given his contemporaries a thorough ethics, as he has given it a thorough esthetics and philosophy of religion. For the thought held by many, that his teaching on the state should be able to take the place of an ethics, does not allow itself to be well realized. This teaching surely contains a classical development of morality's relative stages, but it does not show morality in its absolute meaning. Moral consciousness has its end in the Absolute, being in its essence just as ideal and infinite as the esthetic, the speculative and religious consciousness, and therefore has the same right as these to be classified under the kingdom of Absolute Spirit, although it certainly does not as these have its home exclusively in the Absolute but lives just as much in empirical finitude. It would already in-and-for-itself be peculiar if modern thinkers after the wisdom of the ancients would allow morality to be concluded in the state and posit its ideal in bourgeois righteousness, although no doubt the latter, which Hegel above any other has shown, ought to be seen in a more spiritual light than people until now have been wont to see it. But I see Hegel's own works containing nothing other than [vii] the refutation of that view. Everyone who has studied attentively the *Philosophy of Religion* and the *Aesthetics* will have had ample opportunity to be persuaded that Hegel has known a higher morality than that whose end is absorbed in the state. These works contain the clearest indications of a higher ethical knowledge and especially the *Aesthetics* contains significant contributions to knowledge of the purely ideal meaning of the moral personality. That Hegel has *not* given a comprehensive ethics can only have its basis in the fact that he, who was called to supplant the onesided systems of subjectivity and thereby also contentless morality, had to become absorbed most intensely in the theoretical knowledge of objectivity, of the historically concluded forms of the state and religion, of science and art, and necessarily had to place the emphasis on the proposition that "the actual is the rational," while this proposition's practical complement, that we ourselves must produce the rational actuality, was less vigorously accentuated. He necessarily had to emphasize more strenuously the moment of substantiality than that of individuality and personality, for the empty, formal personality first had to be destroyed before the true personality could be posited. But surely more people [viii] on the whole are accustomed to considering this philosophy as a finished, concluded result, so that it is often misunderstood by friends and foes alike, who hereby fly into dead, fatalistic modes of construing. Indeed, the more one realizes that one has only understood the results of philosophy when one in addition has been able to grasp them as living starting points for a new development, then the more it will become manifest that this philosophy has freedom as its principle, the more vividly apparent will become its great ethical views, and the more determinately it will point to the idea of personality as the gravitational point of thinking. Ethics will then arrive at its entire comprehensive meaning as the presentation of the absolutely practical Idea, as the science of the personality's free self-development toward its ideal through the rational necessity of objectivity. Both in our scientific and poetic literature and in our not only "fateful" but freedom-filled actuality is found a scattered wealth of ethical elements, on which we need only deliberate in order to actually make them our possession.

If the present little writing dare have hopes at all of being even a small contribution to science, then this lies only in the fact that perhaps it can serve to make the peculiar task of [ix] ethics more recognizable. I have here sought to sketch the fundamental types according to which I am convinced science must be developed. In spite of the compressed conciseness, in spite of each paragraph awaiting the complete execution, I yet hope that there will have been enough provided so that experts will be able to see that on which the work here developed most closely depends. They will naturally consider this writing more as a possibility than as an actuality. Now if there is a great step from possibility to actuality, from principle to execution, I console myself on the other hand with the thought that the philosophical possibility, provided this is only granted here, merely as such is already a reality.

I have made use of what the modern literature offers, and have thus paid regard to the works of Schleiermacher as well as Daub, Michelet, and Rosenkranz. Daub's lectures on ethics, which are the most comprehensive ones furnished in this science by the modern school, are still not published entirely, and a survey of the whole is not yet possible. However, nobody will be able to fail to appreciate that it is an exceedingly instructive, thought-provoking work, which moreover has the beautiful advantage that the author's energetic [x] individuality which is penetrated by the moral Idea everywhere steps animatedly toward the reader. But it seems as if Daub's original Kantian orientation has been too forceful for him to be able to allow his latest orientation to have a radical influence on the construction of the whole. Michelet's moral philosophy is only a historical-critical work drawn up, it seems to me, under a far too narrow horizon, and Rosenkranz has only given individual hints and suggestions. Schleiermacher's ethics contains, as one could expect, many fine observations on the individual but will hardly be able to have the significance for the present science that his epoch-making critique of various √ systems of morality did in its time. In this artificially complex ethical system one will search in vain for great, stimulating views; the reason for this cannot lie merely in the fact that it belongs to a by-gone stage of development, for this applies also to the works of Kant and Fichte in moral philosophy, and surely nobody can study these, especially the latter's, without each time receiving a fresh inspiration. To the development of the concept of freedom I have found a welcome contribution in Daub's writing on the hypotheses of freedom. Also in Fischer's brilliant investigations on freedom (in his metaphysics) I have found several *fermenta ethices* [things to enrich ethics], just as I [xi] have never allowed to go unnoticed investigations, which—in some cases going back years—are transmitted in our literature on the freedom of the will.

The assertion, that morality's philosophical types are the same ones upon which theological ethics ought to be developed, I base on the general relation which more and more comes to exist between philosophy and the positive sciences. When philosophy no longer is an empty construction *a priori* but knowledge of actuality, and when the positive sciences allow themselves to be penetrated by philosophy's method, then the old contrast has to offend. To write an *ethica naturalis* [natural ethics], which is to exist along side of the Christian as another sort of ethics, belongs to the attempts which have been tried for a long time. If there is any science which must have its roots in living, present actuality, then it is above all practical philosophy. But a moral philosophy which ignores Christianity also ignores actual morality, and thereby only makes itself impractical. On the other hand if ethics is penetrated by the principle of Christianity, then it will never be able to refrain from entering into morality's religious moments, which formerly were ascribed exclusively to the theologian, such as the doctrine of the relation of the law to the gospel, [xii] conversion and the imitation of Christ, the means of grace, etc. If there is still to be a difference here between theology and philosophy, then it can only appear in the fact that philosophy sticks to the universal and general, while the theologian gives the religious-ethical points their development through the relevant biblical, church-historical, and dogmatic moments. Not by a method differing from philosophy but by the concrete individualizing of the universal shall the distinctively theological character and tone be brought to light. At the same time ethics cannot restrict itself to the religious moment of morality alone but must in addition comprehend its secular moments. The family and state, for example, no doubt contain a religious moment, but their meaning will really no more be able to be exhausted by religious categories than, say, by biblical ones. Christianity itself has surely not concluded its activity inside the precincts of religion and religious morality, but over the course of time has in addition constituted a secular morality, which certainly has its final ground but precisely therefore not its most immediate ground in religion. That is why ethics just as surely cannot stay within the religious sphere alone. Knowledge of the relative self-subsistence and independence of morality from religion has arisen [xiii] in Protestantism and has received a practical expression in the emancipation of the state from the church. In Protestant science this knowledge more or less explicitly underlies the independent separation of ethics from dogmatics, while Catholicism acts most in harmony with its nature when as a matter of course it incorporates ethics into dogmatics or at least dogmatizes ethics from top to bottom. The autonomy of ethics culminates in Kant and Fichte, who assert that moral concepts have unconditional validity in themselves, and demand that they should be presented in their own pure light, not in the colored light of religion. In spite of the onesidedness, one can no longer fail to appreciate the truth. On the other hand if it is now the theologian's concern that religion shall be known as the ground and principle of morality, then this central meaning of religion can really only be scientifically known when morality's relative, secular forms are developed with philosophical necessity into that religious morality which is their highest truth, just as inversely it must be shown how this religious morality must seek its full actuality in the finite life of the world. Through this dialectical interaction of morality's religious moments and its secular moments the system must progress, and to the same [xiv] degree that the consideration has philosophical universality will it be able to develop its theological individuality.

On its religious points ethics enters into an inner relation to dogmatics. But in order for the precincts of dogmatics and ethics not to be unduly confused, the knowledge of dogma must here be restricted to knowledge of its relation to the practical, its meaning *ad extra* [externally]. In ethics dogma must be known more in its effects, in its being for the other, than in its metaphysical being in itself. The highest metaphysical fundamental-truth which supports the ethical system can therefore not be justified on the precincts of ethics, although ethics certainly carries an indirect argument for its validity.

This is the essential thing that I thought should be said in order to meet the most obvious objections. [xv]

Contents

B.

THE GOOD AS IDEAL.. 280

The divine ideal
The mystical and moral unity of God and the human
The personal unity of God and the human

The ideal of the world
The present and the future
Optimism and Pessimism
The romantic and the humorous view of the world

The ideal of individuality
Salvation and virtue
Activity and enjoyment
Freedom and dependence

C.

THE GOOD AS KINGDOM OF PERSONALITY........................... 298

The kingdom of personality in its immediate actuality
The Family

The kingdom of personality in its reflected actuality
The State
Art
Science

The kingdom of personality in its absolute actuality
The spiritual communion [Menigheden], *The kingdom of God as such*

Introductory Reflections on the Concept of Moral Philosophy

§ 1.

Since the concept of a science is no different from the fully-developed science itself, the concept cannot be known at the system's beginning but only at its end. Therefore, at the beginning merely a preliminary account can be given of the science which is to be interpreted. We describe moral philosophy or ethics as the science of the Good, insofar as this is posited as the unending *practical* task for the human and is actualized by the free will's ideal striving. The ethical task places the free individual in indissoluble union with free social life, and the science of the Good is developed therefore not merely as the teaching on duty and virtue [*Plight-og Dydelære*] but equally as ethics [*Sædelære*].

> *Note.* Insofar as there is a distinction between the designations "morality" and "ethics," then the latter, which has its origin from the ancient world, expresses the closest consideration for the social idea, while the former, in following a more modern usage, expresses the most attentive concern for the single individual. In the present exposition these two viewpoints are combined. [2]

§ 2.

Moral philosophy presupposes that actual morality which in all nations is intimately connected with religion, in which it has its final ground. The first immediate manifestations of moral reflection are found in the practical rules, proverbs, and gnomic sayings in which people have expressed their moral experiences. In earliest antiquity there had been those regarded as wise, who gained distinction by devising and stating in a concise way such moral thoughts, in which a people recognized its own consciousness. On a higher stage of cultural development moral *raisonnement* [reasoning] is a correlative ingredient in the general education. But moral *raisonnement* is not moral philosophy. The latter does not remain content with single points of view and aphoristic reflections, but seeks to perceive the whole domain of morality in the concept's comprehensive system.

§ 3.

Moral philosophy's peculiar domain and scientific limits are firmly established by considering it in relation to other cognate sciences. The idea of the Good, which is moral philosophy's subject-matter, is considered also in *the science of religion* but from another point of view. That is to say, the science of religion considers the Good such as it is presented for the religious consciousness or for faith. Therefore, it considers the Good as primordially realized in God and in the world's reconciliation with God. But that fundamental contradiction of life, which is solved originally for the religious consciousness, the moral consciousness *must* only successively solve through an entire system of tasks. The religious and [3] the moral consciousness are related to each other as life's peace and repose are related to its struggle and work. *Ore & labora!* [Pray and work!] Their difference is a dialectical one of such a sort that just as much must be posited as is sublated. The sharper the moral consciousness declares the ideal's *demand* the more the religious need for reconciliation will manifest itself, and the deeper the consciousness is of *being* reconciled the more again will the demand be manifested to give the religious principle its development and actual implementation in the world. Precisely in their sharpest contrast do the law and the gospel mutually confirm each other. It is the same Idea comprehending the entirety of life which is to be lived under a double form by the finite spirit [*Aand*]. From this originates both the distinction and the unity of the modes of reflection of the teaching of religion and that of morality.

§ 4.

Anthropology, which shows what the human is immediately by nature and also what according to its original essence it can become, considers the Good only as an intrinsic possibility of human nature. Moral philosophy, on the other hand, considers the Good in its transition from possibility to actuality through the will's free self-determination. The human's entrance into the moral order of the world is its retirement from the state of nature, where the Good is only a possibility. Whereas anthropology considers the human as part of the total organization of nature, ethics considers the human as part of a total organization which the spirit [*Aanden*] itself has constructed, a world which through its various [4] moments expresses freedom's own system. (Family, State, Church.)

§ 5.

As practical philosophy the science of morals must be distinguished from the *theory of right*. The idea of right is the idea of freedom's outer existence and recognition of this as the ground of reason's necessity. The objective order of right finds its expression in the state, which comprises the whole system of freedom's outer forms. The entirety of human life—morality and religion, art and science—moves inside the circumference of the state and is the object of its interest. *Nil humani a me alienum puto* [I consider nothing human as outside my concern] is its motto. However beautifully its end can thus be said to be all-embracing, it is yet again restricted and finite because it confines itself to the *external side* of freedom's life. The end of right has its deeper ground in freedom's absolute end or in the Good. At all times the form of a state has been determined by the moral and religious principle which has permeated that particular nation.

§ 6.

The question of moral philosophy's *method* is the question of how this science can develop its true content in the form which is satisfactory for absolute thought. Reflective thought has sought to give the grounds for and develop this science by putting forward either dogmatically or critically a *moral principle*, that is to say, a supreme practical maxim in which the highest end and the final basis of decision for the [5] human will receives expression. Along this line reflective thought has indeed made every effort to derive (deduce) in a logical manner the whole system of duties and virtues. But such a general principle is abstract and tautological, and is not able to support any positive content by itself. Moral philosophy achieves a positive content only when the moral is known not merely as an abstract *requirement* of reason for the single individual, but also is perceived as a *world-historical actuality*. While morality is produced by single individuals, it can just as well *be found* by them in the historical life of society. Just as much as its end *ought* always to be enacted, so must it be seen as already having been enacted. As this knowledge lies immediately in the religious belief in Providence, so does it find its scientific foundation in speculation's teaching on the unity of the subjective and the objective, thought and being, practical and theoretical reason.

Instead of the deductive method which wants to derive the totality from a single theorem, there is the dialectical or the conceptual method.

In this method every single theorem appears only as part of the totality and is known both on its own and in light of the whole. Since the single understandings appear as *moments* (*movimenta*), they are seen not merely in their repose but in their *movements*; they are considered in their inner-connectedness and mutual limitation, in their contrasts and their unity, in their struggle and reconciliation. Through this discussion, where every relative truth finds its definite place and limit, there results the free, all-embracing and penetrating comprehensive knowledge or *the concept*. [6]

> *Note.* The philosophers, who sought to put forward a moral principle, can be classified in a twofold manner, namely, insofar as they went either the way of empiricism or rationalism. The former holds true of the English and French moral philosophers, who derived the moral principle from the instincts and feelings of human nature. Although along this way one can by no means penetrate into morality's essence, the truth of these efforts still gave support to the fact that moral determinations must be drawn from the human's own nature, not from any external authority. But the human's true nature is not conceived under the form of instincts and feelings but under that of thought. This is known by Kant who reformed moral philosophy by tracing this principle back to the universality and necessity of reason. He knew the law's unconditional self-validity, its independence from the instincts and inclinations of the natural human, and declared unqualified respect for duty as the single valid motive for human conduct. But as Kant in following his metaphysical principles onesidedly divorced practical reason from the theoretical, he placed morality in an oblique relation not merely to religion but to the whole of reality.
>
> Spinoza's ethics contains the great general fundamental-features of the *speculative* presentation of the moral Idea, which he comprehended in its unity with the idea of God. Practical reason [7] is here in inseparable unity with the theoretical, and subjective thought seeks the fullness of substantial thought. God is known as the highest Good, freedom as the unity of the thinking will with the divine Essence, and salvation as virtue. But Spinoza's ethics stays in the colorless generality of pure thought and does not come to comprehend actual human life because his God cannot be revealed *in history*, since the highest Good is only communicated to the solitary thinker, not to *the community* [*Samfundet*]. Ethics can only achieve life and fullness by presupposing the personal incarnation of the highest Good in history, and that social life established by Christianity. [8]

Moral Philosophy's Presupposition or The Teaching on the Human's Free Will

§ 7.

All moral concepts find their living center in the human's free will. The fundamental moral view in every philosophical system is determined by its teaching on the freedom of the will. Insofar as freedom is considered in the pure universality of the concept (the metaphysical determination of freedom), it must be thought of as the principle of absolute independence from all alien causality, as unconditioned self-subsistence, infinite self-determination and self-activity. Freedom is no immediate being or becoming. It is distinguished both from "things," the world of dead objects, and from the life of nature, since it determines its own being [*Væren*] and its own becoming [*Vorden*]. Freedom's development is not as the plant's growth nor as the animal's instinctive manifestation of life, but it is and becomes only what it *makes* itself into. The concept of freedom is one with the concept of spirit, self-consciousness, *I*. Each of the spirit's expressions is an expression of freedom, each act of self-consciousness is an act of freedom. [9]

§ 8.

As the free spirit makes its own self-activity its *end* and aims at enacting its thought in the world, it determines itself as *willing*. The free will objectifies itself in actions. Without free will there would be no actions but only events.

The Fundamental Features of Free Will

The essential will and the subjective will. The natural barriers of freedom. Its dependence on the divine will.

§ 9.

The free will's self-determination is no formal, contentless, and indeterminate movement, but can only be thought of as the self-determination of the spiritual *being* [*Væsen*]. The *essential* will has an eternal, universal content, is destined only toward its immanent end or toward its Idea and is consequently its own necessity. As essential, freedom is at the same time still not determined as actual. It becomes actual only when it passes over into the human's *subjective* will, when the human's universal will becomes one with its *individual* will. But freedom is a real possibility for the human, a possibility which with inner necessity brings along with it its actuality. The human *must* realize its essential freedom, but that necessity whereby the human is situated is no physical necessity but a metaphysical and moral one.

> *Note.* Insofar as humankind is considered according to its essential will, one must consequently say that all [10] humans have the will toward the Good,

toward the rational. At the same time this cannot be reckoned to them as merit because it came to them in their purely metaphysical quality as free spirits. The good will first receives a moral and personal worth when it is the human's subjective will which is penetrated by the rational. Concerning the subjective will religion bears witness that in its natural state it is evil. If the human's substance were evil, then the concepts concerning sin and guilt, punishment and responsibility, salvation and damnation would lose their meaning. All these concepts presuppose, namely, that the human's essence is good or, as religion expresses it, that the human is created in God's image.

§ 10.

The will could not experience an actual development of freedom if it were not possible for it to negate its own essence. The subjective will must be able to separate itself from the essential, must be able to fall away from [*affalde fra*] the Idea of freedom. The will must therefore determine itself as *freedom of choice* or as the ability to choose between opposite ends. The antinomy between the proposition that the will can only determine itself toward its Idea, and the opposite, that it can also negate it, is annulled by the recognition that the latter contains the negative condition for the actuality of the former. Only by overcoming the possibility of its opposite can freedom actually substantiate itself. [11]

§ 11.

Amidst its striving to actualize its freedom the will must enter into a system of conditions and barriers. Not merely the external powers of nature and relations of the world, but also the human's own nature-determined individuality are barriers for freedom. The antinomy, which occurs between the free will and the necessity of nature, is annulled by the recognition that nature only has the destination to serve the spirit for its revelation. The natural individuality, the external human, is only the matter through which the inner human shall give shape to itself as the moral work of art (Socrates); the outer nature has meaning insofar as it is an element and building-material for the spirit's temple. But freedom's victory over both the outer and the inner necessity of nature is achieved only by a successive progression, and while the human will according to its essence is absolutely free, as a phenomenon in time it is more or less unfree. Its unfreedom does not lie in the fact that it is limited, which it must be in order to be a determinate will. But it is unfree insofar as it still has its limit outside itself and has not taken this up into itself as an inner immanent limit, as its own rational necessity.

Note. It is Fichte's immortal contribution to have made it evident once and for all that a not-*I* only exists for and to the *I*, and that consequently there is nowhere a barrier which in-and-for-itself is invincible for freedom. But he failed to appreciate nature, as he only construed it [12] as a negative barrier for the spirit. He did not know that nature itself contains a rational development, through which there runs a vague striving after freedom, and that consequently nature in addition gives a *positive* testimony to human freedom. This knowledge was initiated by Schelling.

§ 12.

As the human's free will cannot be thought of as absolutely presuppositionless but presupposes the creative will of the Godhead [*Guddommen*] as its innermost ground of determination, a new antinomy appears, namely, the antinomy between dependence of human freedom on God [*Gud*] and its own unconditional self-determination. But this dependence must be seen as freedom itself. That is to say, as the human will is *essentially* determined by the creative will, it *must* realize this; but since it herein is determined as its own self-determining, it is determined as the absolutely free. As the human does God's will, the human in addition carries out its own essential will.

Note. In its sharpest form this antinomy has appeared in the contrast between Spinoza and Fichte. The *thesis* which lies at the foundation of Spinoza's entire system is this: that God is one and all, and that outside God there is nothing (*praeter deum nihil* [besides God there is nothing]). The human *I* therefore has no actual, independent existence, no true self-activity, but is only a [13] transient modification of the impersonal, divine substance which works all in all.—Antithetical to Spinoza is Fichte, for whom the *I* is one and all, (*praeter me nihil* [besides *myself* there is nothing]), and where all becomes a product of the *I*'s self-activity. Since Fichte's *I* is absolutely presuppositionless, it becomes the self-and-all-positing *I* = God. The complete solution of this antinomy must be sought in the development of the Christian teaching on the personal God, who reveals Godself in a kingdom of free spirits.

THE NEGATION OF FREE WILL

The Teaching on Arbitrariness and the Teaching on Coercion.
(Indifferentism, Determinism, and Fatalism)

§ 13.

When a single side of the antinomies presented here is maintained such that it excludes its contradiction, the negation of the true concept of freedom is introduced. Every negation of freedom is at the same time always the affirmation of a single side of the concept, and the freedom-negating system therefore contains only a partial truth. The true concept of freedom can be annulled [*ophæves*] in a double way. Either the moment of necessity is negated as incompatible with freedom, which then is construed only as a purely formal and *arbitrary* self-determination. This is the standpoint of indifferentism, according to which the will hovers interestlessly and indeterminately over all motives. (*libertas indifferentiae* [freedom which comes from indifference]). Or the will's [14] unconditional self-determination is negated, while abstract necessity becomes the all-determining. Then arises determinism and fatalism.

§ 14.

Indifferentism posits the will's freedom in its unconditional ability to choose and arbitrariness, or in the fact that in every moment it can act contrary. It asserts that the very concept of morality has validity only under this presupposition. Although experience shows that human actions are inconsistent with the idea of morality [*Sædeligheden*], indifferentism asserts (particularly in its theological form of Pelagianism) that in every moment it must be just as much possible for the will to fulfill the law as to negate it. It appeals to how the law unceasingly renews its demands on the human, but how this would contain a contradiction if it were not possible for the human in every moment to satisfy this. It appeals to the immediate moral consciousness and refers particularly to the facts of responsibility and repentance as proof for the view that the human not merely *should* but also *could* have acted otherwise.

   This concept of the freedom of the will is an unreal thought because it considers the will in its abstraction both from the human's essence and from the nature-determined individuality. Since this system does not realize that arbitrariness and freedom of choice have only a purely dialectical meaning, have only the destiny of being the vanishing transition-point for the development of freedom's *character*, it annuls the unity [15] and coherence in the moral life. Since according to this view it is possible for the human in every moment to act otherwise than he or she acts, the virtuous in every moment must be able to will the evil and unworthy and the depraved in every moment must be able to will the noble and praiseworthy. The individual's actions thus appear only as an accidental series of discrete and atomistic points which lack the connecting thread of continuity. The inference which is made from the law's pressing demands regarding the possibility of their fulfillment is in-and-for-itself true and right; but the onesided advocates of *liberum arbitrium* [free choice or will] err in the application, as they confuse the essential possibility with the empirical. Neither does indifferentism penetrate deeply enough into the fact of

repentance nor that of responsibility. The thoroughly repentant consciousness does not feverishly question whether it had the empirical possibility
to act otherwise. The essential thing is that it has acted as it *ought* not
to have acted.

§ 15.

In contrast to the doctrine of arbitrariness determinism assumes *principium rationis sufficientis* [the principle of sufficient reason] and points out
the will's total dependence. Raw, immediate determinism teaches that
human character is only a product of the outer surroundings, of natural
and historical causes. What are actually the outer *conditions* of free will
are here considered as its reason and *ground*. The more developed determinism considers character not as a product of outer influences but
as the physically necessary development of the human's own spiritual
organization, and views *the sequence* of the human's actions as [16] the individuality's necessary self-unfolding. But this empirical consideration
grasps only the individuality's phenomenon, and does not penetrate into
the individuality's universal *essence*, which is one with freedom itself. This
is known in speculative determinism, which in the essentials, but also
only in the essentials, is in agreement with the true teaching on freedom.
Speculative determinism knows *the Idea's* necessity as the one true reality, and since this is posited as the individual's *own* necessity, essential
freedom is secured. But it is overlooked that the individual's essential
freedom can be mediated to actuality only through *freedom of choice*. Since
the dialectical validity of freedom of choice is not recognized, the moral
development of character receives a onesided emphasis on nature and is
considered more as an evolution than as a continuously self-subsisting
position of freedom.

> *Note.* Speculative determinism's dialectic can only be completely developed
> through the Christian teaching on divine grace and human sinfulness. It ap-
> pears then as Augustinianism, which struggles for the Idea of freedom, but
> does not allow the Idea to find any point of contact in the human's empiri-
> cal will because it denies freedom of choice. Freedom of choice is claimed by
> Pelagianism, but instead of being considered as a point of contact for the en-
> trance of divine grace into the human, it is taken as the entire essence of
> freedom. Modern speculative determinism is declared by Schleiermacher.
> Schleiermacher [17] is so far from denying the validity of the concept of
> freedom that he much more considers the actualization of freedom in all
> human individuals as history's purpose. His denial of freedom is restricted
> only to arbitrariness and *freedom of choice*. With him freedom's eternal pos-
> sibility passes over to actuality without having gone through the crisis of
> freedom of choice.

§ 16.

Determinism has its final presupposition in fatalism. That is to say, *principium rationis sufficientis* [the principle of sufficient reason] is not able to be implemented except by transcending physical connections and the finite causal nexus, and ascending to the very all-determining ground and cause of physical connections, which is to the Godhead [*Guddommen*]. When the Godhead is posited as the absolute power in which the independence of the human will is destroyed, as the dark necessity to whose lordship the human unavoidably is reverted, then this divine power and necessity appear as fate (*Fatum*—εἱμαρμένη). Determinism proceeds from a cosmological and anthropological standpoint, fatalism from a mythological and theological standpoint. Fatalism contains the consciousness of God [*Gud*] and faith, although its God is only a demonic power and its faith superstition. It is developed in a double direction. That is to say, if the fatalistic power is posited as the world's immanent *ground*, then pantheistic fatalism appears; on the other hand, if the power of fate is posited as the world's transcendent and supernatural *cause*, then appears theistic fatalism. In its immediately religious form fatalism omits all [18] empirical secondary causes and ascribes the events of the world and human actions to the irresistible influence of the Godhead. (It stands written in the book of fate, it is determined in the stars!) Insofar as it is substantiated in philosophy, fatalism is given its intelligent execution in determinism.

Note. Blind power is fatalism's characteristic. Therefore, chance, fortune, and misfortune are fatalistic gods. Every philosophy, which has not risen to a genuine teleological worldview and does not know God as eternal *Wisdom*, contains a partial fatalism because its thought in addition stops at a groundless necessity in which is seen neither plan nor purpose, neither means nor end. Where there is not any τελος [telos], the human must give up on conceiving. One must be content precisely with the tautological understanding that that is the way it is because that is the way it is.

§ 17.

Pantheism, which in its severe form considers the Godhead as the world's unconscious ground and the world as the ground's necessary result, can only construe the world as an eternal development of nature, and therefore, considered from the ethical point of view, becomes fatalism. That is to say, since human individuals are only considered as non-independent points of passage for the divine, the concept of freedom and accountability are abolished. Since it is not the human who acts [19] but the Godhead of necessity who works all in all, the existence of the single individuals, their virtue and vice, their fortune and misfortune are only considered as their inevitable fate.

Note. Pantheistic fatalism has its world historical existence in all *pagan* systems of religion whose development moreover displays a striving after being liberated from the fatalistic power, a presentiment of the wise and loving God, and a seeking after the human's essential freedom. In its harshest and most repulsive form fatalism appears in the religious systems of *the Orient.* On the other hand, in the religion of *the Greeks,* which is designated the highest stage of paganism's development of freedom, the faith in Fate appears in a more pure and enlightened form. First by the Christian revelation, whose God is a light in which there is not ever any darkness, is Fate totally destroyed.

§ 18.

Theistic fatalism proceeds from the thought about God as the world's *Creator* and *Ruler,* and as it construes God's omnipotence and inscrutable wisdom exclusively as the all-determining supernatural *cause,* it posits the world's independence as a mere appearance and denies the will's freedom.

Note. This principle in its realistic form has ascended in the history of religions as *Islam.* Islam's empirical mode of consideration restricts [20] fatalism to the will's objective moment but maintains the subjective moment in the will's freedom. It does not deprive the human of the ability to will and judge, but it denies the will the ability to objectify itself in free *actions* because everything which *happens* is absolutely independent of the human and only caused by Allah's unalterable will, which from eternity has predestined it. In thus admittedly placing the free *resolve* in the will's power while deriving all its deeds from divine predestination, it makes the will into an inessential and powerless principle, just as on the other hand it abolishes all organic connection and living reciprocity between the human and the outer world.

In its idealistic form theistic fatalism steps forth onto the domain of Christianity itself. Here the interest of thinking is focused most sharply not on the external human life, not on events and deeds, but on the *inner human.* The human heart, the will itself with its innermost emotions and most secret intentions, becomes here the essential object of divine omnipotence. When then in the Christian teaching on sin and the workings of grace divine omnipotence is accentuated, so that the human will's independence is annihilated, there arises the fatalistic teaching on *the choice of grace.* According to this teaching God pursuant to an inscrutable decree has predestined some humans [21] to faith and eternal salvation, others to unbelief, misfortune, and eternal damnation. Like the foregoing fatalistic theories, this system also ignores the will's essential freedom, according to which *all* humans are not merely predestined for salvation but have an inner, immanent destination for it.

THE AFFIRMATION OF FREE WILL

Divine Providence. The Good.

§ 19.

The freedom-denying systems are sublated and receive their subordinate validity in Christianity's teaching on divine Providence, which unites human freedom with the divine without the one being absorbed by the other. Fatalism's God is too powerful to grant its world freedom, but the God of Providence according to its free love has released both nature and the human for free existence and fulfills its eternal decrees of wisdom through the very dialectic of human *freedom*.

Note 1. Providence does not exclude human *arbitrariness*, and does not prevent it from bringing itself into contradiction with the law of the Good. But there is care taken that this contradiction be resolved, because it is already originally resolved in the very essence of human freedom, which does not permit the will to stay in any particular direction but incessantly [22] drives it to seek agreement with its own universal nature. Since Providence has not merely granted the human but also its *environs* independent existence as a system of living, freely operating powers, it does not exclude the dependence of the human individual on nature and history. *Chance* and *Fate* are understood as actual powers, however not as absolute powers. In a religious and moral respect one human is born under a more favorable star than another. But the natural and historical barriers are only vanishing moments in the idea of Providence and means in the teleological governance of the world, which also can be expressed thus: that they are vanishing moments in the Idea of human freedom and means for the will's self-liberation toward its own end.

Note 2. The complete knowledge of Providence contains the knowledge of the human's redemption and reconciliation, of the highest Good's personal incarnation in Christ, and of the kingdom of God's coming in the middle of the finite and sinful world. God's kingdom is the full actuality and revelation of Providence, for the reason that the humans who are in God's kingdom *believe* in Providence and *act* in this belief. But this belief and action are moments in Providence itself; only in these does Providence step forward *as* Providence. What many humans call faith in Providence is only an unconscious fatalism. They do not bear in mind that the will of Providence [23] is only realized through human striving, and they will only have God's support as a Fate, not as a grace. For grace and blessing include the activity of human freedom, Fate excludes this.

§ 20.

With knowledge of the free will is given knowledge of the Idea of *the Good*. Nothing can be called good except the good will. (Kant) The universal representation of the Good is the representation of the infinite *end*, but only for freedom can there exist an actual end, and only freedom itself can be its own final end, the one thing which must be desired for its own sake. Consequently, the Good is the free will itself in its developed *fullness of essence*, and its Idea coincides with the *divine* will. *Nothing is good except the One, who is God.* But since the divine will only is revealed by communicating its own essence to the human, the Good must be determined more precisely as the human will's unity with the divine. It is thereby at once the essential presupposition for the human's objective will and the infinite end for its striving. As life's all-comprehensive Idea, as the end which includes all others in itself, the Good is *the human's destination. All* human's must and are able to reveal the spiritual in the form of the Good, because it comprehends not a single side of life but the human itself. [24]

§ 21.

In its actual relation to the Good the will determines itself as *personality*. Personality is the free-willing *I*, insofar as through its empirical actuality, through all its phenomenal spheres of life, it determines itself in relation to its *essential* destination toward life's total Idea. Personality is therefore neither this nor that individual form of the *I* as it is determined by the individuality, talent, special relations of life, etc. It is rather the *I* as in this its peculiar individuality, in these determinate relations of life, it is in addition seen as a link in the *system* of freedom. To consider the human individual under the category of personality is therefore to gather the entire ensemble of its multifarious relative moments of life under the one absolute viewpoint. There remains then not the question of what the individual is in its determinate forms of activity, but how through these it relates itself to life's fundamental requirement, how hereby it solves life's *universal* task.

§ 22.

Just as nothing is good except the good will, so is nothing actually evil except the evil will. Evil, which is not merely the Good's quantitative antithesis but its qualitative antithesis, can only be thought of as the human will's denial of the divine [*den guddommelige*], or as the human's fall from its own Idea, that is, from the Idea of freedom. It has its origin in the subjective will, which determines itself as wilfulness [*Egenvillie*], in egoity [*Egoiteten*], which is determined as egotism. [25]

> *Note 1.* Every theory which seeks the origin of evil outside the creaturely will and posits its source either in God [*Gud*] or in nature is fatalistic. This takes place in paganism, whereas the revealing religion derives evil from *the created spirit's* subjective will. Evil is certainly represented as having intruded into the human paradise in a natural form, as the snake. But the religious representation also holds that this was only a form which the evil *spirit* had taken upon itself, and that consequently the natural has been an instrument of *the will.*
>
> *Note 2.* Since evil is only subjective and lacks all substantiality, it is absolutely powerless against the Good, and only has temporary and transitory meaning. Evil can only achieve a negative, but not a positive, personality. *"Le mal ne peut pas prendre nature."* [It is not possible for evil to take on a nature.]
>
> *Note 3.* Evil [*Det Onde*] must not be confused with the *bad* [*det Slette*]. The bad does not express most precisely the fall of the finite from the Good but its fall from the Idea altogether. In nature there are many bad existents but nothing evil. In the kingdom of the spirit on the other hand the bad and evil continually cross over into one another. When we said above that evil lacks substantiality, then this can also be expressed in such a way that evil is bad. The philosophers, who immediately identify evil with finitude which has forsaken the Idea, have only risen to knowledge of the bad, [26] for which reason they also only determine evil as the unreal. But they overlook the actuality which lies in the subjective will merely as such. In *the will* the bad crosses over into evil, which language also indicates by using the expressions "a bad will" and "an evil will" as synonymous.

§ 23.

The ground-relations, under which the Good's end presents itself for the human will, determines the content of moral philosophy. The first relation is the Good's pure universality and objective necessity in contrast to the human's natural individual will [*Enkeltvillie*], the Good as *the law*. But the Good does not remain in this relation of contrast to the subjective will. Through the destruction of egoism it is revealed as the will's essence, gaining a living, personal shape in the human individual. The Good becomes the human's *ideal*. This subjective unity with the Good is at the same time insufficient, so long as it has not been developed through the objective forms of the life of society. The virtuous individual can only reach its destination and realize its ideals in the world of *morality* [*Sædeligheden*], in the *kingdom* of personality.

Note. If the here-asserted tri-partition is traced back to the categories of religion and dogmatics, then the first part corresponds to the *kingdom of the Father*, where the human through the law and knowledge of sin is led to *the Son*, the second Adam, in whom the human shall view [27] the ideal of human nature and gain its own personal fulfillment. The kingdom of morality has its religious expression in *the Spirit's* or *God's kingdom* as such, which takes up into itself and clarifies the entire life of the world. [28]

THE SYSTEM OF MORAL PHILOSOPHY

A.

The Good as Law

§ 24.

The moral consciousness contains the sublation of the state of innocence or the spirit's natural life, where the contrast between good and evil does not yet exist. As the human's eyes are opened in the world of freedom, the law steps out to meet the human as that demanding necessity of reason which is opposed to its natural will. Next it appears as the existing reason of social life, as the universal spirit's practical wisdom which is expressed in the existing order of folk-life and family-life, and becomes an object of the individual's respect and veneration. But as the *moral* law (in a more restricted sense) it appears only when it not merely steps forth under the positive form of outer authority but when it is found in consciousness itself, when it is "the law written in the human's heart." Then it steps forth in the universality of thought as the pure, the in-[29] and-for-itself law of God. This knowledge of the law has first become universal with Christianity, and this becomes the starting point of the consideration.

THE INNER RELATION OF THE LAW TO THE WILL

Duty

§ 25.

The immanent, morally necessary relation between the law and the human's subjective will is *duty* [*Plighten*]. The representation of duty implies that the Good's fulfillment *is an essential* necessity for the human will, and thus presupposes the will's *possible* identity *with* the Good. The human's obligation to do its duty is the human's obligation toward its own higher self.

Note. The great enthusiasm for duty which Kant evoked in his age originated from this knowledge of the law's immanence in the human soul.
The human's respect for the majesty of duty coincides with the purest
self-respect.—Christianity's teaching on the intensity of the law or on duty
stands in contrast to the *legality* of Judaism and the *civic* morality of the
Greeks.

§ 26.

Although the law is innate to human consciousness, its final principle
cannot really be sought in human consciousness itself. Subjective *autonomy* (as in the Stoics and Kant) cannot get beyond the universality [30]
and formalism of the command of duty. Since this self-legislation is not
able to give itself a positive content, the self bears witness to its limitation.
Just as little can the law have its final principle in the substantial rational
will of the historical human race; for the objective spirit or the spirit of
the human race is just as much as the single individual subordinate to a
spiritual *development of nature*, and only successively arrives at *knowing*
what it properly *wills*, for which reason it cannot in the strictest sense
of the word be *legislating*. The legislating will can only be thought of as
the self-thinking and penetrating *creative* will or God [*Gud*]. Through this
knowledge the moral consideration of duty passes over into the religious.
In all peoples the law's origin is traced back to the gods [*Guderne*].

> *Note 1.* That the law is grounded in God's will is not to say that it is a prod-
> uct of God's arbitrariness. When it is said that something is good because
> God wills it, it must equally be said that God only wills it because it is con-
> sidered good in-and-for-itself.

> *Note 2.* Because the law is grounded in God's will, it does not cease being the
> human will's own law. In the genuinely religious consideration of the con-
> cept of duty lies the view that the law is neither an abstract divine law (as in
> the Jewish Decalogue), nor an abstract human law (as in Kant), but a divine-
> human [*gudmenneskelig*] law. The contrast between divine and human [31]
> laws has no validity in the highest standpoint.

§ 27.

The will's duty cannot be thought of without its *right* or its rationally-
grounded claim on external freedom and the recognition of the same.
What from one viewpoint is duty, from another viewpoint is right, because both concepts are expressions for the same necessity of freedom to
realize itself. Just because Christianity led the human spirit back to its
deepest obligations, it emancipated the same to its original rights.

§ 28.

Considered in its pure universality duty is only one. But the one duty must step out into the *many* duties, which receive their determinate content from the system of actuality. The old division of duties toward God, toward others, and toward ourselves can be justified as true insofar as it proceeds from the ground-relations of life and considers duty under the viewpoint of the individual spirit, the objective spirit, and the Absolute Spirit. Only through the determinate, human *individuality* and its actual life in *the state* and *religion* can a concrete content of duty be developed.

> Note 1. The division of the content of duties into positive and negative, perfect and imperfect, etc. is merely formal.

> Note 2. That all duties are duties toward God is to say more precisely that the entire life of the world must be traced back to [32] God, or that the human's consciousness of the world has its final anchoring in the human's God-consciousness. But just because duty has its *final* basis only in religion, it must be enjoined that the system of the human's duties toward the world has its relative independence and self-validity, and consequently shall not be deduced nor immediately derived from religion but shall be reduced or be led back to this through its inner development. The deeper conception of duty *toward* God, not merely with *reference* to God, depends on knowledge of the *personal* interchange between God and the human.

> Note 3. The duties toward nature are indirect duties toward the spirit. They are not so much duties toward the individual beings of nature as toward the Idea which expresses itself through these.

Conscience

§ 29.

The human's immediate *certainty* of the Good, of duty and right as the absolute reality for the will, is conscience. Conscience is not merely the individual's co-knowledge with itself of the Good; it is in addition its co-knowledge with the moral consciousness of society and its co-knowledge with God in religion. Only the complete unity of these moments is the true conscience or its concept. When the conscience is defined as an immediate knowledge, it must be observed that its genuine *immediacy* [33] and *security* appear only through the most comprehensive mediation, results from only the richest and most radical life in actuality. The subjective conscience must have the attestation of the objective spirit and the Absolute Spirit.

> Note 1. It is the case with the conscience as with feeling that both can be the lowest and the highest, depending on whether it is considered in its primitive natural coarseness or in its transfiguration. In the latter case it is the

expression for the fact that the Idea, the in-and-for-itself rational, has merged with the human individuality, and indicates thus the deepest unity of the divine and the human. The merely subjective conscience on the other hand is atomistic, sectarian, and fanatical. The atomistic conscience is right-squandering and at best can only be tolerated.

The conscience is only *unfailing* where the human's subjective knowledge of the Good is one with its essential knowledge. In its empirical appearance it can be *failing*. It can be both *skeptical* and scrupulous or totally *indifferent*.

Note 2. The proposition: "One shall obey God more than humankind," which is generally cited for the human's right to exclusively follow its conscience, first receives its proper truth by the [34] divine or universal worth which is granted in the conscience. In its most eminent meaning this proposition is expressed in the great world-historical collisions where a new order of things is struggling forth in opposition to the old which now has only the right of antiquity. Thus in the Apostles and Luther. The conscience of these men was not atomistic but contained in itself the most universal of all. It was God's kingdom, the spirit of true society, which achieved a breakthrough in their individualities.

The Determination of Duties' Limit

§ 30.

Duty and conscience comprehend the human's *entire life of freedom*. It is its demand that the human's life present a moral *unity* in which no spiritual moment falls outside the determination of the law. Therefore, duty cannot be comprehended in a circle of abstract commands but is *the individuality's* all-determining spiritual law, or its ideal expressed in the imperativistic form. The spiritual comprehension of duty consequently requires that the individual's life shall be a moral work of art, where even that which is in-and-for-itself accidental receives meaning by becoming the Idea's reflection. Therefore the concept of the *accidental* or the morally *trivial* has no validity and is only the expression for lacking knowledge of the concrete duty.

Note. The spheres of the morally trivial and the closely-related moral license are restricted by [35] the advancing culture. (What in social life is called convenience receives a moral meaning with this viewpoint). In crude humans duty is restricted to a certain quantity of commands, which they often conscientiously observe, while outside of this they abandon themselves to the greatest licenses. In cultured, *flexible* characters the most accidental and the most trivial often assume a mark of higher necessity. At the same time since no human in its praxis can totally liberate itself from the morally trivial, this only shows that no individuality corresponds to its ideal.

§ 31.

If in the arena of the free will there is nothing too trifling to be determined by duty, so too is there nothing too great or too distinguished to be expressed under the form of duty. Duty is morality's absolute measure, and this leaves no more room for *adiaphora* [the inessential] than it does for *opera supererogatoria* [works of supererogation]. A morality which in its practitioner wants to outbid the demands of duty is not freedom but arbitrariness, and will easily be able to be shown as dereliction of duty or as neglect of the necessary.

§ 32.

When by *adiaphora* and *opera supererogatoria* a broader sphere is opened for the will's activity than that which is determined by duty, then by the *collision* of duties the will's sphere of efforts becomes so narrowed that it not merely [36] does not see itself as being able to fulfill its duty but its *fulfillment of duty becomes separated from violation of duty*. The collision of duties can be subjective and illusory, and can then be overcome by a more complete insight; but it can also be *objective*, grounded in the complications of the world's life, which the individual cannot shirk, and by which it inevitably enters into discord with its environment and with itself.

> *Note.* In most of the moral systems the collision is presented as merely subjective, because reason is not able to contradict itself by commanding the human to do the opposite. There is established then a number of *rules* for overcoming the collision, which rules however at the same time have the flaw that they themselves come into mutual collision with each other.— Without objective collisions there would be neither any world history nor any dramatic poetry. Both tragedy and comedy depend on collision. A deeper penetration into the essence of collision leads to the consideration of the *finitude* of the world's life. If paganism considers the tragic collision as a fate, Christianity makes it originate from the general sinfulness and guilt of the race, and hereby opens a higher sphere of consideration than the immediately moral.

§ 33.

Reflection on the limits of permissibility and the compulsory sublation of collision has given rise to *casuistry*, whose [37] purpose is to quell [*løse*] the doubt of conscience in the particular case (*casus conscientiae* [an occasion for the conscience]). But since the accidental and purely individual according to its nature eludes the consideration of science, casuistry is not a true science but only a failure to appreciate the limits of science. It is a moral atomism which detaches the individual from continuity with life's individual unity. The settling of the casuistic case cannot be sought in any sort of *rule* but only in the individuality's own freedom, in its moral *genius* and *tact*.

> *Note.* Casuistry was developed especially by the Jesuits who sought to quell the doubt of conscience by their teaching on probabilism. On the whole casuistry belongs more to Catholicism than to Protestantism because the positive law and the moral rule, not the Spirit's law, is the prevailing. In the ancient world it was especially cultivated among the Jews. As the written *letter* of the law came to be employed in individual cases of life, the casuistic question necessarily had to arise, whose solution became a task for the rabbinical spirit of subtlety.

THE WILL'S SELF-DETERMINATION IN RELATION TO THE LAW

Action and Responsibility

§ 34.

As the will reaches a decision and steps out into the outer world, *action* appears. Action is distinguished [38] from event by the fact that it has *freedom* as its principle, and from the deed by the fact that it is undertaken with *intention* and *purpose*.

§ 35.

With action is given subjective *responsibility* which expresses that the free, *self-conscious* will is the subject of the action and as such is *answerable* to the law. Subjective responsibility presupposes the reality of freedom of choice and temptation. Temptation is not evil, but has the meaning of being the will's test and trial, the transition point for its corroboration in the Good.

> *Note.* Christianity has given fundamental importance to freedom of choice and subjective responsibility. Both the first and the second Adam *are tempted* and must choose between good and evil. In the poetic work about Hercules at the crossroads this idea shone forth in paganism; but in general it is downplayed. There is no distinction made between action and deed, and the subject takes credit for its deed independently of whether it was intentional or not. (Oedip.)—The *exclusive* concentration on subjective responsibility and freedom of choice is that onesidedness which in Christianity's standpoint is called Pelagianism. [39]

The Conflict and Reconciliation of the Will with the Law

Sin

§ 36.

The will's conflict with the law is seen from the purely moral standpoint most precisely as originating from its own free choice. And although the individual action has its relative self-subsistence and independence, it can really not be detached from character; but character cannot be separated from the natural ground of individuality. The acting will's conflict with the law attests to an original conflict in *being* with the law. Hereby the moral consideration of evil passes over into the religious teaching on original sinfulness or original sin, which states that the subjective will prior to every free choice or by *nature* is evil.

> *Note.* Just because Christianity emphasizes free choice so pointedly, it also emphasizes the opposite side or the teaching that both good and evil in the human are independent of its free choice. The first side expresses, namely, the moment of *individuality*, the second that of *the race*. In a more restricted sense the one is the moral viewpoint, the other the religious viewpoint. In a moral respect Christianity requires "actions" instead of the old world's "deeds," emancipates the individual from its entire environment, and places its fate as it were into its own hands. But through this moral standpoint it leads the individual to the religious standpoint, as it teaches that the human's [40] most intrinsic worth depends not on what one does but on what one *is*, and that the quality of the fruit depends on the tree's roots. The individual is hereby able to gain an insight into its *nature* and trace this back to its unity with *the race*, to the universality of sin and reconciliation, which are conditioned by the fact *that the individual has become sharply differentiated from the race.* Only the self-subsisting individuality who is entrusted to its personal self-determination will be able in the struggle of temptation to experience sin and grace as *universal* powers which stir in the innermost quarters of the soul, and place it in indissoluble connection with the entire race. The antinomy between Pelagius and Augustine is this contrast between the individual and the race, between the abstract moral consideration and the religious consideration of sin and responsibility. The Pelagian *thesis* states: "Only the free action can be sin, and I allow nothing else to be reckoned to me as guilt than what I myself have resolved and carried out." Augustine's *thesis* states: "We have all sinned in Adam and his offense is reckoned to us as guilt." Consequently, it is not the individual self which sins, but the race, the universal nature, which sins in the individual.—Both propositions are true only in their unity and reciprocal transition into each other. The ancient world does not know this antinomy. Just as it does not know the idea of a comprehensive human *race* but only the idea of various folk-races, so [41] neither does it know the free, personal *individual*. Personal

freedom is never presented in an unadulterated differentiation because the individual is only considered as a link in the mass of people and state. It knows only the righteousness of deeds or civil righteousness, but moral righteousness of duty-consciousness as well as religious righteousness or righteousness before God is unknown.

§ 37.

That *evil* is *sin* means that it has its origin neither from God nor from nature but only from the human will itself. That the will's natural depravity which is independent of free choice is *sin*, and that the individual reckons this to itself as guilt, is grounded in the fact that it is *the will* which is corrupted, not anything different from the will and the *I* itself. Just because the human is will, *I*, it cannot shift the guilt from itself over to God or nature. Sin is no *stuff*, no "thing," but a movement in the will. Sin exists only insofar as it is willed; outside the will sin is not at all. Consequently, it is *I* and no other who thinks and wills evil. We are all without excuse. As we reckon our will's original depravity to ourselves as guilt, it is no more moral responsibility which is talked about. It is the absolute responsibility, the religious responsibility. Essential freedom pronounces condemnation over the entire natural and empirical condition of the subjective will. [42]

§ 38.

Insofar as sin is considered only from the viewpoint of universality, the proposition can be put forward that all sins are equal. But the one, universal essence of sin is seen only in the *different* sins. The immediate difference is the quantitative or the difference in *degree*. But the difference in degree passes over into the qualitative or the essential difference, which denotes the stages of inner development in the *self-consciousness* of evil.

§ 39.

The first form in which self-will enters into conflict with the law is that in which respect for the law in an immediate, non-reflective way is disregarded for natural and secular interests, for pleasure and earthly possession. But the reflection and idealism of evil begin when the self-will—leaning on subjective conviction, pure intention, and the good heart—disappoints *itself* with the *mere appearance* of the Good, and in a supposed concern for the Good withdraws before the knowledge and ful-fillment of its objective law. When the knowledge of the law's universal validity and necessity is pressed onto the consciousness but the self-will nevertheless will not abandon its direction, it becomes evil for itself but must then strive to seem good for *others*. Consequently, the egoistical self-consciousness reduces the good and true to a mere appearance and a mask. It becomes dissimulation, hypocrisy, and falsehood. Through this the diabolical standpoint is developed, where the evil spirit appoints itself as such as its end and opposes the Good on the exclusive grounds that it does not tolerate [43] any higher power over itself, but itself wants to be the absolute lord and master. The devil appears in part as titanic defiance, in part as Mephistophelean irony.

Punishment and Conversion

§ 40.

The evil will's striving after liberating itself from its dependence on the Good is absolutely fruitless. It has offended the Good's necessity and this necessity or the divine righteousness *must* be restored. Evil cannot escape its *punishment*. As the punishment reveals the sinner's wrong, so too is it the sinner's *right* to be punished; as the punishment reveals the sin-ner's dishonor, so too is it the sinner's honor. The real possibility of pun-ishment lies in this: that the necessity of righteousness is the necessity of self-consciousness itself, that the divine law is the human being's own law. Sin is punished not only by its consequences, but the evil con-sciousness contains the immediate punishment of an inner discord and self-contradiction, lack of true satisfaction, and positive unhappiness. However, this is only the objective side of punishment; the subjective side is the consciousness of *guilt* and *culpability*, the knowledge of sin and *re-sponsibility*. In this way is developed conversion, and punishment passes over into forgiveness.

§ 41.

If the evil consciousness did not arrive at knowledge of the emptiness and inessentiality of its striving, of its own unworthiness and guilt, then its inner unhappiness would have been comprehended as [44] its punish-ment only by others but not by itself. Guilt then would have only been reckoned to it by the spectating observer, and punishment would not have been executed *as* punishment, for which the subjective moment or self-responsibility is unavoidably necessary. But it is self-consciousness's concept not to be the self which is secret, but the self which is clear and revealed. Self-consciousness cannot remain concealed before that which it is, and just because the self, essentially considered, is good, it must also become conscious of the Good as its essence. *Knowledge* of sin is the first act in the inner crisis of consciousness, whereby the self posits a separation between good and evil, light and dark. The practical side of knowledge of sin is responsibility, the assumption of guilt and punishment, whereby the subject declares God as righteous. Carried-through self-responsibility is repentance. This entire inner movement of punishment's subjective moments must in addition be seen as moments of conversion or as different points of the *coming* of the Good and forgiveness into the human.

§ 42.

Punishment culminates *in repentance*, as the completed self-responsibility; but repentance is precisely the end of punishment and the actual beginning of conversion. In that living resentment over sin the will expels evil from itself and joins hands with the divine will and its own eternal essence. Repentance is this dialectical transition from punishment into grace, from the divine righteousness into the divine love, from liability into deliverance. But since it is only the dialectical *transition*, [45] since liability is *still not* overcome in deliverance, since deliverance just as much is not as is in repentance, this crisis must not be maintained but comes to *rest* in the *new human*.

> Note 1. The philosophers, who like Spinoza and Fichte reject repentance because a done deed cannot be changed and the human does not have time to repent, are no less onesided than the humans who transform repentance into an uninterrupted vain brooding over sin. Both overlook that on which it really depends, namely, the dialectical meaning of repentance and its necessity as a *transition point*.

> Note 2. To assert that there are sins which are not able to be repented is the same thing as asserting that the self-responsibility of sin and guilt cannot here be carried through. But this is the same thing as asserting that punishment and righteousness can be accomplished only onesidedly, i.e., merely from the *objective* side. For the guilty subject the merely objective punishment would more or less have the worth of a fatalistic power, and only by a higher observer could be seen *as* punishment or as a moment in the world-order of freedom, in the world-order of righteousness. The concept of the merely objective punishment perishes before the representation of the eternity of hell's punishment.

§ 43.

Religious repentance is distinguished from merely [46] moral repentance by the fact that it is not exclusively a sorrow over individual sins, over deeds and actions or individual conditions of life, but over the will's *natural* condition. The individual grasps itself here in its unity with the race and reckons to itself the depravity of human nature as its innermost personal guilt. Subjective and relative responsibility passes over into absolute responsibility. Here there arises not the question of the individual's knowledge and free resolve, whether it could have acted otherwise or not, whether sin could have been avoided, etc. For the Idea of freedom and its fundamental requirement have absolute validity, independently of the individual's subjective knowledge concerning this, because it is the human's *essential* nature. The empirical will cannot escape from being judged according to its absolute measurement, which asks not merely about what the will does but what it is. The original unrighteousness, the inner contradiction in the human's nature which receives its barb by the fact that it is *willed*, is destroyed through religious suffering and contrition.

> *Note.* The religious knowledge of sin and repentance become totally incomprehensible in a standpoint which stops at action and subjective responsibility. This is the case in the Jesuits' superficial ethics which defines sin as "a voluntary transgression of God's command." The less *consciousness* of sin, the less guilt and responsibility. To the same extent as the human's insight is eclipsed by its passions, to the same extent has it lost control over itself, accountability vanishes, and the circle of [47] excuses is enlarged. *The law's validity and obligatedness for me consequently depend on my knowledge of the law.* But since our subjective knowledge is variable and changing, and since human reason must humbly recognize its limits and dare not presume to decide what is in-and-for-itself true and good, one must be satisfied with moral *probabilism* or the doctrine of probability. On the other hand Christianity does not allow the validity of the law to be dependent on the subject's fortuitous knowledge of the law. It pardons not a tittle of the law but insists on it in its total severity. Because I do not know the law, it does not then cease to be my law, to be the fundamental requirement of the divine righteousness for my personality.—"The servant who *does not know* his or her master's will, but does what deserves a thrashing, shall receive a thrashing" (Luke 12:47); although in addition it says, that he or she shall receive fewer thrashes than the servant who *knows* the master's will but does not do accordingly, whereby then in addition the relative validity of subjective responsibility and excuse is recognized.

§ 44.

Religious repentance only comes to rest in faith in Christ as the objective justification of the human race before God. This consideration is carried through in speculative theology, which develops the doctrine of the human's reconciliation with God, of justification by *faith* alone, of the contrast [48] between law and gospel, of the law's cancellation and the imputation by Christ's righteousness. The standpoint of morality is abandoned. The relative difference between sins, which is posited in the moralistic standpoint, is sublated in the standpoint of religion. *All* have sinned and fall short of the glory they should have before God. There is no difference.

> *Note.* The proposition that all sins are equal receives its highest speculative meaning in the doctrine of justification by faith alone. The thief on the cross and the Lord's apostle on the cross are alike insofar as they are considered under the viewpoint of justification; for they both are delivered by faith alone, without their own striving and deeds, which even in the most pious and best people are only a patchwork. On the other hand insofar as they are considered under the viewpoint of sanctification and morality, and placed together in the domain of *relativity*, there is an essential difference between them.

§ 45.

In the new human egoism is broken in principle and the subjective will is reconciled with the essential will. The Good has become the will's *nature;* the will's relation to the Good is not merely an inner relation of dependence but a relation of identity; necessity, duty is reconciled with freedom. For the human's practical striving now determines the Good itself as *the ideal.* [49]

B.

The Good as Ideal

§ 46.

When the human spirit knows the will's absolute end or *the highest Good* as its own essential end, then it views the Good as the ideal. Only for freedom can there exist an ideal, and where the reality of freedom is negated, faith in the ideal must also vanish. The ideal has no existence outside of freedom and *is* only insofar as it in addition is *brought forth* by freedom's striving. Just as on the one hand it is the object of the human's greatest enthusiasm and longing, so on the other hand is it the object of the human's deepest *obligation*, since the divine law requires the ideal's actuality of the human. The will's movement toward the ideal is *virtue* [*Dyden*].

> *Note 1.* The antinomy which frequently is put forward between acting out of virtue and out of enthusiasm is annulled by the insight that duty is the moment of necessity in the freedom of enthusiasm and love. A striving after the ideal to which I am not obligated is only a striving after a false, self-created ideal.

> *Note 2. Antinomianism* or the rejection of the standpoint of law and duty only has validity insofar as duty is construed as the abstract rule, as the external statute. From this point of view Christianity transcends Jewish law; the Protestant conscience transcends [50] the traditional precepts of Catholicism, and the living, moral individuality is validated over against the abstract moral category. The human does not exist for the sake of the law, but the law for the sake of the human. (Cf. e.g., Jacobi's famous letter to Fichte). But love is in-and-for-itself so far from excluding the law that it much more is *the fulfilling of the law*, and contains the finest, most conscientious consciousness of duty.

§ 47.

As was the case with duty, so too here the ideal is considered under a threefold point of view, as God, the world, and the individual are viewed under the form of the ideal. Consequently, as practical ideals, God, the world, and the individual should all receive their true actuality by virtuous striving. But on the other hand this striving itself depends on the religious belief and knowledge that the ideals already *are* realized and only because of this are able to *become* realized. Therefore, the ideal's determinate content must be developed by the *historical view of the world*.

THE DIVINE IDEAL

§ 48.

In the Christian view of life God is not only life's creative beginning but also its result, its final all-embracing end. As such or as *the highest Good* God is to be realized by human freedom. The divine end is nothing different from the very self of God [51] and the meaning of all God's demands on the human is that the very self of God will be all in all, that God will gain personal shape in the human individual. The very self of God is that which God commands, by every imperative God means only Godself.

"God commands love, justice, mercy, etc., but all this is God Godself."
Consequently, God or the highest Good wants to become human and
thus requires a *God-human* of every individual. But this *demand* would be
empty and meaningless if it did not presuppose as its possibility that originally *existing* [*værende*] unity of the divine nature and human nature.

The mystical and the moral unity of God and the human

§ 49.

The true union of God and the human is *not the mystical*. The mystical is,
namely, only the abstract-*essential* unity, where the difference between
God and the human does not receive its *due*, where the subjective will and
the natural individuality become absorbed. This unity appears both in the
pre-Christian and the Christian mystics as pantheism and denies the practical concern of morality. But just as onesided is the abstract-*moral* unity,
which merely consists in the fact that the human does God's will. God's
will cannot be separated from God's essence, and it becomes unattainable
in all eternity for the human to carry out God's will if God is not permit-
ted *essentially* in the human soul. The true ideal requires the combination
[52] of the mystical and the moral union and the latter's elaboration of
this in the human's nature-determined individuality. In this way the unity
becomes *personal*.

> *Note.* In Spinoza's ethic the highest Good is determined as God and the
> human's unity with God is determined as an intellectual love which is a
> part of the infinite love by which God loves Godself. This statement in-and-
> for-itself can be considered perfectly Christian. But in accordance with the
> system's pantheistic character this intellectual love contains only the essen-
> tial or the mystical unity, not the personal unity. Since the consideration
> dwells exclusively on the one substance and renounces the world and all
> human independence, it makes both the ideal and love impossible. For the
> ideal presupposes the free independence of the striving will; it presupposes
> an actual contrast and tension between the Infinite and the finite; and love is
> a union in which two live. This twoness is lacking in Spinoza's system. The
> impersonal Substance cannot love, for which reason Spinoza also so mag-
> nanimously does not demand reciprocated love of his God. Consequently,
> Spinoza's intellectual love is *onesided* and does not originate, as in Chris-
> tianity, from the fact that God loved us first.
>   Although Fichte in contrast to Spinoza in the most powerful way asserts
> the free [53] independence of the human will, his moral view of the world at
> its highest point of development really turns into mysticism. For since the
> God of the moral world is actually only *actu* [acting] in the human individ-
> uals' virtuous striving, since God only exists as "the series of moral actions"
> and "only is, insofar as *we* produce God," so hereby is produced a unity of

essence of God and the human, which cancels the fundamental difference and annihilates the concept of a community [*Samfund*] and a cooperation [*Samvirken*] of God and the human. Neither is God here actually thought of as an ideal nor is any personal unity brought about.

The personal unity of God and the human

§ 50.

The religious ideal is absolutely realized by God's personal incarnation in Christ, by the entrance of the second Adam into history. His unity with God is not only the moral agreement in the will but the metaphysical consubstantiality [*Væsenseenhed*]. But the eternal, super-historical consubstantiality is not, as in the descendants of the first Adam, in original conflict with his empirical actuality, with his natural and historical individuality, and his unity with God must therefore in addition be seen as resting with him by *nature*. The second Adam is born without sin. It is his immediate natural destination to reflect the Godhead's fullness, to be freedom's new point of creation in history. On the other hand his unity with God must be seen just as much as that [54] which *is produced* by the subjective development of his freedom. Through temptation he makes evident the unity of the natural with the spiritual and realizes then at every point of his history the eternal unity of essence as the personal unity.

> *Note.* Had Christ's unity with God been only a substantial unity of essence, then he would have been only a mystic, such as he is represented by Fichte, but not the incarnation of the eternal Logos. Had it been only the abstract moral unity, which he himself had to conquer through the overcoming of a reluctant naturalness, through the ennobling of an individuality encumbered with natural depravity, then he would have been only a Socrates on a higher scale. And had his unity with God been only the immediately natural except that in addition this is viewed as a moment in *freedom's* ideal, then he would have been only a Dalai Lama. His God-humanness would then have no ethical substance and could only take a place among the incarnations of paganism. But these moments, which in the descendants of the old Adam are found only parceled out and dispersed, are in the new Adam in indissoluble association and inter-penetration. Moreover, Christ's personality is first seen in its complete light when it is seen as the center in the revelation of the triune God. Ethics cannot consider Christ in his purely metaphysical meaning but only in *relation* or in such a way that [55] his personality shines into the practical life of the world.

§ 51.

As the absolute mediator between God and humankind, as the prototypical personality of the human race and the one who alone is capable of redeeming the human will from its natural depravity, Christ is the object of faith's unconditional appropriation. In a practical respect the ideal is determined then as *the imitation of Christ*. But the imitation of Christ is accomplished only by this: that the individual settles on a particular vocation in God's kingdom. In this way the religious ideal passes over into the larger context of life-in-the-world.

> *Note.* We see how the imitation of Christ has been given shape in history when we find on the one hand an immediate, empirical construal, a believing imitation of his person, but a lack of consciousness about his Idea as in the Apostles before the spirit's outpouring; on the other hand we find an abstract spiritual construal, a striving towards the Idea with a disregard for the person. The extreme of the empirical imitation is seen in many martyrs, who aspired to repeat the passion of Christ in a carnal manner; in monks, whose entire life, as, e.g., the holy Francis of Assisi, had as its exclusive purpose to copy Christ; finally, in the Protestant sects, for which the gospel is a Jewish law, and who are not able to be secure of any moral [56] truth unless they are able to refer to a Bible passage or find something empirically equivalent to Christ's example. Since then the multiplicity of life in the world cannot establish its Christ-likeness in such an immediate way, they get into disputes over this. They retreat from life in the world and imitate the Redeemer along the obscure way of *feeling* [*Følelsen*]. The abstract spiritualistic imitation is in part mystical, which only wants to merge with Christ's essence, in part moral, which only wants to follow the universal in his example and teaching. The former developed especially in deeper dispositions in the Middle Ages as the highest achievement of the monks' life; the latter came to prominence in the eighteenth century with Kant. The contrast indicated here in the concept of the imitation of Christ is the practical side of the dogmatic contrast between the historical and ideal Christ.

THE IDEAL OF THE WORLD

§ 52.

The true faith in the religious ideal leads to considering the development of the world as the development of God's kingdom. Therefore it becomes the practical task for the human to transform the world into God's kingdom, or to liberate it to its ideal, which happens not only by immediate religious activity (Apostles, Missionaries, etc.) but by every free activity, which is conceived as a cooperating moment towards the absolute end of history. The developed striving after [57] the ideal of the world presupposes knowledge of history's present stage of development, vital and variegated participation in the concerns of the world, and deliberate relating [*Henførelse*] of this participation to the infinite end. No individual is excluded from participation in the task of history. In the moral order of the world a direction for everyone's activity has been provided.

The present and the future

§ 53.

As the temporal development of freedom, history must be viewed as a successive actualization of the ideal. Therefore it becomes the task of the individual to understand the existing ideal in actuality; but just as the ideal must be already presupposed as actualized, so must a new moment of its actuality be produced by the overcoming of the barriers, which freedom finds in a few respects. The present receives full life by that rich futurity which stirs in its interior, and every time a new "fullness of time" occurs, a new promise and a new hope are also born.

> *Note.* Hegel's celebrated claim that one must acknowledge the actual as the rational is inseparable from the claim that one must oneself *produce* the rational actuality. Otherwise his thesis would contain a denial of freedom and the ideal. Moreover, if Hegel has so powerfully polemicized against subjective arbitrariness which does not want to acknowledge the *existing* ideal of the world, then this polemic on every occasion [58] has its application because there are always humans who will not accept reason and truth in this way, as it is revealed, but want to have a religion, a philosophy, a state according to their own fancy. With this misunderstanding of the present are always associated fantastic and lofty hopes concerning the future. Not only in the domain of religion but also in all other domains, there are false messianic expectations and chiliastic hopes.

Optimism and Pessimism

§ 54.

The ethical view of the ideal of the world is incompatible with pagan *Optimism*, which ignores the imperfection, badness, and depravity of the earthly life, and finds absolute satisfaction in the present life and the present condition of things as that in which all perfection is realized (*Quod petis, hic est* [That which you seek, is here]). Similarly, the ethical view of the world's ideal is incompatible with *Pessimism*, which considers the bad [*det Slette*] and evil [*det Onde*] as an invincible barrier, and allows the human to lose itself in faint complaints or in an indifferent resignation, or finally makes the human seek satisfaction in sheer irony. Both Optimism and Pessimism destroy all energetic striving and deny true faith in the ideal. [59]

The romantic and the humorous view of the world

§ 55.

Since the nature of Optimism and Pessimism is pagan (Docetic and Manichean), both are refuted by the Christian view. Christianity's *romantic* view of the world depends on the contrast between the ideal and actuality. Certainly the reconciliation has been essentially accomplished in the world, but the world's actuality does not correspond to its essential truth. Now although this view, if it is not to dissolve in a vague poetic vapor, must recognize actuality as the successive revelation of essence, it really always contains the consciousness of the ideal's secret glory which has not yet broken through temporality's larva, which prevents it from being optimistically satisfied by *this* life but on the contrary must consider this life as a point of passage to the full actuality of the ideal of the eternal world. Consequently, the romantic view of life depends on the dialectical contradiction that God's kingdom has already come and that it has not yet come. Therefore the Christian disposition [*Gemyt*] contains in the middle of the joy over God's kingdom an unresolved sadness, a transfigured sorrow over sin and the world's misery, a longing for the fragmentary to be dissolved by the perfect. Far from being unpractical, this view rather contains the most powerful ethical impulses toward a chivalrous struggle on behalf of the ideals of life. No barrier is absolutely invincible, for the essential victory has been won. [60]

§ 56.

If the romantic consciousness becomes deeply absorbed in the *contemplative joy* over the ideal's essential victory or, what is the same thing, over the essential reconciliation of eternity with time, then appears the *humorous* view of the world, which *anticipates* the goal toward which all of life strives, as already attained. What the romantic longing only has in hope, humorous joy deals with as present. The existing contrast between the ideal of the world and actuality, which the romantic consciousness longs to annul, the humorous consciousness allows to stand, because in its inner self it accomplishes the solution. The humorous is deservedly called the "world disdaining idea" (Jean Paul), because it calls to attention the moment of finitude and nothingness in everything and views actuality as *the unnaturally-wrong world*; but it is not merely the world-disdaining and world-judging but also the world-reconciling idea, because it knows its own unity of essence with this world and in finitude is reflected its own infinitude. The humorous is an outflowing emanation of the highest

Good, of the eternal love which cannot do without the contrast of finitude and which gladly forgives and suffers everything because by this it can reveal the superfluity of its kingdom. The humorous is the innermost background in all Christian considerations of the world. Where under the movement and labor of life the humorous gushes forth, there acts the absolutely liberating and redeeming because it sublates [*ophæver*] all the barriers of actuality and allows the soul to breathe in a blessed world. But since this joy over the world is the anticipation of the development's highest achievement, since life here is viewed from the standpoint of the blessed spirit, [61] the humorous can only appear as a moment and not be maintained because the conflict still continues, and actuality with its unresolved tasks and singular end is called to serious action.

> *Note.* The ancient worldview knows neither the properly romantic nor the humorous (the romantic-comical, as Jean Paul calls it), because it does not, as Christianity, know two worlds but only one, and is lost in an immediate Optimism. It certainly raises itself to *irony* over its onesided optimistic view, but this irony lacks the joy of the gospel and even in its most spiritually robust pronouncement has a bitter aftertaste of pessimism. Likewise the humorous is alien to the Jewish hypochondria, which is expressed in Ecclesiasates' complaint that everything is vain. Christian humor is neither irony nor hypochondria, but genuinely speculative Optimism, because it contains life's entire reflection as conquered [*overvunden*] and through the experience of the Fata Morgana of illusions, through the pain over the entire spiritual and natural distress of existence has been preserved the imperturbable joy over the fact that the absolute Good is really the substance in this world. Therefore this view will especially be able to appear in an age which, after a life torn to pieces by reflection, returns to the peace of reconciliation; and in the individual it will especially be able to appear in the old person, who through the many [62] experiences of life has confirmed her or his faith in the ideal. As an immediate practical view of life, the humorous is the same thing that speculation is as a comprehending theory. Speculation views the movement of the world in the repose of eternity and in thought possesses everything as present, which for empiricism is a future reality. However this is only the one, the *essential* side of speculation; for it might just as well demand that finitude actually should be united with the ideal, whereby it points to the romantic view of life.

§ 57.

Since the kingdom of freedom is history's absolute end, but freedom is not without nature, then nature must be seen as a moment in the ideal of the world. Christianity perceives in nature a prophecy concerning itself and concerning nature's own liberation from service to corruption to the glorious freedom of the children of God. Therefore it becomes the task of the human to *ethicize* nature and thus to actualize nature's destiny. The ethical relation to nature [63] excludes both the materialistic idolization of nature and the spiritualistic contempt for nature.

> *Note.* In the pagan religions a sensuous cult of nature alternates with a pessimistic aversion to nature. So long as the human has not grasped its own destiny, neither can the human grasp that of nature.

§ 58.

The Christian view of the world's ideal sublates the consideration of the history of the human race according to which this is either only a tautological cycle without an actual progressive development, or a development which struggles forth in an infinite progress without ever reaching its goal. To the contrary, history will one day obtain its end, God's kingdom will not for all eternity be only a *coming reality* but is revealed in its perfection as the life of the blessed individualities in God.

> *Note 1.* According to Fichte's teaching infinite progress must be maintained, because the life of freedom would stagnate if it did not always find new limits for its activity. Freedom must incessantly struggle, for otherwise it dies. Consequently, fruitless activity becomes the highest, and after the present life there is opened to us only the prospect of a moral Valhalla, where blessedness consists in combat. What Fichte carried out from the subjective standpoint has also been manifested from the objective standpoint. Life in the universe would stand still if it did not continuously develop, and if under this development there were not continuously produced new negative moments (Fichte's "limits"), which could incite and solicit the Idea to produce a new dialectic. History is therefore the opposite of being a teleological development and really eternally having its telos outside itself. Ever unsatisfied it shatters [64] what it has itself constructed in order to create for itself higher forms, which yet again are encumbered with the general ground-contradiction [*Grundmodsigelse*]. But with this contradiction it must purchase its existence. (Thus a certain section of Hegel's school). This view of the history of the world as a restless *becoming*, where the perfect is only a *coming reality* but is never granted in its actuality, depends, just as much as Fichte's restless *acts*, on a presupposed indissoluble dualism of the Infinite and the finite, a disguised Manichaeism. The Infinite *demands* unity only with the finite, except that this demand can be satisfied. But the fear, that by attaining the goal life and movement should stand still and be transformed into a dead consequence, is groundless. There cannot only be thought of a fighting and a struggling, a suffering and a dying, but also of an eternally regenerating and rejuvenating life which is an inner harmonious fullness.

Note 2. The indissoluble connection between the natural and the ethical, without which Christianity cannot complete the ideal of the world, Kant came to see along the way as he was obliged to postulate a future harmony between the kingdom of nature and that of freedom. [65]

THE IDEAL OF INDIVIDUALITY

Salvation and virtue

§ 59.

As the individual realizes the world's ideal, it realizes in addition its own. In as much as it views itself under the form of the ideal, it views its own salvation or the sublation of the contrast between its eternal and its phenomenal individuality, between its inner and its outer human. If salvation, considered from the standpoint of faith, is absolutely independent of the individual's deeds, then from the practical standpoint it must be seen as that which is successively effected and produced by the individual. This in-itself undying *striving*—which, insofar as it is construed in its points of rest, must be seen as a *condition*—is virtue. For the ethical consideration virtue is no different from salvation. It is the subjective moment in the highest Good.

> *Note.* Christian virtue is essentially different from the ancient, which does not know the deep contrast between the inner and the outer human, between the spirit and the flesh, and the representation of salvation as the sublation of the sharpest contrast that coheres with this deep contrast. Ancient virtue depends on the harmonious satisfaction of the instincts, on an immediate esthetic equilibrium of the human's rational and sensuous nature, and has therefore an erotic and phenomenal character, which is also manifested in the well-known Aristotelian [66] definition of virtue as the middle of two extremes, a determination which is only quantitative, not qualitative. Since pagan virtue does not presuppose the depravity and redemption of nature but is immediately satisfied in its own autonomy, a Christian thinker, who did not measure the pre-Christian world with its own relative standard but with the absolute standard, could advance the thesis that the virtues of the pagans are brilliant vices.

§ 60.

The question, whether there is only one virtue or many virtues, is answered analogously with the question of duty's unity. The ancient's division of virtue into four cardinal virtues is an attempt to present the fundamental psychological moments in one virtue. The Middle Ages added to this the three so-called theological virtues, which are to give those general virtues the higher spiritual quality.

> *Note.* One can thus trace *wisdom* or the knowledge of the highest Good back to faith, *justice* or wisdom's practical side back to love, *courage* or stead-fastness in conquering the outer barriers and hindrances back to hope, and *moderation* (σωφροσύνη) or inner self-control back to humility. Among the Christian cardinal virtues humility ought not be missing. For of all the Christian virtues it is the one which most nearly and most sharply expresses the contrast to paganism, because it points directly [67] to the insufficiency of human nature, to its craving for divine grace.

§ 61.

Virtue gains actual shape *in character*. Character is not only the inner disposition but the *marked* will, the unity of the outer and the inner human. Genuine character is not only the formal consistency of the will, with which it is often confused, but the beautifully-modelled elaboration of an eternally universal content. The more character is considered as an instrument of the universal and is determined by life's objective powers, the more free is its self-determination and the more versatilely virtue can be revealed.

§ 62.

If the independence of thought and the originality of the will's determination are singled out from the concept of true character, then virtue cannot be taught. The problem of virtue is unique to every human individual and cannot be expressed in a general theoretical formula. Virtue can certainly by means of theory and lively presentation awaken the soul, but as the production of the individual ideal it must be considered as a divine art, and its originality must be seen as a gift of divine grace.

> *Note.* Virtue's independence and originality shall only rarely appear as the conspicuous and extraordinary. In this immediate, visible form it can only occur in the heroes, [68] who appear at the great turning points in the development of the moral order of the world. These are in a more restricted sense ideal figures in the drama of history; they form a necessary contrast to the customary and they are as it were the points of visible revelation of the ideal. The Apostles, e.g., Luther, are such ideal figures, because they are to introduce a new state of things, which is the proper task of the heroes. If this state of things is well-founded, if the society's new life is organized, then the

individual, visible ideal retreats before the spirit's general activity. Now the individuals are only able to arrive at their destination in a cooperation with all, and must more inwardly than outwardly seek to lift up their peculiarity. To strive after the visible ideal, when the whole state of the world has made this striving futile, is ridiculous. Don Quixote is the representative for the knights who aspire to historic greatness and fame but could not find any place in actuality.

§ 63.

To consider virtue as a *merit* is only to consider it under the viewpoint of freedom of choice and subjective accountability. But if this viewpoint does not comprehend the entire idea of freedom which in its highest development must be seen as one with the divine necessity of nature or grace, merit has only a relative meaning. The absolute viewpoint is that virtue has an unconditional *worth*. [69]

> *Note.* Just because virtue has an unconditional worth, it cannot be compensated for by any sort of *price*. A price can be given only for the finite and the impersonal, whose worth is never unconditional.

§ 64.

The representation of virtue's *reward* must not be classified merely according to merit but according to worth. The false representation of reward is considering it as something which exists outside virtue's own concept. *Beatitudo non est virtutis praemium, sed ipsa virtus* [Happiness is not the reward of virtue, but virtue itself] (Spinoza). But to say that virtue can be self-sufficient in the bare awareness of its own worth is onesided, because virtue cannot dispense with a *world* in which the Good is both possible and actual, because it requires a corresponding objectivity in which it can accomplish its concept.

Activity and enjoyment

§ 65.

Since the highest Good is both actual and in addition something which first has to be produced, virtue as its subjective side must consist at once in enjoyment and activity. If one onesidedly posits the essence of virtue in activity, in the overcoming of the striven-against barriers, then one makes life's reflection into everything and never arrives at life's paradise or at

the moment of immediacy. If one onesidedly posits with Eudaimon-
ism the essence of virtue in enjoyment, in a harmonious state where
all practical barriers are annulled, [70] then it is overlooked that genuine immediacy must always *result* from [*resultere af*] reflection, that life's
paradise only goes forth from life's striving, and that enjoyment, in order
to be spiritual, must itself be *productive*. The virtuous and blessed life consists in the rhythmic exchange of activity and enjoyment. Activity is not
merely for the sake of enjoyment, and enjoyment is not merely for the
sake of activity. Although they are mutually sublated into one another,
each of them in addition has its unconditional self-validity. It is just as
much the human's duty to enjoy as to act.

> *Note.* Fichte's virile but onesided way of thinking posited the essence of
> virtue in activity and consequently has to regard every enjoyment, even the
> esthetic, as merely means and impulses to renewed work. But life hereby
> takes on the character of a boring, practical seriousness, and receives a dras-
> tic lack of irony and humor. The opposite extreme to Fichte's energetic
> industry (he posited the essence of sin in laziness and inertia) is developed
> by F. Schlegel, who posited the highest ideal of virtue in *et dolce far niente*, a
> brilliant idleness, "*eine gottliche Faulheit*" which had its pattern in the Epi-
> curean gods; while one allows the others to work, one must oneself be the
> brilliant irony over the whole. In Goethe's practical wisdom on the other
> hand we find the harmonious crossing over of enjoyment and activity into
> one another. [71]

§ 66.

In the moral order of the world activity and enjoyment *correlata* [are
correlated]. It is the eternal law of justice that a rest is only given for the
working, and that only the one who seeks can find. Only for the spirit
who works on his salvation does the comfort of reconciliation and joy
over God's revelation exist; only for enthusiastic striving does science and
art open a world of realized ideals; and only the sacrificing love and faithfulness knows the blessings of life in society. For the individual, who,
inside the sphere that is entrusted to its free self-determination, shirks
from freedom's work, there is given only an insipid enjoyment.

§ 67.

Ethical activity and enjoyment has the Good in-and-for-itself as its end
and content, but just as much seeks and finds the individual in this itself.
True self-forgetfulness is inseparable from true self-respect. It is only an il-

lusion that there should be any enjoyment of the substantial, in which the human did not in addition have enjoyment of its own *I*, that the human should be able to posit its life for the ideal, if in a higher sense it does not maintain its individuality. Self-respect only becomes false when it wants to be more than a moment which is ever sublated and passes over into its opposite.

> *Note.* Just as the individual who seeks God does not seek God only but in addition seeks its own *I* as maintained [72] and certified in God, so the same moment of self-respect is repeated by all other ends of life. As the religious individual wants to know it is recognized by God, so does the moral individual want to know it is recognized by the community of spirit. What the claim to eternal salvation is in the religious, the individual's claim to honor is in the secular. This is determined further as the individual's claim to power and influence, as a concern for possession and property, life and health, etc. The concern for these goods, both for the religious and the secular, can be egoistic, but is in-and-for-itself legitimate. For true self-respect is not merely the *I*'s self-certification but in addition its self-denial. In this way the infinite self-esteem of salvation has its inner limit in *humility*, in which the individual acknowledges its own nothingness as over against the everythingness of grace. The feeling of salvation and humility are the positive and the negative moments of the very same thing. In the very same way in which the individual places its honor or its title to a positive recognition in the community lies the basis for its *modesty* or its knowledge of its limited and relative importance in the whole, etc. [73]

Freedom and dependence

§ 68.

Because of the contrast still existing between actuality and the ideal, virtue is bound to come *into collision* with its surroundings, and freedom is bound to develop into the antinomy between τα ἐφ᾽ ἡμῖν and τα ἐκ ἐφ᾽ ἡμῖν [those things which are within our power and those things which are not within our power].

§ 69.

Practical *prudence* seeks to annul the collision between the subjective and the objective so far as possible by establishing an *equilibrium* and a mutual accord between them, and in this way to secure its bliss. But prudence will come to have the experience that the relative harmony is dissolved and needs to be restored in the Infinite; and if it does not want to abandon wisdom and lose freedom, its teaching on bliss must be sublated into the Stoic way of thinking.

> *Note.* In the ancient world Aristipp represents world-wise virtue. The teaching of Epicurus on bliss ends with the achievement of Stoicism.

§ 70.

The Stoic way of thinking cuts the knot in two by onesidedly maintaining inner freedom and independence. The true sage gives up on all bliss, and in order to be fully liberated from the vicissitudes of this world, the sage tears to pieces all the bonds which tie him or her to objectivity. Life's [74] sympathetic moment is destroyed, and the *I* strives to hold itself firm like an immovable atom in the universe. Every feeling and passion, even the religious, must be excluded by the soul, for in feeling the soul is suffering and affected by a foreign power. This freedom is only negative and has not been released from dependence, for as its contrast it has an invincible and irreconcilable barrier outside itself. In its consistent striving after abstract independence this standpoint may result in the abandonment of individuality itself.

> *Note.* In the ancient world this standpoint appears as Cynicism, as Stoicism proper, and as Skepticism, which with the abandonment of every concern for reality only strives to preserve the *ataraxia* or the soul's inner security and uninterrupted conformity with itself. Monastic life and the mysticism which grew out of this is its Christian modification.

§ 71.

This dialectic is first resolved for the Christian consciousness. Παντα ὑμῶν ἐξι [All things within our power are permitted], says the Apostle to the Christians, and thereby sublates the dualism between τα ἐφ᾽ ἡμῖν and τα ἐκ ἐφ᾽ ἡμῖν [those things which are within our power and those things which are not within our power]. *All things* work for good for those who love God. While the contrast between the ideal and actuality stands as a fatalistic necessity for the pagan consciousness, the Christian consciousness is reconciled with it. Pain, suffering, and death are acknowledged as freedom's own necessity, as means to the individual's eternal salvation. "It is proper for us through adversity to enter into God's kingdom." The contrast between the ideal and actuality, the cross, is itself a principal [75] moment in Christian optimism. Instead of Stoic resignation, love's submission to a personal providence now sets in. Temporal bliss is known in its merely relative and minimal insignificance, for Christian skepticism has liberated the soul from every concern for finite reality. But Christian skepticism rests in the substantial certainty of faith and knowledge. It apprehends essence in mere appearance, in temporality's most fleeting shapes it detects the image of eternity and in the world's vanity the hidden seeds of God's kingdom. In activity and enjoyment, in suffering and delight, in life and in death the Christian sage preserves a blessed ataraxia, a peace of mind, which cannot be taken from her, because in her innermost self she is one with the power which conquers the world and knows the eternal personality as the absolute reality in the universe.

§ 72.

Since on the one hand virtue may be seen as the expression for the will's most free self-determination, but on the other hand depends on the individuality's original talent and in its deepest meaning must be understood as a divine gift of grace, so hereby is repeated in a new form the antinomy between τα ἐφ᾽ ἡμῖν and τα ἐκ ἐφ᾽ ἡμῖν. The contradiction is now put into virtue's own concept. It is no longer virtue which struggles with an outer necessity and which therefore can seek a way out in resignation and the consciousness of its inner freedom. It is virtue, striving freedom, which relates itself to itself as to that which does not exist in its own power. But virtue [76] and the ideal is the single thing which the will dare not give up.

§ 73.

The most immediate way out of this antinomy is for the subject to soothe itself with the thought that the will really is capable of *something*, and that more cannot be required of it than exceeds its ability. *Ultra posse nemo obligatur* [Nobody is obligated regarding that which is beyond one's ability]. But hereby is mitigated the ideal's absolute demand, and virtue compromises with nature's frailty.

> *Note.* This satisfaction by a relative "something" is common in the ethics of Catholicism. When this ethics teaches that the true ideal must be posited in the union of human freedom and divine grace, then it means, according to its Semi-Pelagianism, not the actual identity of freedom and grace, but only freedom + grace. Freedom does something, and grace does something; τα ἐφ᾽ ἡμῖν and τα ἐκ ἐφ᾽ ἡμῖν are only mechanically connected without deeply penetrating each other.

§ 74.

On the other hand if the subject will not give up on the ideal's perfection, and it becomes absorbed in a continuous reflection on its own incompetence and sinfulness, then appears that moral and religious brooding, an incessant occupation with the soul's inner state which removes the human from the life of society. The single thought which fulfills the individual is the thought of its own salvation, and the single praxis [77] which has worth for this one is working on its own virtue and perfection. However, if the individual is not virtuous, but has its virtue and its perfection outside itself as the abstract *object* of its striving, then this striving or the "something" which the individual itself contributes to its salvation can only be of a negative nature. This striving cannot be actually virtuous but only a means of transmission, an exercise and pre-school for virtue. It is only *asceticism*, a moral regimen and exercise-program, which has as its end to facilitate the breakthrough of the ideal in the soul by eliminating and removing the hindrances which the secular principle puts in the way in and around the human.

> *Note.* The thorough asceticism of monastic life ends with the relinquishment of individuality in the mystical unity with God. The ideal, which eventually breaks through, can only be the purely abstract essence, because the ascetic subject has appointed itself as the epitome [*Abstractum*] of freedom. The mortification of the flesh here becomes in addition a complete spiritual emptying. In Catholicism ascetic austerity accompanies secular irresponsibility. On the one hand the flesh has died, on the other hand its weakness becomes an excuse for lacking virtue. This morality has at once a onesidedly pessimistic and optimistic view of the human individual.—The immediate asceticism of the Middle Ages recurs in a more idealistic and reflective form in the pietism of modernity. [78]

§ 75.

Both onesidednesses, both secular austerity which soothes itself with the frailty of nature and ascetic and pietistic scrupulosity which struggles with nature as a hostile barrier, are destroyed in the standpoint of the ideal, because grace has here arrived at a breakthrough as freedom. Everything that is freedom's is God's, and everything that is God's is freedom's. Here also applies the Apostle's word: Everything is *yours*! Certainly this absolute freedom is the only essential principle of virtue, and as striving this virtue cannot escape the contrast between τα ἐφ' ἡμῖν and τα ἐκ ἐφ' ἡμῖν [those things which are within our power and those things which are not within our power]. But as this contrast is essentially solved in the standpoint of the ideal, in this way the ideal striving consists in the successive sublation of freedom's "something" by grace's "everything."

§ 76.

The successive actualization of personal perfection is obtained so little along the way of asceticism that this actually leads away from such perfection. Ascetic striving has only the abstract ideal, empty virtue and the *I* which is occupied exclusively with itself as its content. But the individual's concern for its own perfection and salvation is egoistic and unwarranted, its virtue lacks worth, when it does not contain self-forgetfulness and submission to a universal substance. The way of freedom to God passes through the eventful, significant secular life, and it only finds itself by going out into the community and assuming its share of the race's work for the world's [79] ideal. It must allow itself to be penetrated by the world-historical Substance which it encounters in the family, in the state, and in the spiritual actuality which is developed on the basis of the state. As the subject abandons itself to the service of these powers, it works itself free not merely from its spiritual but also from its natural dependence on itself. By ethicizing or by becoming the physical side of moral freedom, the satisfaction of the natural inclinations is legitimated.

§ 77.

When one admits an ascetic moment inside actual morality, because in particular cases it can be necessary for the individual to undertake a special self-purification and to place its life under a rule in order thereby to make itself more fit for the fulfillment of the end of its moral life, then such an ascetic moment is really only considered from the standpoint of legality as a remnant which is incompatible with the concept of virtue, and can therefore only have the destiny to disappear. From the standpoint of the ideal no moment of life may be merely a means but must in addition be an infinite end in itself.

§ 78.

Asceticism, as a science of virtue's means of transmission, like casuistry [*Casuistiken*], depends on a misunderstanding of the nature of science and individuality. The immediate individual does not allow itself to be determined by general rules. The only *universal* means of transmission of virtue are the family [80] and the state, art, science and religion, because virtue's means are here in addition its highest goal. In this kingdom of freedom significant work and substantial enjoyment are the soul's rightful and only κάθαρσις [catharsis]; practice in virtue is here no empty gymnastics, but actual action and spiritual achievement; school coincides with life. Asceticism may therefore be destroyed in objective ethics. [80]

C.

The Good as Kingdom of Personality

§ 79.

Although on the one hand the system of freedom may be considered as a work of the freedom of all, on the other hand it may be seen as that totality which freedom itself presupposes and develops. The ethical life of society is developed through family life and national life with its end in state, art, and science into church life [*Kirkelivet*], where it receives the meaning of the community of saints. Each of these forms of objective life can be considered as stages in the individual's way to its ideal, and as the *means* to the actualization of the individual's personal perfection. But if in this way, on the basis of the individual's infinite significance, society can be said to exist for the sake of the individual, then on the other hand the individual may just as well be seen to exist for the sake of society. For in each of those spheres of life reigns eternal deities [*Guddomme*], essential and self-valid powers, which are the object of the individual's unbounded awe and abandoned devotion. As these general structures are communicated to the individual and initiate it into their own eternity, they demand the individual's [82] complete resignation and self-denial, and are to be honored and loved for their own sake.

> Note. If one assumes the Christian view of the church as the kingdom of absolute redemption, then all the spheres which are presuppositions of the church's life can be seen as relative forms of redemption, namely, insofar as they have an end to liberate the natural human from its false dependence on itself and the world, a liberation which can only be seen in its full light from the standpoint of the church [*Kirken*].

THE KINGDOM OF PERSONALITY IN ITS IMMEDIATE ACTUALITY

The Family

§ 80.

The family is the most immediate form of the kingdom of the Good because it is just as much a work of nature as of spirit, because its members are just as much united by the bond of blood and natural sentiment as by the universal power of morality. The family is the cradle of personality; in its midst takes place not merely natural birth but also the moral birth of the individual. As the individuality comes into the world with the family's natural characteristics, so are the first elements of character developed by the moral spirit of the family which as a well-formed, active force imparts to the individual its spiritual mark, a determination which [83] must not however be separated from the individuality's self-elaboration and self-determination.

§ 81.

As the first link in the system of society's life the family already contains in germ the final and highest end. In the ancient world, where the life of society concludes in the state, the family is considered only as a point of departure for political life. But by Christianity, which distinguished between the inner and outer human and viewed the kingdom of blessed personalities as the purpose of the life of society, the family has also received a self-contained meaning which is not dependent on the state, an introspective and esoteric side. In the natural and moral common life the family is to express the eternal destination of personality. Through awe and piety, confidence and love, which are the elements of family spirit, the corresponding *religious* elements are to be developed and engendered in the soul. As religion in this way takes root in the most natural communal feelings of the human, the life of the family becomes the basis of the life of the church.

> *Note.* The consideration of the family and especially of marriage, which is developed in Plato's *Republic* where the individuals are only means for the state, seems to us as only a paradox, because we take for granted a completely other view of the human's destination and are not able to think of the life of society as concluding other than with the church [*Kirken*]. If we look away from this view, the Platonic *Republic* becomes quite intelligible. [84]

§ 82.

The center of the family is marriage. The basis of marriage is the difference between the sexes, which in addition is a difference in the individuals' spiritual determination. By joining the two individualities into one personality, marriage annuls both spiritual and natural one-sidednesses, which are given with the difference between the sexes. Just as incorrect as it is to appoint the physical side of marriage as the all-embracing point of view, equally incorrect is it to emphasize exclusively the spiritual side. Conjugal love hereby loses its *limitation* and becomes no different from other forms of love. It is precisely the entire *natural determination* of man and woman which in marriage is to display its moral significance.

§ 83.

The necessity of *monogamy* is grounded in the concept of conjugal love, in which the individuals grasp their natural determination in indissoluble unity with their moral determination. The onesided physical view of the human individual underlies polygamy, where love is impersonal because the individual only represents its sex and lacks self-worth. The human individual is here placed on an equal level with natural beings, who are only means and points of transition for the life of the race. But the free moral individual cannot be a means for *the race*, except insofar as by this it is confirmed in its unconditional self-worth as an *individual*. Christianity, which in all spheres of life preserves individuality [85] from being lost in the generality of the race and of natural life, also developed the monadic love, where submission requires unconditional *faithfulness*. By introducing monogamous marriage, Christianity accomplished the emancipation of women. Love's *freedom of choice* became the point of departure of marriage.

§ 84.

Marriage is not merely the individuals' relation *to each other* but also their relation to the objective idea of the family. Love may be developed through a common life toward a universally valid, moral end. Therefore, the woman may become the organizing center in a moral home, and the man through the struggle and work of life shall fulfill his destiny as the head of the family. By being brought into connection with the entire system of actuality love receives true validation and underlies his existence. The individuals first receive true significance for each other when in their peculiarity they express the common morality. Love achieves the proper depth through the earnestness of actuality.

Note 1. The antinomy between the inclination-grounded-match and the reason-grounded-match finds its resolution in the concept of marriage, which contains both aspects. The individuals are just as much for the sake of marriage as marriage is for the sake of the individuals.

Note 2. The prohibition against *divorce* is based not merely on the fact that the individuals are obligated to each other, but that they are obligated to the moral [86] order of the world. That the individual is not happy in marriage as a reason for divorce can only originate out of a lax teaching on blessedness. Only where the fulfillment of the moral determination of marriage—not merely in a subjective but in an objective respect—is made impossible, is divorce not merely permissible but a duty.

Note 3. When Catholicism presents celibacy as a higher stage of moral perfection than married life, then it shows by this that it has not comprehended marriage as idea but only considers it under the natural point of view. When in contradiction with this it declares marriage as a sacrament, then this is only an attempt at giving with one hand what has been taken with the other.

§ 85.

The moral household is further developed in the relation between parents and children, and in the relation between master and servant. As Christianity, which everywhere takes onto itself the poor and despised of the world, emancipated women, so too does it emancipate the children and the slaves to their essential human rights. By the education of children the family certifies its spiritual coherence with the state and the church.

Note 1. The infinite meaning which the child has in the Christian family is expressed by infant baptism, which is in addition an object of the Christian state's care. The child's destination is not absorbed in [87] the family, but by being born into the family it is in addition incorporated into the larger systems of the state and the church. The higher spheres of the system of freedom, to which the child belongs just as much as it belongs to the intimate sphere of the family in which it is born, are immediately active at its birth. The child is posited at once as belonging to the family and entrusted to the care of the family's love, and in addition as emancipated from the family, because also in those higher spheres of a universal love and justice there is an account made of its freedom.

Note 2. Every family life may be developed into an individual type, but in addition may contain the endeavor to take up the common social elements. The family consciousness becomes dull when it is not stimulated by the general substance of society. Onesided love of family delimits the soul and kills the sense for the ideal, while true love of family develops the soul's sympathy for everything that has worth in life.

§ 86.

Both by the mutual relation of families to each other and by the same among individuals there is cultivated a sphere of more free social relations which develop the ideas of hospitality, friendship, and companionship. These relations receive their ethical meaning by the mutual spiritual communication and the substance of *personality* which is developed through them. The [88] outer limit, inside of which these forms of society are able to be developed, is determined by the different stages of *culture*; the inner limit is determined by the individuals' own sympathies.

> *Note 1.* Human love can only be immediately brought to light *in special* social relations as love to certain, definite individuals. On the other hand, insofar as it shall embrace all humans equally, it is either an empty abstraction, or it may be thought of as an intellectual love for the ideals of the human race. Just as there are individuals who have chiefly cultivated individual, empirical human love, and therefore find their proper sphere in the family and special relations, so are there individuals who are inspired by a high intellectual love for *the race*, which they bring to light by self-sacrificing activity for ideals of the arts and sciences, of the state and the church, but which have not in the same degree cultivated the concern for persons. Christian striving toward God's kingdom contains the equal cultivation of both aspects indicated here.

> *Note 2.* In special personal social relations the task becomes to develop the sense for the specific in every relation, to acquire an immediate proficiency in comprehending each relation in its *limit*. What one calls good tone, delicacy, discretion, depends on this proficiency in observing the limit, which [89] is required no less in the most intimate relation of love, the most confidential relation of friendship, than in purely formal companionship.

§ 87.

Individual social relations, where the multitudinous subjective concerns cross each other, point to a higher substantial world of reason which is reflected in culture. As culture is the common element in which individual relations transpire, so does culture itself receive its color and its contents by the political and scientific, the artistic and religious life which is stirring in the age.

THE KINGDOM OF PERSONALITY IN ITS REFLECTED ACTUALITY

§ 88.

In order that personality might come of age it must pull out of the individual sympathies, of the kingdom of piety and love, and both in a practical and in a theoretical respect become self-conscious of its general content in its pure *objectivity*. It must enter into the world of the state, art, and science, whose ideals form a relative contrast to the ideal of the Good, because they do not like this contain explicit respect for the individual's subjective will. The Good is certainly granted in these spheres, but in an indirect way. It appears here through an *other* [*Andet*] than itself and therefore has only a reflected, a sublimated or mirrored actuality. But the Good has only given itself this sublimated actuality because through this reflected actuality the Good will [90] be developed into its *true* actuality, into the spiritual communion [*Menigheden*], God's kingdom as such.

> Note 1. The family and the spiritual communion [*Menigheden*] are the extremities in the system of social life and the only general forms of society which express immediately the idea of the Good. But in order to develop the Good in its true spirituality they need the intermediate link of reflection. Where this is lacking, so that the family and the spiritual communion immediately coincide, is found only the patriarchal, idyllic condition.

> Note 2. The assertion that the state shall have a purely moral purpose, that the more art and science approach this ideal the more they develop life's moral and religious substance, and the opposite assertion that these spheres shall be developed according to a sheer autonomy without any moral and religious secondary consideration, are mediated in the consideration suggested here. For it is only as an *other* than the Good that these ideals may contain *essential unity* with the Good. The personality should not seek its own thing, but should be educated to unselfishly love and give itself completely to the Good by viewing this under another form than its own. To know the Good in its immediate revelation, where it applies directly to our personality, be it as the commanding and threatening law or as consoling, protecting love, is not difficult; but to know the Good in its indirect [91] revelations where it directly ignores our personality, in the necessity of history which overlooks the individual, in the rigorous forms of science which are indifferent towards our subjective wishes and longings, in the beauty of art which pays no heed to the astonished beholder, is the more difficult and presupposes the higher culture.

The State

§ 89.

The state is the kingdom of personality in its formal universality and necessity. The right of individuals to universal freedom and equality is realized through their necessary inequality, through the *systematic* limitation of their freedom. Therefore the life of the state is organized in different estates [*Stænder*], and in the relation between government and subjects. The developed system of the powers that be is the state's constitution.

§ 90.

The concept of the state is inseparable from the concept of the people. The folk-spirits or spirits of the people, whose natural boundary lines are language, are given a right to external existence in the states. Only when a people arrives at an actual condition of rights does it come into possession of its spiritual property, does it come to feel and know itself *as* a people. By the life of the people the state receives its *individual* type. But the individual spirit of the people cannot develop its peculiarity except insofar as it posits itself as a link in the *system* of folk-spirits, and in living interaction [92] with the other folk-spirits participating in the *universal* development of history.

> *Note.* By the higher general content of life which Christianity imparted to people, the state also received a higher significance than the merely national. States in the ancient world, on the contrary, are *only* national; everything is "folksy," even all the way to the gods. When in modern times one sometimes has wanted to make the national into the all-embracing point of view, then such an endeavor can only be regarded as an after-effect from paganism and Judaism. On the other hand, only a onesided cultural understanding will disentangle the *cosmopolitan* from the national.

§ 91.

The connection of the state with the idea of the Good appears in this, that outer justice finds its deeper basis in the inner, that the system of rights is guaranteed by the system of inner obligations, by the moral disposition, mutual confidence and recognition. Nevertheless the state is not the kingdom of sentiment and love. The state as such actualizes only factual justice and allows this to enter into power in rational *institutions and forms*. As the state's constitution is conditioned by morals, so are morals conditioned by the constitution. Through the view of lawfulness and necessity explicated in the state is developed the subjective consciousness of justice, just as on the other hand this consciousness is weakened and eclipsed [93] where justice does not press against it as a self-subsisting power which is independent of the individual.

§ 92.

In order for civic virtue to be developed the individual must belong to a definite *station* [*Stand*], appoint itself as an instrument for one of the general ends of the life of the state. Virtue appears then as a definite *competency* and the loyalty corresponding to this. But the state's different stations are not *castes*. The activity of the individual station is only collaborating with the whole, and therefore civic virtue contains the developed social consciousness. Justice and spiritual love-of-country are the essential elements of this social consciousness.

Note. Patriotism is not merely the immediate feeling and urge, not merely the power of custom, which imprisons us to this nature and this national life, but free, conscious life on behalf of the *ideals* of the spirit of the people. In the knowledge of these ideals the people shall judge and estimate its own actuality, and in this natural patriotism finds its proper goal and its limit. Ancestral heredity has true worth only insofar as in this the *essential* spirit of the people has been explicated, and historical memories instigate true enthusiasm only as they in addition instigate the higher self-understanding of the people. But the national ideals of the modern world do not differ from the general ideals of the race. Patriotism therefore is only the spiritual form of nature for that higher, general [94] love. Nationality is sacred because it is the means through which the in-and-for-itself sacred, the eternal and universal shall be taken up and appropriated. For if the spiritual is to become our actual property, if it is to become life and nature in us, then it must be presented for us in a native form.

Inseparable from patriotism is piety and admiration for the nation's great individuals. In admiration we feel our own smallness, our distance from the spiritual greatness to which we look up, but in addition the admiration raises us above ourselves and assures us of the actuality of our own ideal. Admiration contains not merely the difference but also the unity with the admired. The admired heroes are our own, our brothers and sisters. It is our own essence which shines in their radiance. As we spiritually bind ourselves to them, we are united more fervently with the ideal itself. When a people loses admiration and piety for its great individuals, it negates its own spirit and loses the higher self-respect.

§ 93.

The individual's destination is not absorbed in the state, for through the state the individual stands in relation to the kingdom of the absolute ideals, the kingdom where the ideals are actual in their pure ideality. As the spheres in which the spirit of the people arrives at consciousness of the Infinite, art, science, and religion are ends of the state, but in such a way that the state by positing these ends in addition *presupposes* their inner [95] independence and self-subsistence, and hereby points beyond itself.

Note. Just as Christianity gave rise in the individual to the double-consciousness of the outer and the inner human (which incidentally it not merely separates but also combines), so also did it separate the social consciousness into a double kingdom, namely, the outer world of the state and the inner world of the absolute ideals. *Inside* this inner world of absolute ideals art and science are again to be construed as the spiritually outer reality and religion as the inner reality, because the actuality of the ideals of the former is purely objective, while the actuality of the ideals of the latter is subjective and personal. By this introspective, self-intensifying development of the social consciousness, the Christian period is distinguished from the ancient period, where life in its entirety is immediately manifested *ad extra* [externally] without having any mystery. Therefore the state becomes the entire actuality of the ideal. In Plato's famous work on the state this view is clearly brought to life. Religion and poetry, art and science are determined only as moments and means in the political work of art.

Art

§ 94.

In the kingdom of art or the kingdom of beauty the absolute ideal is viewed as *actual*, but in such a way that this actuality, [96] this union of the ideal's essence and its phenomenal appearance, *is itself phenomenal*. The world of beauty is only a world of mere appearance [*Skinverden*], but this mere appearance is itself that of the ideal and freedom. Every nation's art corresponds to its consciousness of the ideal of freedom. The different views of freedom underlie the qualitative difference between ancient and Christian art.

§ 95.

Since freedom is the principle in all spiritual beauty, the various arts receive their meaning by being different stages of development in the beautiful elaboration of the ideal. Poetry is the universal art, the art which no cultured nation can do without because it has personality itself as its content. The other arts contain more a prophecy of the revelation of personality than this itself and are related to poetry as promise to fulfillment. In poetry art unfolds its entire, complete essence.

> *Note.* The kingdom of free personality has its highest *represented* actuality in dramatic art. The living, *national* instrument for the presentation of dramatic artwork is the *theater*.

§ 96.

Although art's innermost essence is freedom, it yet forms a pure contrast to the ethical. In the enjoyment of art the human forgets the empirical imperfection of freedom, its own defective morality and becomes absorbed exclusively in the spectacle of its essential glory, in the joy over possessing all the possibilities of freedom as actualities in [97] the realm of the imagination. On the other hand, where the ethical idea as such appears, there art contains explicitly the serious *practical* consideration of the *empirical* human and does not allow itself to be satisfied with the merely essential and *represented* glory. But ethics requires the very independence and self-subsistence of art. Were there no free self-subsisting art, or were art *only* a means to a moral purpose, then the human would not be liberated from immediate *dependence* on the Good, from the limited respect for its finite personality, and not arrive at pure joy over the ideal's own perfection. Therefore the Good must be transformed into the beautiful and conceal practical earnestness.

Note 1. The Good as such, the moral and the religious, is always *argumentum ad hominem* [an argument against the person, or deriving its force from the situation of one's opponent]. Thus, the purely religious consideration of Christ is inseparable from the individual's consideration of its own sinfulness and desire for Christ, and Christian preaching essentially reaches out in order to bring the listener to apply the teaching to itself. To the same extent as this personal reference is neglected, the consideration will cease being religious and take on an esthetic or scientific character. That there is then a purely esthetic and scientific consideration of Christ's glory, that there is a joy over Christ which is of another sort than the joy the sinner feels over its deliverance, and that that consideration and joy are legitimate, must all be acknowledged as grounded in ethics' own demand. [98]

Note 2. The denial of the ethical validity of art originates in part from a selfish love of the Good, in part from a crude representation of the true. But the denial of art can also originate from a higher consciousness of truth, when art wants to confer onto itself another substance than the phenomenal. From this point of view one may consider Plato's denial of the art of poetry. He wants to have the poets excluded from his state because they taught the people the untrue and imparted false representations of the gods. That is to say, antiquity attributed immediate religious meaning to the fabricating representations of the imagination. Art had not grasped itself as art and had not arrived at a clear consciousness of the nature of illusion. Plato's polemic and therefore the polemic of thought is against mythology. The same thing recurs at the time of the Reformation in the Protestants' rejection of the Catholic images which play so important a role in ecclesial mythology. In Catholicism and paganism art is confused with religion and in this fantastical light appear the forms of mythology and superstition. First in Protestantism does art find its proper limit and only in this distinction can religion be reconciled with it and science justify it.

§ 97.

As art is an end in itself it in addition [99] becomes a true means for the moral life. Esthetic enjoyment, which has moral worth in-and-for-itself, contains in addition the impulse to moral *activity*. The human's joy over its essential glory, over the reconciliation of freedom and necessity, spirit and nature, may awaken the effort to sublimate the ideal's merely represented existence and give it real existence, transforming the esthetic into the ethical. Art's tacit demand on the human is that it should execute that about which art itself is only a prophecy, and art itself sends the human back into the practical life of the world. Individuals, who only indulge life in esthetic enjoyments, who only want to rejoice in the enchanting mere appearance of ideals and in the images of freedom but shirk before work in serious actuality, have just as little grasped the meaning of art as the meaning of life. Only the individuals who both outwardly and inwardly live for actual freedom are able to grasp true joy over the esthetic ideal.

Science

§ 98.

In science the absolute ideal has discarded the mere appearance, and personality itself becomes objective in the pure forms of thought and the concept. As the conceiving knowledge of the actuality of the ideal, of the absolute reality of freedom, science is determined as *idealism*.

§ 99.

The different links of the carried-out system of idealism are relatively complete forms of the presentation of freedom [100] as the Absolute. The speculative logic ends with knowledge of the category of freedom as the category which concludes the entire system of thinking. *Teleological* thought is known as the all-encompassing ground-thought [*Grundtanke*] which makes comprehensible actuality in its entirety, because this thought is the rational, the comprehensible itself. The philosophy of nature reproduces nature's inner idealism, transfigures matter into spirit, necessity into freedom, but ends with the insight that teleological thought is not concluded inside the circumference of nature, that nature has its end outside itself. The philosophy of spirit has personality itself as its object, presents the different stages of its development, and concludes with knowledge of God's kingdom as the centralization of the entire universe, its perfect concept.

§ 100.

What the beautiful form is in art, the free necessity of *method* is in science. The concern of science for its object is not the subjective, personal concern, but the logical and metaphysical concern. The Good itself only has worth and meaning for pure science insofar as it is known as the highest *true reality*, as the highest metaphysical reality. In this purely theoretical freedom, which is independent of all practical ends, science asserts its independence as over against the state and the church.

§ 101.

If science is treated only as a means for the state, then appears practical barbarism. But the intelligent [101] state knows the free-born right of science, considers it as an end in itself, and thereby derives the full *benefit* from science. The purely scientific way is here the only practical way. The citizens of the state who are not working merely for secondary and particular ends but for general ends, who are to have an educating, guiding, and ordering effect on life, must have taken possession of *the principles* for this activity, must be able to draw their insight from the living, original source. But the true principles are obtained not in the half-hearted science, but the fully-rigorous science. The meaning a state confers on science is manifested practically in its relation to *the university* and *literature*.

§ 102.

If science appoints itself only as a means for the church, then appears scholastic, medieval barbarism. In the Protestant church, where faith has been liberated from the authority of the visible church, where certainty is grounded in faith's own saving power, freedom of thought is inseparable from that of faith. In the church, where faith is found in its deepest inwardness, science is also instigated to its most profound doubt. As little as science may be scholastically constructed on the authority of the visible church, just as little may it be pietistically constructed on the dispositional states and feelings of the believing personality. A merely "upbuilding" science is only an echo of faith, its tautological paraphrase, instead of faith gaining true justification and freedom by the fact that its truth is certified for it along another and opposite way, that it is attested to by a voice other than that of faith. [102] The truth must be seen doubly, in part from the practical standpoint of faith and life, in part from the standpoint of truth itself. To assert that it is only the human's duty to believe but not to know is the same thing as denying the truth's own *right* to be known by the human.

§ 103.

As scientific theory in-and-for-itself is moral praxis, so must it in addition contain the impulse to shape the understood ideal into life's individual actuality. Art contains this demand only latently, but science expresses it explicitly since it is not merely theoretical science but practical science or *ethics*. Although ethics expresses its demands in the pure universality of thought, it yet in addition is at every point *argumentum ad hominem* [an argument against the person, or deriving its force from the situation of one's opponent], insofar as it calls the individual to liberate the ideal from its imaginary existence and give it living, personal actuality. Pure thought must be reborn in the pure heart, the idealism of thought must be transformed into the idealism of the will.

§ 104.

The idealism of the will, which possesses power over the world because it centralizes all objectivity into the center of personality, presupposes that reconciliation and redemption established by Christ, and is obtained only by life in the Christian spiritual communion [*Menigheden*], the kingdom of the *holy* will. The mystery of the will is hidden in all pre-Christian times. The pagan world is absorbed in the political, the esthetic and scientific ideal, but is not able to trace [103] the glory of the world back to the pure heart, to the hidden human of the will. The people of Israel are certainly directed toward the religious ideal, but the spiritual communion is snared in the political barriers of the national spirit. God's kingdom has only a latent, a bound existence.

THE KINGDOM OF PERSONALITY IN ITS ABSOLUTE ACTUALITY

The spiritual communion [Menigheden], *God's kingdom as such*

§ 105.

The personal unity of God and the human which is revealed in Christ is developed in the community of believers. From the second Adam as the point of birth of the holy will in history, there is a spreading out of God's kingdom, whose most precise end is not the culture of the human race, its cultivation and enlightenment, but its deliverance and salvation. As the race is reborn as God's spiritual communion [*Menighed*], as the Lord's mystical body, it is raised not merely to a higher stage of knowledge but to a higher stage of existence and life. God as the Holy Spirit takes up residence in the human race; and in as much as God as the Spirit of the spiritual communion is entirely and undividedly admitted into every *individually* [*enkelt*] believing soul, God consummates Godself as eternal love. The Lord's spiritual communion is the most holy reality of creation, the point where the development of the world reaches its conclusion, because life here first discovers itself in its fullness.

§ 106.

As the community of faith and love whose life in God is hidden, the church [*Kirken*] is invisible; but [104] the church makes its invisible essence visible by taking shape in a definite confession and cultus, whereby it in addition enters into a definite relation to the state.

§ 107.

In order that God's kingdom can be revealed as the centralization of the entire life of the world, the life of the world must be developed in its free independence as an other than God's kingdom. The development of the spiritual communion is conditioned by the free development of the state, art, and science. To the same extent as the consciousness of the world reaches a comprehensive unfolding, *the gifts of grace*, faith, hope, and love, are also able to unfold the entire inner richness of their heavenly powers.

Note 1. It lies in the nature of the case that the first apostolic spiritual communion [*Menighed*], although prototypical according to its essence for all succeeding times, cannot be prototypical according to its form, insofar as the spiritual communion in its beginning could only be presented under the type of *the family.* "The believers were of one heart and one soul and no one had any property for herself or himself, but they had everything in common." (Acts of the Apostles, 4:32). As beautiful as this image is, that condition really only has vanishing importance. As the spiritual communion enters into an inner relation to *the state*, it makes the great *qualitative* advance in its development, whereby its concept is first *posited*.

Note 2. The state's Christianness depends not on the fact that it assumes [105] an immediate religious character, as the Catholics and the pietists demand; but on the fact that the same general *principle*, which the church develops through the categories of religion, is developed through the peculiar categories of the state. It is a lack of spiritual freedom not to be able to know the Christian principle in forms other than the religious.

§ 108.

The confessional difference between Catholicism and Protestantism receives ethical significance by the fact that the concept of the development of spirit, of the relation between the ideal and actuality is determined in different ways. Catholicism's development is only quantitative because it essentially rests content at [*slaaer sig til ro ved*] a definite historical form, at a relative stage of development of the ideal. It fails to appreciate the negative moment of development and dares not posit its temporal life in order to gain the eternal. In Protestantism every advance is qualitative; the ideal is developed through an unbroken metamorphosis, through a continuous death and resurrection. Out of the deeper consciousness of the distance of actuality from the ideal originates Protestantism's moral earnestness, which is consecrated to the work of thought and will.

> *Note.* Confessional difference in the religious is the same thing as national difference in the secular. Although the confessional difference is developed out of the religious idea itself, it is yet closely connected with the national difference. Thus, [106] Catholicism is closely related to the nationalities of the south, Protestantism to the nationalities of the north.

§ 109.

To the confession is joined the ecclesial cultus, in which the spiritual communion is gathered from the life of the world in order to be built up by the immediate *presence* of God's kingdom. This living and actual presence of God's kingdom is effected by means of the word and the sacraments. Christian preaching is not the expression of a speculative wisdom but the believing proclamation of the truth of the gospel unto salvation, and the sacraments are not esthetic symbols but living means of grace, by means of which the human personally participates in the mystery of reconciliation. The Protestant cultus thereby is distinguished from the Catholic in that it allows religion to operate by its own power and assigns the esthetic a relative and subordinate significance in the church, whereas in the Catholic cultus upbuilding is supplanted by esthetic enjoyment.

> *Note.* Although Christian preaching is to produce neither the effects of philosophy nor those of poetry, it must yet stand in an inner relation to the scientific and esthetic consciousness of the spiritual communion. But the speculative and the esthetic must here, as well as in the remaining cultus-moments, have a latent presence, a sublimated presence; it no more dares to step forth independently in religion than the religious and the moral dare step forth independently in art. [107]

§ 110.

The immediate presence of God's kingdom in cultus contains in addition the promise of eternal life as a reality yet to-come. To the promise of religion is bound the ethical obligations, and the church sends the faithful back into the life of the world in order to work in the hope of God's coming kingdom.

Index